THE TIME OF THE

BUFFALO

Tom McHugh

THE TIME OF THE

BUFFALO

with the assistance of Victoria Hobson

ALFRED · A · KNOPF / New York

1 9 7 2

This is a Borzoi Book
Published by Alfred A. Knopf, Inc.

Copyright © 1972 by Tom McHugh

Library of Congress Cataloging in Publication Data

McHugh, Tom   The time of the buffalo.

Based on the author's thesis, University of Wisconsin.
Bibliography: p.   1. Bison, American. I. Title.
QL737.U53M3   1972   599′.7358   72–2242
ISBN 0–394–47618–2

Manufactured in the United States of America

First Edition

To my mother and father

ACKNOWLEDGMENTS

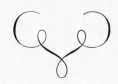

THIS BOOK OWES ITS GREATEST DEBT TO COUNTLESS IN-dividuals who cannot properly appreciate their due—the buffalo in several refuges who patiently, stoically, sometimes indignantly permitted themselves to become subjects of my investigations. To the directors and managers of these refuges, however, I would like to express my gratitude:

In Yellowstone National Park, observations were carried on with the cooperation of Superintendent Edmund B. Rogers and his staff, most particularly Chief Park Naturalist David de Lurie Condon. Additional assistance came from Head Animal Keeper David W. Pierson, biologists Robert E. Howe and Walter H. Kittams, as well as Mary Meagher, W. Verde Watson, W. Leon Evans, Stanley McComas, John S. Bauman, Frank T. Hirst, Joseph Way, and Lee L. Coleman.

In other refuges, ready assistance was extended by Earl Semingsen and H. R. "Bob" Jones of Wind Cave National Park; by Gordon Powers and Clark Stanton of the Bureau of Indian Affairs at Crow Agency, Montana—and also by the Crow Indian Tribe; by Ernest J. Greenwalt, Claude A. Shrader, and Richard J. Hitch of the Wichita Mountains Wildlife Refuge; by John Schwartz, Cy Young, and George E. Mushbach of the National Bison Range; and by Eliot Davis and K. C. "Sunny" Allan of Grand Teton National Park.

Acknowledgments

For their inspiration, understanding, and many helpful suggestions, I am especially grateful to Paul Brooks, John Livingston, and Roger Tory Peterson.

Many other persons have most generously furnished information and reference material for this study: Margaret Altmann of the University of Colorado; Georgia and Bud Basolo of the B-Bar-B Buffalo Ranch; Oliver Burris of the Alaska Department of Fish and Game; Robert A. Elder, David H. Johnson, Margaret Halpin, and Meredith Johnson of the Smithsonian Institution; Jack Hogben of Walla Walla, Washington; Julian Howard of the Wichita Mountains Wildlife Refuge; Barbara Lawrence of the Museum of Comparative Zoology, Harvard University; Raymond J. Parker of La Grange, Illinois; H. R. Peters and J. B. Campbell of the Canada Department of Agriculture; Zdzislaw Pucek of the Mammals Research Institute, Polish Academy of Sciences, Bialowieza, Poland; C. Bertrand Schultz of the University of Nebraska State Museum; and Michael Z. Zablocki of the Central Bison Park, U.S.S.R. Still other persons have been helpful in both thought and deed: Henry Babcock, Harry Brown, Frank and John Craighead, Cally Curtis, Jack Douglas, Robert C. Fields, Warren Garst, George Hobson, Allen Keast, Jane Kinne, Reginald Laubin, Holly Leek, Ruth Laurie, Roberta Mayo, S. J. Olsen, Morris F. Skinner, and Tom Smith. I am also indebted to numerous scientists and chroniclers whose writings have yielded much information; most of these observers are listed in the bibliography at the end of the book.

Photographs from the files of *The Vanishing Prairie* were kindly furnished by Tom Jones and George Sherman of Walt Disney Productions; credit for the original work goes to the photographers themselves—James R. Simon, Hugh Wilmar, and Warren Garst.

This book had its beginnings in a research study I undertook for a doctorate at the University of Wisconsin. Funds for the project came from the Jackson Hole Biological Research Station of the New York Zoological Society; the director of the station, James R. Simon, lent considerable support to the endeavor.

For his assistance in the execution of the research and for his advice on the book that eventually resulted from it, I am most deeply indebted to Professor John T. Emlen of the Department of Zoology, University of Wisconsin. His guidance, aid, and en-

Acknowledgments

couragement deserve major credit for bringing this study to fruition.

The text itself owes much to the labors of Victoria Hobson, who, over a period of years, unselfishly devoted her time to improving the style, structure, and organization of my original chapters. Her way with words has illuminated the writing and added immeasurably to the final work.

CONTENTS

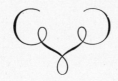

Contents

ILLUSTRATIONS

*Additional illustrations appear
throughout the text.*

MAPS

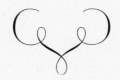

35,000 YEARS AGO: *Bering Strait separated Asia and North America*

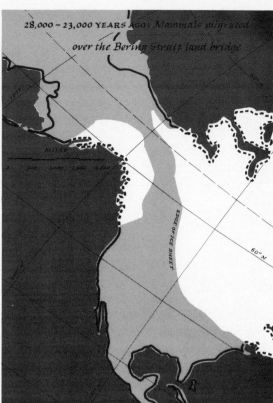

28,000 – 23,000 YEARS AGO: *Mammals migrated over the Bering Strait land bridge*

The Bering Strait Land Bridge During the Last Part of the Ice Age

NOTE: *Time spans are approximate, as are the general shapes of the land masses and ice sheets.*

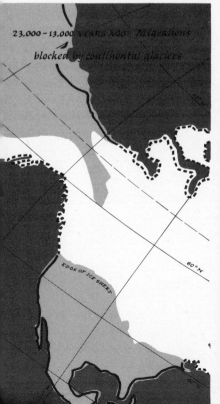

23,000 – 13,000 YEARS AGO: *Migrations blocked by continental glaciers*

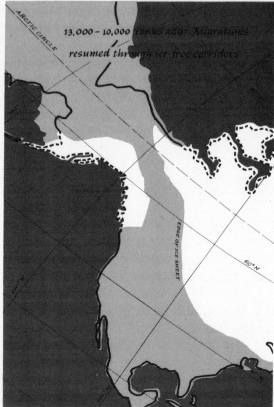

13,000 – 10,000 YEARS AGO: *Migrations resumed through ice-free corridors*

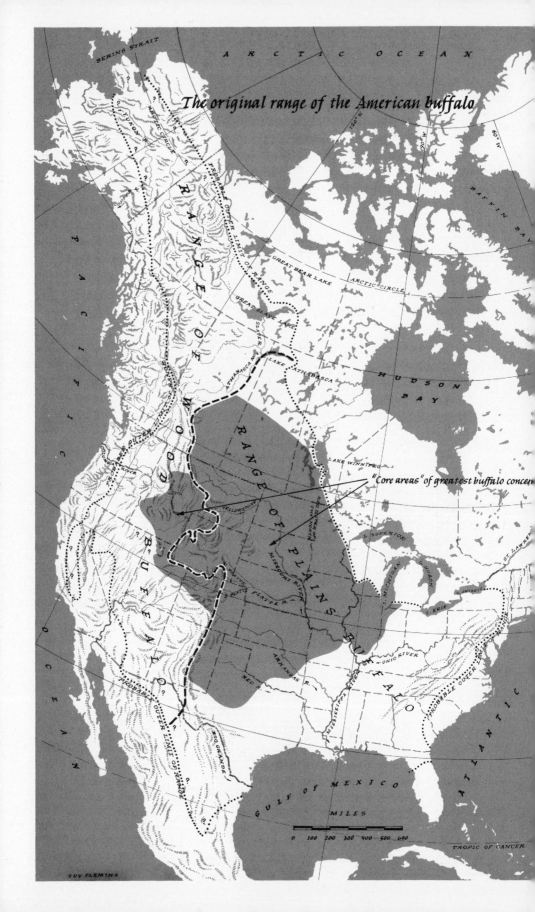

The original range of the American buffalo

"Core areas" of greatest buffalo concen[tration]

GUY FLEMING

WOOD BUFFALO NATIONAL PARK

ELK ISLAND NATIONAL PARK
EDMONTON
WAINWRIGHT

PORTLAND

MANYBERRIES

PABHEAD R.R.
NATIONAL
BUFFALO
RANGE

PONDEROSA
RANCH

WINNIPEG

FT. UNION
MILES
CITY
GLENDIVE
FROMBERG
YELLOWSTONE
NAT. PARK
JACKSON HOLE

NORTHERN PACIFIC R.R.

BISMARCK

PROMONTORY PT.
SALT LAKE CITY

FT. LARAMIE

CUSTER STATE PK.
WIND CAVE NAT. PK.

TRIPLE "U" ENT.

QUEBEC
MONTREAL
OTTAWA

FT. NIOBRARA
NAT. WILDLIFE REF.
NORTH PLATTE

SIOUX CITY

CHEYENNE

UNION PACIFIC
R.R.

COUNCIL
BLUFFS

CHICAGO

BOSTON

DENVER

HOUSE ROCK

KANSAS PACIFIC R.R.
ATCHISON, TOPEKA & SANTA FE R.R.

KANSAS
CITY

NEW YORK

RAYMOND
RANCH

SANTA FE

OLSON, N.M.

DODGE CITY

WICHITA

ST. LOUIS

WASHINGTON

ADOBE WALLS

KIOWA AGENCY

EL PASO

FT. WORTH & DENVER R.R.

WICHITA MTS.
WILDLIFE REF.

DALLAS

TEXAS & PACIFIC R.R.

MISSOURI & PACIFIC R.R.

FT. WORTH

M E X I C O

NEW ORLEANS

MILES

0   100   200   300   400   500   600

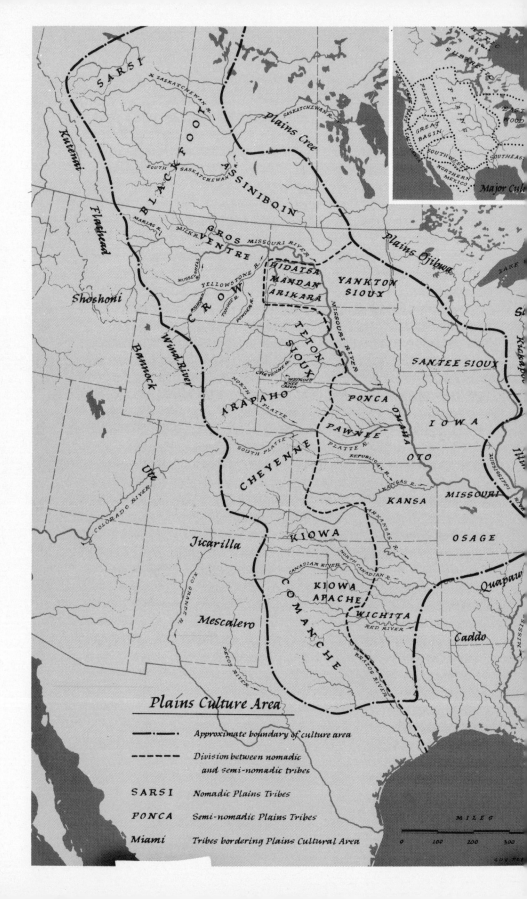

Plains Culture Area

— · — · — Approximate boundary of culture area

— — — — Division between nomadic and semi-nomadic tribes

SARSI Nomadic Plains Tribes

PONCA Semi-nomadic Plains Tribes

Miami Tribes bordering Plains Cultural Area

MILES

0   100   200   300

Major Cul

SARSI

Kutenai

Flathead

BLACKFOOT

Plains Cree

ASSINIBOIN

X SASKATCHEWAN R.

SASKATCHEWAN R.

SOUTH SASKATCHEWAN R.

Plains Ojibwa

LAKE

Shoshoni

MARIAS R.

MILK R.

MUSSELSHELL R.

MISSOURI RIVER

GROS
VENTRE

YELLOWSTONE R.

CROW

TONGUE R.

POWDER R.

HIDATSA
MANDAN
ARIKARA

MISSOURI RIVER

YANKTON
SIOUX

TETON
SIOUX

SANTEE SIOUX

Su

Kickapo

Bannock

Wind River

North
Platte
R.

CHEYENNE R.

WOUNDED
KNEE CREEK

ARAPAHO

NORTH PLATTE R.

PONCA

OMAHA

IOWA

Ute

SOUTH PLATTE

PAWNEE

PLATTE R.

OTO

Illin

REPUBLICAN R.

COLORADO RIVER

CHEYENNE

KANSAS R.

KANSA

MISSOURI

MISSISSIPPI RIVER

Jicarilla

KIOWA

OSAGE

ARKANSAS R.

CANADIAN RIVER

NORTH CANADIAN R.

Quapaw

KIOWA
APACHE

COMANCHE

WICHITA

RED RIVER

RIO GRANDE R.

Mescalero

PECOS RIVER

BRAZOS RIVER

Caddo

MISSI

INTRODUCTION

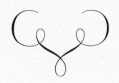

EARLY IN THIS CENTURY, THE NATIONAL MUSEUM OF
Canada sent an anthropologist to the plains of Alberta to record
what he could of the native culture of the Sarsi before the tribe
took up the ways of the white man. As the Indians described
customs and beliefs that dated back to the time of the great buffalo
hunts, they related their particular version of the hereafter. They
imagined that a deceased man's soul and shadow wandered away
to a cold sandy land far to the east, there to dwell with other departed tribesmen, to sit around a campfire in the center of a ragged
tipi and gnaw on the parched bones of buffalo that had perished
long ago. Sarsi warriors accepted the possibility of death and a
journey to this barren Elysium stoically, even without fear. Perhaps because they had been living comfortably off the meat and
hides of the buffalo roaming the northern prairies, the mythical
tableau of a wasted plain filled only with the bones of the once
great herds was no more than a remote vision, a bleak conjuration of aging shamans.

In the closing years of the 1800's, however, the Sarsi vision
came depressingly close to reality—the millions of buffalo did
indeed vanish from the North American grassland. Before this
annihilation ran its course, however, few men who had set their
eyes upon the vast herds could ever imagine total extinction. To

the pioneers who led wagon trains through the heart of the buffalo country, these herds were "an insufferable nuisance." Seemingly endless hordes drifted around their caravans, trampling the moist and grassy soil into a muddy paste and so polluting the streams and springs that voyagers often had to travel for miles to locate drinking water. As far as the eye could see the country was a heaving mass of buffalo, the plains a veritable brown mantle of fur. When the wagon teams advanced along the trail, the droves quietly separated to right and left, leaving a lane through which the men could travel, a space within the herds that shifted westward with the caravan as it steadily pushed across the prairie. Most buffalo appeared to be docile; all they asked, apparently, was to be left alone.

For centuries before the white man set foot upon the continent, the great herds had been coexisting with the Plains Indians in a rare balance between nature and man. The Indian societies lived harmoniously and respectfully with their environment, taking what buffalo they needed for food and shelter, gearing their rhythms and rituals—their entire mode of life—to the ways of the roving herds. In this ecological scheme of the primitive American grassland, the Indian was a prominent partner in the natural community, a predator, one might say, who harvested a share of buffalo as methodically as the wolves that also stalked the open plain. In the legends the Indian wove about the herds, in the countless artifacts he manufactured from the hides and horns and hoofs of the animals, in his constant and varied use of buffalo meat, in his understanding of buffalo as a spiritual force of his prairie world, he maintained the close relationship between man and beast. In short, the Plains Indian culture *was* the buffalo culture.

A tribal adaptation to the nomadic herds, the buffalo culture was an ancient way of life, a rich heritage of customs and a pattern of living that made the tribes self-sufficient in the harsh setting of the exposed plains. We have only recently begun to understand and appreciate the values of a society that lived at peace with the earth, for in its day the Indian culture was considered strange and barbaric by outsiders. The white invaders of the continent used their own European standards to judge these native Americans, condemning them as uncivilized because they were different. As pioneers pressed westward across the continent, bartering for or simply grabbing the Indian land in their path, the tribes could consider two fates. They could shed their own culture and try to accept the civilization of the white man, or they could resist and chance possible death. The Indian was fortunate in at least having the choice, however distasteful, of accepting European ways, for the tribes' cohabitant on the plains, the buffalo, faced but one fate —certain extermination. Under a relentless tide of explorers, sportsmen, settlers, and hunters, the American buffalo was due to perish in an orgy of marksmanship.

As surely as the herds disappeared from their prairie homelands, as surely as the tribes were forced onto reservations, the plains themselves were transformed from grassy wilderness to urban and agrarian sprawl. Prairie gave way to wheat field, wheat field to shopping center. Billboards, smokestacks, and power poles now line highways and railways carved from the old buffalo and wagon trails. The wild Missouri of song and legend is today a tame river, with levees to keep it on course and giant concrete dams to turn its rapids into slackwater lakes. And the threat of extermination still haunts numerous plains creatures as sheepmen and government trappers mount programs of wildlife extermination aimed at animals branded egregious predators. Drenching the West with poison, these guardians of livestock have brought whole species to the brink of extinction and killed thousands of other innocent mammals and birds.

As each year sees new species added to the endangered list, it is of some comfort to know that a once-threatened animal like the buffalo has been securely saved from possible extinction. The rescue began in earnest in 1905, when a group of dedicated conservationists banded together to form a society to save the diminishing herds. Alarmed that they could locate no more than a few hundred wild buffalo on the entire continent, they began to arouse public support for the beast. After establishing and stocking several buffalo refuges, they became so successful in their efforts that they eventually disbanded their organization for lack of interest. Today buffalo number over thirty thousand and are increasing so steadily that hunting or herd reduction is necessary to keep the animals in balance with their range.

And so the saga of the buffalo is a living legend, its actors relegated to scattered refuges, perhaps, but far from vanished still. Several years ago I was attracted to the story of this uniquely American mammal, this carryover from an age when Indians and outlaws, six-shooters and horses created a legendary West. Searching at the time for a species upon which to concentrate my research for a doctoral thesis in zoology, I found in the bison an almost perfect subject. My program of observations on herds would take me out of the confines of the laboratory and into a series of adventures in the western mountains and plains. Furthermore, the vast literature on the beast had left a legacy of questions that might be answered by detailed studies on present-day herds:

How were Indian decoys disguised under buffalo hides able to lure herds into a trap? How were hide-hunters able to slaughter scores from a single group without frightening the survivors into flight? Is the oft-reported lone bull an outcast from the social herds or simply a voluntary recluse? Is it possible for one bull to kill another during the vicious battles of the rut? Can we believe reports of thousands of buffalo deaths from blizzards, drownings, quicksands, and prairie fires? Exactly how many millions lived in the aboriginal herds? Did these multitudes wander erratically or make precise annual migrations in search of temperate weather and lush forage?

My years of observations not only helped me to arrive at some decisions on these and other questions from the past, but also gave me a thorough insight into the behavior and ecology of the species. As I studied these buffalo, my quest for wilderness adventure was thoroughly satisfied. Hiking daily within sight of some herds, camping next to others for weeks at a time, I came to know and love these magnificent animals. From my field notes and from my own analysis of the reports of plainsmen, hunters, and other chroniclers of the frontier West, I have been able to write about the character and life of this bull of the plains—his community of grassland creatures, his yearly cycle from the rutting season through the time of winter hardships to the calving season, his daily habits and travels, his spirit of play, his inclinations to attack man or beast, and his highly developed social organization, including a clearly defined order of rank. To supplement this natural history, I have written of the buffalo's place in the Plains Indian culture, his role in the early frontier, and his near extermination and dramatic rescue, with the intention of building an inclusive work on the mammal that has figured so prominently in the history and prehistory of the continent.

THE TIME OF THE

BUFFALO

. . . the hunters were galloping their horses around and driving their whizzing arrows or long lances to the hearts of these noble animals, which in many instances, becoming infuriated with deadly weapons in their sides, erected their shaggy manes over their bloodshot eyes, and furiously plunged forward at the sides of their assailants' horses; sometimes goring them to death at a lunge, and putting their dismounted riders to flight for their lives. Sometimes the dense crowd was opened, and the blinded horsemen, too intent on their prey, amidst a cloud of dust, were hemmed and wedged in amongst the crowding beasts, over whose backs they were obliged to leap for security, leaving their horses to the fate that might await them in this wild and desperate war. Many were the bulls that turned upon their assailants, meeting them with desperate resistance; and many were the warriors who were dismounted, saving themselves by the superior muscles of their legs. Some who were closely pursued by the bulls wheeled suddenly round, and snatching the half of a buffalo robe from around their waists, threw it over the horns and eyes of the infuriated beast, and darting by its side, drove the arrow or lance to its heart. Others suddenly dashed off upon the prairies by the side of the affrighted animals which had escaped from the throng, and closely escorting them for a few rods, caused their hearts' blood to flow in streams, and brought their huge carcases to the ground.

GEORGE CATLIN, *among the Hidatsa in 1832.*

1

THE BUFFALO CULTURE

IN THE FALL OF 1907, A ROLLING TRACT OF OKLAHOMA prairie lay still and unused under the October sun. The choice area of mesquite grass and bluestem in the southwest corner of the state had not been grazed by buffalo for almost thirty years, and the old wallows of the bulls had long been overgrown with grasses and weeds. But in the nearby town of Cache, Oklahoma, local residents stirred with excitement. The eight thousand-acre prairie tract had been selected and fenced to become the nation's first buffalo refuge. Due to arrive at any moment were fifteen buffalo specially chosen for the range by the director of the New York Zoological Society. The animals had covered the eighteen hundred-mile journey in two Arms Palace horse cars, in lavish passenger-style accommodations donated by the express companies.

The return of these buffalo to the pastures of their ancestors was a momentous occasion for everyone within miles of the refuge. Word of the special train had quickly spread, and already a mob of cowboys, ranchers, and Indians lined the rail siding.

Some of the Indians had trudged into Cache on foot; others had journeyed in on ponies or in mule-drawn wagons. Many of the women, dressed in their richest blankets, carried papooses on their backs, and a number of men wore colorful tribal regalia. Present in the crowd were distinguished leaders of several tribes; even Comanche Chief Quanah Parker, famous for his raid on Adobe Walls, was on hand.

At last the train pulled in, amid the cheers and bustle of the crowd. No group of spectators was more excited than the large gathering of Indians. They swarmed around the cars to get a look at the new arrivals, the veteran tribesmen regaling their sons with fond tales of the wild, free days of the herds and the hunt, when the Indians and the buffalo still ruled the land.

Decades had passed since the Indians had seen buffalo, but memories of the great beasts were fresh in their minds. For several years after the disappearance of the herds, stunned tribesmen had made forlorn treks out onto the prairie and found no more than scattered skulls of the quarry they sought. Grain crops flourished, and the white man's cattle and sheep now chewed a placid cud on these plains where the Indians had once pitched their tipis and the bison had wandered in massed herds.

To the Indians, the loss of the herds had been devastating. Long before the white man colonized these shores, the buffalo, in the words of an early explorer, were "the food of the Natives, which drinke the bloud hot, and eate the fat, and often ravine the flesh raw." They were "meat, drink, shoes, houses, fire, vessels and their Masters whole substance."

In later years, the legions of buffalo sustained the explorers, frontiersmen, and settlers who led the way west. Without the herds, many of these pioneers would not have survived the raw environment on the open plains. Buffalo nourished the men who plied cargo to remote outposts, stocked the larders of early homesteads and settlements, and provisioned wagon trains, private expeditions, and government survey teams. In short, no other wild animal was so important to the development of the North American continent as the massive, long-haired beast of the plains.

When Lewis and Clark set forth along the Missouri in the spring of 1804, buffalo meat sustained them through the early part of their odyssey. But as the corps reached the Rockies, they found the herds thinning, and Lewis was prompted to note in his journal: "I know when we leave the buffaloe that we shall some-times be under the necessity of fasting occasionally." His predic-tions were borne out when his party came close to starvation in the Bitteroot Mountains. Several months passed before the two ex-plorers again mentioned buffalo in their journals, each in his preferred spelling. (Lewis wrote "buffaloe" and his second-in-command "buffalow." To this day there remains some confusion about the name of the beast. "Buffalo," through long, continued usage, is the popular term; in scientific parlance, however, the ani-mal is properly known as a "bison.")

To other pioneers struggling to survive on the broad expanse of grassland, the American buffalo was a welcome source of com-fort and life. By day the animal furnished them with an abundant supply of meat. At night and in winter, he sheltered them with rich robes. And on the open plain, where there was not a stick of wood to burn, he provided them with fuel—durable buffalo chips kindled many a campfire that otherwise would have necessitated the transporting of logs for many miles. The trails of buffalo often indicated the best wagon routes across rugged terrain or turbulent rivers, or led parched travelers to waterholes. During the winter, the herds trampled such firm paths through deep snow that men could travel unencumbered by snowshoes.

Despite their indebtedness to the buffalo, voyagers on the plains often discovered that the animals could also create danger-ous and frustrating situations. Parties in wagon trains and stage-coaches were sometimes greatly inconvenienced when vast num-bers of congregated buffalo blocked the trails. As Brigham Young led his string of seventy-three pioneering wagons across the Platte River valley toward Utah, there were times when he had to dis-patch advance runners to sweep masses of buffalo from the route so the main column could pass.

Plains caravans were also endangered by stampedes, and the mass of galloping animals presented an even greater hazard if vis-ibility was low, when dust was thrown up from pummeling hooves or darkness rolled in. To prevent livestock from being swept away or wagons from being overturned, the men sometimes had to cor-ral all vehicles and drive the stock inside. At times they would even fire rifles into the approaching herd, in an effort to divert it from the livestock. Some of the lead animals would fall; the rest of the onrushing buffalo, blocked by the carcasses of their companions or alarmed by the noise of the shots, would peel off in two columns and pass on either side of the camp.

When the railroads reached the plains, the buffalo met the invaders face to face. Crossing the tracks in masses, they enlightened many an engineer on the matter of bisontine right of way. Steamboat captains had equal respect for herds swimming in the Missouri. Sometimes deck hands could push small bands of buffalo away from bow or wheel with long poles, but larger herds often made it necessary for the captain to tie up along shore until all had swum past.

Although white men with their vessels and vehicles often clashed head on with the buffalo, Indians maintained an orderly relationship with the animals. The tribes became as much a part of the plains community as the grasses, the pronghorn, the prairie dogs, and the buffalo themselves, for they learned how to belong to the land as well as take from it. The buffalo with whom they shared their domain became linked with them in a unique physical and spiritual kinship.

Buffalo were the Indians' commissary, furnishing food, clothing, shelter, and a remarkable range of luxury articles; but there was more to the relation between Indian and beast than such material considerations. The daily thought and ceremonial practices of the tribes—indeed their very culture—developed out of their response to the buffalo. The random wandering of the herds across the plains forced the Indians to settle on nomadism as the most practical way of life. Tribes adapted their possessions—everything from tableware to tipis—so that all could be easily moved where the grass was greenest and the buffalo thickest.

Crucial to Indian nomadism were the buffalo-hide tipis, which could be collapsed within minutes of a signal from the village chief. With horses and dogs secured nearby, the women then began to load all their belongings. Tying several tipi poles together at the thin ends, they balanced them over the shoulders of the horse, running an equal number of poles back along either side with the butt ends dragging on the ground. Just to the rear of the horse they lashed a brace crosswise over the two bundles of poles, creating an A-shaped frame, or "travois." The crosspiece locked everything in position and formed a small platform on which could be heaped the rolled-up tipi cover, household effects, furniture, and as many as four women or children.

Once everything was loaded, each woman guided her string of horses into the main caravan, to be joined there by the men of the tribe on their own mounts. Bringing up the rear of the procession was a large pack of dogs drawing miniature travois similar in construction to those trailing behind the horses. Thus the tribes pursued the roaming buffalo across miles of plain and prairie, some changing camp so often that their tipi poles would wear down and need replacement several times a year.

Without buffalo, it is unlikely that many of these Indians could have survived the rigors of the plains; with them, they achieved the rich, colorful life described by artist George Catlin when he visited the area in 1832: "The several tribes of Indians inhabiting the regions of the Upper Missouri . . . are undoubtedly the finest looking, best equipped and most beautifully costumed of any on the Continent. They live in a country well stocked with buffaloes and wild horses, which furnish them an excellent and easy living . . . and they are among the most independent and happiest races of Indians I have met with . . ."

They were indeed independent. Although hunting buffalo was a continuing responsibility demanding both skill and toil, most Plains Indians were able to maintain a full larder so easily that they could afford the luxury of waging almost continual warfare. They resisted European invaders for two and a half centuries, stoutly defending their territory against the Spanish, French, English, Mexicans, and Americans. Wealthiest, proudest, and probably wildest of all Plains tribes were the Sioux, based on hundreds of miles of choice northern range, enriched by thousands of horses and furnished with an almost unlimited supply of food by millions of buffalo.

The war operations of the Plains tribes were sustained by herds of bison that were often themselves the cause of dispute. The Assiniboin gave as the reason for their parting from the Sioux a legendary quarrel over a buffalo heart. According to the story, when the delicacy was claimed simultaneously by the wife of an Assiniboin chief and her Sioux counterpart, a struggle ensued between them. Before long, the chiefs themselves entered the fracas with warriors. The two leaders eventually split and took their people into separate camps, where they dwelt "in lasting discontent." Quite possibly the legend had its origins in a real misunderstanding over the apportionment of the herds.

7

When the Winnebago left their own territory on the western edge of Lake Michigan to hunt buffalo, they took along extra warriors, knowing that a chase after the herds might turn into a fight with inimical neighbors as well. The returning hunters would bring back enemy scalps along with their buffalo meat and hides, making a dual celebration of the Victory Dance that followed.

Such quarreling over buffalo had probably been going on for many centuries, for as long as rival tribes had been pursuing the herds. The first written records of this hunting on the North American plains came from Coronado, whose scribes wrote of roving tribes that lived "like Arabs," and drew their main sustenance "entirely from the cows, because they neither sow nor reap corn." Clearly this flourishing society of buffalo hunters had been established at least some time before Coronado's visit, but its duration on the plains was not known until recently.

In the early part of this century, archeological discoveries indicated that a nomad people had hunted a species of giant bison as much as ten thousand years ago. Both the beasts and hunters had originally arrived on this continent in waves of migrations from Asia, over land that has since become submerged in the sea. As the climate changed in the millennia that followed, a severe drought coupled with hunting pressure helped to bring about the extinction of these early, long-horned bison. Relics from a later period beginning some three or four thousand years ago provide the first traces of the forefathers of the Indians we know and the type of bison they hunted.

Some of the artifacts found near the remains of the more recent group, the "Early Indian" ancestors of the North American tribes, reveal that two types of native culture developed during the last millennium on the Great Plains. Each of these groups adapted itself to the limitations and opportunities presented by its own region. On the western plains, where an arid climate made agriculture precarious, the Indians embraced the nomadic life, trekking many miles to hunt the wandering herds; on the eastern plains, where climate was more conducive to agriculture, the tribes developed a way of life as semi-nomadic villagers, supplementing their buffalo hunting with the growing of crops.

This separation into nomadic and village cultures began many centuries ago and occurred in two phases. The early phase can be examined only through artifacts unearthed at ancient sites; the more recent has been directly observed and studied in the field. The papers of numerous historians and anthropologists have detailed the varying habits and customs of a vast array of tribes that moved back and forth on the North American continent, dividing, merging, and adopting new customs with the new lands they settled.

The greatest tribal shifts in history occurred after the Spaniards introduced the horse onto the continent in the 1500's. By the end of the next century, stray, stolen, or bartered horses had worked their way from Spanish outposts into most tribes on the grassland, and the Indian way of life started to change. The historic village tribes extended their hunting range in summer with a mounted trek after buffalo, although they continued to cultivate their fields of maize. Other tribes, such as the Cheyenne and Crow, completely abandoned their villages and farming and reorganized to move their belongings by horse caravan. Now highly mobile, they could pursue their buffalo quarry with ease, shifting their camps to keep up with the largest herds. As an Indian culture built up around the buffalo and the horse began to climb toward a glorious peak, the original Plains tribes found their homeland invaded. Some became displaced and others intermixed as Indians from bordering areas pushed into the grassland. Warfare broke out here and there as hunters ranging the open plain raided neighboring camps and villages to steal horses or grab a supply of maize.

The plains eventually became a giant melting pot where tribes spoke more than thirty different tongues derived from six major language families. Across all of North America, of course, there was an even greater diversity, with native peoples speaking some 550 separate languages. But much of this seemingly bewildering multiformity can be unscrambled if all tribes are analyzed according to their principal foods. Each can then be classified as belonging to a certain "food area." Thus, some thirty-five tribes of the northern tundra can be grouped in the Caribou Area. The Pacific slope centering in the Columbia River region becomes the Salmon Area, the eastern United States the Eastern Maize Area, and the grassland the Buffalo Area.

Classification by principal food acquires greater meaning when the ways of life of individual tribes are taken into account. If the areas are revised according to such cultural traits, all boundaries shift but one—the grassland. This region maintains its integrity under both formulas, and the Buffalo Food Area becomes the Plains Culture Area.

The dominant role of the buffalo in this area determined not only the food of the tribes but also most aspects of their life and culture. The Indians' dependence on buffalo for clothing and wares led to the development of special skills involving the use of parts of the animals for raw materials. The tribes became proficient in the art of leathercraft, learning to fabricate a multitude of objects from green skins—or "rawhide"—and dressing other skins into luxurious, soft-tanned robes. By piecing a number of tanned hides together, they fashioned the collapsible tipis that, borne overland by dog- or horse-drawn travois, so simplified their moves from camp to camp.

In addition to the material aspects of their culture, the Plains tribes had other traits in common. Most formalized their ideology of war with military societies for men; they organized a police force for control of hunts; and all of them took part in a number of complex ceremonies culminating in the annual Sun Dance.

From Alberta to Texas, the uniform distribution of these cultural traits is significant in light of the mixed origins of the tribes involved. Some had been on the plains or prairies to begin with and others moved in from bordering forests or deserts, yet all achieved a remarkable homogeneity within a few generations. Although they spoke no common tongue, they communicated with each other by a sign language comparable to that used today by deaf-mutes. This great leveling of cultures over the immensity of the plains was possible only with the advent of the horse, which facilitated contact with tribes that until then were remote and foreign. Long before the horse appeared in the area, however, the basic ecological pattern had been established in the exploitation of the buffalo. Once equipped with mounts, the hunters could more easily follow the great herds and thus realize the full potential of the grassland.

Exhibiting the basic customs of this culture area were the nomadic Plains tribes, the "typical" grassland Indians familiar to any schoolboy. There were eleven groups in all: the Arapaho, Assiniboin, Blackfoot, Cheyenne, Comanche, Crow, Gros Ventre, Kiowa, Kiowa-Apache, Sarsi, and Teton Sioux.

These nomadic tribes populated the western half of the grassland. In the eastern half lived fourteen semi-nomadic tribes sharing most of the traits of the nomads, including particularly the dependence upon buffalo, but differing in certain other habits. More sedentary than true nomads, many of these Indians engaged in farming and lived in permanent lodges for part of the year. Some took up travel by boat, and abandoned the Sun Dance for other ceremonies. These tribes of wandering villagers were the Arikara, Hidatsa, Iowa, Kansa, Mandan, Missouri, Omaha, Osage, Oto, Pawnee, Ponca, Santee Sioux, Yankton Sioux, and Wichita.

Living around the edge of the Plains Culture Area were still other Indians whose principal food was buffalo, but whose cultures differed somewhat from the plains norm. Notable among these marginal tribes were the Plains Cree, Plains Ojibwa, Shoshoni, Caddo, and Quapaw.

Beyond the northwest corner of the Plains Culture Area a few buffalo-hunting tribes inhabited the Plateau, the region named after the plateaus drained by the Columbia River system, straddling the borders of British Columbia, Washington, Idaho, and Montana. Plateau tribes included the Kutenai and the Flathead as well as a few of lesser importance. Since buffalo were scarce in their territory, these tribes were forced to cross the divide into inimical Blackfoot country to hunt. Some tribes moved swiftly and cautiously back and forth, aware that the Blackfoot, their faces painted and their weapons readied for battle, would be lying in wait at the margins of their territory. The Kutenai and the Flathead, on the other hand, forged across in warlike formation encompassing so many lodges that they had little need to fear Blackfoot attack.

Despite the great variety of tribal life patterns in the huge area inhabited by the Indians of North America, a significantly large number of tribes used buffalo for at least part, if not all, of their provisions. Pursued by native hunters before the coming of white man and horse, the great American bison was the material and spiritual focus of plains life and culture for thousands of years. When explorers began to probe the continent, the animal made possible many early expeditions that led to the settling of the west. And in more recent times, as prey of hide-hunter and subtenance

for early plainsman, the buffalo played out his final role, influencing the affairs and hastening the growth of two young nations,
until the danger of his extinction forced both governments to establish game preserves where he could live at peace on the margins of the modern world.

2

IN NUMBERS—

NUMBERLESS

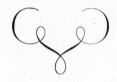

"... I REACHED SOME PLAINS SO VAST THAT I DID NOT find their limit anywhere that I went, although I traveled over them for more than 300 leagues. And I found such a quantity of cows (buffalo) . . . that it is impossible to number them, for while I was journeying through these plains, until I returned to where I first found them, there was not a day that I lost sight of them."

The report is from one of the first white men to view the American west, Francisco Vásquez de Coronado, who set forth from his base in Mexico City in search of treasure for his patron, King Charles V of Spain. Although his letters to the king describe an awesome number of buffalo, they are not unusual in plains lore. Such accounts of enormous populations have abounded since the beginning of European explorations on the continent. The immensity of the herds constantly astounded early witnesses, who jotted down glowing descriptions of what they had seen.

When chronicler-zoologist Joel Allen examined these reports, he suspected some of exaggeration; in a monograph he expressed ". . . slight misgivings in respect to their thorough truthfulness." Only after he himself had witnessed similar multitudes on the plains of Kansas in 1871 was he "convinced of the possibility of the seemingly most extravagant reports being true." A few excerpts from this collection of historical notes speak for themselves:

> There is such a quantity of them that I do not know what to compare them with, except the fish in the sea . . .

> . . . numerous as the locusts of Egypt . . . they were crowded together so densely that in the distance their rounded backs presented a surface of uniform blackness.

> We could not see their limit either north or west.

> The plains were black and appeared as if in motion . . .

> The country was one robe.

Some pioneers and explorers, their imaginations exhausted, drew from the pages of literature. The Reverend Robert Rundle leaned on Milton and declared that the animals were "in numbers —numberless." Father Pierre-Jean de Smet described "whole bands . . . lying amidst flowers on the grass," a scene that "realized in some sort the ancient tradition of the holy scriptures, speaking of the vast pastoral countries of the Orient, and of the cattle upon a thousand hills."

Only when observers scanned the herds from an elevated position were they able to grasp the true scope of the populations. In North Dakota one railroad surveyor "ascended to the top of a high hill" where "for a great distance ahead every square mile seemed to have a herd of buffalo upon it. Their number was variously estimated by members of the party, some as high as half a million. I do not think it any exaggeration to set it down at 200,000."

Even half a million was entirely conceivable, as Canadian frontiersman John McDougall came to appreciate. After having remarked how trifling a certain group of domestic cattle looked on the open plain, he was startled to learn from the local wrangler that the herd numbered twenty-three thousand head. McDougall began to think back on the size of buffalo herds he had seen. Only then did he realize the number of animals involved: "Many times, from hills and range summits, I had seen more than half a million of buffalo at one time . . ."

Another way to comprehend the immensity of a passing herd was to measure its dimensions. In a letter to his family, Nathaniel Langford, the first superintendent of Yellowstone National Park, described an almost unbelievable swarm of buffalo.

First of all, and before you repeat to your friends my buffalo story, I want you as a preliminary, to season their imaginations with a recital of your own experience with the (passenger) pigeons in St. Paul, in 1857. You remember that enormous flock of them. Did they not darken the air at times?

In our trip across the plains in 1862, after crossing the Red River of the North, buffaloes abounded everywhere.

We thought the herds of 5,000, 10,000 or more, very large herds, until we got beyond the second crossing of the Cheyenne River, where the herds increased in size . . . I well recall the day when we camped for the night. The sky was perfectly clear, when we heard a distant rumbling sound, which we thought was thunder but our guide, Pierre Botineau exclaimed, "Buffalo!" and as we could see no sign of them, he said that they were a few miles away . . . Soon we saw a cloud of dust rising in the east, and the rumbling grew louder and I think it was about half an hour when the front of the herd came fairly into view. The edge of the herd nearest to us was one-half to three-quarters of a mile away. From an observation with our field glasses, we judged the herd to be 5 or 6 (some said 8 or 10) miles wide, and the herd was more than an hour passing us at a gallop. There seemed to be no space, unoccupied by buffaloes. They were running as rapidly as a horse can go at a keen gallop, about 12 miles an hour . . . the whole space, say 5 miles by 12 miles, as far as we could see, was a seemingly solid mass of buffaloes . . .

Langford multiplied his estimate for the herd's area by the approximate density of the animals and came up with a staggering figure for the total population: "I have no doubt that there were one million buffaloes in that herd."

An even larger herd was seen by Thomas Farnham as he traveled west on the Santa Fe Trail in 1839. For three days he passed through country "so thickly covered with these noble animals, that when viewed from a height, it scarcely afforded a sight of a square league of its surface." He then began computing: "We traveled at a rate of fifteen miles a day. The length of sight on either side of the trail, 15 miles; on both sides, 30 miles: $15 \times 3 = 45 \times 30 = 1350$ square miles of country."

That came out to be a block of buffalo a little larger than the state of Rhode Island.

Plains literature is filled with such estimates, leaving no room to doubt that the aboriginal populations numbered into the millions. But how many millions? Most writers have proposed figures of sixty or seventy million, but these seem excessive to me. For my own estimate, I have relied heavily upon the capacity of the grassland, multiplying its magnitude (1,250,000 square miles) by the maximum number of buffalo a single square mile could have comfortably supported. For this last figure I have borrowed methods used by range managers in allocating quotas of domestic grazers to measured plots of ranch land. When regulating stock densities, these men use the principle of "grazing capacity," specifying the maximum number of animals that can forage for one year on a given tract without misusing it. Quotas are conservative, taking into account both wet and dry seasons, to guarantee their validity over a number of years. Though based on the grazing of cattle, the quotas apply equally well to buffalo, since the two species are roughly the same size and can be expected to exert about the same amount of grazing pressure.

But no single figure can accurately cover the entire range of the grassland. A mere four acres of rich prairie in Illinois would have supported one buffalo for a year, whereas a hundred acres of arid range in New Mexico could barely have sustained the same animal. We must therefore attempt to arrive at an average by sampling some typical areas from east to west.

On the lush eastern half of the tall-grass prairie, one buffalo could have lived for a year on about ten acres; on the westerly half a single animal would have needed twenty acres; within the mixed prairie of the central plains, twenty-six would have been required, and on the short-grass plains, where conditions were drier, forty-five. This averages out to about twenty-five acres per buffalo, or twenty-six buffalo per square mile. The estimate for the entire grassland population is then thirty-two million. Another two mil-lion probably lived in wooded areas bordering the plains, bringing the total to thirty-four million.

From this total I have subtracted four million to allow for competing big game animals such as elk, deer, and pronghorn. This leaves a final estimate of thirty million. I cannot visualize the available range supporting many more buffalo than this.

But the exact figure is hardly necessary in order to realize that buffalo wandered across the land in astonishing multitudes. No matter what figure is accepted for the aboriginal population, to early spectators on the plains the great animals were indeed "in numbers—numberless."

3

GRASSLAND AND BUFFALO

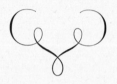

WHEN LEWIS AND CLARK JOURNEYED ACROSS THE
North American grassland in the early 1800's, they passed
through a vast and fertile wilderness; for mile after mile they
found grasses so tall that a man on horseback had to stand up in
his stirrups to see over the rank growth. But in the course of the
next hundred years, the rich fabric of plains life had become tat-
tered almost beyond recognition, as settlers pushing westward
tamed the wilderness with ruthless zeal. Civilized man wrought
more destruction upon the grassland than upon any other natural
realm on the continent. His assault with rifles and poisons left
local wildlife so ravaged that many species exist today only as
natural curiosities. He carried out an equally thorough exploitation of the land itself. Developing the fertile portions into rich and
productive farms for corn, wheat, and soybeans, he sectioned the
arid lands with barbed wire to make ranches for his livestock.

A similar exploitation has transformed most of the world's

grasslands, which once covered almost half the earth's surface, and included such regions as the pampas of South America, the velds of Southern Africa, the *pusztas* of Hungary, and the steppes of Asia.

Despite their scattered locations, all of these regions share certain identifying characteristics. Rainfall is generally sparse on the grassland, and its effectiveness is diminished under the drying forces of wind and sun; sufficient to favor grasses and prevent the formation of deserts, it is nonetheless inadequate for trees. Animal life in the varied regions has also evolved along strikingly parallel lines. Though often members of different biological families, creatures continents apart have adjusted to their environment in closely corresponding fashion. For example, similar forms of burrowing plant-eaters developed on different continents separated by thousands of miles—there are the cavies of South America, the hamsters of Asia, the wombats of Australia, and the prairie dogs and ground squirrels of North America.

The sweeping expanse of North American grassland is properly called prairie in the east and plains in the west. Together, the two parts blend into one sea of grass, the heartland of the former buffalo range, a vast tract of some 1,250,000 square miles. When the early explorers first came upon this region, it stretched about twenty-four hundred miles from Mexico north to Saskatchewan; at its greatest width it ran continuously from Indiana over a thousand miles into Wyoming. Large portions even extended from the Rockies westward into California, Oregon, and Washington. For the prairie schooners pressing across this sea of grass the distances were so great they were measured not in miles but in months. Pioneers traversing from east to west moved from one extreme of country to another, from towering grasses eight feet high to short, scrubby blades of not more than a few inches.

The range in climate on the grassland is equally great, passing from the heavier rainfall area of the eastern prairie to the drier region near the center. At the western borders of the Dakotas and Kansas, rainfall becomes sparser still. From here to the Rockies the plains are deep in the "rain shadow" cast by the high peaks, which squeeze moisture from eastbound clouds.

This wide range of grassland climate is also marked by striking local extremes. The winds blow more strongly than anywhere else in the country, except along certain seashores. In summer they are dry and hot, licking moisture from the soil, crumbling it to dust; in winter they drive great blizzards, slashing a knife-edged blast of snow across the plains, heaping flakes into monumental drifts.

No condition in this land of excesses is more erratic than the rainfall. At times it comes in such heavy showers that most of the water runs off the soil; hail storms pit the ground, frazzling and beating down plants. At other times there may be no rain at all— Weather Bureau records in western Montana indicate that drought ravages the area about once every five years. The earth may become so dry that some plants fail to put forth any new growth at all.

Fortunately, grasses in these semi-arid regions are extremely hardy, and can withstand severe pressures from creatures and climate; although their leaves may wither and die during dry seasons, their deep, extensive root systems send up fresh shoots with the return of warm, rainy weather—even when drought lasts for years. They are equally resistant to prairie fires, which merely char the blades and shoots above the ground, leaving the perennial bases largely untouched.

The strength of the grasses is most striking in their ability to withstand heavy grazing. Their growth tissue—unlike that of shrubs or trees—lies close to the ground, thus remaining active after the tops of blades are broken off. Just as a lawn continues to grow after repeated mowings, the grassland maintains a rich carpet of herbage after light to moderate grazing; in certain species of grasses, grazing may even stimulate the roots to send up a denser, more succulent growth.

Over the years, this abundant herbage has fostered the evolution and spread of large plant-eating animals, which attain their greatest densities on the grassland. Foremost among the wild animals of the North American plains are the great bison, which once roamed in throngs so dense they blotted every glimpse of greenery for miles. In many grassland refuges, although today's groups are no more than a shadow of the historic herds, the round of life goes on largely unchanged. A capsule sketch of the seasonal cycle among the buffalo should help introduce the more detailed material of future chapters. The story logically begins with a month in spring.

Grassland and Buffalo

———◆●◆———

As the drifting herds walk among the windflowers and prairie buttercups that dot the new grass carpet, each pregnant buffalo cow begins to search for a spot to bring forth her single calf. The infant, awkward and gangling at birth, coordinates his actions within an hour or two and is soon kicking his hind legs playfully in the air and running circles around his mother. He grows rapidly in the first weeks, and after about three months his juvenile coat of reddish-orange begins to darken to the deep brown of his elders.

By that time it is midsummer and the herd is engrossed in the rut, as individual bulls vie with each other over the chance to mate with a chosen cow. Rival bulls bellow threats across the plains in guttural blasts, paw the ground, and lie down to wallow furiously in the dust. At times they even thrash their horns into small trees as though dealing mortal blows to a host of adversaries. Occasionally an exchange of threats erupts into battle, as enraged bulls butt furiously, each trying to position himself for a debilitating stab into his opponent's flanks. In most contests, the weaker bull yields before any real damage is done, and the victor, his status assured, is free to court the cow of his choice.

Toward the end of summer the rutting season wanes; the grasses cure to a rich, golden brown, asters and goldenrod bloom, and the ever-shortening days and crisp evenings presage a time of frost and hardship for the herds. The animals meet the first snowfall stoically, foraging patiently through the drifts; but toward the end of winter a few of their number will weaken and perish.

In this seasonal round on the grassland, the herds of buffalo mingle with a diverse assemblage of other creatures, both large and small. Stocky badgers waddle across the open country in search of ground squirrels to eat; pocket gophers nibble away at roots and tubers in their underground tunnels; colonies of ants drill nine feet down in the prairie sod; and rough-legged hawks soar and circle high above the land. From time to time, from havens in wooded stream bottoms or other forested areas, whitetail deer, mule deer, and elk wander out to graze the meadows, and groups of agile pronghorn range across the plains.

It is the majestic buffalo, however, that establishes the special character of the American grassland. The great beast is more than up to the standing physically. The largest land mammal in the New World, a buffalo bull weighs half a ton more than his closest rivals, the moose and the big brown ("Kodiak") bears. When giant marine mammals are included in the rankings, he is surpassed only by the whales and an occasional bull walrus.

A full-grown male plains buffalo weighs between fourteen hundred and twenty-two hundred pounds, stands between five and a half and six and a half feet high at the shoulder and measures from nine and a half to eleven and a half feet in total length, including about a foot and a half of tail. The horns may be as much as three feet apart at their widest spread.

The cow is smaller, weighing from seven hundred and fifty to eleven hundred pounds, standing four and a half to five and a half feet in shoulder height and measuring less than ten feet in length. Less shaggy on head and chin, she has a smaller hump, and her horns are more slender and curved than those of her mate.

The coat of a buffalo attains prime condition during the winter months, then sloughs off in clumps during the annual molt in the spring. The biggest chunks come from the hump and shoulders, where the fur is two to five times thicker than the hair on the slimmed hindquarters; this difference in thickness of pelt serves to accentuate the formidable hunchbacked shape of the buffalo. Other hair on forelegs, throat, chin, crown, and forehead reaches astonishing lengths, especially in older animals. The longest masses, dangling from between the horns and upper forehead, have been known to grow to a length of twenty-two inches.

Differences in color and texture of coat are useful in separating the two subspecies—*Bison bison bison*, the plains buffalo, and *Bison bison athabascae*, the wood buffalo. Darker coloration and a woollier fur are identifying characteristics of the wood buffalo. Wood animals are also greater in size, the bulls reaching twenty-five hundred or more pounds and the cows about sixteen hundred. Because it is difficult to establish these differences in the field, positive identification is possible only in the lab, where other features can be used to identify the wood buffalo, with its larger and broader skull and its stubbier horns. Once common in Canada's Wood Buffalo National Park, the subspecies was virtually wiped out in the 1920's when misguided officials introduced several thousand plains animals onto the range. The two subspecies started crossbreeding almost immediately; today most of the residents of the park are hybrids.

Wood buffalo also inhabited much of the early Canadian and American west. Beginning in the area around Great Slave Lake, they ranged south through the Rocky Mountains to Mexico and west to parts of the Pacific states.

Frontier trappers referred to the wood subspecies as "mountain bison," apparently with good reason. These bison regularly wintered in valleys or open parklands of the Rockies and then moved into mountain meadows or tundra as the snow melted. The discovery of skeletons in alpine regions and the statements of early observers indicate that mountain bison were nimble crag dwellers. On the slopes of Pikes Peak one group often negotiated a neighboring twelve thousand-foot pass. And in Rocky Mountain National Park, several buffalo skulls have been discovered close to or above timberline, the highest one at 12,200 feet.

The most surprising evidence on the mountaineering activities of wood buffalo comes from Wyoming's Medicine Bow Range, an isolated group of peaks that slope up from the seven thousand-foot Laramie Plains to reach an elevation of twelve thousand feet. As geologist Fritiof Fryxell studied records of the herds that once swarmed on the plains below, it occurred to him that certain animals might have attempted an ascent to the higher crags. After hiking into the range, he found enough skeletal remains to indicate that buffalo had indeed wandered up to timberline.

Near the crest of the range Fryxell made a startling discovery. To reach the area, he had to negotiate rocks so massive and angular that he could advance only by leaping precariously from one point to another. At 11,500 feet, he came upon a decayed skeleton scattered among great quartzite boulders. The geologist was perplexed: "How a buffalo could get over a surface of this character to such an astonishing altitude without breaking a limb or becoming entrapped among the boulders is well-nigh incomprehensible."

Climbing another 150 feet, Fryxell found evidence to suggest just such an accident. As he examined two skeletons whose bones lay strewn among the rocks, he noticed that the leg bones of one protruded at a sharp angle from between two large boulders: "They were wedged so tightly that only with the greatest difficulty could they be extricated. All other bones were lying loose around them. Their position strongly suggested that the bison became trapped between the boulders and, too exhausted to work itself loose, perished there."

It is clear that the animals were not after food, since both skeletons were near a crest far above the limits of alpine vegetation. What prompted them to clamber so high in the Medicine Bow Mountains remains a mystery.

In prehistoric times, herds of wood buffalo roamed the arctic meadows stretching from the Yukon to the Bering Strait. But by the time white men arrived in the country, only a scattering of skulls remained, the animals having already made their unaccountable retreat southeastward to their current habitat near the Great Slave Lake.

Other wood buffalo were then occupying the western two thirds of Alberta, leaving the eastern part of the province to their plains relatives. A reasonably distinct dividing line between the territories of the two subspecies can be followed southward along the eastern foothills of the Rockies to the New Mexican border.

East of this line, the range of the plains buffalo stretched across the continent to the Atlantic Ocean. Its heartland was the Great Plains, home of literally millions of buffalo, extending from the tip of Texas all the way up to southern Alberta, Saskatchewan, and Manitoba.

Around the borders of this vast area, in forested regions east of the Mississippi and west of the Rockies, buffalo are known to have penetrated marginal localities. The precise limits of this outlying range are difficult to delineate, but the zoologist's task has been simplified by the discovery of some important clues. The unearthing of skulls in a given area helps to establish range, as do the statements of early explorers. (Historic journals must be carefully interpreted, however, since travelers could not always pinpoint their location and sometimes used vague terms to relate what they saw—one English explorer clouded his account by describing both deer and buffalo as "Beasts.")

Many of the grounds for delimiting range are purely circumstantial. Meager evidence to support the presence of buffalo in the northwestern corner of Nevada forced historians to turn to old

A coastal setting with a pelican, palm trees, and an opossum dangling from a branch surrounds Father Louis Hennepin's rendition of an American bison, first published in 1683.

maps for additional clues. They soon discovered a Buffalo Spring, a Buffalo Salt Works, a Buffalo Cañon, a Buffalo Creek, and a Buffalo Meadows.

Other circumstantial evidence has come from the careful sifting of antiquated records. Thus the presence of buffalo in an area of Mexico just south of the Rio Grande was corroborated by the discovery of a document written in 1806: "Buffalo hunting expeditions in the settlements of this province are the cause of neglect of families," complained a local official. "The expeditions cause settlers to lose interest in stock raising (and) disrupt friendship with the Indian tribes."

With these additional bits of evidence, we can extend the known range of the bison almost to the borders of the continent—west to parts of Washington, Oregon, California, and Nevada, south to central Mexico, and east to the Atlantic states, from much of Florida to central New York. But despite the presence of buffalo in these marginal areas, the fabled myriads roamed only on the Great Plains. East of the Mississippi, the herds that seemed immense to local residents actually represented no more than an incidental overflow, too small to exert a real influence on the customs of local tribes.

A section of the Ohio River basin was said to be the home of the legendary "Pennsylvania bison," a subspecies first described in 1915. It was reputed to be very dark—even "coal black"—in color, and to dwell in dense forests. Those who claimed to have a reliable knowledge of the animal stated that in the Pennsylvania bison, "the hump, so conspicuous on the western bison, was notable by its absence." Such particulars came not from the early settlers, who were supposed to have seen the real animal, but from their grandchildren. These third-hand reports appear to be no more than hearsay, for they have never been substantiated by a hide or skeleton. Zoologists have therefore ruled that the variety is hypothetical.

Thus the wood and plains buffalo remain the only two valid subspecies of bison in North America. Their family tree, however, supports branches of eight American fossil bison and traces its roots back into geologic time for more than a million years.

4

ANCESTORS AND

RELATIVES

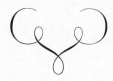

THE MOST STRIKING DEVELOPMENT OF THE LAST SEV-
enty-five million years of evolutionary history has been the rise and
specialization of the mammals. Originally shy, small, and primitive, early mammals survived the tyranny of the dinosaurs by
huddling amid the shadows of marshy glades or in the leafy
undergrowth of softwood forests. With the rapid extinction of the
dinosaurs, however, they ventured out to seek new ways of life,
evolving into the largest and most intelligent of terrestrial or
marine creatures.

Scientists have traced the buffalo back through this evolutionary span to the twilight of the Pliocene epoch, the last temperate
period before the continental ice sheets began creeping down from
the north. This pre-glacial epoch was characterized by a rich variety of fauna, the product of evolution of primitive forms into di-

versified ones, small mammals into large. On the prairies and in
the forests of Pliocene North America, a hippopotamus-like rhino
developed to immense proportions. Towering above this amphib-
ious giant was the shovel-tusked mastodon, whose scooplike lower
incisors were ideally suited for dredging roots from marshy
ground. Despite its huge size and thick hide, the slow-moving
mastadon was manageable prey for carnivores like the saber-
toothed tiger, a feline larger and more formidable than any now
living, which stabbed its victims to death with a pair of six-inch,
scimitar-like fangs.

Among smaller Pliocene mammals, one fossil gopher evolved
into the largest known rodent, the only one ever to grow horns.
Also dwelling on the Pliocene plains was an animal closely resembling the mythical unicorn: this deerlike cud-chewer sprouted a
set of antlers on his crown and a single horn on the bridge of his
nose.

Toward the end of the Pliocene, the earliest known ancestors
of the buffalo appeared in southern and eastern Asia. Fossil remains of these primitive bison have been unearthed near Peking,
China, and on the northwest frontier of Pakistan, along the foothills of the Himalayas. Though small and slender compared to
present-day forms, they displayed all the characteristics of the
genus *Bison*.

During the next million years of geological history, an interval
known as the Pleistocene epoch, or Ice Age, bison grew in size
and spread out over much of the northern hemisphere. In time,
they left behind an assortment of buried skulls and other bones, a
fossil record of their pattern of evolution. Yet for years the interpretation of that record has been shrouded in controversy. As
paleontologists have traced early bison through the Ice Age, they
have based their findings on the most variable characteristic of the
genus—the shape and size of the horns. And there lies the crux of
the difficulty, for the horns exhibit great differences not only from
one species to the next but also within each species. In addition to
increasing in size with the age of an individual, the horns may
change according to diet, physical accidents, and general health.
Despite the inevitable variations, however, the skull and horns remain the best features for classifying the fossil species, and they
figure prominently in the latest and most complete survey of bison
evolution. Although some chapters of this history may yet be re-

vised as investigators unearth further evidence, we now have a fair picture of the pattern during the million years of the Ice Age.

In the early part of this epoch, a small-horned primitive bison spread west and north into Europe and Siberia from its homeland in central Asia. Somewhat later, this bison evolved into a larger-horned form, the steppe wisent (*Bison priscus*), which continued to occupy the same range and even passed over into Alaska. The steppe wisent thus became the first bison in North America, its arrival on the continent made possible by changes in climate and land mass occurring in the middle of the Ice Age. As vast glaciers thickened and pushed across much of the northern hemisphere, amassing and compacting the snows of countless winters, the ice cap grew to a thickness of several thousand feet. So much of the earth's water was locked up in this mass of ice that the ocean level fell drastically. Although fifty-six miles of choppy water now separate Alaska and Siberia, the lowering of the sea during the Pleistocene exposed a bridge of land that was at some points wider than Alaska itself. This land bridge formed first between about fifty thousand and forty thousand years ago and again between twenty-eight thousand and ten thousand years ago. During the latter period there were several thousand years when Alaska, cut off from the rest of the continent by a giant barrier of ice and still connected to Siberia by the land bridge, was actually more a part of Asia than of North America.

The Bering Strait land bridges soon became busy causeways over which the animals of the Old and New Worlds passed back and forth. Camels and horses that had been evolving for millions of years on the Great Plains now migrated to Asia, leaving their remnants to become extinct in North America. (Horses did not reappear on the continent until brought here by Spanish explorers in the sixteenth century.) Moving in the opposite direction were species that had developed in the Old World—mammoths, musk oxen, mountain sheep, moose, deer, caribou, cougars, jaguars, and the first bison. These migrations were blocked for only one extended interval by the ice sheets covering the northern half of North America. For most of the duration of the land bridges, ice-free corridors through Alaska and western Canada furnished access to the rest of the continent.

Bison made their major penetration of North America about two thirds of the way through the Ice Age, when a temporary warming trend caused the glaciers to recede, thus laying bare great portions of the continent. An initial chapter of this colonization in the New World was uncovered recently in southwestern Kansas. One day in 1947, a cowboy coursing through a pasture known locally as the "Jinglebob," was attracted by a bony object half buried in the gravel at the side of a dry creekbed. Digging around the bone, he uncovered what looked like an elephant skull. The owner of the ranch sent for scientific help, and a paleontologist arrived some days later to examine the find. Close scrutiny revealed that the skull was indeed that of an elephant, or, more precisely, a Columbian mammoth. After further investigation along the creekbed, the scientist uncovered other fossil bones, evidence of an early community of animals, which he named after the nearby pasture—the Jinglebob fauna.

The present-day Jinglebob is an impoverished, semi-arid plain supporting only short grass and sagebrush; by contrast, the fossil fauna of the earlier epoch, identified as the Pleistocene, points to a moist and temperate period with fertile soil and a lush cover of tall grass, shrubs, and trees. The fossil forms, unlike the animals currently residing on the thirsting pasture, were types characteristic of a coastal-plain habitat: shrews, rice rats, meadow voles, bog lemmings, jumping mice, and plentiful varieties of mollusks.

In addition to the Columbian mammoth, which reached a height of eleven feet, the Jinglebob fauna included other giants of the Pleistocene epoch. The large and clumsy Harlan ground sloth, restricted by its short limbs and recurved claws to lazy rambling, was nonetheless remarkably adept at browsing the swamplands. Using its massive tail as a prop, it could rear up into an erect position and nimbly pluck twigs and leaves with its handlike front feet. Another giant, the huge short-faced bear, had jaws so abbreviated its face resembled that of a bulldog.

Prominent in the Jinglebob fauna was the largest American bison, a hulking beast designated as *Bison latifrons*, from the Latin for "wide forehead." Its horns measured about nine feet from tip to tip, a span fully three times that of present-day buffalo. This giant-horned bison evolved from the early Alaskan colonies of steppe wisent, which had migrated south and then become isolated in the heartland of the continent as the great ice sheets again swept out over Canada.

In their invasion into the temperate zones of North America, the giant-horned bison met with a community of horses and other grazers. Apparently the competing animals were no match for the huge bison, for fossil evidence seems to suggest that the horses declined in numbers as the bison increased. During the same period in Europe, however, competition was keener; bison did not expand their range to any extent and did not increase comparably in size. Although the same steppe wisent were abundant in the northern parts of the continent, they were stopped in their southern migrations by numbers of wild cattle. Nor were the cattle able to push northward, for the bison were firmly entrenched in this colder habitat. Only in one limited case, in the highlands of Asia, did they penetrate the range of the bison. There a line of cattle evolved into the yak, a form adapted to the colder alpine climate. Some even crossed into North America, where a few fossil remains have been found.

In the late Pleistocene, bison and other ungulates streaming across the Bering Strait land bridge were trailed and shadowed by early men, who were thus stumbling upon the same portal to the New World that innumerable other mammals had found before them. No one definitely knows when the first human beings crossed over the land bridge, and any evidence at the site is buried under a heavy layer of sediment at the bottom of the sea; but recent findings elsewhere on the continent suggest that men first arrived as much as forty thousand years ago.

Although it has long been assumed that early inhabitants of North America lived off surrounding big game, scholars have had little evidence to support such speculations until this century. In 1926, startling clues about the hunting activities of some primitive American peoples came to light, upsetting archeological theories of the day and establishing beyond a doubt the connection of these hunters with the big game animals on the early plains. In that year, J. D. Figgins of the Denver Museum of Natural History led a party of paleontologists into northeastern New Mexico to begin excavations in the region. At a site near the Cimarron River, the men discovered bones of a number of fossil bison, which had apparently been attracted to a waterhole or bog that had once existed in the area.

In the clay surrounding a rib bone of one bison, excavators detected what they thought was a small piece of neatly chipped flint. After dissecting the mass of clay in the laboratory, they were able to see clearly that a stone point was imbedded in the matrix next to the bison bone. This leaf-shaped projectile, distinctive in its fluted or hollow-ground flaking, they named a Folsom point after the town nearest the diggings. As a bison-hunting weapon, the point had probably been mounted on a thrusting spear and hurled or driven into the animals. The victims, a smaller form that had replaced the giant-horned *latifrons* late in the Ice Age, were eventually named after the Denver paleontologist—*Bison antiquus figginsi*.

The discovery of an extinct bison in direct association with a weapon fabricated by man severely shook the archeologists of the day. Since current theories held that the first human being had appeared on this continent only three or four thousand years before the arrival of Coronado, the scientists were reluctant to accept the authenticity of the Folsom point in a deposit estimated to be about ten thousand years old. They chose instead to believe that the point was an artifact of more recent hunters, and that its presence among the bones of the earlier bison was purely accidental.

Undaunted by their skepticism, Figgins ordered further excavations for the following summer. When his team uncovered another point embedded next to a bison bone, he stopped all work and telegraphed invitations to several museums. Three institutions sent experts to view the site containing the undisturbed Folsom point. After detailed inspection, each representative accepted as authentic the relationship between point and bison. When the scientists returned to their institutions, however, their colleagues were still dubious.

It was not until the following year, after a third expedition to the Folsom site and more telegrams and more visits by experts, that the scientific community was finally convinced of the validity of the evidence.

In the years that followed, excavations at other sites corroborated and extended the Folsom finds. The unearthing of numerous points demonstrated that various groups of early bison hunters had thrived on the plains, each developing a different style of flaking. During the millennia in which these hunters prospered, their prey gradually changed, from *Bison antiquus*, slain by Folsom men, to *Bison bison occidentalis*, brought down by more recent hunters.

The new, smaller-horned *occidentalis* evolved in Siberia from the steppe wisent that had been inhabiting northern regions of the world for much of the Ice Age. When the last continental glaciers began receding, *occidentalis* migrated southward from Alaska through ice-free corridors. Current evidence suggests that this bison moved into the Great Plains after its predecessor, *Bison antiquus*, had already become extinct. Once the dominant member of the plains grazing community, *antiquus* was probably done in by early big-game hunting societies. After the hunters helped to eliminate this old resident, the smaller *occidentalis* took over the vacated habitat. Evidently it was better adapted to withstand the hunting pressure of the prehistoric Indian cultures, for it not only survived a period when many local associates—camels, horses, sloths, and mammoths—became extinct, but also extended its range over most of the continent.

Much new information on the hunting of *occidentalis* was brought to light recently in an excavation 140 miles southeast of Denver. At this site near the Arkansas River, evidence for the slaughter of 193 bison is so complete that the moment of the hunt some eighty-five hundred years ago virtually comes to life on the spot. From the arrangement of bones at the dig, scientists were able to deduce not only the season of the kill and the direction of the wind, but also the number of hunting people present, their method of ambush, and their patterns of butchering their prey.

The site of the kill is a V-shaped arroyo about two hundred feet long, shallow at one end and extending to a depth of seven feet at the other. The disposition of the twisted and massed skeletons indicates that hunters stampeded the herd into the chasm, causing the front-running buffalo to fall in first, only to be buried under the bodies of companions plunging in after them. Proof for this mode of entrapment is clearest in the bottom layers of the remains, where the lead animals, too deeply buried for butchering, were left as they had fallen. Some of the carcasses are grotesquely twisted, and two on the bottom of the heap are lying on their backs. We know from the south-facing position of most of the skeletons that the herd was driven in from the north. In all probability the hunters had attempted to prevent their quarry from sensing their approach by moving in against the wind, and thus we can assume the wind on that day was blowing from the south. The presence of sixteen calves in the kill, including a few very young ones, dates the ambush at late May or early June.

In the upper layers of carcasses in the arroyo, the careful organization of certain bones indicates that hunters butchered methodically, beginning with the forelegs, working up to the hump, hindquarters, and spine, and finishing with the neck and skull. Apparently they snacked on raw tongues as they worked, for the tongue bones, instead of appearing in a single layer of the deposits, are scattered throughout the piles.

Evidence accumulated at this and other sites has demonstrated that early big game hunters lived comfortably on the Great Plains twelve thousand years ago, roaming in tribes of considerable size and impressive organization, preying on a seemingly limitless supply of primitive bison. The last of these early species died out about eight thousand years ago and was replaced by the modern buffalo (*Bison bison*). In a new series of sites on the plains dating back some three or four thousand years, the buffalo has been recovered in association with relics of hunters whom we can finally —and properly—label "early Indians."

The types of bones found at the locations of these different kills enable us to distinguish the butchering sites of nomads from those of villagers. Nomads discarded heavy bones that bore little meat, like the skull and the pelvis, evidently considering them of too little value to transport on extended treks, but villagers often carried these pieces for the short stretch back to their lodges, where they could work them over to remove tiny scraps of meat. The relative quantities of skull or pelvic bones can be used to differentiate the two kinds of settlements. Thus studies of bison remains found at kill sites can teach us much about the early tribes; the bones lying in the different locations also help us to trace the evolution of the bison in North America.

As the end of the Ice Age saw the evolution of the buffalo in North America, a close relative was developing in the Old World. Both forms can be traced to common ancestry in Siberia, where a reservoir of *Bison bison occidentalis* furnished migrants that dispersed into Europe and across the land bridge into America. Subsequently these new bison followed parallel lines of evolution, developing horns smaller than those of their ancestors. In both the Old and the New World, the end points of this evolution are remarkably similar. The European bison, or wisent, closely resembles the American bison in skeleton, general appearance, and many other features. So close is the kinship, in fact, that the two animals, once classified as separate species, have recently been re-grouped as mere subspecies: the plains buffalo is now *Bison bison bison*, and the wisent *Bison bison bonasus*.

In the scheme of natural classification, both buffalo and wisent belong to the group known as ruminants, those species that re-work their food by cud-chewing. Thus, in common with other ruminants, bison swallow large quantities of forage after only superficial chewing, storing it in the rumen, or paunch, the first sac of the four-chambered ruminant stomach. By the time they retire to digest their food more thoroughly, soaking and churning have run their course in the rumen. The food is then regurgitated wad by wad for rechewing before being swallowed again. There-after it passes from the second stomach (reticulum) to the third (omasum) and finally the fourth (abomasum), where most of the digestion takes place.

Among ruminants, bison fall into the family *Bovidae*, and within that, into a still more refined grouping, the tribe *Bovini*. This is a collection of genera related through the common charac-teristics of horns on both sexes, long tufted tails, and broad moist muzzles.

Included among the bison's immediate kin under this category are the African Cape buffalo, the wild Indian buffalo, the domesti-cated water buffalo, the dwarf water buffalo, or anoa of Celebes, the tamarau of the Philippines, and all true cattle. In the last group are members of the genus *Bos*, compromising two kinds of cattle with a worldwide distribution, as well as five other species dwell-ing mostly in southern Asia—the yak, the gaur, the gayal, the banteng, and the kouprey. The genus *Bos* also included the aurochs of Europe (*B. primigenius*), a recently extinct (1627) long-horned ox believed to be the wild ancestor of domestic cattle. (The animal is also known as the urus, a term that appears in the classical Latin writings of Julius Caesar and Virgil.)

Even the American buffalo was once grouped with cattle in the genus *Bos*, although the designation was later changed to *Bison*. Traits that separate bison from other bovines are their sin-gular appearance, certain peculiarities of their skull structure, and their fourteen pairs of ribs against the thirteen found in cattle.

At the same time, the similarities between the genera *Bos* and *Bison* are equally striking. For example, their individual bones are easily confused unless examined in detail, their chromosomal structures are quite similar, and their blood has been shown to bear an extremely close relationship. Recent serological studies, including examination of antigens and antibodies in the blood of both cattle and bison, have disclosed numerous distinctive characteristics, most of them involving the biochemically complex red corpuscles. Just as the blood of human beings can be divided into different blood group systems by the ABO, Rh, and other factors, that of bovines can be classified into at least sixty different categories. When the blood of bison and cattle is tested for these factors, the results provide a reasonable measure of the extent of kinship of the two groups.

An analysis of such evidence accumulated over the past few years has revealed few differences and many strong similarities between *Bos* and *Bison*. In fact, so close is the affinity between the two genera that serologists proposed placing bison back again in the same genus with cattle. Support is given to their proposition by the observation that bison can successfully cross with members of the genus *Bos*, in particular with domestic cattle, humped cattle, and yaks.

In all of these crosses, however, the male offspring are sterile, preventing any further breeding of a line of hybrids. On the other hand, American buffalo cross freely with European wisent, yielding offspring that are fertile in both sexes, thus indicating the closer relationship of buffalo and wisent, the only other living member of what is still labeled the genus *Bison*.

Though very much alike in many ways, the two forms of bison still have distinctive features. In contrast to the American buffalo, with its ponderous, front-heavy proportions, the wisent is streamlined, with longer legs, a longer and lighter body, and a less-pronounced hump. The feeding habits of the two species are also dissimilar, for buffalo graze grasses or herbs while wisent browse the leaves of trees or shrubs. The European animals favor willow, aspen, and ash, whose shoots, branches, and bark supply about half their diet. Among shrubs they prefer mistletoe, blueberry, raspberry, and blackberry. They even relish acorns; in the fall, when the fallen oak nuts are abundant, they may eat nothing else.

Despite these differences, wisent and buffalo share many traits in the field of behavior, especially in the activities of rutting bulls and in the organization of social groupings. Herds formed by wisent are not nearly as large as the masses of buffalo on the

North American plains. They congregate in groups of between six and twenty and occasionally as many as forty individuals. These small gatherings are dictated by the wisent's choice of a woodland habitat, which restricts space and visibility and thus limits herd size.

Both European wisent and American buffalo have been similarly persecuted by man and his encroaching civilization. Although buffalo were not doomed until farming and ranching took over their historic grasslands in the last century, wisent lost ground much earlier as an expanding populace slowly destroyed their native forests. Toward the end of the Middle Ages they were exterminated from most of their original range—in France before 1400, in Austria and Hungary during the 1500's, and in Germany in the 1700's.

By the beginning of the First World War, the largest remaining group of wisent, a herd of over seven hundred, lived in the Bialowieza Forest of northeastern Poland. Wartime hostilities soon depleted the ranks of the unprotected herd—when the Kaiser's troops marched into Bialowieza thirteen months later, they found only 120 survivors. The decline of the wisent, according to the German officer who took control of the forest, occurred "partially in consequence of poaching by the retreating Russian troops, but particularly by the Russian deserters and scattered bands . . . hiding in the forest in the fall of 1915 . . . , which, together with the forest peasants, slaughtered the half-tame animals." The Germans soon issued and enforced an order forbidding the killing of bison, except by special permission from the commanding general of the East, Prince Leopold of Bavaria. Permission was granted in only about a dozen cases—"exclusively for royalties and specially meritorious high ranking generals." Under this legal protection, the Bialowieza herd increased to some 175 head by December 1918. But in that month the Germans retreated, and the resulting chaos and lawlessness again left the herd at the mercy of poachers. Within a year every wisent in the Bialowieza Forest had been slain.

This was the last remnant of free-living European bison. Four years after the slaughter, an official census revealed that there were only sixty-six wisent left in the world, all of them descendants of individuals given to zoos and wildlife preserves by nineteenth-century Russian czars. In 1923, these animals were scattered in eight European countries. And the meager number of survivors included several cattle-bison hybrids, which had to be stricken from the meticulously kept stud books of purebreds.

By 1939, the surviving wisent had increased to some one hundred animals, and a new herd of sixteen had been reestablished in Poland's Bialowieza Forest. With the outbreak of World War II, however, the forest was again caught up in hostilities. The area was first occupied by Russians, who soon forbade the killing of wisent on pain of death: during their occupation, only one animal was shot—a crime for which three Soviet soldiers were executed. When the Nazis invaded the area, several wisent were slain before order was restored and edicts were again issued to protect the herd. The preservation of the Bialowieza wisent was assured by the efforts of a group of naturalists and the concern of top-ranking members of the party—Hermann Goering personally owned four purebreds and a few hybrids. Even Hitler took an interest in Bialowieza wisent, and ordered several transferred to Berlin.

When the Bialowieza Forest changed hands for the third time as Russians reoccupied the area, a local Polish forester brandished the same Russian decree that had earlier guaranteed protection to the wisent; thus the herd managed to come through the war with sixteen members, as many as it started with in 1939.

Other wisent that had survived the war in zoos and refuges brought the worldwide population to eighty-four. In the years that followed, the survivors bred with notable success, increasing their numbers each season. Today there are close to a thousand wisent in the world, more than half of them in Poland and Russia. The largest single herd is again living in the centuries-old homeland of the species, the Bialowieza Forest. In this area Polish mammalogists are making steady progress in their efforts to transform a once captive group into a free-living herd as natural and wild as the primeval forest in which they roam.

5

EARLY CHRONICLES

MAN MADE HIS FIRST GRAPHIC RECORD OF BISON MORE than twenty-five thousand years ago. Deep in the chambers of caves in France and Spain, Cro-Magnon peoples carved and daubed images of the big game animals that furnished them with meat and skins. Foremost among the creatures depicted in many underground galleries was the giant, hunchbacked steppe wisent (*Bison priscus*).

The Cro-Magnon artists recorded their bison with a skilled hand, outlining the musculature with accurate, stylized lines, smoothly shading the body with masses of color and making use of rocky bumps and clefts to give the figures a three-dimensional aspect. Absorbed by the limestone and preserved by the sheltering climate within the caves, the pigments survived the passage of thousands of years, retaining much of their original brilliance until their discovery in modern times.

The purpose of these prehistoric murals must have been spiritual rather than decorative, for they were generally hidden in the remotest corners of caves, at the end of passages that could only have been penetrated by Cro-Magnons carrying fat-filled lamps or torches. In the French cave of Niaux, a visitor today must trek more than three thousand feet through twisting, stalactite-strewn corridors before finally coming upon the gallery of drawings.

Among the many bison on the walls at Niaux are several depicted as victims of the hunt, their bodies pierced with spears and spewing reddish blotches of blood. Just as the artist put his bison to a symbolic death on the rock wall, the hunter was expected to go forth with confidence and duplicate the feat in real life. The paintings and carvings were thus a vehicle for magic, transforming the caves into subterranean shrines. Through them, Cro-Magnon hunters apparently hoped to gain power over their quarry, rendering the bison vulnerable to the thrust of their spears.

Thousands of years after these rough beginnings in cave art, the contemporary bison of Europe, or wisent, were appearing regularly in the annals of the continent. In the fourth century B.C., Aristotle included the wisent in his history of animals, referring to the beast by the Greek *bonasos* (a term that has since become part of the animal's scientific name). Some three hundred years later, the wisent figured in games in the Roman arenas and was described in the works of Pliny and Seneca. In the sixth century A.D., Theodebert, King of the Franks, was fatally gored by a wild bull while on a hunt. The classic reference to the chase appears in the *Nibelungenlied*, the German epic poem in which the hero, Siegfried, slays a wisent in the mountains bordering the Rhine Valley. Later chroniclers described how Polish kings presented neighboring monarchs with gifts of salted bison meat, considered an "exquisite dish."

The recorded history of bison in Europe spans many thousands of years. By contrast, the annals of the American buffalo extend back only four centuries, to the time of the first European explorers in North America. But in this comparatively short period, an astonishing amount of historical literature has accumulated—more, in fact, than exists for any other mammal on the continent.

The tale of the first white man ever to gaze upon an American buffalo comes out of the twilight period of the Aztec empire. In November of 1519, the reigning monarch of Mexico, Montezuma II, greeted Hernán Cortés and his troops with elaborate ceremony.

The Aztec emperor, soon to lose his kingdom and die at the hands of the conquering Spaniards, apparently treated the ambitious intruder to some sightseeing, including a visit to the royal zoo in what is now Mexico City.

There, it was reported, Cortés viewed an impressive menagerie. In the vicinity of the palace buildings he discovered elaborate galleries faced with rare stones and holding hundreds of birds, mammals, and reptiles. Within low wooden cages made of massive beams were cougars, jaguars, and bears; some were seen feeding upon the meat of deer and rabbits or the intestines of human sacrificial victims.

In other cages, Cortés came upon additional beasts "of the savage Kind which New-Spain produc'd; among which, the greatest rarity was the *Mexican* Bull; a wonderful composition of divers Animals: it has crooked Shoulders, with a Bunch on its Back like a camel; its Flanks dry, its tail large, and its Neck cover'd with Hair like a Lyon. It is cloven-footed, its Head armed like that of a Bull, which it resembles in Fierceness, with no less Strength and Agility."

The sighting of this "Mexican" buffalo by Cortés has been standard fare for the past century, although the captive specimen was never described by the explorer himself. The original report comes instead from a Spanish historian, Antonio de Solís y Rivadeneyra, who wrote from an isolated station in Spain without ever having visited Mexico—and composed his story 164 years after Cortés' sojourn with Montezuma. Other reports coming out of Mexico in the same period made no mention of buffalo. In a personal account of his visit to Montezuma's zoo, one of Cortés' soldiers described cougars, jaguars, foxes, rattlesnakes, and a great variety of colorful birds—but no animal that sounded like a buffalo; and Cortés himself failed to mention buffalo when he returned to Spanish court circles nine years after his arrival in Mexico. The Mexican bull of Solís thus appears to be chimerical.

With the elimination of this report, the first record of a sighting by a white man is that of another explorer, Alvar Nuñez Cabeza de Vaca. In his wanderings across the plains of Texas in 1533, the Spaniard observed "oxen" that had "little hornes like the Moresche cattle, and very long haires . . ."

Since Cabeza de Vaca did not publish a report on his travels for twenty-two years, credit for the first printed description of buffalo goes to his countryman, Gonzalo Fernandez de Oviedo y Valdes. Between 1535 and 1537, Oviedo brought out a twenty-volume history dealing primarily with the West Indies but curiously devoting one chapter to "the Cows of the Land to the North." Among his remarks was the following observation about the behavior of the herds: "They will not walk, nor will they move at a fast pace or faster gallop, unless united, as though tied together like horses; but they are nimble and swift animals, and very savage, and innumerable in quantity."

Francisco Lopez de Gomara published this earliest known likeness of an American bison in his Historia General de las Indias, *1552–3.*

Continuing the Spanish tradition of exploration, Francisco Vásquez de Coronado headed north from Mexico, departing on February 23, 1540, in search of the fabled riches of the "Seven Cities of Cibola." He rode at the head of some 250 horsemen, 70 foot soldiers, more than 300 native allies, and at least 1,000 Negro and Indian servants.

The following July he reached, assaulted, and penetrated Cibola, but the treasure remained illusory; the seven splendid cities turned out to be no more than a cluster of shabby pueblos in the Zuñi country of New Mexico.

Coronado's obsession with treasure persisted. So intrigued was he by reports of a new El Dorado in the region of Quivira that he gave scant attention to a report that one of his scouting parties had sighted the expedition's first buffalo. After wintering his troops, he set forth in pursuit of the mirage of wealth in Quivira, leading his entire army eastward through the Staked Plain of Texas. There the men met with this new breed of cow, "wilde and fierce, of which they slue 80 the first day for provision." The expeditionary forces might well have starved had it not been for those buffalo killed along the way to Quivira.

Coronado's army was impressed by the size of the herds they encountered as they headed east: "All the Plaine is as full of hunch-backed Kine (buffalo) as Serena in Spaine of Sheepe," came the expedition's report. The record also took note of an unexpected bonus provided by the herds. Shortly after setting forth on their trek, the men discovered that small piles of buffalo chips could be laid along the route "for way-markes against their return."

Quivira was attained at last, but proved to be a mere tipi village of Wichita Indians located near the present site of Great Bend, Kansas. After exploring the surrounding country for several days, Coronado returned to Mexico, "very sad and very weary, completely worn out and shame-faced."

Quivira had yielded no riches, but a vast portion of America had been explored and described. Among the other documents of the trip, the men brought back new and valuable information on the herds of buffalo that roamed the pristine plain. Contained in the report were some remarks about the impressive mien of the bulls: ". . . there was not one of our horses that did not take flight when he saw them first, for they have a narrow, short face, the brow two palms across from eye to eye, the eyes sticking out at the side so that, when they are running, they can see who is following them . . ." (The veracity of this observation about the vision of buffalo was not confirmed until almost four centuries later, when anatomists noted that the eyes of buffalo were indeed more wide-angled and mobile than those of domestic cattle.)

Coronado's report contained an elaborate description of the

new beast with "a great hump, larger than a camel's," and went on to discuss certain physical and behavioral traits of the herds:

> In May they change the hair in the middle of the body for a down, which makes perfect lions of them. They rub against small trees . . . to shed their hair, and they continue this until only the down is left, as a snake changes its skin. They have a short tail, with a bunch of hair at the end. When they run, they carry it erect like a scorpion.

The peculiarities of French Anarctica, otherwise called America, and of the several lands and islands discovered in our time, *published by André Thevet in 1558, contained this primitive drawing of an American bison. The beast shown looks much like a camel, and the accompanying text even makes note of the resemblance.*

About fifty years after Coronado's trek, Captain Juan de Oñate, a descendant of both Cortés and Montezuma, inherited the Spanish thirst for conquest. In 1598 he arrived at the Rio Grande and took formal possession "of all the kingdoms and provinces of New Mexico . . . in the name of our Lord King Philip." Establishing a colony at El Paso, he turned his attention to exploration, commanding his nephew, Captain Vicente de Zaldívar, to take sixty men on a buffalo-hunting expedition.

Zaldívar's party came across numerous bands of Indians in what is now the southeastern corner of New Mexico. These nomads lived in tipis of tanned buffalo skins, shifting their "rancherias" to follow the herds of buffalo. Zaldívar was particularly awed by the size of the herds they pursued. After sighting an estimated hundred thousand buffalo, he was confident that his men could capture at least ten thousand.

Constructing a corral of cottonwood timbers, the Spaniards soon managed to drive a herd toward their trap. But as the beasts headed for the enclosure, they suddenly "turned back in a stampede towards the men . . . rushing through them in a mass," and fled in all directions: "It was impossible to stop them, because they are cattle terribly obstinate, courageous beyond exaggeration, and so cunning that if pursued they run . . . and if their pursuers stop or slacken their speed they stop and roll, just like mules, and with this respite renew their run."

Despite this rout, Zaldívar's men managed to kill some buffalo for food. "The meat of the bull is superior to that of our cow," they reported, "and that of the cow equals our most tender veal or mutton."

The members of the Zaldívar expedition thus joined the ranks of other early visitors from the Old World in expressing their opinion of a native American food. Indeed, the matter of buffalo meat would be a frequent topic of plains conversation over the next three centuries, for thick, lean cuts of the animal were to become standard fare on the American frontier. The herds would supply a ready means of sustenance to explorers, military expeditions, fur traders, voyageurs, sportsmen, railroad builders, villagers, and even steamboat captains, who kept crews of hunters scouring the river banks for buffalo to provision their vessels.

When George Catlin paddled hundreds of miles down the Missouri in a canoe, he made his bed every night in the grass "amongst the lilies and other wildflowers," and for food used "simply buffalo meat, without bread or coffee." As the virgin heartland of America was gradually broken up into homesteads, early settlers had to depend on buffalo meat to carry them through the first few years of frontier farming. Daniel Boone and his party subsisted almost entirely on such meat during their first winter in Kentucky.

Hotels in pioneer towns served cuts of buffalo instead of beef, and visitors from the east seldom knew the difference, often commenting upon the fine flavor of the steaks in front of them only moments after asking whether buffalo meat was fit to eat. Long before the hotel chefs learned to rely on buffalo, most frontier gourmets had given their vote of praise: "The cow buffalo was equal to any meat I ever saw," wrote Zebulon Pike, "and we feasted sumptuously on the choice morsels." And Father Hennepin thought "the flesh of these Beasts . . . very relishing, and full of Juice, especially in *Autumn;* for having grazed all the Summer long in those vast Meadows, where the Herbs are as high as they, they are then very fat."

But this fine reputation would be blighted whenever a greenhorn made the mistake of trying meat from an old bull. "The entire flesh was surprisingly elastic—indeed, a very clever imitation of India rubber," wrote one disenchanted gourmet. "It recoiled from our teeth with a spring, and just then I should scarcely have been surprised had I seen those buffalo, which were feeding in the distance, go bounding off like immense foot-balls." Later, however, on sampling some cuts from young buffalo, the same writer became sold on the virtues of the meat.

Plainsmen sampled many parts of buffalo, roasting, baking, boiling, salting, or drying the tongues, humps, livers, and of course the prime cuts. Especially appetizing were the marrow bones, broiled over a plains fire and cracked open to expose the soft, rich center. Many cooks made passable buffalo sausage from minced tenderloin and fat, but the dish attained epicurean perfection with the French touch of Toussaint Charbonneau, the interpreter and sometime cook for the Lewis and Clark expedition and the husband of the expedition guide, Sacajawea. As the party proceeded westward away from "buffalo country" in the summer of 1805, Meriwether Lewis lamented leaving the buffalo and Charbonneau's *boudin blanc:*

This white pudding we all esteem one of the greatest delicacies . . . About 6 feet of the lower extremity of the large gut of the Buffaloe is the first morsel that the cook makes love to; this he holds fast at one end with the right hand, while with the forefinger and thumb of the left hand he gently compresses it, and discharges what he says *is not good to eat,* but of which in the sequel we get a moderate portion; the mustle lying underneath the shoulder blade next to the back, and fillets are next saught, these are needed up very fine with a good portion of kidney suet; to this composition is then added a just proportion of pepper and salt and a small quantity of flour; thus far advanced, our skillful operator Charbonneau seizes his recepticle, which has never once touched the water, for that would intirely distroy the regular order of the whole procedure.

After detailing Charbonneau's technique for pressing the stuffing into the intestine, Lewis went on to describe the final stages of the preparation:

It is then baptised in the missouri with two dips and a flirt, and bobbed into the kettle; from whence, after it be well boiled it is taken and fryed with bears oil untill it becomes brown, when it is ready to esswage the pangs of a keen appetite or such as travelers in the wilderness are seldom at a loss for.

Although meat was the most frequently discussed product of the buffalo, it was only one of a number of benefits derived from the beast, ranging from emergency water rations to navigational aids. The list includes such diverse plains lore as the pit-like buffalo wallows used as makeshift foxholes in time of Indian attack and the boats fashioned from buffalo hide for floating the wares of fur traders downriver. Even the meat itself was often cooked with fuel furnished by the herds, for the dry, weathered dung stoked many a campfire on the treeless plains. "Wood now is scarce," wrote Mrs. George Donner, heading west in 1846 with the ill-fated Donner party, "but buffalo chips are excellent. They kindle quickly and retain heat surprisingly. We had this morning buffalo steaks broiled upon them, that had the same flavor they would have had upon hickory coals."

Buffalo chips also kindled frontier humor. "It is a common joke upon the plains," remarked an overland traveler, "that a steak cooked on these chips requires no pepper." And one authority, his tongue planted firmly in his cheek, gauged the value of the famous buffalo by-product: "As . . . westward the course of empire takes its way, the buffalo chip rises to the plane of the steam engine and the electric telegraph, and acquires all the dignity which is supposed to enshroud questions of national importance or matters of political economy."

Buffalo also provided emergency water rations, thus rescuing an occasional thirsting party in arid regions devoid of waterholes. As the inaugural wagon caravan traversed the Santa Fe Trail, the voyagers ran out of water on a "pathless desert" between the Arkansas and Cimarron Rivers. They were finally reduced "to the cruel necessity of killing their dogs and cutting off the ears of their mules, in the vain hope of assuaging their burning thirst with the hot blood." They might well have perished had they not discovered and shot a wandering buffalo—from the paunch of the animal they were able to drain enough of a certain "filthy beverage" to sustain them until the next waterhole.

John Townsend, an early plains traveler, left a record of how this liquid was procured. Once, when suffering from an intolerable thirst several miles from the Platte River, Townsend and a hunter named Richardson encountered and shot a stray buffalo. Without hesitation, the more experienced Richardson walked up to the carcass, rolled it over on its side, and cut it open "so as to expose to view the great stomach, and still crawling and twisting entrails." Staring in astonishment, Townsend watched Richardson "plunge his knife into the distended paunch, from which gushed the green and gelatinous juices, and then insinuate his tin pan into the opening, and by depressing its edge, strain off the water which was mingled with its contents." The extraordinary liquid was apparently quite potable, for Richardson "laughed heartily before he applied the cup to his own mouth . . . then drank it to the dregs, smacking his lips, and drawing a long breath after it, with the satisfaction of a man taking his wine after dinner."

In still another benefit provided by the herds, travelers in the wilderness were indebted to the buffalo for making it possible to journey with relative ease through rough country. When stymied by a maze of sharp-walled bluffs bordering certain rivers, pioneers chose buffalo trails as sure, if sometimes tortuous, passes through these confusing natural barriers. In some areas, the animals had whittled fifteen-foot river banks into passably graded approaches.

Buffalo trails were judged by George Washington ·to be "crooked and not well chosen." But he was in a minority. Countless other travelers used the trails and praised them highly. Lewis and Clark, for example, felt that the animals had "a wonderful sagacity in the choice of routes," and remarked, "The coincidence of a buffalow with an Indian road was the strongest assurance that it was the best . . ." Another observer considered such a trail, though not a "good waggon road, the best route to be had."

Certainly there were times when the trails were questionable routes for wagons or even for riders on horseback. Some travelers became confused by the welter of interlacing paths and lost their way. Others were inconvenienced by dangerously bumpy trails; passing wagons broke axles as they bounced over the deep ruts, especially in places where their course cut across parallel rows of buffalo trails. But the works of the buffalo were the only natural roads in the wilderness, and if sometimes rough, they were plotted well. According to one enthusiastic traveler, the animals selected "routes, even in the roughest districts, which the tripod of the white man cannot improve upon." Buffalo have even been credited with the groundwork for several notable engineering achievements: the Wilderness Trail from Virginia through the Cumberland Gap to Kentucky; the rail line over the most feasible portage between the Potomac and Ohio Rivers; and the Union Pacific route across wide prairie expanses along the Platte River.

Some of the most spectacular of all the buffalo trails were those converging upon mineral licks—the natural salt deposits found in certain marshy areas. In parts of Kentucky, herds heading for favored licks made trails that were sometimes five or six feet deep and "spacious enough for two wagons to go abreast." Around one lick in the region, chronicler John Filson, writing in 1784, described "the prodigious roads they have made from all quarters, as if leading to some populous city, the vast space of land around these springs desolated as if by a ravaging enemy, and hills reduced to plains."

In addition to acting as compass lines for colonial migration, the trails influenced the patterns of settlement in the heart of the Ohio River valley. By 1790, Lexington, Frankfort, Louisville, and Cincinnati had developed along the old paths. Although the buffalo disappeared soon afterward from most of this area east of the Mississippi, the herds had already stamped the country with some distinctive signs of occupation that would persist for centuries.

6

PREPARATION FOR THE

KILL

When the buffalo population was at its height and the animals moved in herds of hundreds of thousands across the plains, the lives of the Indians who depended on them for their existence and culture were carefully arranged around the elaborate proceedings of the hunt. A complex fusion of practical habit and religious ritual attended the quest, killing, and consumption of the animals.

Among the Blackfoot and the Hidatsa, it was said that supernatural power for controlling the herds was invested in *iniskim*, or "buffalo rocks," special trinkets that derived their magic from a resemblance to people or animals. Certain *iniskim* were referred to as "buffalo"—in the irregularities of their shapes the Indians perceived legs, tail, hump, and head. Naturally such "buffalo" were prized above all other *iniskim*.

Legend relates that the first buffalo rock was discovered long ago during a severe winter, when the disappearance of the herds had brought the Indians to the brink of starvation. One day, a young woman walking near camp heard a beautiful song. Searching for the source of the music, she traced the strain to a curiously formed rock sitting on a bed of buffalo hair in the fork of

Protuberances on this Blackfoot iniskim *give the rock the crude shape of a buffalo.*

a tree. As it finished singing, the rock spoke to her and said, "Carry me to your lodge, and when it is dark, call in the people and teach them the song you have just heard. Pray, too, that you may not starve, and that the buffalo may come back." When the woman took the *iniskim* back to camp, she bade the old men gather and pray in the lodge, just as the rock had instructed. Before long, they were rewarded with the arrival of a great herd, and from that time on, they revered the power of the buffalo rock.

Iniskim were usually painted red, swaddled in a nest of buffalo wool, and wrapped in the skin of an unborn calf. Each bundle was then encased in a fringed pouch along with two bags of paint included for their purported magic. The pouch hung on a tripod behind the tipi, where tribute was paid morning and evening with a smudge of sweetgrass.

Many believed that stones left undisturbed for a time would

bear offspring. As proof, they flourished small pebbles or fossils similar in shape to the "parent" stone, claiming that these had appeared mysteriously at the unwrapping of the bundle.

Iniskim were occasionally honored in special ceremonies inside the lodge, where the owner prayed and practiced magic over them in an effort to entice buffalo into the neighborhood of the camp.

The buffalo rock ritual was only one aspect of the complex repertory of charms, superstitions, and ceremonies brought into use before each hunt. The proceedings emphasized that the hunt was less a sporting venture than a solemn undertaking controlled by the supernatural. So vitally did the outcome of a hunt affect the entire tribe that the matter could not be left to chance. The Indians appealed to their spirit powers to induce the herds to come near the camp, enter a trap, or fall easy prey to hunters. Triumph in their efforts was naturally attributed to strict observance of the shamanistic procedures. Failure was passed off on some defect or omission in the ceremony. And failures there were: the winter of 1871 was designated on the Sioux tribal calendar by the most significant event of the season: "Buffalo Ceremony Failed."

Each tribe had its own special conjurations for buffalo, traditions that had been a sacred heritage for generations.

The Hoof-Rattle Society of the Cheyenne relied upon a section of elk antler carved to look like a rattlesnake, its back notched with a line of grooves cut at half-inch intervals. When members wished to entice large herds of buffalo near their camp, society members congregated, chewed herb medicine and spat upon the snake to activate it. Pressing the snake's head against a resonator of buffalo rawhide, they rubbed its corrugated back with the shinbone of an antelope. This produced a loud, shrill call reported to be highly effective in luring herds.

The Mandan fashioned a case of parchment about six feet long, decorating the top with seven gourds, each ornamented with a tuft of red-dyed horsehair. Inside the case they placed a set of mounted birds. A hunter seeking supernatural assistance would lug a whole buffalo—minus head and viscera—to this "bird case" and deposit it as an offering. Four such contributions were supposed to guarantee a sufficiency of buffalo to the supplicant.

To the Pawnee, success in hunting depended in great part on the care and respect lavished on "buffalo staffs," slender spruce poles wrapped with red and blue streamers and elaborately decorated with beadwork and eagle feathers. Priests and shamans fasted for several days to consecrate the staffs. Then, inside the medicine lodge and in the presence of twelve buffalo skulls, they offered sacrifices to *Atíus Tiráwa*, the Spirit Father, fervently intoning: "Father, you are the Ruler—We are poor—Take pity on us—Send us plenty of buffalo, plenty of fat cows . . ." As they prayed, they blessed their bows and arrows, devoutly depositing them next to the buffalo skulls to await the commencement of the hunt, when the consecrated staffs would be borne in a procession toward the herds.

The Blackfoot placed their faith in the "Beaver Men," special shamans who used sacred bundles to lure buffalo. They were called upon in severe winters, when the buffalo drifted far from camp and the snow was too deep to mount a hunt. Each bundle of the Beaver Men contained a small bag of rattles, a string of buffalo hoofs, and a tail. The incantations of the shamans and the magic of the bundles were expected to charm the herd into moving near the camp.

The Beaver Men began their ritual by lighting a smudge of sweetgrass and inviting participants to sit inside the tipi. Then they sang the first of seven "charming-the-buffalo" songs:

". . . Man, he has come in with happiness.
Buffalo, them I have taken . . ."

By the end of the fourth verse, the Beaver Men had propped up a large chunk of buffalo rawhide shaped like a profile of the real animal. The raising of this effigy ushered in the second round of songs, which were chanted to the accompaniment of rattles. Next, the flourishing of the sacred hoofs and tail indicated that it was time for one shaman and his wife to commence their mimicry. Bellowing, butting each other, and slapping their hands on the earth as if preparing to wallow, they imitated the actions of their noble prey. Then the head shaman dipped the buffalo hoofs into a snow-filled bowl and proclaimed that wind would come from the direction of the nearest herd, bringing a blizzard to drive the animals toward camp. The sessions were concluded with a prayer and a final song.

Such ritual acts reached their pinnacle in the buffalo-calling ceremonies of the Mandan and Hidatsa tribes—the men's Bull Dance and the women's White Buffalo Cow Dance. In normal times the men performed, in order to charm nearby herds into coming closer to the village; in periods of dire famine in winter, the women were pressed into service to summon back long-departed herds. Two early observers have reported that the spiritualists were always successful, since they danced on and on—for several weeks if necessary—until the buffalo appeared.

The men commenced their Bull Dance in front of the medicine lodge, accompanied by an orchestra of four men with red-painted bodies. As most of the tribe gathered to watch, the four men thumped mallets and drumsticks against sacks of water, shook rattles, and blended their voices in high-pitched yelps. Ten to fifteen dancers stomped into the square, their faces and bodies daubed with identical patterns of red, white, and black, their ankles adorned with locks of buffalo hair. Each man wore a mask made from the complete skin of a buffalo with the horns fastened to the sides and a tail braided onto the back; in his hands he carried rattles and a favorite bow or lance. Stamping, grunting, and bellowing, the men danced before the medicine lodge, in graphic imitation of a group of buffalo bulls.

Hour by hour the ceremony wore on, until at last one dancer after another signified his exhaustion by bending forward and sinking toward the ground. As each performer flagged, an associate fired a blunt arrow at him. Struck with the harmless missile, the Indian collapsed on the ground like a slain buffalo. Immediately bystanders seized him, dragged him out of the arena by his heels, and brandished knives about him as though skinning and cutting up a genuine carcass. When they released him to rest, a fresh dancer pranced into the ring to take his place. In this manner, relays of dancers kept the performance going day and night until herds were finally sighted near the village.

The group of Bull Dancers had its feminine counterpart in the White Buffalo Cow Society, a club of forty or fifty older matrons, the most exalted group of women in any Mandan or Hidatsa village. When called upon to lure buffalo, they prepared themselves with face paint, daubing one eye with azure and the other with vermilion. The chins of most were already marked with the tattoos distinctive of their society.

The entire group was outfitted to represent a buffalo herd. The leader wrapped herself in a treasured robe from the rare white buffalo, the seat of the "medicine" alleged to bring in the herds.

Most of the women wore hats of white buffalo hide decorated with owl and raven feathers.

Inside the women's lodge, a small group of male musicians beat on drums, shook a rattle of buffalo skin, and chanted an overture. Then, after forming a circle, the women responded to the men's chants with some loud shrill whoops and began to dance, keeping time to the drum beats by rocking from side to side, always remaining on the same spot.

Carl Bodmer, the artist traveling with Prince Maximilian of Wied, sketched this group of women from the White Buffalo Cow Society while visiting the Mandan in the 1830's.

After each night's session, one of the musicians gathered the women's buffalo costumes and attached them to a long cottonwood pole; this he fixed above the doorway of the lodge as a charm to summon a blizzard and drive the buffalo close to the village. Then all the performers slept in the lodge.

In addition to their varied dances, both the Mandan and the Hidatsa occasionally tried to attract buffalo with a sexual sacrifice, in which the young men surrendered their wives to tribal patriarchs—or even visiting white men. While wintering with the Mandan in 1805, Captain William Clark reported on this "curious

Custom," dutifully following President Jefferson's instructions to "acquire what knolege you can of the state of morality, religion & information" among the tribes.

"The old men arrange themselves in a circle," wrote Clark, "and after Smoking a pipe which is handed them by a young man Dressed up for the purpose, the young men who have their wives back of the Circle go each to one of the old men with a whining tone and request the old man to take his wife (who presents herself necked except for her robe) and Sleep with her. The Girl then takes the Old Man (who verry often can scarcely walk) and leades him to a convenient place for the business, after which they return to the lodge." Each young man, believing that the spirits will be summoned only if the patriarch is gratified, "begs him not to dispise him & his wife."

Clark's delegate to the Mandan ritual was thorough in his research: "We Sent a man to this Medisan Dance last night," went the report, "and they gave him 4 Girls; all this to cause the buffalow to Come near So that they may Kill them."

If some Indians used dances and charms, others in every plains tribe relied on supernatural visions to summon the buffalo spirits. These last, who became known as "dreamers," sequestered themselves in lonely retreats to fast and thirst for several days, imploring the spirits to accept their sacrifices and grant them special powers. An occasional man further humbled himself by cutting off a finger joint or enduring other forms of self-torture. Once he had made contact with the supernatural, an Indian was eligible to receive dream-sent disclosures about the location of the herds. (This privileged information then brought the man under the restrictions of a taboo, for he was not permitted to kill any animal he had dreamed of. Many bypassed the taboo by limiting their dreams to buffalo of a certain age; in this manner, they retained the right to kill all other animals during the forthcoming hunt.)

Still another stratagem for calling buffalo was the two-man "hoop-and-javelin game." As one player rolled a hoop over the ground, his partner tried to throw a light javelin through the hole. Points were scored according to the accuracy with which the player wielding the javelin directed his missile through the center of the hoop. Many tribes played the game for sport, and in addition, a few thought the game had magical power to attract buffalo. Pawnee storytellers, in particular, recounted a myth that gave the origin of the hoop-and-javelin game. Recital of this tale, they believed, would influence the spirits to charm buffalo into approaching and permitting themselves to be slaughtered. Other tribes had similar myths for attracting herds.

Few Indians doubted the efficacy of these myths or other methods of invoking buffalo. If a certain ritual did not produce the animals, its various steps were repeated under stricter supervision.

When at last a herd materialized, the Indians announced the event with assorted signals. Omaha runners and Pawnee horsemen crossed back and forth on a prominent ridge where they could be seen by those in camp. Sioux scouts conveyed more complete information by riding across a distance approximating the span of the herd. The Kutenai relayed the message by sign language, sending the word back to camp through scouts spaced a quarter of a mile apart. (After white traders supplied them with mirrors, they signaled with flashing beams of sunlight.) Cree scouts waved a robe, and if they spotted large numbers of animals they threw up handfuls of dirt as well; at times they even broadcast the discovery by setting fires.

As a returning Assiniboin scout neared camp, tribal leaders set up a pile of buffalo chips on the prairie. If the scout bypassed the pile, the Indians knew the search had failed; but if he rode straight through it, knocking chips in all directions, his companions could be assured that his reconnoitering had resulted in the discovery of a herd.

Even when they had received signals indicating the proximity of a herd, most camps did not rush immediately into the hunt. Instead, they set into motion an elaborate sequence of events planned days in advance. Such a serious undertaking as the hunt, upon which the livelihood of the entire tribe depended, could not be gambled on the whims of the individual hunters. If several hundred Indians were to spread out indiscriminately over the prairie, each trying to slay a buffalo for his own lodge, a few would succeed at the cost of routing every animal in the area and depriving the rest of the tribe. The scattering of a major herd might well leave the camp teetering on the brink of starvation.

Group effort, then, was essential. To ensure cooperation, a governing council planned and disciplined each hunt as rigidly as a group of military tacticians might plan a maneuver. Thus supervised, the tribe was more likely to succeed in ambushing large herds and supplying each camp with enough meat and pelts to last until the next outing.

Some of the best information on pre-hunt activities comes from the Omaha, whose ancient rites and rituals were described in 1905 by anthropologists Alice Fletcher and Francis La Flesche; both spent over twenty-five years in their studies, and La Flesche, the son of a principal chief of the tribe, actually witnessed many of the original ceremonies connected with the buffalo hunt. In their detailed accounts, Fletcher and La Flesche relate how the Omaha's "Council of Seven" and other tribal officials met several days before the commencement of a hunt. Each delegate wore a buffalo robe with the shaggy side out, the head portion on the left arm and the tail on the right. To inaugurate the meeting, they selected a single man from a group of nominees, investing him as *wathon*, or director of the hunt, a position of high honor and grave responsibility. After everyone had smoked from a pair of sacred tribal pipes, the Council of Seven agreed upon the day of departure and the route for the hunt, all speaking with "but one heart and as with one mouth." Then, as a crier proclaimed the decisions of the council through the camp, the delegates concluded their meeting with a feast of sacred buffalo meat served from seven wooden bowls.

During the four days leading up to the departure for the hunt, the *wathon* fasted. When the grand cavalcade set forth at last, he trailed behind, walking barefoot as further proof of his humility, beseeching the Spirit Father to grant him wisdom to lead his people well. In the days that followed, the *wathon* steered the tribe's march, selected overnight camping places, and dispatched some twenty runners to search for buffalo.

As the hunt drew closer, the *wathon* met with other officials to appoint a number of "police," choosing from among the bravest and most trusted warriors. Commissioned in the Sacred Tent of the White Buffalo Hide, the police were instructed to "recognize no relatives in performing your duties—neither chiefs, friends, fathers, brothers nor sons." During the hunt they exercised absolute control, dominating troublesome tribesmen whom even the chiefs would hesitate to discipline in normal times.

Control by the police intensified as the tribe settled within earshot of the buffalo. Marshals quickly silenced any sounds that might spook the herd—the noise of dogs barking, horses neighing, or people shouting. Women were forbidden to chop wood—all fires had to be made from dry brush or twigs that could be broken by hand with little noise.

In addition, the police watched carefully to prevent hunters from slipping away and killing on their own. Renegades imperiled the entire endeavor, and were dealt with violently. Sometimes a troublemaker would be used as an example, to heighten respect for the command of the hunt. After flogging him, marshals confiscated or killed his dogs and horses, cut his lodge into pieces, burned his tipi poles, broke his bow or gun, took his meat supplies, and ripped his hides, reducing him to total beggary.

If the victim accepted his penalty with composure—perhaps even standing aside and managing to laugh at the proceedings—he was reinstated a few days later. The police gathered together and took up a collection for the dispossessed Indian, each officer contributing some article of his own; in some instances the aggregate gifts amounted to more than the goods destroyed. But if the reprimanded man showed anger or tried to reclaim his possessions, there was no restitution; often he would be flogged again.

Police had to be especially watchful when the hunters began the final march toward the herd. Whips in hand, they intensified their control, forbidding any man to break toward the buffalo before the official signal. Transgressors were quickly lashed, the rawhide thongs whipping across their almost nude bodies in stinging rebuke. Occasionally a miscreant was literally pounded to death.

Discipline before the hunt was unquestionably harsh, but the strictness is understandable in the light of the deprivation and suffering likely to follow on the failure of an important campaign—only small numbers of buffalo would be killed and the remainder of the herd would be frightened beyond the reach of the tribe. The buffalo hunt was a major economic venture upon which depended the happiness, the welfare, possibly the very existence of the Indian camp. Each man's awareness of the stakes helped him to endure the rigid controls, and made even the extreme punishments an acceptable part of Indian life. With the laws of the hunt enforced and respected, the camp could look forward to an abundance of meat.

7

INDIAN HUNTING

TECHNIQUES

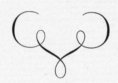

As seven Flathead Indians returned in triumph from a tribal hunt in December 1841, the local missionary questioned them on the details of their kill. In all they had slain 189 buffalo, they reported, but they wished to highlight the exploits of one daring hunter, who had distinguished himself with "three remarkable coups."

Pursuing his first cow on the run, this versatile Indian had dispatched her with a direct hit between the horns—with a powerfully thrown rock. The second buffalo he had knifed. The third, a large bull, he had crippled with a thrust of his lance, finishing the kill by strangling the beast. (The missionary did not explain precisely how one went about the task of wringing the life from a buffalo, although he did add that the hunter "looked like a Hercules.")

Indian Hunting Techniques

To accomplish his "remarkable coups," this one Indian had used several of a possible multitude of techniques. Although no details on buffalo-strangling have ever come to light, other styles of hunting and killing were colorfully described in scores of plains documents. Techniques ranged from the simple shooting of the animals with arrow or bullet to complicated systems involving decoys and carefully constructed traps. Individual hunters pursued the beasts on foot, and large groups, sometimes entire villages, united in collaborative hunting ventures to slay great numbers of animals in a single outing.

In a hunting technique employed occasionally by several tribes, expert swimmers were able to slaughter buffalo taken at a disadvantage while crossing large rivers. The above drawing from an 1874 issue of Harper's Weekly *depicts such a scene on a wide expanse of the Missouri.*

One of the earliest methods of group hunting was the foot surround, in which a long line of Indians gradually encircled a herd and then moved in for the kill. The surround was best held on a still day, when the animals would be less likely to scent the hunters; if forced to work on a windy day, the Indians planned their

trap so that the windward side took shape last. As the line of hunters drew around the herd, the men gradually moved closer to each
other and to the buffalo, setting an increasingly impenetrable ring.
When at last the animals became alarmed and tried to break
through the trap, the Indians yelled and tossed robes in the air;
loosing arrow after arrow into the herd, they fired almost continuously until all the milling buffalo were slain.

Though effective, the surround on foot had a serious draw-
back: on occasion, frantic buffalo would succeed in searching out
and escaping through weak points in even the tightest line of foot-
men, sometimes drawing the other animals after them. To eliminate such breakouts, the Indians gradually learned to take advantage of features of the surrounding landscape. Deploying the line
of men around one side of the herd, they drove the animals into
natural traps where they were likely to flounder and present easy
targets. In summer they guided them into bogs or blind canyons,
or onto necks of land jutting into lakes, and in winter they maneuvered them into deep snowdrifts or onto thin ice.

From these rudimentary beginnings, the Indians developed
a highly successful system of "impounding." A herd would be
driven or lured into the wide mouth of a funnel formed by two
lines of crouching, camouflaged braves; as the buffalo approached, the hidden tribesmen arose one by one to direct them
down the narrowing corridor into an enclosure at the spout. Once
corralled, the entire herd was easily slaughtered. The method
sometimes netted the hunters three hundred to six hundred animals in a single campaign.

The Assiniboin and Plains Cree were particularly proficient in
impounding, and other northern tribes, including the Blackfoot,
Gros Ventre, Sarsi, Crow, and Cheyenne, commonly used the
technique. The following is a composite description assembled
from the more popular patterns of impounding.

First the Indians built a corral, a walled enclosure generally
circular in shape and 30 to 250 feet in diameter. It was situated in
a hollow between two hills or in a clump of trees, where it was
obscured from the sight of the approaching buffalo until they were
right on top of it. The entrance, about twenty or thirty feet across,
faced the open prairie. Leading up to it was an inclined ramp, a
platform of logs covered with soil. The ramp presented a gentle
aspect to inbound buffalo, but it terminated at the lip of the pound

in a sheer drop; once the animals tumbled into the pit, the lip prevented them from running back out again.

Extending in a V from either side of the entrance were two wings of spaced stations manned by camouflaged Indians. These lines stretched out into the prairie for a distance of one or two miles; the open mouth of the V was about one mile across, a sufficient span to prevent the wary buffalo from sensing a trap. Individual stations were positioned 50 to 150 feet apart at the outer ends of the wings; the distance between them gradually narrowed to 20 feet or less at the approach to the corral, a critical channel where the herd might begin to feel hemmed in and attempt a breakout.

When it came time for the actual hunt, lone hunters would conceal themselves in the stations, transforming the lines into living fences. To avoid detection by the buffalo, they remained motionless, camouflaging themselves with whatever material they could find nearby—bundles of brush or branches, small tipilike structures of sticks, mounds of earth, and sometimes piles of stone, snow, or even buffalo chips. Some Indians carried their camouflage with them from camp, hiding under a robe or behind a leafy branch tied to the head.

After the completion of corral and wing stations, the Indians were ready to begin the preliminaries. A shaman consecrated the venture, beseeching the spirit powers for good fortune in the hunt. From a tall pole in the center of the corral, he hung three charms purported to attract buffalo—a streamer of scarlet cloth, a piece of tobacco, and a buffalo cow's horn. At the foot of the pole he placed a ritual offering to propitiate spirits of buffalo; among the specially selected artifacts were two buffalo skulls painted red and dressed up with feathers, and several kettles adorned with red cloth.

The pound having been consecrated, the shaman sent four scouts after buffalo. Throughout their forays, which sometimes ranged forty or fifty miles from the pound, these men carried the sacred Wahkon Ball, a rounded mass of buffalo hair covered with hide, revered for its power to charm the herds. Only after the scouts had sighted a group of buffalo near the pound could they return this magic sphere to their spiritual leader in camp.

As long as the mystical Wahkon Ball and thus the buffalo— were out of sight, the shaman beat his drum, sang hymns of conjuration, and vowed to abstain from all meat except that of buffalo killed in his pound. Since a month or more might pass before a herd came within range of camp, an occasional shaman, to avoid starving, must have learned to compromise with his conscience. One missionary even dared to suggest such a sacrilege in 1854 after contemplating the robust good health of a local shaman: "It is probable that he eats stealthily at night, for he has no more appearance of fasting than his brethren in camp."

At long last the scouts would return with the Wahkon Ball, indicating the discovery of a herd in the vicinity of the pound. As soon as a favorable wind blew from herd toward pound, the shaman made his final offerings to the medicine pole and committed the tribesmen to their positions in the wings. If there were not enough men to fill all stations, he sent out women and even children.

When the stations were manned, the shaman dispatched several hunters to drive the herd into the fatal angle between the wings. This was a tedious task, demanding both skill and patience. The chosen youths had to push the herd slowly along, never frightening the animals into flight with a hasty advance. On some occasions they waited for hours for the wind to change or for the buffalo to drift into favorable terrain; at other times they were forced to race miles ahead of the herd to swing it into the proper direction. If the herd was uncooperative, they might even kindle small fires of dung or grass to prod it onward. Each youth had to work calmly and without rest, nettling the animals into drifting leisurely toward the wings.

Occasionally these "guides" worked at night, slapping their folded robes on the ground to make a sharp report and startle the buffalo into shifting in the desired direction. When the herd had settled down again in the interval of calm between reports, the young men slapped the robes again and pressed the animals forward a little more. As daylight returned, they resumed their patient nudging, popping up now and then to wave their robes for an instant, then rapidly ducking back behind cover. And all along, the herd headed slowly toward the pound.

Buffalo driving must have been an uncertain procedure at best. Present-day handlers are all too familiar with the slippery maneuvers of buffalo that balk at being herded. The Indians, perhaps frustrated by their stubborn prey, eventually conceived another method for bringing the buffalo within range. Instead of forcing the animals to head in the desired direction, they lured them in. Indian decoys disguised under buffalo hides—and even mimicking the actions of the animals—would pass near the herds in an attempt to guide them toward the pound.

Such buffalo masquerades have been reported from the earliest times; later, when the Indians secured horses, they used their buffalo decoys to deceive neighboring tribes. Blackfoot scouts piloting their horses on reconnoitering jaunts into enemy territory often disguised themselves under large buffalo hides; when viewed from a distance the draped, crouching figures on horse-back looked every bit like buffalo. In 1832, artist-explorer George Catlin described them while visiting a Mandan camp. He was present during a buffalo-luring ritual when sentinels reported sighting a small group of animals on a distant hill, prompting over-anxious tribesmen to rush out in anticipation of a glorious hunt. Their "buffalo" turned out to be Sioux warriors camouflaged under robes, and the gullible Mandan were tricked squarely into the center of an ambush.

It is difficult to imagine duping nearby tribes in this manner, but apparently the decoys became so skillful that they even learned to foil the buffalo themselves. Donning tanned robes often topped with headdresses complete with horns, the decoys approached the herds slowly, taking great pains to move against the wind and keep the animals from catching their scent. Some hunters crouched on horseback; others advanced toward the herds on foot or on all fours. Occasionally they used a highly effective form of pantomime. "Their gestures so closely resembled those of the animals," declared an observer, "that had I not been in on the secret, I should have been as much deceived as the buffalo."

A few decoys even mimicked buffalo calls. In one report the Indian actually bellowed; in another he made a sound like the bleating of a calf "being devoured by a wolf and crying for help."

Present-day buffalo mothers and at times their herd mates respond immediately to a calf's call for help. Perhaps the act of the Indian decoy was so authentic as to prompt members of the herd to attempt a rescue; or the animals may simply have been attracted by the novelty of the decoy and sufficiently reassured by his appearance to dare an approach.

Once the decoy had won the buffalo's attention with his calls and antics, he began to move toward the wings of the pound. The herd usually followed, advancing slowly at first, then speeding up to a trot or a gallop as the decoy increased his pace.

After luring the herd to the entrance or even into the corral itself, the decoy slipped away. If still outside the walls, he threw himself down in the grass or escaped into one of the wing stations; if he had been forced into the corral, he leaped over the fence or ran out through a special gate. His exit in the close proximity of the herds was "extreamly dangerous," as Meriwether Lewis has suggested. "If they are not very fleet runers the buffaloe tread them under foot and crush them to death, and sometimes drive them over the precipice also, where they perish in common with the buffaloe."

Occasional tribesmen developed their own variations in the decoying technique. A Blackfoot decoy named Apauk described how he concealed himself on his horse under the usual buffalo robe and mimicked the actions of a panicked cow. Guiding his mount slowly toward the herd, he advanced until they raised their heads and stared at him. Then he prodded his horse to a gallop, luring the herd after him in a boisterous stampede. (This technique would have been feasible, since I have occasionally observed a single alarmed cow bolting away from the herd and starting a stampede.)

Certain Blackfoot decoys worked without camouflage, wearing only a loincloth. Advancing slowly on the herd, they would wheel in circles, alternately coming into view and hiding. As the buffalo, their curiosity whetted, moved closer to investigate, the decoys withdrew toward the wings of the pound, and the inquisitive herd trailed conveniently after them.

Curiosity motivated the behavior of the buffalo that attended my own primitive effort at decoying, an experiment prompted by the whim of a production manager at the Walt Disney studios. Learning of the Indian decoying techniques, he listened with interest to a suggestion that a photographer might take close-up shots of the herds while concealed under a buffalo hide. The cameraman could get some interesting footage for the feature film *The Vanishing Prairie*—and pictures of him in action could be used for superb publicity releases about the making of the film.

Consequently, with buffalo hide draped over head and body, a photographer whom a magazine later dubbed "Buffalo Tom" was to be seen a short time afterward creeping toward a herd in Wind Cave National Park. (I might mention that crawling under a hide is not the most comfortable way to traverse a prairie. The fur hanging over my face restricted my vision, and I could see very little through the small opening where the sides of the robe met— at one point I planted my hand squarely on top of a cactus.) When I neared the herd, the animals stared for a moment, then backed off in hesitant flight, watching me closely as they retreated. Within ten minutes, however, they had grown accustomed to my presence; approaching in clusters, they began to treat me, so it seemed, as one of their own. Soon there were buffalo all around me.

Several buffalo, a few young ones in particular, advanced to within four feet to investigate. The herd seemed to accept me as a bisontine creature, for there is no doubt that I could move closer to the animals in my disguise than I had been able to without it. In my unaccustomed garb, if I advanced slowly and steadily, I could sidle up to any buffalo.

But I was in a vulnerable position. The small opening through which I peered afforded no view of the animals beside or behind me. I was also concerned about several buffalo in my range of vision that looked as if they'd like to give my robe—and its contents —a good hook in the side. One angry, or perhaps merely curious, bull circled around me, regarding me with such a menacing glare that I finally lifted a corner of my robe in his direction. He backed up and moved off a few paces when he found out it was only me.

In another part of the herd, an old bull inspecting a cow from time to time had been punctuating each investigation with a round of vigorous bellowing. No sooner had I tested my own guttural rendition of a bellow than two animals in front of me parted to reveal this very bull staring directly at me. He answered my bellow and walked a few feet toward me, still bellowing. We glowered at each other for a moment, then I backed up hastily, grabbing one end of my hide to avoid tripping over it. My masquerade as a decoy had gone far enough.

From this experiment I learned that a costumed decoy will provoke bold inspection in buffalo, and that the animals will more readily accept a man under a robe than one in everyday clothes. Their response to my ploy convinced me that the reported successes of Indian decoys were indeed feasible.

When the Indians did finally maneuver a herd into the wings of a pound, the buffalo would begin to scent the tribesmen hiding in the nearby stations. By then, however, any effort to escape would be futile—already headed in the direction of the pound, and closely pursued by hunters, the animals would only work themselves farther into the trap. All the way down the wings, Indians concealed in the stations would pop up one by one, waving their robes and shouting to frighten the buffalo onward, not letting up the pressure until their prey had reached the pound.

It was a perilous operation. On occasion the onrushing herd would veer off course into a wing, sometimes trampling Indians to death. The only hope for an endangered hunter lay in the solidity of his station. If he was lucky, it was made of stone—the sturdy rock pile sometimes used to construct a station afforded better protection than the usual bundle of brush, branches, or sticks.

To eliminate breakthroughs as the buffalo converged in the narrow bottleneck at the mouth of the pound, large numbers of Indians gathered at this danger point; their wild demonstrations usually succeeded in forcing the herd into the enclosure.

The drop from the mouth of the pound into the corral was six to eight feet. Because of the great distance, and because the ground below was often cluttered with stumps purposely left in place by the Indians, many buffalo broke their legs as they tumbled in. Those that were still fit thrashed about inside, severely testing the walls of the corral, especially if the pen was filled to capacity. As the hunters closed off the entrance with a barrier of hides, women and children gathered around the top of the fence, waving skins and yelling at the beasts to prevent them from pushing against the walls or jumping over. If but one buffalo punched a small hole in the fence, the herd would quickly widen the breach and dash to freedom. Occasionally animals poured into the pens in such numbers that the last ones escaped easily over the walls of the corral by running across the backs of those already trapped.

As the impounded buffalo raced around inside the corral, hunters perched astride the fence felled passing animals with arrows, lances, or, later, bullets. (Cree hunters killed only the adults, to give the boys of the tribe a chance to enter the pen and fight the calves; many a young buffalo put up a fierce stuggle, sometimes even driving its assailant up onto the log walls.) Amid the jubilant cheers of the tribe, the slaughter continued until the last writhing survivors had been clubbed to death with stone-headed mauls.

In Blackfoot country, a pound was referred to as a *pis'kun*, a "deep blood kettle." And so it was. The tribes killed every buffalo inside the enclosure, in the belief that survivors would warn other herds, which would then avoid the area of the pound and make future catches impossible. To this superstition was added a practical reason for the annihilation: only when all the buffalo were slain was it safe for butchers to enter the pen.

Occasionally impounding was supplemented by grassfiring. During the dry season, as an alternate means of driving buffalo toward the corral, selected hunters might set fire to patches of the grassland. Grassfiring was also used as a hunting pattern by itself, in a technique similar to that of the surround; instead of controlling the buffalo with a cordon of men, the Indians surrounded them with a ring of fire. Hunters encircled the herd and kindled the grass on every side; as the burning circle squeezed the animals into an ever-diminishing area, the men moved in to slaughter their terrified prey.

Now and then the Indians modified this surround by fire, leaving unburned exits where hunters could ambush the fleeing buffalo. Father Louis Hennepin witnessed the technique among the Illinois in 1683:

> When the Savages discover a great Number of those beasts together, they likewise assemble their whole Tribe to encompass the Bulls, and then set on fire the dry Herbs about them, except in some places which they leave free; and therein lay themselves in Ambuscade. The Bulls seeing the Flame round about them, run away through those Passages where they see no fire; and there fall into the Hands of the Savages who by these Means will kill sometimes above sixscore in a day.

"Sixscore" was a modest estimate for a grassfire kill; other writers told of slaughters of anywhere between two hundred and two thousand. Hunting by this fire-surround was most popular on the prairies of Minnesota, Wisconsin, Iowa, and Illinois, where it was practiced by the Ojibwa, Winnebago, Santee Sioux, Iowa, Illinois, and Miami.

Several other tribes burned off sections of grassland for a totally different purpose. They believed that scorching the prairie in fall, winter, or spring stimulated a premature crop of fresh green grass that would lure herds to the area. Lewis and Clark reported on the technique while on the Upper Missouri: ". . . it is Said to be common for the Indians to burn the Plains near their Villages every Spring for the benefit of their horses, and to induce the Buffalow to come near to them."

Even today, grassfires that are invariably started by humans influence the movements of hundreds of thousands of wild ungulates in East Africa. Several species of antelope, particularly wildebeest, shun the rank grass of unburned areas—not only because the forage is unappetizing, but also because it may hide lurking predators. The antelope have distinct preferences for young sprouts and blades no taller than four inches, and will migrate hundreds of miles to savor the flush of new grass on a burn.

Controlled firing of grasslands is also popular today on cattle ranches in southern Africa and Brazil, and on the southern plains of the United States. In this country the practice has suffered from a Smoky Bear sentiment against any kind of burning, which is unfortunate, for ecologists are gradually learning to work with fire as a useful tool in managing the range.

Actually, fire started by lightning was a natural force on the grassland long before man ever ventured into the area. The vegetation, subjected to repeated and extensive burning for thousands of years, gradually became adapted to such blazes as a normal feature of the prairie environment. Unlike forest fires, which inflict heavy damage by consuming trees that have taken years to reach a substantial size, prairie fires destroy only one season's growth. Although grasses and other plants are burned to the ground, the perennial roots escape largely unharmed, ready to put forth fresh growth within weeks.

In some northern and eastern regions of the historic prairie, this frequent natural burning was clearly beneficial to the grassland as a whole. Along the margins, where prairies touched forests of oak, hickory, or aspen, periodic fires did not damage the root systems of grasses, but killed sprouts and seedlings of trees

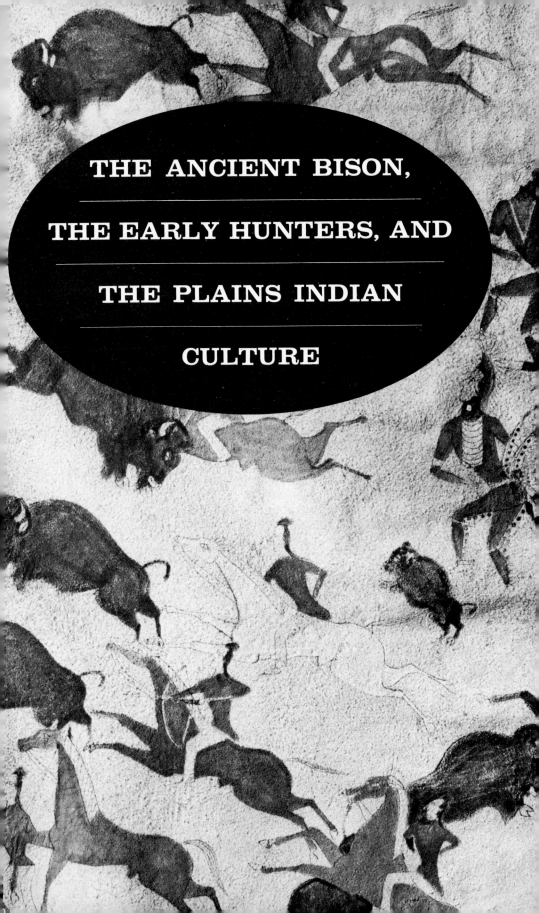

THE ANCIENT BISON,

THE EARLY HUNTERS, AND

THE PLAINS INDIAN

CULTURE

At left, a paleontologist measures the horn cores of a *Bison latifrons* skull from Ohio. The skull would have an even greater span if the horn sheaths of the living animal were growing over these bony cores.

The sketch of a steppe wisent (*Bison priscus*) wounded by spears (below) is from a cave at Niaux, France. By overlapping the form of one animal upon another, the prehistoric artist gave his bison an impression of being two-headed.

Deep inside a cave at Tuc d'Audoubert, southern France, Cro-Magnon men modeled these clay bison (left) about fifteen thousand years ago. They located their flattened relief sculptures in the most remote chamber of the cave, reachable only after crawling through narrow tunnels and navigating an underground river.

In the center of an ancient arroyo in southeastern Colorado (right) archeologists unearthed this long row of bones of *Bison occidentalis*, many of the skeletons lying in a tangle as the bison had perished after being stampeded into the natural trap some eighty-five hundred years ago. The arrangement of the bones in the upper layers suggests that the early hunters had hauled several bison into position and cut them up at the same time; later, they systematically dumped similar groups of cleaned bones back into the arroyo. In the foreground, for example, is a pile of skulls that was built up in this way.

The Teton Sioux (above) felt spiritually prepared for the chase after a visit to their "medicine buffalo," scraped from the earth in the pattern of a bull.

Mandan Bull Dancer (left) performed during the tribe's annual Okipa, an elaborate and mystical ceremony held to insure an abundance of buffalo for the hunt and to keep bad luck away from the village. Over his head the dancer wore a buffalo hide replete with horns and tail; on his back he carried a bundle of green willow boughs to symbolize the ebbing of a giant flood—a chapter in a tribal myth about the creation of the earth and its creatures.

Members of the Mandan Bull Society (right) also wore buffalo headdresses. Carrying buffalo-hide shields and their favorite hunting lances, the men danced whenever the tribe was threatened with starvation to lure the herds near the village.

Drives over cliffs were usually held in the fall, when buffalo could be herded more easily than during the calving or rutting seasons.

This 1823 sketch of a buffalo pound shows fences built from logs.

Hunters from the plains Cree drive a herd of buffalo toward a pound.

Buffalo-running: Cheyenne warriors penciled the above sketch while being held as prisoners of war. At right, a wounded buffalo charges a hunter in a scene drawn on an elk skin by a Shoshoni (see also Plate I). Charles M. Russell painted the canvas below.

At left, the three scenes of Indian hunting were painted by artist-explorer George Catlin while visiting the plains in the 1830's.

Commenting on the top drawing, Catlin said that buffalo "are aware of their own superiority in combined force, and seem then to have no dread of the wolf, allowing him to sneak amidst their ranks, apparently like one of their own family. The Indian . . . profits by these circumstances by placing himself under the skin of a white wolf, with his weapons in hand, in which plight he often creeps over the level prairies (where there is no object to conceal him) to close company with the unsuspecting herd."

In the center plate, a mounted Indian with a lance runs buffalo, pressing one individual to the edge of the herd for his kill. Because buffalo came together into massive rutting herds during the summer months, small bands of Indians—in a parallel social cycle —united into larger camps at this time in order to prey on the bison.

Snowshoe-clad hunters (bottom) nimbly run across the icy crust to bear down upon a buffalo mired in a deep drift.

A Crow Indian (above right) proudly posed for this photograph while holding his buffalo-hide shield, which is actually wrapped in a cover of soft deerskin painted with the design.

At lower right, the magical power attributed to this Pawnee shield came from the ceremony associated with curing the disk of buffalo rawhide as well as from the drawing of a bull's head painted on the deerskin cover. After seeing the bull during a vision quest, the owner considered the animal a special guardian who would look after him in times of danger. Decorating the rim of this shield are several eagle feathers.

Rope from hair (Pawnee)

Rope from strips of hide (Caddo)

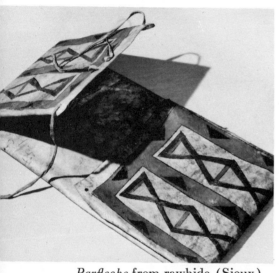

Parfleche from rawhide (Sioux)

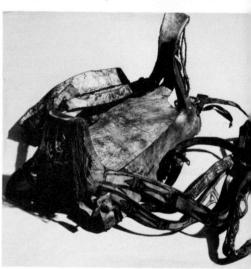

Saddle from rawhide (Cheyenne)

Tinder holder from horn (Sioux)

Ladle from a horn (Comanche)

INDIANS FASHIONED A MULTITUDE

Brushes from bones (Blackfoot)

Skinning blade, used in working
up hides. Made from a shoulder
bone.   CROW

Skinning blade from a bone (Crow)

Snow sled from rib bones (Sioux)

Vessel from a scrotum (Kiowa)

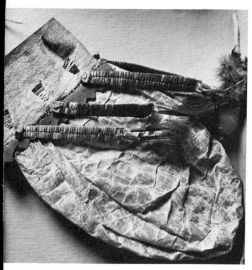

Food pouch from bladder (Sioux)

War charm from piece of intestine

OF OBJECTS FROM THE PARTS OF BUFFALO

The buffalo skull painted in the Sioux manner (above) was carefully positioned in the center of the tipi next to the fireplace, there to be looked upon as a sacred totem of the animal and the herds, a dedicated helper to the owner of the lodge.

Buffalo skulls suspended from skewers piercing the flesh (right, above) were part of the torture rite of the Mandan Okipa ceremony. A supplicant was twirled with a pole, "faster and faster," stated artist George Catlin, "until the brave fellow could control the agony no longer and burst out in the most heart-rending cries . . ." From this ordeal a man was said to acquire powers of good fortune.

In the Cheyenne Sun Dance held in 1901 (right), a priest kneels to apply a decoration to the sacred buffalo hide while five dancers in the background paint their bodies for the ceremony.

On a mountain peak in Wyoming, rocks outline the spokes of a giant "medicine wheel"; the hub is a buffalo skull. The tribe is unknown.

The buffalo mask from the Seneca (above) was donned by a dancer who impersonated the animal by mimicking its actions.

In the Catlin painting at left, Pawnee warrior "Buffalo Bull" wears the outline of the head of his namesake painted on face and chest and holds a buffalo robe.

that were invading the area. Thus burning helped to maintain rank, grassy prairies in areas of moist climate that would otherwise have grown up to woodland.

Controlled firing, as practiced by Indians or by ranchers, can indeed help to produce a lush cover of new grass. Initially the burning hastens the breakdown of mineral matter in the dried plants, thus enrichening the soil. Deep black in color and unshaded by foliage, the charred earth soaks up the maximum heat of the sun, further stimulating spring growth. Cattle can readily graze the new grass without having to fight through a tangle of dried stalks left over from the past season, and they seem to find the fresh sprouts more alluring than the usual fare—in the occasional meadow where only a part of the old grass has burned, the stock demonstrate their preference by forsaking the unburned areas for the richer forage of the burned section. Recently range managers have also discovered that the new grass is more nutritious, with a higher-than-normal content of proteins and minerals.

Burning does have drawbacks, however, for the new grass is sensitive to abuse by excessive numbers of cattle or wildlife, especially in the semi-arid grassland of the western Great Plains. In this region of sparse, short grass, firing that initially produces an increase in forage may sometimes be accompanied by a reduction in over-all yield. Perhaps it was for this reason that many Indian tribes in the area enforced strict laws against the practice.

In firing selected tracts of land to improve forage and attract the herds, the Indians had discovered a useful principle of plains agriculture. Applying it as a hunting method, they became so sophisticated in its practice that they knew when it would be effective and when not.

In other buffalo drives on the northern Great Plains, Indians used the rugged terrain to assist them in killing the animals, as their remote ancestors had done thousands of years before. Most effective for such slaughter was a steep cliff or cut-bank, toward which the hunters would direct the herds by means identical to those used in impounding. Once the lead animals reached the edge of the chasm, they were powerless to turn back. Pressed over the lip by the animals immediately behind them, they fell, bumping, sliding, bouncing down the cliff, followed shortly by the rest of the herd. By the time all the animals had slammed into the bottom, many were already dead or disabled. The remaining badly bruised buffalo were easily dispatched by hunters. Only at locations where the drop-off was slight did the Indians bother to construct any kind of corral at the bottom.

To be successful in this method, the Indians naturally had to know the configuration of the land far better than their quarry, for it is unlikely that the buffalo would have allowed themselves to be driven toward a precipice they knew, no matter how well-concealed the drop-off. One herd of seven hundred that until recently roamed over a thirty-four thousand-acre range in Montana was surrounded on three sides by cliffs dropping precipitously into the Bighorn Canyon. Obviously familiar with their range, these

Closely pursued by Indian hunters mounted on horseback, a herd of buffalo begins to tumble over the edge of a cliff in this drawing from an 1869 issue of Harper's Monthly.

buffalo never plunged off any of the cliffs, even in time of the annual slaughter, when they were relentlessly driven by hunters in jeeps. But bygone herds probing their way through unfamiliar territory might well have been ignorant of canyons in the region. Because of the immense size of the terrain they traversed, the great herds must often have been easy prey for Indians attempting to drive them over the cliffs.

At the base of certain cliffs in the northern plains, early explorers chanced upon great heaps of skulls, mute remains of former Indian drives. Lewis and Clark, progressing up the Missouri River, sighted "a vast many mangled carcases of Buffalow which had been driven over a precipice of 120 feet by the Indians and perished." Clark described the grisly scene:

> The water appeared to have washed away a part of this immence pile of slaughter, and still their remained the fragments of at least a hundred carcases. They created a most horrid stench. In this manner the Indians of the Missouri distroy vast herds of buffalow at a stroke . . .

Traces of the old impounding sites are visible even today. In Wyoming, Hell's Half Acre is a highly colored, badlands-like chasm that splits the rolling grassland near the city of Casper; the locale has yielded Indian artifacts that identify it as an important drive-off site. Other sites are located in the vicinity of several Montana towns lying east of the Rockies; extensive digging at the base of nearby cliffs has revealed layers of bones and other debris one to four feet deep.

The same techniques that proved successful for driving herds over cliffs or into pounds worked just as well during special winter campaigns. Encircling small groups of buffalo, tribesmen drove them out onto the slippery ice of frozen lakes and rivers. The helpless creatures skidded and lurched about, some breaking legs or hips in falls; but their suffering was brief, for all were rapidly slaughtered by the Indians. The Plains Cree dubbed this technique a "wolf pound," explaining that they had conceived it after watching wolves maneuver buffalo onto ice to make easy victims of them.

These various techniques of surrounding or impounding were clearly effective when conducted by men on foot; the tribes dwelling on the plains brought down a supply of buffalo sufficient for food, clothing, and other needs. But the techniques were to prove spectacularly successful after the introduction of the horse.

This took place around the middle of the sixteenth century, when Plains Indians obtained their first horses from Spanish colonists. The animals made their initial appearance among southern tribes such as the Kiowa, Comanche, and Caddo, gradually spreading northward throughout the grassland during the next two hundred years. Tribesmen of these regions soon learned to use the horse so effectively in surrounds and buffalo-running that they were able to come by enough meat and hides to satisfy their own lodges and supply the mounting fur trade of the white man. In an astonishingly short period of time, the Plains Indians became one of the foremost equestrian peoples in the history of the world.

The horses were first employed in an improved version of the surround. For magnitude, swiftness, and efficiency of kill, this hunt on horseback outclassed all other methods. The highest known take, made in 1832 by some five hundred Yankton Sioux armed with bows and arrows, was numbered at fourteen hundred animals, a figure confirmed by the local trader as he totaled the tongues brought in by returning hunters. Other tribes often fielded about a hundred men to slay from one hundred to five hundred buffalo in less than an hour.

In the typical horseback surround, two columns of mounted hunters—like the lines of walking hunters in the foot surround—formed twin crescents, approaching and enclosing the herd in a giant circle from one to two miles in diameter. Gradually they tightened the ring, converging upon the animals until the herd, smelling or sighting the oncoming tribesmen, dashed off in a stampede. At once the horsemen darted in from all sides to spring their snare and commence the slaughter.

Before advancing on the herd, hunters would shed almost all clothing, for articles like jackets, leggings, or even shields would be encumbrances during the chase. Most men kept only a loincloth; a few rode completely naked. In their left hands they grasped their bows with a cluster of arrows ready for instant firing, and in their right, whips to prod their steeds alongside the buffalo. Horses were likewise stripped for action; many bore no saddles, and bridles were simple ropes looped about the lower jaw.

The final approach was made with the utmost caution, under the cover of coulees or bushes and against the wind, to keep the animals ignorant of the human presence until the last minute, for the tribes had a great respect for what the Arikara called the buffalo's "exquisite degree of scent." A surround would be ruined if the animals were prematurely alerted to the approach of the men by a message on the wind.

After being caught in the tightening cordon, the herd, suddenly aware of its plight, would attempt to escape by probing for weak places in the line. Ricocheting from point to point as the ever-tightening circle of Indians drew in, the terrified animals were soon trapped within the pincers. Bunched tightly together, they became a frenzied, milling mass. Now the hunters galloped from animal to animal, loosing a barrage of arrows and lances. Buffalo by the score fell under the withering assault, littering the arena with carcasses that tripped pursued and pursuer alike; other victims, arrows dangling from their sides, lashed back at their assailants, leaving here a horse ripped apart by slashing horns, there a rider mangled by trampling hooves. Sometimes, as the herd eddied chaotically, horsemen were swept up in the turmoil; forced to abandon their mounts, they clambered over the backs of the buffalo to escape from the melee. But other hunters kept up the pressure, and wherever the animals turned they met arrow and lance. In time, almost all perished.

So many animals could be slain in a successful horseback surround that the Indians were now able to stock up against a time of shortage. Even when larders were full, however, tribal leaders were likely to organize a hunt as soon as a herd was sighted in the vicinity of the camp. A chief of the Teton Sioux once articulated the philosophy behind their haste: buffalo were like cherries—they didn't stay around very long, so the tribes should take plenty whenever they had the chance.

But even the brilliant horseback surround was not foolproof. For although the lines of encircling horsemen were tightly interlocked and tribesmen struck at the trapped buffalo with great speed and sureness, occasional animals still contrived to dash through gaps and escape. At such moments the surround moved into a new phase—buffalo-running. With their specially trained horses, Indians pursued the renegade animals across the prairie, pulling up alongside to fell them with arrow or lance. Buffalo-running soon proved such an efficient means of catching escapees that it outgrew its original function as an emergency measure and evolved into a style of hunting in its own right.

The buffalo-running Indian, relying on the superb reflexes and stamina of his mount, followed a wildly stampeding herd across the plain, at intervals overtaking and bringing down individual animals. In effect, horse and rider worked together as pilot and co-pilot—one concentrated on navigation toward the target and the other focused on the strike.

Bending his mount's course toward a particular buffalo, the

hunter separated his target from the herd to avoid being trampled in the surging throng. The horse careened after the fleeing buffalo without further guidance, his halter lying loose and untouched, for an experienced buffalo-runner seemed as willing to close in on a savage cow as to join a band of horses on the plain. As the mount drew alongside the buffalo at a breakneck gallop, the hunter launched a lance or an arrow (in later years a bullet), striking the animal in the heart. The victim usually fell within a few leaps.

An Assiniboine running a Buffalo.
Drawn by an Assiniboine warrior
and hunter. Fort Union, Jan 16.1874.

A white trader stationed with the American Fur Company collected this sketch of a hunter wearing his typical regalia for buffalo-running.

After the first kill, the Indian dashed on to single out a second target, possibly even a third. A horse that endured to carry his rider through three kills was highly esteemed. Kutenai hunters insisted that buffalo-running called for a "five-mile horse."

When his horse became too exhausted to gallop in pursuit of fresh buffalo, the hunter abandoned the chase. Reining in his mount, he guided the animal slowly back through the area to finish off any buffalo that still lay wounded on the prairie.

On occasion, the Indians also used horses in impounding: in place of the usual foot hunters, mounted tribesmen would bear down on the herds to funnel them into the corrals. But as soon as the tribes acquired enough horses to provide all hunters with mounts, it became obvious that buffalo-running surpassed impounding. To impound a herd, it was first necessary to toil for days to construct a trap; hunters were then dependent on the whim of the herds, for their pound confined them to one locale. Horses made it possible to keep up with the herds, permitting completely movable hunts. The gradual increase of horses among the tribes thus marked the end of impounding as an important hunting method.

As buffalo-running slowly increased to become the predominant hunting technique on the plains, the prosperity of the Plains Indians evolved toward its peak, and tribal customs began to change. In the 1800's, the demands of fur traders for more and more hides soon elevated the status of the Indian women, who prepared most skins for market. A hunter with a good horse could bring down enough buffalo to keep many women occupied; and the more wives a man had, the more hides he could get tanned. As a result, the number of wives to an affluent man soared in this period from a maximum of five to as many as twenty or thirty. A man made this increase in his family through outright purchase, exchanging horses for additional wives, thus transforming idle capital in the form of surplus horses into productive capital in the form of toiling spouses. As his ever-increasing number of wives turned out more and more buffalo hides, the head of the household was enriched in proportion. He acquired bartering power for procuring guns, ammunition, tobacco, revered medicine bundles —and sometimes even additional wives.

As a new concept of personal property began to take hold among the tribes, the well-trained buffalo-running horse became the supreme status symbol in Indian society. The distinction was even more important in horse-poor tribes—among the Plains Cree, for example, only one tipi in ten had a good buffalo horse. The owner of such a horse became the provider for a number of neighbors, who followed him wherever he moved his camp and shared any buffalo he brought down. Dependent on him for meat, they were naturally eager to carry out his orders. Thus served, he became a kind of local lord.

The valuable buffalo-runners were pampered as lovingly as a treasured thoroughbred. Some Indians spared their finest mounts until the commencement of the chase by riding pack horses out toward the herd; others marched forth on foot, escorting their buffalo-runners. Just before the hunt, they would address the favored steeds as they would a father, brother, or uncle, calling upon them to run well and keep close to the buffalo, and at all costs to avoid being gored.

Some of these remarkable horses were so imbued with a passion for the chase that they stirred impatiently before each outing. The Gros Ventre said that buffalo-runners bound for the herds pranced "as if their hearts were glad." Many a horse that lost its rider during the hunt continued the pursuit alone.

This equine passion for the chase once proved a nuisance for the Lewis and Clark expedition. As the group made its way east in the summer of 1806, one of its members, Sergeant Pryor, was charged with the responsibility of returning some borrowed horses to the Mandan. On the way to the Indian camp, the horses broke free, and Pryor discovered to his chagrin that he was leading some strong-minded buffalo-runners. Clark related the incident in his journal:

> . . . the loos horses as soon as they saw the Buffalow would immediately pursue them and run around them. All those that had speed sufficient would head the Buffalow and those of less speed would pursue on as fast as they could. [Sgt. Pryor] at length found that the only practiacable method would be for one of them to proceed on and when ever they saw a gangue of Buffalow to Scear them off before the horses got up.

The buffalo-running Indian used many different weapons over the years. At first the lance was favored. With its light wooden stem from ten to fourteen feet long and its blade of bone, stone, or, later, steel, this shaft was lethal in the hands of a practiced hunter. But success could be achieved with a lance only if the horse could position his rider just ahead of the buffalo. From this vantage point, the hunter could thrust his weapon behind the buffalo's shoulder blade and make use of the forward surge of his victim to drive the point down to the heart. The lance was then as deadly in the chase as it was in battle.

Because of the difficulty of positioning a lance for the throw, and because only one could be launched at a time, the weapon was soon superseded by the bow and arrow as the most effective means of downing buffalo from a moving horse. But when the muzzle-loading rifle was first introduced into the tribes, many Indians were attracted by the novelty of firepower. Individual hunters learned to use the weapons with great skill, and soon acquired the knack of reloading a rifle while careening across the prairie. After the first shot of each run, the hunter stopped using wadding to hold in the charge. From then on he primed his rifle on the gallop only a few paces from the buffalo, tipping the powder horn hanging from his shoulder to pour a wildly guessed measure down the barrel. Then he spat a ball down the muzzle from the supply he carried in his mouth and rapped the butt on his thigh to settle the charge, counting on saliva to hold the ball until it was fired. If the barrel was tipped too low before shooting, the pull of the trigger produced no blast, for powder and ball would already have fallen to the ground.

Although many Indians became proficient with the rifle, the bow and arrow was soon reinstated as the preferred weapon—the rifle just didn't do the job as well. An Indian could aim his bow more surely than his rifle, and he could fire it more rapidly: for every lead ball he shot from a rifle, he could let fly six or eight arrows, each a more effective killer than the ball. Two or three one-ounce bullets shot through a buffalo often failed to lay it low, whereas a single arrow launched with skill and force caused the buffalo such distress that it soon came to a standstill. Furthermore, an arrow wound bled profusely, leaving behind a useful trail.

The average Indian hunter used a short bow (under three feet) because it was easy to handle on horseback. He selected his arrows with care, tipping them with flint, bone, or steel. Arrowheads used in the hunt were much broader than those intended for tribal wars, and consequently produced a more lethal discharge of blood. Each hunter carried about fifty arrows and could launch them rapidly enough to keep at least one in the air at all times. He aimed for the buffalo's heart, calculating by a point just behind the shoulder, firing as the beast made its forward stride—at the instant when the ribs reached their maximum separation and thus permitted the surest passage of the arrow. If the missile didn't strike accurately or penetrate deeply, the hunter sometimes rode up to the enraged animal, yanked it out, and tried again. Mortally wounded buffalo usually betrayed the gravity of their injuries by frothing blood through mouth and nostrils; a buffalo that failed to exhibit these signs was pelted with a second or third arrow.

The power of a bow in expert hands was tremendous. The practiced archer fired his shafts so forcefully that most sank clear to their feathers; some penetrated so far as to stick out a foot or more on the opposite side. An occasional arrow even passed clear through the buffalo and lodged in the earth, forcing the hunter to circle back to retrieve his blood-spattered missile. Several expert marksmen boasted about launching arrows with such force that they sped through one buffalo with enough momentum to wound and, very rarely, kill another.

It is not difficult to imagine the precariousness of firing an arrow from a churning mount while dashing alongside an enraged buffalo. In spite of artful maneuvering by buffalo-runner and rider, accidents in the course of the hunt were routine. Choppy terrain and treacherous buffalo were obvious unpredictables; these were compounded by an exhilaration for the chase that often drowned prudence and reason alike. An occasional hunter was maimed or killed by the animals themselves, but the greater number of casualties derived from falls or faulty firearms. Bullets sticking in dirty barrels caused guns to explode, destroying fingers, hands, arms, or legs—and sometimes taking lives.

Wounded or harassed buffalo were likely to charge abruptly and gore or trample their pursuers. During a winter campaign in the 1860's, chronicler Henry A. Boller watched one Gros Ventre hunter guide his mount close to an injured cow and prepare to fire; just as he pulled even with her, his horse plunged into a snowdrift and floundered. The man was thrown clear, but the cow charged in to slash the belly of the horse. The animal sprang up with a convulsive bound and dashed wildly over the prairie, treading on and tearing out its own entrails; after only a few moments, it dropped dead.

Tumbles from horses were natural consequences of the wild chase across prairie terrain pockmarked with mammal burrows, creased with trails or rivulets, and littered with rocks. The hazard of these obstacles was aggravated by the screen of dust raised by the racing animals. But a practiced rider regarded a mere fall as a lesser danger than the dread possibility of having his horse, or even a buffalo, fall on top of him. Equally grave were spills that threw him against some piece of gear—a bow, arrow, or gun.

Although an occasional fall was unavoidable, the hunter could take precautions against the additional plight of losing his horse. Looped about his mount's lower jaw was a simple rope halter with a loose end between thirty and sixty feet long that he coiled and tucked into his loincloth (or even left to drag on the ground). Whenever he was thrown, he caught this thong instantly and pulled his mount to a stop. Within moments he was back on and into the chase again.

These numerous and varied techniques of communal hunting provided meat and supplies for several lodges at a time—or for entire tribes. But an individual hunter could still go out on his own to provision himself and his family. On his solitary mission he might try to ambush animals at a waterhole. More often he would stalk his quarry on foot, wearing a light-colored outfit that blended into the surroundings.

Recumbent buffalo were preferred targets, because their low position restricted their field of vision. If the hunter was not so fortunate as to find a buffalo reclining, he crept forward at moments when the animals' heads were lowered for grazing or turned away from him. Whenever they glanced in his direction, he kept perfectly still. In this manner he advanced slowly until he came within firing range; then he launched his arrows and felled his prey.

In the northern range, where snow accumulated to a fair depth, stalking took on a winter variation with the first big storm. Fastening snowshoes to their feet, hunters moved easily over the snow-covered ground to bear down on the mired animals. Many were able to approach close enough to kill with lances as well as arrows.

Hunting on snowshoes was so simple and safe that even women and boys were able to bring down animals. The promise of an easy kill brought by the first big snowfall was celebrated joyfully among the Chippewa with a Snowshoe Dance. Singing gratitude to their spirit powers, the Indians clomped about on their webs, waving gaily decorated standards and circling around a post from which dangled a pair of snowshoes.

Stalking took still another form with the addition of some clever camouflage. Indians were aware that buffalo massed under the protective canopy of herd life seemed to have no fear of the wolves that haunted their fringes and even moved among them. Taking advantage of this complacency, hunters disguised as wolves were able to move toward the herd with ease. Wrapped in skins tied at the neck and waist, they crawled on hands and knees, perhaps even howling like a wolf if a buffalo cast a suspicious glance in their direction.

A Cree named Jacob Bear teamed up with a cohort to bring the wolf-skin subterfuge to the point of melodrama. Jacob bundled himself in a white blanket to simulate a wolf, and, as reported by anthropologist Alanson Skinner, "attacked his accomplice, who was clothed in the hide of a buffalo calf." The ersatz calf bleated so pitifully that nearby cows and bulls came to its rescue—and within shooting range.

From the histrionic wolf skit of Jacob Bear to the efficient mass kill of the surround, the Indians developed a remarkable gamut of hunting techniques. Their inventiveness brought a life of excitement and plenty. Until the time of change came west with the white man, their cleverness in the hunt guaranteed them an abundance of materials for apparel, for the construction of dwellings, for playthings, for food. These articles they prepared and enjoyed with the same rich imagination they had used in procuring their raw materials.

8

INDIANS AS CONSUMERS

THE SPIRITUALISTIC INDIANS OF THE PLAINS ENDED their communal hunts as they had begun them, with elaborate ritual. Even as the leading wave of Omaha hunters charged in to slaughter the surrounded herd, two specially chosen boys started preparations for the Feast of the Sacred Tongues to crown the day's hunt. As the first bull fell, the boys rushed into the melee, dodging between hunters and buffalo, hastening to collect tongues from the slain before any were touched—and thus contaminated —by the butcher's blade. After they had gathered the required twenty tongues and a single heart, they carried the lot to the Sacred Tent of the White Buffalo Hide to await preparation for the ritual feast.

When dusk fell over the Sacred Tent, the Seven Chiefs and the director of the hunt assembled inside in reverence, each cloaked in a buffalo robe with the fur facing out. At the back of the tent, the White Buffalo Hide occupied its place of honor, mounted on a frame and facing east.

After the sacred buffalo tongues and heart were boiled, the crouching delegates partook of the feast. The consecrated food was highly valued, said to bring good health and long life to those who ate it; if any remained when the celebrants had finished, it was passed around among a few lucky outsiders. Then, as the feasting drew to a close, the delegates sang the ritual song of the White Buffalo Hide and smoked from the sacred pipe to conclude the ceremony.

Tribal hunts were usually capped with such ritual feasting and celebration, as the Indians gave thanks to their gods and consecrated the spoils of the chase. But before general rejoicing could begin, there was a practical matter to attend to. The aftermath of a successful hunt was a prairie littered with slain buffalo, and carcasses had to be sorted before butchering could proceed. Although the chase and killing of buffalo was a communal affair, the processing of the meat, once divided, was the responsibility of individual families.

The rights to a buffalo went to the slayer, whose identity was confirmed by his arrow, distinguishable by the particular characteristics of its handcraft. Each man could identify his personal arrows as easily as we recognize our own handwriting.

In most cases, ownership was easily established. Dispute arose only during the largest surrounds, when several hundred buffalo were slain—some with arrows from the bows of more than one hunter. After all the missiles had been identified, the carcass was consigned to the man who was judged to have made the first mortal wound. If the owners of the arrows could not agree on who had made the fatal strike, the matter was settled on the spot by the tribal police. But serious controversy was unlikely, since in these larger hunts the Indians usually brought down more than enough buffalo to supply the entire camp.

———◆◆◆———

Depending on the tribe, the task of butchering fell either to men or to women—or to both. The Blackfoot believed that the job called for the strength and dexterity of a man, but the Hidatsa and Miami, classing the work as mere drudgery, assigned it to the women. From the remarks of Father Louis Hennepin, it is clear that Miami women were equal to the chore: "These women are so lusty and strong, that they carry on their Back two or three hundred weight, besides their Children; and notwithstanding that Burthen, they run as swiftly as any of our Soldiers with their Arms."

The site of the butchering soon became a tumult of Indians cutting and slashing carcasses, shouting clamorously, quarreling and laughing with neighbors.

As they worked, most of the participants snacked on raw morsels taken still warm from the slain buffalo, including livers, kidneys, tongues, eyes, testicles, belly fat, parts of the stomach, gristle from snouts, marrow from leg bones, and the hoofs of tiny unborn calves as well as tissue from their sacs. A sprinkling of bile from the gall bladder—used as we would use mustard on a hot dog—was said to improve the taste of liver. Hunters bashed holes in the tops of skulls with their tomahawks and scooped out the fresh brains. Once the belly was slit and the entrails removed, the men ladled up and drank handfuls of warm blood, the Cree in the belief that this would prevent them from being perturbed by the sight of blood in battle. The elderly sometimes sliced the nipples of lactating udders and drank the tepid milk. Those who were ailing coveted the kidneys.

These wild blood feasts after a hunt are not surprising in light of the arduous efforts of the day. In relief, in celebration, and in hunger, workers craved a snack of some kind as they butchered, and the various raw organs were perhaps tastier than we might imagine. John James Audubon, for one, came to appreciate the Indians' relish for the uncooked parts. After killing a few buffalo one day, he and some companions were startled when several tribesmen asked for "certain portions of the entrails, which they devoured with the greatest voracity." The naturalist was intrigued. "This gluttony excited our curiosity," he wrote, "and being always willing to ascertain the quality of any sort of meat, we tasted some of this sort of tripe, and found it very good, although at first its appearance was rather revolting."

Certain uncooked morsels also satisfied another need. The heat of a summer day and the hard work of cutting up the carcasses left the Indians with parched throats. If water was not available, the next best relief came from chewing the gristle of a buffalo's snout.

Furthermore, many Indians, conditioned to eating in enemy

territory, where the smoke of a fire would betray them, were accustomed to making a complete meal out of raw buffalo. Using a section of the ribs as a bowl, they made a pudding of marrow and brains; other organs were devoured raw as garnish, and the blood used to wash down the meat.

Most Indians relished raw viscera, but a few tribes abstained from them. The Kutenai, in particular, threw out most of the entrails, saving only the highly prized heart. They considered crude organs repugnant, and held the neighboring Blackfoot in contempt for eating raw liver.

When all carcasses were skinned and cut up, the meat was distributed according to the regulations of the individual tribe. Among the Assiniboin, the tongue, four of the choicest cuts, and the hide were set aside for the man who had slain the animal; the remainder—actually the greater part of the carcass—went to the skinners and butchers. The chiefs also made arrangements to distribute surplus meat and hides among the poor and the infirm, among the men who had no horses for hunting, and among the men who had remained in camp to guard tribal belongings.

To ready a butchered buffalo for transport, a hunter spread out the hide and piled the cuts of meat on it; then he wrapped everything into a bundle and loaded it onto the horse. The meat and skin from a single buffalo cow was considered a fair load for one horse; if the distance to camp was short, the Indian often added another half a cow or hopped on himself. When hauling his kill by dog-drawn travois, he loaded about a quarter of a carcass or one hide onto each frame, tying the mass securely with a rawhide rope.

Soon the route between butchering site and camp was jammed with a bustling line of people, horses, and dogs, all passing and repassing as they bore home the harvest of the hunt. As hunters loaded the last of the meat an ever-growing band of wildlife gathered at the kill site. Wolves, kit foxes, red foxes, coyotes, and badgers skulked impatiently just out of bow shot; when the last Indian had left, they would move in to feast on the bones and scraps, often joined by ravens, golden eagles, vultures, and occasional hawks. If the kill had taken place near an Indian village, packs of dogs would rush out to gorge themselves as well.

Eventually the last pack horses straggled into camp. Night usually overtook the operation as the Indians unloaded the final

This pencil sketch by a hunter named To-oan illustrates how men of the Kiowa tribe packed their buffalo meat from the butchering site back to camp.

batches of meat and hides onto the mounting piles in front of each lodge. As women and children picked over the day's haul to search out tiny morsels for grilling, the whole village began to glow with the flickering rays of scattered fires.

Now families gathered around the fire at every lodge, and the feasting and merriment began. Marrow bones were tossed among the red embers, calves' heads were baked in the hot earth, meaty ribs were roasted over the coals. Sometimes hunters stayed up all night cooking and eating, each of them consuming several pounds of fresh buffalo steak. With laughter and singing, storytelling and dance, the night quickly slipped away.

All through the next day, the tribe dried, cooked, or cached the stores of meat brought in from the hunt. Caching in particular was prescribed if the Indians were continuing on in pursuit of other herds; they could retrieve anything they left behind on their way back through the area. Techniques for laying away the meat varied from tribe to tribe, especially during the summer months. Some groups simply heaped it under hides. Others buried it in an underground pit; in winter, a similar cache might be dug into a snowbank.

But caching was only a temporary measure for storing buffalo meat. If cuts were to be kept for any length of time, the Indians sliced them across the grain into strips about half an inch thick. The pieces were then hung on a tall scaffold built from a meshwork of thin poles and adorned with streamers; the height of the structure and the fluttering of the streamers safeguarded the flesh from marauding wolves. After several days of exposure the meat became mummified by wind and sun.

An elevated rack of this design was used by the Blackfoot for drying slices of buffalo meat.

The dehydrated meat, called *jerky*, kept for as long as three years without spoiling. One explorer even remarked reassuringly that the preparation could become worm-eaten without turning rancid. Although Indians preferred to toast the strips over a fire or fry them in a pan, jerky was edible in its dried state. Zoologist William Hornaday once described its flavor as being "quite good," although the lack of salt in the curing process left it with a " 'faraway' taste which continually reminds one of hoofs and horns."

Whatever the peculiarities of its taste, jerky was a daily ration for many plainsmen, some of whom apparently grew quite fond of it.

Even with its practical excellence, however, jerky had drawbacks. Although it weighed only about one sixth as much as fresh meat, it was bulky—rather like a bundle of tree bark. In rain or damp air, it absorbed moisture readily, gaining weight as well as molding or decaying, often both. And if completely dry, it was hard to eat, calling for strong teeth and endless munching.

To make jerky less tough, the Indians tried pounding it into shreds: the crushed bits, when dipped into melted grease, were much easier to chew. But the other inconveniences—bulk, dampening in moist air, mold, and decay—remained. All of these difficulties were eventually mastered with the development of pemmican, the product of one of the most effective methods of food processing ever devised.

The processing of pemmican varied slightly from region to region, but the basic steps were the same throughout the Plains Culture Area. After pulverizing jerky, the Indians packed it into bags sewed from buffalo rawhide, each one about the size of a pillow case. Into these sacks they poured hot liquid marrow fat, which seeped through the contents to form a film around each crumb of meat. The bags were stitched up at the mouth and sealed with tallow along the seams. Before the contents had time to harden, each bag was tramped or pressed into a flat shape about six or seven inches thick. A single sack, weighing about ninety pounds, was known as a "piece" of pemmican, and made a convenient parcel for back-packing or portaging. It was also easy to store: placing a row of pieces on rocks or small logs to keep them off the ground, the Indians piled up the remaining sacks like cordwood.

Such was the procedure for making "plain" or "summer" pemmican. Three pounds of fresh buffalo meat could be dehydrated to half a pound of jerky; the jerky, mixed with an equal weight of fat, made a pound of summer pemmican. Or, figured in reverse, each pound of pemmican contained the equivalent of three pounds of lean buffalo steak. Some tribes, like the Blackfoot, used still less fat, making a pound of pemmican with the nourishment of five pounds of fresh meat. No wonder, then, that pemmican was considered so remarkable an advance in the field of food preservation. The process has even been ranked above canning, which merely reduces the likelihood of spoilage—pemmicanization reduces bulk and weight as well.

Other grades of pemmican differed in composition from the summer type in their proportions of fat, additives, or moisture. "Winter" pemmican was processed when the proper drying of meat was difficult; the resulting dampish jerky made the final mix heavier and bulkier. Still another form was the "berry" type, prepared with wild cherries or saskatoon berries for extra flavor.

Although additives improved the taste of pemmican, they tended to increase spoilage in the long run. Plain pemmican, if made properly with only dried lean meat and rendered fat, lasted almost indefinitely. The desiccated meat endured as though mummified; protected from moisture or air by its coating of fat and encased in its sealed rawhide bag, it kept for as long as thirty years and remained as good as the day it was mixed.

The excellent preservability of pemmican made it possible for Indians to store meat from a season of plenty to one of scarcity. And the remarkable food kept as well in Texas as in Manitoba. It was so condensed in weight and bulk that it formed the perfect travel ration for Indian scouts and raiding parties—a man could carry enough food to last him several days and eat it without building a single telltale fire. The preparation was so nourishing that the hard-working transportation crews of the fur trade were able to subsist on nothing else for weeks at a time.

This long list of virtues would seem to make pemmican an ideal ration for war. Indeed, in 1810, at a post on the North Saskatchewan River, a trader advertising the qualities of the product remarked: "Even the gluttonous french canadian that devours eight pounds of fresh meat every day is contented with one and a half pounds per day. It would be an admirable provision for the Army and Navy." Some sixty-two years later, in a neighboring region, a member of a Scottish expedition expressed this same view, but remarked indignantly: "The British Gauvirmint won't drame of pimmican till the Prooshians find it out."

It took time, but the "Prooshians" did find it out: in World War II the German army issued pemmican to soldiers. One might suppose that the American services would likewise order large quantities of this strikingly native invention. After all, pemmican had sustained American Indians, plainsmen, and fur traders until the end of the buffalo era, and later beef pemmican had been vital to balloon excursions, arctic expeditions, and camping trips all over the country. Fortifying their arguments with such known historical successes, the promoters of pemmican tried to sell the army and the navy on the idea of the product as a lightweight, compact emergency ration. A few officers in the field even made official requests for it. To the bewilderment of its champions, however, dietitians ruled in 1942 that pemmican was unsuitable for servicemen. Laboratory technicians had analyzed the ration and decided that it simply wasn't wholesome; and other experts who had sampled it didn't like the taste.

It is perhaps fitting that the final downfall of pemmican came as a result of its flavor, for no characteristic of the product was more controversial. The newcomers who rushed westward with the California gold rush found it unpalatable, even revolting. And a visiting Scottish nobleman was hardly complimentary: "Take scrapings from the driest outside corner of a very stale piece of cold roast beef, add to it lumps of tallowy rancid fat, then garnish all with long human hairs . . . and you have a fair imitation of common pemmican, though I should rather suppose it to be less nasty."

A few army regulars who ate pemmican during the last century's Indian wars deemed it "not particularly agreeable" on the first taste, but liked it once they got used to it. Peary used the preparation on his arctic explorations and considered it the only food that could be eaten twice a day for a year and taste as good at the last mouthful as it did at the first. After innumerable marches in bitter temperatures, he looked forward eagerly to his half-pound lump of pemmican: "By the time I had finished the last morsel I would not have walked around the . . . igloo for anything . . . the St. Regis, the Blackstone or the Palace Hotel could have put before me."

So much for pemmican. Although Plains Indians thrived on it, they ate fresh buffalo meat when it was available, preparing it in many different ways. Cooking methods varied from tribe to tribe, from tipi to tipi, and included roasting, broiling, stewing, and smoking. The pot was always bubbling, waiting to be sampled by any hungry tribesman, whether from the household or from a neighboring lodge. Soups were popular, some brewed with fleshy ribs and assorted bones fractured to render up their marrow, others with buffalo meat, berries, fat, and the roots of jack-in-the-pulpits. The women also boiled food in an earthen pit lined with fresh buffalo hide; after placing meat, roots, and water in the pocket, they rolled in heated stones to bring everything to a simmer. Another kind of pit, dug in the tipi floor, was used as an oven—the meat was placed in the pit and covered with hot ashes to bake for a few hours.

No matter how their meat was cooked, most Indians preferred it rare. And it did not have to be particularly fresh—many tribesmen favored hanging their cuts of buffalo until decay set in; some became notorious for their fondness for the putrid meat of carcasses conveyed downriver by the spring breakup—apparently they consumed it with relish even when fresh meat was plentiful.

Tribes reveled in other buffalo delicacies unlikely to appeal to non-Indian palates. The Cree savored fat from the udder, and the Hidatsa grilled the whole organ full of milk. Both the Cheyenne and the Pawnee liked the lungs either roasted alone or boiled with corn.

If they did not enjoy such unusual dishes, early traders and travelers who sampled Indian cookery did praise certain specialties. George Catlin greatly esteemed three Indian dishes: dog meat, beaver tails, and buffalo tongues. Grantley F. Berkeley, an English sportsman touring the plains, was more impressed with another part of the buffalo: ". . . and oh, shade of Eude, the marrow bones!" These were buffalo thigh bones that had been stripped of all but a few layers of tender inner flesh and placed on stones arranged at either side of the fire; after roasting for a time, the bones were cracked open and the marrow pried out, to be savored together with the crisp meat clinging to the surface.

Other frontier gourmets believed that the choicest part of a buffalo was the hump. In Indian cooking, this strip of muscle was cut from the spine and sewed up in a fold of hide to make a bundle resembling an oversized, elongated football. The bundle was placed in a preheated earthen pit, covered with layers of coals and soil and, finally, a vigorous fire. There it baked until noon the next day, when the cooks opened their furnace and took out the cocoon.

The hump of the buffalo also bore a unique strip of fatty tissue along its crest. This piece, known on the frontier by the French term *dépouille*, ranged up to two inches in thickness and weighed from five to eleven pounds. The Blackfoot and a few other tribes stripped it from the carcass, dipped it in hot grease, and hung it in the smoky apex of the tipi for a few hours. The finished specialty was tender, sweet, and nourishing, and it kept indefinitely. Indians ate *dépouille* along with pieces of jerky, using it in place of—and in preference to—bread. Raiding parties lived on jerky and *dépouille* alone for weeks at a time.

Among several northern tribes, a favorite dish was concocted from the fetal calf of a buffalo. In 1868 a local trader described this specialty and the method of its preparation among the Gros Ventre:

> . . . a young calf, before it is born, is considered the greatest delicacy of all. When first eaten, early in the winter, it is never larger than a kitten, and gradually increases in size until near spring, when it becomes too large and coarse. The idea of eating such a barbarous dish was at first revolting, but afterward, when better able to appreciate these Indian luxuries, I found it very palatable, particularly the natural liquor or broth in which it was boiled; which, with the addition of salt and pepper made an excellent soup.

Many tribes had formulas for brewing the blood of buffalo into pudding or soup. The Cheyenne cooked it in a pouch made from a buffalo stomach; the Blackfoot used a coarser technique. Removing the entrails from a slain buffalo, they turned the whole carcass over on its back; in this position, the rib box formed a natural cauldron that already contained a quantity of blood and fat. Adding a little water, the cooks dropped in some preheated stones to produce a rich broth in what was probably the largest soup bowl on the plains.

For still another kind of blood broth, Buffalo-Bird-Woman, a distinguished elder of the Hidatsa tribe, had her own approach; late in her life she related the recipe to an anthropologist in a general description of a hunting campaign she had been on in 1870. To obtain a base, she tapped blood from a pool that settled between the lungs and diaphragm of a slain bull (throwing away the clotted blood, which was difficult to cook and likely to ruin the broth). With this select fluid, she proceeded according to her recipe: Pour one and a half to two gallons of blood into a large kettle. Add one cup water, one piece of buffalo marrow-fat twice the size of an egg, and two handfuls of dried cooked squash. Bring to a boil. Prepare a stirring paddle from a two-foot length of chokecherry sapling, fringing the bark at one end to render a cherry flavor. Prepare another stick by stripping the bark from a small twig. Dip this into broth and remove. If red blood clings, continue boiling. Broth is ready to serve when stick emerges clean and white. (Buffalo-Bird-Woman added a warning for prospective chefs: the blood broth was a "delicate dish," and would spoil if left too long over the fire.)

This versatile Hidatsa cook was also skilled at making blood into a pudding, which she stuffed into a section of buffalo intestine. In like fashion, Crow chefs filled an intestine with long strips of meat and called their creation—one hopes only in the home market—"Crow-Indian-Guts." Other tribes made similar sausage-like puddings from stuffings of chopped meat.

From bile to bones to brains, few parts of the buffalo escaped the Indians' culinary experimentation. Bypassing only the hoofs, horns, and hair, they even cooked up skin, at times because they relished it and at other times out of desperation, when no other food was available. Against such emergency, the women saved and cached scrapings from the hides they tanned. Boiled with berries, or sometimes ungarnished, these leftovers made a palatable soup or jelly.

The Cheyenne also cooked fresh hides, baking them in a saucer-shaped oven excavated in the ground; all hairs were scraped off before the cooked skins were served. The dish was reported to be "quite tender and very good." (Even today, in parts of Nepal and Thailand, natives relish pieces of water buffalo hide cooked in deep fat.)

———————•◦•———————

No matter how tasty the skins might have been, few ended up in the kitchen. They were of much greater value in the domestic economy—as personal wealth in the form of robes, as raw materials for about half of the Indians' possessions, and as prime property for commercial trading.

The dressing of hides was almost always done by women, whose expert workmanship turned the bulky, heavy (about eighty pounds) green skins into finely tanned leather. It was toilsome, monotonous work, but it was an important skill. Girls accomplished in skin dressing were able to attract desirable husbands; older women boasted of their handcrafted leather tipis as proudly as warriors bragged of valorous deeds.

Two women dress a buffalo hide staked to the ground while another works over a hide stretched on a pole frame in this Catlin sketch of a Sioux camp on the upper Missouri. On a rack in the background, strips of buffalo meat dry in the sun.

All Plains tribes dressed skins in a similar fashion, with slight variations in tanning substances and in the time devoted to the task. The process had seven separate stages—fleshing, scraping, braining, stripping, graining, softening, and smoking—each distinguished by its own tools and techniques.

First, working with a chisel-like scraper made from the serrated end of a buffalo leg bone, the hide-dresser gouged from the hide any scraps of flesh and fat that remained after the hunter's hasty stripping. Then she laid the skin aside for the next step—scraping.

Her scraping tool was a short adze, a metal or flint blade right-angled into a handle. Laying the hide out on the ground, she planed the surface to an even thickness. Hides that were destined to become robes she worked only on the flesh side; all others she turned over to remove the hair as well.

In the third step, braining, the hide-dresser anointed the skin with a paste of fat, cooked brains, and liver, using a rounded stone to work the greasy blend into the hide. When the skin was thoroughly oiled, she set it aside to dry in the sun; later she saturated it with warm water and rolled it into a bundle to soak overnight in preparation for the next stage—stripping.

For the stripping operation, she wrung out the surplus moisture and stretched the skin onto a frame. Grasping a squeegee-like instrument in both hands, she pressed its edge forcefully against the hide and drew it steadily from top to bottom; a ripple of water oozed out with her every stroke. After working over the whole surface, she left the skin suspended in the frame to dry and bleach until it was ready for graining.

The graining step called for a rasplike stone or a globular piece of bone sliced to expose its sharp, spongy inner texture. As if wielding sandpaper, she rubbed this tool over the hide to remove any excess fibers and implement a uniform smoothness. After further drying, the skin was ready for the softening process.

Now the woman stretched a sinew between two trees and draped the hide over it like a freshly laundered sheet. Seizing an end in each hand, she seesawed the hide back and forth over the sharp edge of sinew. The friction of the operation built up considerable heat, which helped to dry and limber the leather. With the completion of this sixth step, the hide was "soft-tanned" and ready for use.

Skins intended for clothing usually received one last treatment —smoking—to give them the virtue of drying soft and pliant after any number of wettings in rain or snow. The hide-dresser built a smokehouse, erecting a domelike or conical framework of sticks over a pit in the ground. In the pit she kindled a fire of rotten wood, with sparse flame and heavy smoke. Overhead on the framework she stretched her skins, pinning or sewing them together to trap the smoke inside, then leaving them in place for several hours to cure. From beginning to end, the smoking process took about half a day.

Dressed hides and meat were foremost among the buffalo products used by the Indians, but the list went on and on. Hair, horns, bones, sinews, viscera, dung, and even tails—all these and still other parts—were carefully laid aside as raw material. From them the Indians fashioned shoes, garments, bedding, tableware, vessels, fuel, saddlery, tools, musical instruments, toys, cosmetics, and jewelry.

A substantial number of these articles was still made from hides. Time after time, from cradle to burial ground, Indian used hides in a variety of different forms. Soft skins of infant calves swaddled the youngest papooses and thick robes of tough bulls shrouded the corpses of departed elders.

Hides fell into two main categories according to type. Skins taken in autumn or winter, when the fur was long and dense, were tanned with the hair on and used chiefly for robes, bedding, winter moccasins, and gloves; those taken in spring or summer were depilated and made into light clothing, body armor, ceremonial masks, snowshoes, utensils, packing cases, bags, ropes, harnesses, saddles, bindings for tools, and covers for tipis.

The number of hides used to make the average tipi ranged from seven to twenty, depending on the size of the individual lodge. Indians fitted the hides together in the most economical fashion, filling gaps with small scraps of skin and joining the seams with sinew. Lifting the finished semi-circular sheet onto a framework of poles, they brought the two loose ends around to the front and fastened them with small wooden pins tacked upward from the doorway; then they staked the rim to the ground with pegs. Some Indians ran an extra lining of hides across the floor and up the sides for four or five feet to make the tipi draft-proof in winter.

Buffalo skins were also used for most of the furnishings inside the lodge. Often painted and embroidered, they were hung like tapestries to partition the tipi into semi-private nooks, or used to adorn primitive pieces of furniture. When tightly stretched between four posts, a buffalo robe provided a luxurious underpinning for a bed; other robes served as covers, and a doubled-over robe made a handy pillow.

Skins also served as covering for another important tribal structure—the sweathouse. This special feature of Indian life operated in the same fashion as the Finnish sauna: participants stripped and entered, sprinkled water on a cluster of heated stones to stir up a dense vapor, then stayed inside to swelter for half an hour or more. Upon emerging, many plunged into a cold stream or rolled over in snow in an early version of the hydrotherapy shock techniques used today in the treatment of nervous tension. Indian hunters relished the sweathouse for reviving tired muscles and relaxing the body, especially after the strenuous exertions of a buffalo chase. Sweating was also prescribed for propitiating supernatural spirits or curing disease.

A standard accessory within the sweathouse was a buffalo tail mounted on a short handle—an efficient counterpart of the birch switch used in the sauna. Tribesmen used it to sprinkle water on the heated rocks and to beat the body in an Indian form of massage.

In addition to providing furnishings for the lodge, buffalo hides were source material for a variety of garments, many so expertly tanned that they were as soft as cloth. Indeed, before the arrival of white traders and their fabrics, the entire wardrobe of most Plains tribes was made from buffalo skins. Among the Blackfoot, for instance, men wore a long-sleeved shirt, a breechclout hanging down from a belt, and leggings; women wore a single garment that draped from neck to ankles, branching at the shoulders into two flowing sleeves and cinched at the waist with a belt. Accessories included caps, mittens, and moccasins—all fashioned from buffalo hides. Articles intended for wear in winter were made from hides with the fur left intact to provide added insulation and warmth; summer wear dictated lighter, depilated skins.

For further adornment, most men wore a buffalo robe thrown loosely around their shoulders; during hunting or travel, it was secured by a belt. For many this furry cape was the only covering for the upper body. With the hair turned outward, the robe gave protection from rain, and when reversed, it provided greater warmth in winter.

Certain buffalo robes brought less tangible benefits through the spiritual and ceremonial illustrations that adorned them. Virtually the sole art form of Plains Indians, the designs and drawings were motivated less by the desire to decorate than by the desire to record. Each was a graphic bulletin documenting real or imagined tribal history—an outstanding annual event, a supernatural vision, or a personal biography.

Biographical paintings originated in the narrative tradition of the warrior. It was the custom and privilege of the Indian fighting man to declaim an account of his deeds in a raid or in battle. If anyone dared question a certain event, the participant could authenticate it by oath, weighting his pledge with a display of the drawings on his buffalo robe. There the heroic acts were clearly enumerated—the wounds suffered, the blood lost, the number of enemy slain, the quantities of arms, prisoners, or horses taken. What was written or drawn was accepted as fact (a practice hardly restricted to the Plains Indians).

Paints for the hide drawings were derived by the artists from iron-bearing clays or from parts of the buffalo themselves. The Blackfoot obtained a shade of yellow from buffalo gallstones, and the Cheyenne concocted a black pigment by stirring cottonwood buds or ashes of burned grass into fresh buffalo blood. The colors were applied with brushes made from bone, horn, or wood.

No matter how magnificent its decoration or how luxurious its fur, the splendid buffalo robe was likely to end its days in exposure and decay; for the favored garment—sometimes accompanied by jewelry, a weapon, and other treasured property—was often used to shroud the corpse of its owner in death. Indeed, the more lush and elaborate it was, the more likely such a fate, for what had been treasured in life was considered even dearer to the dead. Amid the tears and lamentations of friends, the Indian's corpse, swathed in its rich buffalo robe, was hoisted onto an elevated scaffold and fastened there to slowly rot.

Though of great importance in the daily and ceremonial life of the Indians, buffalo robes constituted only a portion of the skins processed. A great number of other skins were put to a more ordinary use as rawhide. These hides underwent only the first two of the tanning operations—the fleshing of meat particles and the removal of hair and leveling of bumps. The resultant green leather, or rawhide, had an extraordinary strength and toughness that rendered it ideal for the manufacture of knife sheaths, cups, dippers, kettles, mortars, rattles, drumheads, cradles, cages, fencing, boats, cases, shields, bridles, lariats, and other pieces of saddlery —including small bags that were wrapped around a horse's hoofs and served as shoes.

In addition, wet rawhide shrank markedly as it dried, and could perform the function of nails, twine, or glue. Applied green

Drawings by a Hidatsa artist show how a mortar was made from a square of rawhide. The piece was first scraped with an ax to remove all hair, then folded double and trimmed to shape at the lower corners. After the edges were sewn together the skin mortar was fitted snugly into a pit in the ground for use in grinding corn or dried meat.

over a rock and a handle, it bound the two into a durable club, maul, or masher. A rawhide cover sewn wet onto the wooden sections of a saddle joined the pieces together in a unified frame.

No article made from rawhide was more useful than the ingenious *parfleche*. The suitcase or packing box of its time, this important piece of equipment was so versatile as to belie the simplicity of its construction. Spreading a flat sheet of rawhide about six feet long and three feet wide on the ground, a woman painted or incised a simple geometric pattern on the surface and creased four lines to mark the folds. Arranging her clothing or foodstuffs in the middle, she brought the top and bottom margins toward the center, folded the left and right sides inward and laced them together to close up the package. The *parfleche* was then ready for storage or travel.

Rawhide was also fashioned into boats with the improbable design of oversized washtubs, a shape that still retains its reputation for tippiness and unmanageability. But it would have been difficult to modify the design of a "bull boat," given the method of its construction. The fresh hide of a bull, hair out, was simply draped over a circular framework of willow boughs; as the hide shrank in drying, it bound firmly to the slender frame, making a watertight shell strong enough to carry as much as one horse or three men. Though perhaps not the most sophisticated or the most stable of craft, it was simple to make and extremely durable and useful. Several Plains tribes acquired a special knack for maneuvering these unstable tubs, and learned to paddle up and down nearby rivers with ease. An Indian woman could propel one across the Missouri with surprising speed: sitting or kneeling close to one side, she merely thrust the paddle into the water ahead and

A series of sketches by a Hidatsa artist illustrate the steps for making a storage sack from the skin of a buffalo calf. To begin, the woman pulled off the entire skin from the neck down and sewed up the small holes where the hoofs were removed and where the vent was cut. Then she blew air in through the neck, closed the opening, and dried the inflated hide in the sun. Finally, she worked the hide with her hands to soften it and turned it inside out for filling with corn.

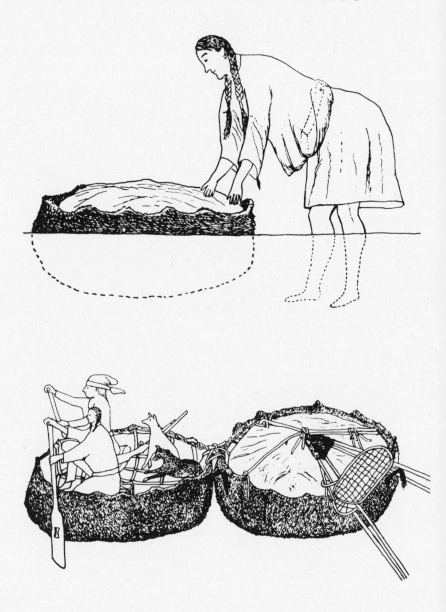

These drawings of buffalo bull boats were made by the son of the Hidatsa couple pictured here. In the upper drawing, the wife covers a load of dried hides and meat with an old skin. With the two dog travois lashed on top, this boat is then towed behind another bearing the couple and their two dogs.

102

pulled the boat forward. She would surely have insisted that she was positioning herself in the "bow" of the tub, and slight irregularities in its roundness might have justified her claim. Many Indians avoided uncertainty by leaving the buffalo's tail intact on the finished craft, thus marking the "stern." Some even attached a driftwood drag to the tail to prevent undue pivoting.

Precarious navigability was not a serious disadvantage, since bull boats were used principally for artless drifting downstream. But even when steered through rough water, the vessels proved a match for turbulent rapids or wind-driven waves—numbers of floating Indians merely drew their tubs together, grasping the rims of neighboring boats to hold them in a tight cluster. Thus bunched, they weathered the tempest like a giant rubber raft. And when it came time to haul the boats back upstream, the round shape and light weight proved ideal—the travelers simply carried them upside down on their heads, appearing to one observer like "huge black beetles crawling along the sandbar."

In still another application, rawhide was cured into rock-hard shields by a process of boiling, steaming, baking, or grilling. The long, tedious heat treatment reduced the chunk of leather to half its original size, forming a circular plate about three fourths of an inch thick and some seventeen to thirty inches across. The finished shield was so tough it could turn an arrow or even deaden the force of a bullet.

Indispensable as a piece of armor in battle, the shield was also highly prized for its spiritual properties, which were established during the curing process through the prayers of the owner's most trusted friends. The chosen tribesmen sang and danced around the disc of rawhide, appealing to the spirit powers to invest the finished shield with a special force that would render their comrade invulnerable in the face of his enemies. Further supernatural protection derived from the shield's decorative paintings of the sun, moon, thunderbird, buffalo, or other figures—whichever spirits had come to the owner in a vision.

Buffalo hair—scraped from rawhide, clipped from the heads of slain animals, or gathered from spots on the plains where large tufts had been shed—gave rise to a virtual cottage industry among the tribes, yielding a long list of products. Few of these fragile articles have survived to take their place in museums and collections; our knowledge of them comes primarily from early journals, which indicate that buffalo hair was used extensively in all tribes, especially those in the southeastern part of the country between the Mississippi and the Atlantic coast. (Buffalo in this region became scarce in colonial days but were a staple of tribes before that.)

Word of the product even found its way across the Atlantic: in a letter to the governor of the French colony at the mouth of the Mississippi, Louis XIV decreed that top priority be given to buffalo wool. Indeed, the prospect of a trade in the product helped to launch the new settlement. But after a series of abortive efforts, the idea was dropped.

Although buffalo wool made little progress in the French economy, it found many uses in tribal camps. The Indians lined their moccasins with the soft fuzz. They also used it for stuffing, packing it into saddles for adults and into balls and dolls for children. Some artisans spun the wool into strands for weaving blankets, scarves, bags, wallets, and—in combination with porcupine quill stiffeners—women's girdles. Strands were twisted or braided into ropes, which served as halters, lariats, belts, and cords. A Shoshoni halter examined by Meriwether Lewis contained six or seven strands woven into a cord "about the size of a man's finger and remarkably strong."

Similar rope was used for a macabre purpose among the Natchez. A witness to the funeral of a tribal chief in 1730 described the rites, in which a group of men submitted themselves to sacrificial death in honor of their departed leader: "After having danced and sung a sufficiently long time, they pass around their necks a cord of buffalo hair, with a running knot, and immediately the ministers appointed for execution of this kind come forward to strangle them."

Buffalo hair was also a popular item in the beauty trade. Quapaw women made loop earrings of it, and other squaws braided it into bracelets or garters.

Even the young men used buffalo hair to promote beauty: when warriors of several southeastern tribes pierced their ears for earrings, they inserted wads of buffalo wool soaked in bear grease to distend the holes until they healed. Indeed, in the plains region, beauty was considered primarily the domain of the male. "The men," reported a visitor to one Hidatsa community, "devote more attention to ornaments and fine appearance than the girls."

Among the Hidatsa and certain other tribes, long hair for the men was the style. Embellished at times with silver buckles or slips of colored cloth, it was very long hair, which flowed in graceful tresses down to the knees or even to the ground. But the abundant locks did not belong exclusively to the owner—the men commonly extended their own hair with sections of hair from a buffalo, sticking the pieces together with tiny daubs of gum or clay.

The articles fabricated from hair and hides, though diverse and plentiful, made up only a portion of the roster of buffalo by-products. The list goes on in astonishing length and variety. From buffalo horns alone, the Indians fashioned arrow points, drinking cups, powder flasks, trimmings for war bonnets, emblems of high office, spinning tops for boys, instruments for flattening porcupine quill embroidery, heads for war clubs, cupping horns for bleeding patients to relieve infections, and—after simmering with spruce needles—a medication for sore eyes. And pieces of the horns, boiled, split, and flattened, were sewn together with sinew to make dishes. The vessels were not watertight, but evidently the slight leakage did not impair their serviceability.

Both the Cheyenne and the Crow made buffalo horns into excellent bows. After a soaking in local hot springs, the horns were cut into strips, pieced together in the contour of a bow, and bound firmly in place with sinew soaked in glue. According to the Crow, these buffalo bows were superior to any made from wood.

Other buffalo horns were fashioned into spoons and ladles. First the gluey matter inside the horns was fried out by scorching. Then the horns were trimmed into shape with a knife and boiled in water; when pliant, they were molded around rocks of suitable roundness and left to harden. After a final smoothing with a sandy rock and a little polishing with the palm of the hand, the hornware was ready for the kitchen.

Another form of spoon was forged from the hoofs of buffalo. The tough hoofs found their most important use, however, as the main ingredient for glue. Other components of buffalo glue included the muzzle, penis, eyes, cartilage from the breastbone, and shavings from the hide. All were boiled down to a gelatinous mass that was skimmed periodically until only a clear adhesive remained. Indians used this mucilage for attaching points or feathers to arrow shafts, for binding components of bows, and, undoubtedly, for "general household repairs." Any glue remaining in the pot was dipped out on sticks, dried in blobs, and laid away. When needed again, it was renewed by moistening. The Cheyenne did not save the excess, however, for they considered the molasses-like mixture quite tasty, and usually devoured any left-overs.

The bones of buffalo were also fashioned into a variety of objects—saddle trees, war clubs, pipes, knives, knife handles, arrowheads, arrow-making tools, and runners for small, dog-drawn sleds. Spades and hoes were shaped from parts of the frontal bones of skulls as well as from shoulder blades. The fleshing tool for the tanning of hides was made from the lower leg bone, and the graining tool was split from the bulbous end of the humerus, which had a spongy inner core that dried to the consistency of sandpaper. Paint "brushes" were made from other cores with a natural porosity ideally suited to picking up pigments; the colors flowed smoothly from the bony reservoirs onto rawhide or leather.

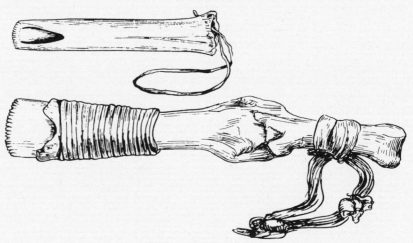

Bones from the hind limbs of buffalo were cut into a chisel-like shape and given a toothed edge to serve as fleshing tools for dressing hides.

Teeth of buffalo served for ornamentation, and were sewn on dresses, dangled as pendants, or strung into necklaces.

One of the most useful of all the products obtained from buffalo was sinew. The large tendons lying on either side of a buffalo's backbone were carefully stripped out and set aside. Whenever an Indian needed thread, he pulled off a strand with his teeth, softened it in water (or even in his mouth), and smoothed it with his fingers in preparation for twisting. Then, grasping one end of the strand in his teeth, he rolled it in his palms to smooth and limber it. Sinew made tough, durable thread for twisting into ropes, weaving into bowstrings, binding the strips of wood or horn in bows, attaching feathers or points to arrows, and sewing tipi covers and clothing.

Assorted internal organs also ended up in the pool of buffalo by-products. Most versatile was the paunch (the first of the four ruminant stomachs). When a carcass was butchered, the organ was cut out, cleaned, dried, and set aside for future use. Filled with water, it made an ideal canteen for treks away from camp. It served just as well in the tipi, where it was suspended from a pole and tapped through a natural valve; in winter it was stuffed with snow and hung near the fire until the contents melted. The paunch case made a handy wrapping for dried meat. And in a practice particularly appropriate to their name, the Gros Ventre stuffed paunches full of meat, blew them up with air, tied the openings, and floated the packets across the Missouri River.

The Blackfoot sewed willow or cherry hoops into the top and bottom of a paunch and added a bail to make a collapsible bucket. In smaller versions minus the bail, the organs were used as collapsible cups. A paunch suspended at the top between four sticks set a few inches apart and driven into the ground made an admirable saucepan; cooks placed ingredients for soups in the bottom, then gently slid heated stones into the pot to bring the liquid to a simmer.

The membranous sacs enclosing a buffalo's heart or bladder were used in the manner of the paunch bags—to hold water or food. In addition, when the bladder was fitted with a nozzle made from a hollow bird bone or a depithed elderberry stem, it served as the bulb of a physician's syringe.

The buffalo's large intestine was also serviceable as a container. Filled with fresh blood and cinched at either end, it was carried about the neck in the style of the leather wine skins popular in Spain. The small intestine could be used to repair broken wooden handles: stretched over the fragments, it dried to bind them firmly together. Among the Omaha, intestines were baked in the sun, then woven into edible mats, which could be cached underground until needed for food.

Diverse parts of buffalo were adapted to several tribal games or sports. "Snow snakes" made from wooden shafts tipped with buffalo horns were cast across the snow or over the ice for an Indian version of curling; similar gliders were also made from rib bones. Frozen ponds were perfect for buffalo-skull skating—the boy seated his girlfriend on a skull, hooked a rope through the nostrils, and towed the contraption over the ice. If the couple preferred coasting down hills, they made their sled from six to ten buffalo ribs lined up side by side and laced together with rawhide; sometimes a section of backbone with the ribs still attached was used for the same purpose. When grassy hills were freshly green in spring, boys slid down them on toboggans of rawhide. And for an Indian version of the trampoline, Crow children took a large hide and laced a rope around its border; playmates were challenged to stay on while their friends bounced them vigorously up and down on the springy sheet.

Indian children incorporated buffalo items into various games of marksmanship. Darts made of willows were trimmed with buffalo tails, a buffalo lung was held aloft on a pole for target practice, and buffalo chips with holes punched in the centers were rolled along the ground as archery targets. Buffalo chips were also handy as ammunition for playful bombardments.

Even musical instruments could be made from various parts of a buffalo. The Sioux beat out rhythms on a chunk of dried hide with sticks made from buffalo tails mounted on handles; other drums were made from hide stretched across sections of hollowed tree trunk. Rattles were fashioned from dried rawhide bags filled with pebbles and equipped with handles; a buffalo scrotum worked even better than rawhide; and a similar rattling effect was achieved with a few hoofs strung off the end of a wand. Several tribes made "bull-roarers" or "buzzers" out of the bone taken from inside the hoof of a buffalo. Suspending the small hoofbone on a sinew between two sticks, they spun it round and round, winding up the sinew until it was tightly twisted along its entire length; then, by moving the sticks in and out, they alternately relaxed and tensed the sinew, causing the bone to whirl rapidly until it threw off a buzzing sound.

Buffalo even furnished the Indians with rudimentary cosmetic aids. Cree women liked the rough side of a buffalo tongue for brushing hair, and many women used other by-products as ingredients for makeup. Buffalo-Bird-Woman once described her personal regimen:

I painted every morning because the wind and air made our faces dark, tanned them as you say, so we painted that our complexions would not darken . . . To paint my face I rubbed grease made from buffalo back fat into my palms and then rubbed my palms over my face. Then I opened the mouth of the paint bag and with the flat of my three fingers I touched the paint . . . Of course, a little of the paint clung to my fingers which were oily with the buffalo fat. I now touched my fingers, first to one cheek and then to the other, and finally I rubbed the paint evenly over my face.

Any list of buffalo by-products would be incomplete without a tally of the uses of buffalo chips. In their most frequent application as fuel, the piles of dried dung burned like chunks of peat and yielded a clear, hot flame, especially if crisped beforehand by sun and wind (during conditions of dampness, they were sometimes too moist to ignite). Shredded dung made excellent tinder for starting a wood fire; a little powdered dung scattered over the pipe bowl made the tobacco mixture easier to light—to say nothing of its effect on aroma. Women gathered thoroughly weathered buffalo chips for pulverizing into quantities of soft, downy fiber, which served commendably as material for absorbent blotters, providing Indian mothers with an early version of the diaper.

This last innovation crowns the collection of buffalo by-products, an endless list, founded on the essentials of meat and hides, branching out into a series of luxury articles of almost unbelievable variety. The total array made the buffalo a tribal department store, builder's emporium, furniture mart, drugstore, and supermarket rolled into one—a splendidly stocked commissary for the needs of life.

9

A PLACE IN SYMBOLISM

AND CEREMONY

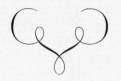

Seldom before in the history of mankind had one species shaped the life of a people as totally as the American buffalo influenced the ways of the Plains Indians. Brought into intimate rapport with the tribes through their dependence upon him, the buffalo became a cherished symbol. His appearance and movements were poetically described. Parts of his body were valued as charms or sacrificed to spirit powers. He figured in dances, superstitions, taboos, societies, visions, and cures. His habits gave names to the months. Ceremonies were held in his honor. In short, the buffalo was worshipped—as no other animal was ever worshipped in the Indians' domain.

Considered the most sacred of wild creatures and a potent force in nature, the buffalo was the highest-ranking figure in many hierarchies of tribal gods, featuring in a large body of religious practices, symbols, and rituals. The Arikara divided their universe into four quarters—Sunrise, Thunder, Wind, and Night. Each quarter also stood for a spiritual being. The tribe dedicated the southwest quarter to the guardian spirit of Buffalo, thus affirming their belief that the herds had been placed on earth for the sustenance and support of mankind.

To the Teton Sioux, the Buffalo God was the patron of chastity, fecundity, industry, and hospitality, the qualities they considered most desirable in a woman. Accordingly, their Buffalo God Ceremony revolved around a girl just reaching puberty. Placing her in the protection of their god, the ceremony confirmed, officially, that she was a woman.

Before the ceremony began, the girl's menstrual discharge was attentively wrapped up and stashed in a plum tree. The attending shaman then donned a buffalo-horn headdress so that he might speak for the Buffalo God, whose influence he sought to draw into the lodge by blowing a few puffs of smoke through the nose of an old buffalo skull. The sanctity of his words was further guaranteed by the wearing of a special buffalo tail, which he dangled from his cap.

Informing the girl that she was now a young buffalo cow and he a buffalo bull, the shaman set forth to show her what the rutting season was like. He walked purposefully out of the lodge, returning a moment later on his hands and knees, bellowing and pawing the ground, in imitation of a ruffled bull. Testing the air with his nose and bellowing again, he crept over to sidle up against the girl. "That," he explained, "is the manner in which the Crazy Buffalo will approach you, tempting you into acts which you will later regret."

After this warning, the Sioux ceremony drew to a conclusion as shaman and girl drank like buffalo from a wooden bowl filled with chokecherries and water, a ritual quaff symbolizing their kinship with the Buffalo God.

Religion among the Kiowa knew no Great Spirit, no heaven, no hell, but was instead a shadowy world of ghosts, witches, and assorted offerings and totems. Polytheists and animists, the Kiowa deified and prayed to all the powers of nature. Their greatest god was the Sun, by whom they swore, and to whom they made sacrifices of their own flesh. Next in order of reverence were the buffalo bull and the peyote plant: the peyote was the Sun's vegetal representative, the buffalo in his strength and majesty its animal symbol.

In honor of the Sun, the Kiowa held their great K'ado, or Sun Dance. Similar ceremonies became the most important annual event for some twenty other tribes—virtually every group in the Plains Nation except a few in the south and southeast. So vital were the Sun Dances to tribal welfare that participation in them was mandatory. Convening at this time was no problem for most Indians, since the dance was usually held just after families had abandoned separate winter quarters and massed for the summer buffalo hunt.

The Sun Dance was conducted in similar fashion throughout the plains region. After officials erected a medicine lodge around a consecrated center pole, they marked out an altar with a circle of buffalo skulls and placed special offerings in a fork in the pole; these sacred objects, along with the sun itself, drew the steady gaze of the celebrants. (Such staring at the sun probably gave the dance its name, since the sun alone did not occupy a key position in the formalities.) Devotees prepared themselves by fasting and thirsting; then they danced and prayed for about four days at the height of the proceedings and concluded the ceremony with a torture rite.

Features of the Sun Dance involving buffalo were more or less consistent from tribe to tribe. Soon after the scheduling of the event, certain participants began to accumulate "sacred" buffalo tongues. Sliced and dried like jerky, the tongues were subsequently put to use as emergency rations during the dancing. An important part of the offering placed on the center pole was the consecrated hide of a buffalo bull. Ritual stipulated that this bull must have been killed by a small band of distinguished warriors; each brave was allowed but a single arrow or cartridge for his part in the killing.

Placed among the buffalo skulls at the Sun Dance altar was a specially decorated skull whose colors and designs bore ritual significance. Among the Cheyenne, the priest who painted the tribal skull drew a black line down the front and two narrower white lines down either side; the eye sockets and nasal cavity he filled with three neatly formed plugs of swampgrass, painting these and the remainder of the skull red. The paint on the skull symbolized the earth, and that on the grass plugs its vegetation; the white lines represented day, the black ones night.

Buffalo skulls were also featured in the torture rites at the close of the Sun Dance. Young men submitted voluntarily, hoping by means of their sacrifice to earn the favor of the spirit powers. A warrior would undergo torture at the commencement of his career, and thereafter before a hazardous undertaking such as guiding a foray against the enemy.

In a drawing made in 1901, a Cheyenne artist shows how buffalo skulls and support ropes were attached to a supplicant's body with skewers of wood.

Skewers were attached to folds of skin on the body of each candidate for torture. The first two were anchored to the man's chest; cords running from these were fixed to the center pole and pulled taut, hoisting him into the air, where he dangled for hours or even days. Buffalo skulls were often hung from additional skewers hooked into the skin on his back. An occasional youth, instead of swinging the full weight of the skulls from his back, chose to fasten the skewers to long cords; with as many as fifteen buffalo skulls attached to the cords, the victim plodded pitifully about the camp, dragging his burden along the ground behind him. The ordeal continued until the man either tore out the skewers or collapsed from exhaustion. When he was fully revived, he was deemed eligible to undertake the most dangerous of expeditions.

A Cheyenne undergoing torture, as drawn by a tribal artist, attached four buffalo skulls to folds of skin in his back and dragged this encumbrance over the ground for an entire day. Afterward, claiming to be in no way fatigued, he told of receiving special spiritual powers from the ordeal.

The buffalo skull, the foremost totem of the animal, was put to many other uses in ceremonial life. Very often the same skull that had been painfully borne in torture proceedings was later placed over the doorway of the lodge, where it would repose in honored calm, daily supplicating the buffalo spirit to watch over and guard all members of the lodge. When the head of the household felt death approaching, he instructed a young man to remove the skull and arrange it on a barren prairie hill; there it was presented with an offering of a pipe with tobacco and abandoned to the elements.

Most tribes placed a buffalo skull on a mound of earth in front of the sweathouse. The Cheyenne smoked a pipe to their sweathouse skull, beseeching it to rise, invest itself with flesh, and come to life to present the tribe with meat for their kettles and skins for their lodges. During ceremonies inside the sweathouse, warriors sometimes sliced sacrificial bits of skin from their arms or legs; these were later deposited under the ever-present buffalo skull at the entrance.

Among the Plains Cree, a single buffalo skull oversaw group confessions. A man would position the skull inside his tipi, then call some friends together and demand that they recount their illicit sexual relations. Fearful of the judgment of the buffalo skull, the men spilled their stories truthfully, aware that disaster overtook all liars, and that those who failed to bare their transgressions were certain to be slain when next they went to battle.

The buffalo skulls revered in camp often served the Indians after death, continuing their vigil at the burial ground. Pawnee tribesmen propped the body of a deceased warrior in a sitting position and surrounded it with a shelter of tightly woven reeds and branches, to keep out wolves. To mark this tomb, they added a few buffalo skulls painted red.

The Assiniboin laid out their deceased on burial scaffolds. Frail in construction, the structures eventually weakened with age and collapsed, dumping the sun-bleached bones to the ground. Relatives then gathered the remains, burying most of the bones and setting the skulls aside for totemic remembrance. After accumulating a number of these skulls, they composed them in a circle on the open prairie with the "faces" turned toward the center. To complete the circle they added a medicine pole and several buffalo skulls. The macabre assemblage was idolized and tended with care.

An Arapaho youth about to join his first war party suspended a buffalo skull at the top of the medicine lodge as a devout pledge to the spirit powers. He was expected to be rewarded for his devotion with a great triumph in the raid. Elsewhere in the land of the buffalo, different parts of the animal were proffered in sacrifice with the hope of some concrete return—health for oneself or kin, a wealth of horses, success in buffalo hunting, or the gift of shamanistic powers. To appeal for such benefits, the Pawnee made a sacrificial bundle containing the heart and tongue of a buffalo, and the Arikara offered the viscera. Most valued of all sacrifices was the skin of the rare white buffalo.

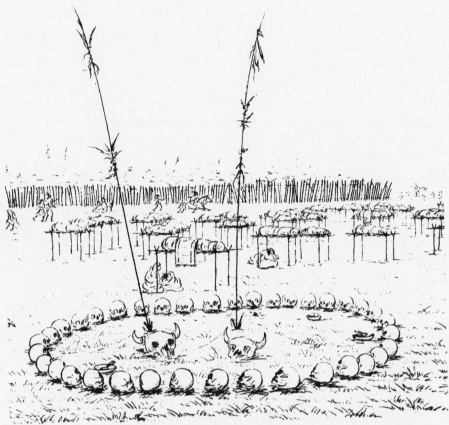

In the background of George Catlin's pencil sketch of a Mandan cemetery are corpses wrapped in buffalo skins resting on top of scaffolds, all with their feet toward the east, "facing the rising sun." After the remains decomposed, the bleached skulls were gathered up and neatly arranged in a large circle with decorated staffs and a pair of buffalo skulls in the center.

Even the lowly buffalo chip was exalted in ceremony. The first scalp taken by a young Cheyenne was sectioned into four quadrants on top of a large chip; after the Indian had invoked the spirits, he deposited the offering on the grassy plain. Buffalo chips were used by other tribes as hallowed resting places for such sacred objects as medicine pipes.

Parts of the buffalo were also treasured for their potency as charms. Among the Creek Indians women wore garters of buffalo hair for adornment as well as for fending off miscarriages, painful labor, and "other evils." Members of the Pawnee Buffalo Society prized maw stones from a buffalo's paunch for preventing sickness, considering them the source of the "wonderful power" of the animal. Assiniboin hunters attempted to stave off buffalo gorings by means of a charm made from a bull's head; to "activate" the piece, they bedecked it with paint, feathers, sticks, and scarlet streamers. The Plains Cree wore buffalo dewclaws for their magic power to deflect bullets.

Not all buffalo rituals were positive in concept; a few taboos were also associated with the animal. A Cherokee under treatment for rheumatism was forbidden to eat the meat, touch the skin, or use a horn spoon of buffalo—the tribe saw an occult connection between the cramped attitude of a rheumatic and the natural hump of a buffalo. The Crow and Cheyenne forbade the eating of meat from a white buffalo, the Crow because they thought it would turn their hair gray prematurely and the Cheyenne because they feared it would forever repel the herds from their locale.

Other tribes observed taboos against ridiculing a live buffalo or its meat. The Flathead feared that speaking irreverently would cause a shortage of buffalo, or perhaps prompt the animals to charge hunters or stampede into camp. The Teton Sioux considered the earth and the buffalo as one; if anyone spoke ill of buffalo, however softly, they believed the earth would hear and tell the buffalo, which in turn would kill the disrespectful person.

The special feeling of Indian for buffalo was reinforced by the wearing of a buffalo robe, which provided a spiritual link with the animal and strengthened the wearer's sense of the deep connection between all living forms and himself. It was only natural that many Indians donned such robes when commencing sacred ceremonies. In the rites preceding an Omaha communal hunt, official delegates huddled in conference like so many crouching buffalo, acknowledging by this attitude the flow of life from buffalo to man.

The empathy of Indian for buffalo carried over into many phases of tribal life. It influenced the names assigned to soldier societies: the Mandan had their "Buffaloes" and the Arikara their "Mad Bulls." In like manner, the Winnebago buffalo clan gave their members titles like "Big-Female-Buffalo," "Suckling-

1 1 7

Buffalo-Calf," "Two-Buffalo-Heads," "Kicking-Up-the-Earth" and "Shaggy-Walker."

The buffalo was further symbolized in the haircuts of the children of certain Osage clans. The heads of the young Indians were shaved bare with the exception of a few tufts of hair whose design had been conceived to represent a buffalo.

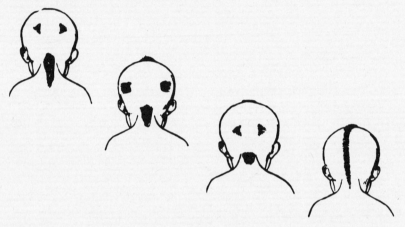

Haircuts on the two Osage children at the left symbolize the horns and tail of a buffalo, while the third child wears a briefer version of the same design to represent a calf. The child on the right has a thin strip of hair representing "the line of a buffalo's back as seen against the sky."

Even Indian calendars were influenced by the buffalo and his seasonal habits. Each lunar period began with the appearance of a new moon and was named after regularly recurring natural phenomena. In the calendar used by the Teton Sioux and Cheyenne, the importance of the buffalo was evident in the series of lunations beginning with the autumnal moon:

1. The moon the leaves fall off.
2. The moon the buffalo cow's fetus is getting large.
3. The moon the wolves run together.
4. The moon the skin of the buffalo fetus begins to color.
5. The moon the hair gets thick on the buffalo fetus.
6. The moon the buffalo cows drop their calves.

Still another way in which tribesmen identified with the buffalo was in the wearing of buffalo headdresses. Fabricated with fur and horns intact, such bonnets virtually fused Indian and buffalo into one being. Not everyone could make the costume—the honor was usually reserved for a man to whom a supernatural buffalo had appeared in a vision. After making his headdress, he could join a Bull Society and take part in the Buffalo Dance with other privileged men.

In special performances before the rest of the tribe, buffalo dancers imitated their animal idols, shaking their horns fiercely, butting one another, and occasionally charging into spectators. Certain performers among the Sioux synchronized their steps to the beat of a drum, stomping first one foot and then the other with an overstated scraping motion. This simulated the pawing of a threatening bull, and was intended to reveal an equally defiant bravery in the dancers. A group of Hidatsa dancers sported stiffly erect buffalo tails like those of charging wild buffalo, signifying their readiness to pursue any foe with the ferocity of the animals they mimicked. Once having worn these tails in ceremonies in camp, the same men were obliged to make good their claims in war, standing firm against any opponent no matter what the odds.

The leader of the Winnebago Buffalo Dance climaxed his performance with a meal of maple sugar, which, for some reason, was considered the cherished food of buffalo. Costumed in his shaggy headdress, the dancer bellowed a few times, then lowered his head to consume the ritual food, lapping up the maple sugar with his tongue "just as buffaloes eat." Other members of the buffalo clan followed him in this bovine banquet.

The buffalo headdresses used in these dances were all cherished for their spiritual power, but none approached the sanctity and eminence of one extraordinary bonnet—the Sacred Hat of the Cheyenne. It was more ornate than other buffalo headdresses. The main covering, cut from the skin of a buffalo cow's head, was adorned throughout with large blue beads. Attached to the sides were two cow horns, each shaved smooth and engraved with geometric designs in red. The custodian of the Hat guarded it by day and slept beside it at night, keeping it always tucked away in its special sack, a crescent-shaped bag of buffalo skin trimmed about the lip with buffalo tails.

The Hat was only taken out on special occasions—when it was needed to bring good fortune in war, to "renew" the sacred Medicine Arrows, and to cure grave illness. Whenever it was placed on public display, it rested on the center of a row of five buffalo chips cushioned on a bed of white sage. It always attracted crowds of idolizers, who filed by and made their prayers, passing their hands over the Hat and then over their children.

Comparable to the potency of the Cheyenne Sacred Hat were the singular powers vaunted by the "Buffalo Doctors" of several tribes. These special shamans had purportedly received instructions in the art of healing directly from the buffalo, by means of a vision.

Men seeking such a confrontation would often fast for several days to tune mind and body for communication with the spirit realm. In the psychic state brought about by this ordeal of starvation and thirst, the supplicant was extremely susceptible to hallucination. Thus primed, he sought to make contact with a spirit buffalo; if a meeting occurred, the particular animal was established as his personal guardian, a patron animal from whom he could learn where to find healing plants.

Materializations took place almost anywhere. Some men reared up in their sleep, asserting that they had heard spiritual voices; later they described cordial interviews with venerable buffalo. When in need of information about medicine, the Pawnee visited a site where spirit buffalo met in council. They knew of five such meeting places in Kansas and Nebraska, including one under a high bluff opposite what is now the city of Fremont. Each man attending one of these occult councils petitioned the assembled buffalo for information about special cures.

Certain Sioux Buffalo Doctors placed absolute faith in their own private buffalo fetishes. Raw liver dipped in bile was considered a cure for tuberculosis. Buffalo hair soaked in medicated water was good for washing wounds. Anyone stunned by lightning was wrapped in one buffalo robe and tossed up and down on another. A man bitten by mad wolves or dogs was tightly encased in a buffalo robe and rolled in a smudgy fire; the smoke, both from the singed robe and from the fire itself, caused the unfortunate victim to vomit and effected the cure.

Buffalo Doctors among the Omaha augmented their fetishes and songs with complex rituals. Records of some of these have come to us through the journals of Francis La Flesche, who spent his childhood with the tribe and then took up anthropology after graduating from college. As a young boy in the late 1800's, La Flesche often passed time in a gambling game with his Indian friends. During one particular round, he was remotely aware of a target practice going on nearby. A few youths were firing their pistols at a mark on the trunk of a large tree while some younger boys looked on. Suddenly the whole village was roused by a woeful wail from one of the pistoleers: he had just accidentally shot one of the boys in the head.

Within minutes the nearest Buffalo Doctor was at the scene, supervising the removal of the wounded boy to the shelter of a lodge. A runner was dispatched to a neighboring village to summon more Buffalo Doctors. These soon came galloping over the hills on horseback, one or two at a time, their long hair streaming over their naked backs as they rode.

Before long, the boy was surrounded by a circle of more than twenty Buffalo Doctors, the so-called *Té ithaethe*—those "to whom the buffalo has shown compassion." The first of the group to try his charms told of the day he had been possessed by buffalo, when his patron animals had come to him in a vision to reveal the mysterious secrets of their medicine and songs. After reciting his story, he wailed a special ballad, to be joined shortly by other Doctors, until the loud strains of their singing carried for over a mile. The song depicted a setting on the prairie, a round buffalo wallow filled with placid water, near which a wounded buffalo was being cured by his companions. Acting on the theory that buffalo healed wounds with their saliva, the first Doctor mouthed bits of roots from ground cherry and hop, took a swallow of water, munched the mixture, and as everyone watched in wonder, advanced methodically toward the wounded boy, pawing and bellowing in imitation of an agitated buffalo. Once beside the lad, he drew in a deep breath and forcefully spat his medicated mouthful into the wound. As the boy winced, the Doctor hooted "He! He! He!" to add a final charm to the potion.

During the four days that followed, each of the remaining Buffalo Doctors treated the patient in similar fashion. At the end of this time, the boy was able to rise feebly and shuffle a symbolic four steps. "Four!" cried the Doctors. "It is done!" At once they broke into the prescribed triumphal chant.

Now all that remained was the matter of payment. For their

services the Doctors accepted horses, buffalo robes, bear-claw necklaces, eagle feathers, embroidered leggings, and other articles of tribal value.

"Within a month," Francis La Flesche reported, "the boy was back among us, ready to play or to watch another pistol practice by the young men."

For the Omaha, another symbolic ritual had worked its magic. Once again the beneficent influence of the buffalo had been revealed to the Indians.

10

THE WHITE BUFFALO

ON THE EVENING OF JUNE 12, 1924, THE FOX INDIANS of Wisconsin held one of their last performances of the White Buffalo Dance. By this time, such intricacies of the Fox heritage were passing out of vogue. To the youths, who had little respect for ritual, the elaborate ceremony was largely a time for feasting and fellowship. The elders of the tribe still revered the White Buffalo Dance, but they would soon die, and with them the solemnities of a ritual that had been handed down for generations.

The main events of the ceremony lasted all night, as participants carried out a program of songs, dances, and feasts. Central to the proceedings was the sacred bundle of the White Buffalo, a magic pack that could be traced to a mythical tribal hero. According to legend, this revered warrior had distinguished himself by massacring singlehandedly a horde of invading Sioux, assisted by a supernatural white buffalo. The striking animal, with red eyes and red horns, had appeared to him in a vision, granting him the power to metamorphose into a white buffalo himself in time of need.

The visitation of the White Buffalo to a member of their tribe impressed the Fox enormously, for no animal was more esteemed than the rare white mutant. In many other Plains tribes, it was considered the sacred leader of all herds. White buffalo robes were supreme status symbols in Indian society. A boy who possessed one, although he might never have seen battle, commanded more respect than a veteran warrior with a number of enemy dead to his credit.

It was said that a man who succeeded in killing a white buffalo received a special blessing from the gods. The Sioux felt they must kill every white animal sighted, in order to fulfill the rites connected with it. So rare was the white buffalo, however, that some Sioux bands often waited years for the opportunity to slay one.

It is hardly surprising, given the rarity of the animal in the immense historic herds, that few white buffalo are found in herds today. The first record of a specimen in this century comes from the National Bison Range, where "Big Medicine" was born in May 1933. Except for a brown patch about the crown, this unusual animal had an "off-white" pelt: his fur was lightly tinged with cream or beige just after the spring molt, but by late winter it had bleached to an almost pure white. His eyes were bluish-gray, lacking the normal dark pigmentation.

When Big Medicine reached the age of four years, he mated with his own mother. She gave birth to a pure albino, a male calf with white fur, white hoofs, and pink eyes. Soon afterward, the rare baby was abandoned by his mother; deaf and partially blind, he was rescued by attendants and shipped to the National Zoological Park in Washington, where he died within a few months. Big Medicine, however, lived to a ripe age of twenty-six.

To explain the genetic aberration that gave Big Medicine and his calf their distinctive white color, one must first understand the coloration of normal buffalo. The brown fur of an ordinary animal is caused by tiny granules of pigment deposited in hair, skin, and eyes. Known as "melanin," this pigment is widely distributed in the animal kingdom. In buffalo, one form produces the dark brown color of adults, and a related form colors the orange pelts of calves. In human beings, the great range in skin colors of different races is attributable to varying amounts of the same pigment. What we know as freckles are local concentrations of melanin.

Particles of melanin saturate the "ink screen" shot out by an alarmed octopus. Even the blackening of bruised or cut potatoes results from the formation of melanin.

It follows logically that the absence of melanin causes the condition of colorlessness known as albinism. A special enzyme necessary for the manufacture of melanin is missing in the bodies of albino animals, and thus the pigment is prevented from forming. The resulting impression of whiteness is caused not by a white pigment but by the inherent physical structure of skin or hair. A similar whiteness is visible when certain liquids are riled—the resulting foam looks white because it contains a maze of bubbles, which reflect and refract white light; whether the foam comes from colorless water or from yellow-tinted beer, it is still white. By the same principle, tiny pockets of air in the hairs of an albino buffalo give the effect of whiteness; and since there is no pigment to color the transparent interiors of the animal's eyes, the blood vessels become clearly visible, giving the iris its characteristic red tint.

From exhaustive studies of albinism in human beings, we know that the condition is always inherited as a "recessive" trait. As such, it may be present in a person without being visible in any way. The person, a "carrier," can transmit the trait from one generation to the next, without there being any outward expression of albinism. But as soon as one carrier marries another, the chances are one in four that any child will be an albino. And when one albino marries another, all of their offspring will be albinotic.

Albinism in buffalo seems to be inherited in a similar fashion, although the line of descent has seldom been traced. In the National Bison Range, the birth of Big Medicine and his purely albinotic calf indicated that at least a few carriers existed in that herd. Apparently some of them later slipped into a group of twenty-two buffalo that were transferred north to establish the Big Delta herd in Alaska. The presence of these carriers in the herd became evident when several white calves were born. (The emergence of albinism in the small, new herd was not surprising because of the likelihood of mating between relatives.)

The first white calf, a female, was born in 1939, and other white individuals appeared in later years—in 1941, 1949, 1953, 1955, and 1958. The calves bore brownish patches like Big Medicine's, either on the crown or near one eye, and thus they, too, were not true albinos. None of these white calves lived more than a few weeks.

Recent reports from the Big Delta herd indicate a continuing incidence of white calves. Three were sighted during the calving season of 1961, yet all had disappeared when the herd was canvassed three months later. In May of 1963, army helicopter pilots making a routine flight over the range spotted two more white calves. Both were seen again from time to time during the next few months and appeared to be in vigorous health as late as October. When part of the herd was checked three months after that, at least one albino was still alive. But subsequent aerial surveys revealed none. For some reason, the white calves had failed to survive the winter.

We can surmise that most albino buffalo born to bygone herds fared no better than these short-lived Alaskan animals. The low incidence of albino births and the short life expectancy of a white animal probably account for the infrequent mention of white buffalo in the records of spokesmen from past centuries. Between 1783 and 1805, for instance, chroniclers recorded but seven sightings. In the year 1830, the most significant entry in the Sioux tribal calendar was the notation that four white buffalo had been killed that year—"the largest number in history." Speculating on the proportion of albino animals in the herds, George Catlin proposed "not one in a hundred thousand, perhaps." This estimate was reduced still further by a fur trader who, after having seen five in his twenty years of handling hides, suggested "not more than one in millions." The infrequency of the sightings indicates that white buffalo were much more rare than albino humans, currently born at the rate of about one in twenty thousand.

Some of the white buffalo described in historic reports were not pure albinos; the five robes of the fur trader, for example, varied considerably in color: "yellowish fawn . . . dark cream . . . white . . . dappled gray . . . tips of the hair white and the bases black, giving the effect of silver gray." A similar color variation was recognized by the Crow, who distinguished between albino buffalo (*bice-itse*) and a yellow buffalo with dark brown spotting (*nakawate*). In addition, there were records of piebald buffalo, brown animals marked with blotches of white.

Among the Indians, white robes were so rare that they became the most costly articles of tribal barter. Both Mandan and Gros

Ventre especially prized the robe of a white cow not over two years old, tanned with hoofs, snout, and tail intact, and with the horn sheaths sewn back to the head. When offered such a skin by a fur trader, they presented at least sixty normal robes in exchange. To get one from a neighboring tribe, they bartered as many as fifteen horses laden with guns, cloth, blankets, brown robes, and other treasures.

The Cheyenne invested the treatment of a white buffalo hide with complex symbolism handed down from the practices of by-gone war parties. When a hunter had slain a white mutant, he dared not touch it, but set forth immediately to locate a tribal patriarch commanding sufficient spiritual power to initiate the ritual. If the buffalo had been slain with an arrow, this elder must have previously killed an enemy with an arrow. Further prescriptions relating to battle determined the successive stages of the ritual. The skin from the head had to be peeled off by a brave who had scalped an adversary. The hide was then placed on a packhorse by a man who had seized and carried off a captive with his own horse. Upon reaching the village, it was unloaded by someone who had pulled an opponent from his mount. And it was borne into the owner's tipi by a man who had killed inside an enemy lodge. Similar ritual attended the dressing of the skin.

The finished robe was then ready to be offered votively to the tribe's supernatural beings. Attached by its owner to the top of a pole, it was left hanging high in the air, where it eventually crumbled to dust under the force of rain, snow, sun, and wind. If war parties happened by, they dared not touch it for fear of incurring the wrath of tribal deities. To the mind of a materialist, the surrender of so choice an article could only appear wasteful, but to the Indians, it represented the ultimate sacrifice, an offering guaranteed to put them in favor with the spirit powers.

Most elaborate of all rituals connected with the white buffalo was the impressive ceremony of the Hunkpapa, a powerful division of the Teton Sioux, perhaps best remembered for one of their leaders—the famous Sitting Bull. The Hunkpapa White Buffalo Festival was carried out under great secrecy, behind a dense circular wall of interlaced boughs covered over with a tent. Only a few select men were admitted to the proceedings, and guards were stationed outside to prevent eavesdropping.

Despite the clandestine character of the ritual, we have a thorough knowledge of its several stages, thanks to the reportage of anthropologist Alice Fletcher, who wrote an account of a typical ceremony in 1882. After considerable persuasion, she convinced the Hunkpapa that she could not interpret their tribal religion to outsiders without having observed the White Buffalo Festival. Tribal leaders ultimately gave their consent, although several were certain that such sacrilege would invite retribution.

Miss Fletcher's account began with a description of the dressing of the white hide, a ritual performed by a virgin selected by the owner of the skin. While the girl worked, the owner staged two lavish feasts, the second of which culminated in the presentation of the finished robe. Thereafter, no one was allowed to touch this sacred skin with his hands—ritual decreed that it be carried or turned only by means of sticks used in the manner of forceps.

Handling the white hide in this fashion, the celebrants arranged it over a square plot of cleared ground symbolizing the earth's life-giving powers. Two nearby patches of ground were given over for the worship of the other sacred objects of the festival, a decorated buffalo skull and a small heap of coal-black soil.

Positioning himself to the left of the white hide, a priest sprinkled sweetgrass on a few live coals to fill the lodge with an aromatic smudge—a messenger between the seen and the unseen, the Indians and the gods. Around the rim of the lodge sat the chiefs, each in official costume.

Next came the culminating point of the festival. With great ceremony, the priest lifted sixteen tufts of red-tinted goose down from two slabs of wood and arranged them in appropriate positions on the black soil. The chiefs and elders, aware that a misstep would invite disaster, watched raptly as all sixteen were set down in their checkerboard pattern on the consecrated earth. When the last red tuft was in place, they bowed their heads and cried, "Hei-ya!"

To the Hunkpapa, the bits of red down symbolized all living powers—the forces of the earth and the people who lived thereon. The four tufts at the corners stood for the four winds that swept away sickness and granted health; those in between represented the life cycle of the Indians. As the down rested on the black soil, so the people dwelt on the earth. Or, in the words of the Hunkpapa:

The old die, the new are born, and the race lives on forever. The white buffalo is the chief of the herd, and from the buffalo comes our animal food, and this gives life and strength. We put the dish with the cherries and water beside the head of the hide, because the buffalo likes these things; they make him to live. We eat the cherries and drink the water that there may be no end of fruit and water with us.

Near the end of the ceremony, the priest cut the white buffalo hide lengthwise into strips, giving the center piece to the owner and the outer bands to the chiefs in his lodge. These strips were considered the most sacred of personal possessions, to be worn only when searching for game in times of dire scarcity, or when marching against the enemy.

To conclude the White Buffalo Festival, the owner of the hide took off all his clothing and departed naked from the lodge, in a gesture of devotion and humility signifying his renunciation of all personal or worldly possessions and his submission to the spirit powers. Nearby tribesmen immediately brought more clothing to him and presented him with a lodge. Thus humbled and restored, he began life anew, in a higher spiritual state.

11

THE STORYTELLERS

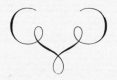

ON A CRISP EVENING LATE IN THE FALL OF 1876, THE
glow of the dying sun lingered along the Montana horizon, outlining the peaked forms of several Blackfoot lodges. Across the top
flaps of a weathered tipi, orange flickers played back and forth as
the woman inside stirred the fire and positioned over it a kettle
brimming with choice cuts of buffalo. Nearby, the man of the lodge
busied himself mixing shreds of tobacco and weeds.

A little later, the Indian gathered his family together and invited a few friends in for an evening of storytelling. Family and
guests were soon settled about the fire awaiting the arrival of
Little Face, a chief of the tribe and an esteemed narrator of sacred
myths. After a few moments, Little Face walked through the doorway. As he took his place in the group, the men made the customary offering of smoke from a pipe, thereby launching the
evening's program.

Little Face began by reciting his version of the creation myth,
the details of which were carefully recorded by Lieutenant James

Bradley. Stationed at a nearby army post, Bradley had been employing Little Face ("aged in the neighborhood of sixty years") as one of his scouts and by thus gaining his confidence had taken notes on many Blackfoot ways before they changed with the coming of the white man.

Long ago, Little Face explained in his narration, there was no earth—just water. The only living things were two spirits who floated about listlessly in the company of a large, duck-like bird. Eventually, however, the spirits grew tired of all the water, and decided to make some dry land to serve as a home for other creatures. They commanded the bird to dive down and bring up a little mud from the bottom. The bird did as he was instructed, and soon returned to the surface with his find. One spirit pressed the mud into a cake and let it dry; the second cast a portion of it over the water, causing land to materialize all about.

Then, rolling some mud in their fingers, the two spirits threw the magic earth upon the ground to create men and women. Next they made earthen images of buffalo, blowing on them to bring them to life. In like manner they molded other creatures to inhabit their world.

The newly created men and women began to marry, rear families, and people the land. For lack of better habitation, they were obliged to dwell in hollow logs and trees. Life was not easy for these early beings, for the buffalo created to coexist with them suddenly turned belligerent and began to drum their hoofs on the logs to drive out the human occupants. The animals continued to persecute the early people, until at last they killed one man, devouring every part of him but an arm.

Alarmed by this turn of events, the spirits made bows and arrows and gave them to First Man. "It is not right that buffalo should kill and eat you," they said. "You should kill and eat the buffalo, for they were given you for food." Thus encouraged, First Man slew two buffalo and wounded a third.

The abrupt attack by First Man frightened the herd away. As the wounded buffalo fled, however, he hooked his horns under the severed arm of the recent victim and tossed it onto his back. Until that time, the buffalo had been without a hump, but as the animal dashed away, the arm became fused to his body. And ever since, said Little Face in closing, "all buffalo have had a hump upon the back."

———◆◦◆———

Such evenings of storytelling were common in the lodges of the Plains Indians. Most tribes had their own versions of the creation myth, based on the same theme of a submerged world brought up from the sea with the help of a diving animal and peopled with creatures formed from samples of charmed soil. The story was but one of a multitude of tales that, taken together, made up the body of Plains Indian literature, a collection of traditions passed down from generation to generation by word of mouth. Through the adventures of animal characters endowed with supernatural power, myths like this chronicled the origin of social customs and tribal rituals; other traditions were concerned with the history of the tribe and everyday adventures among the Indians. The tribe's most prominent consociate—the buffalo— was substance and inspiration for much of this colorful literature. The sacred and devoted relationship of buffalo to Indian was emphasized in legends of marriages and adoptions between the two or in tales of heroic bulls performing astonishing feats and comic individuals falling prey to slapstick trickery.

Recital of tales served as both entertainment and instruction; it was also looked upon as a form of worship, a prayer to the gods and heroes of the tribe. Often a tale would stress a moral: from certain stories, the youths were expected to learn that they could achieve greatness by their own efforts, no matter how humble their origins. The same tales would also warn them against pitfalls laid in the paths of the unwary.

Passed from tribe to tribe over a wide area were several myths with standard plots, each bearing the special stamp of its local narrator. Well known among these were such tales as "The Woman Who Married a Bull," "The Buffalo Boy," and "The Boy Who Was Raised by the Seven Bulls." Among the most widespread was the Pawnee myth of the robotlike buffalo skull that pursued and devoured people.

One day, went the tale, a hungry coyote coursed over the prairie looking for food, singing of his fond desire to run down a few buffalo and make himself a tasty meal. All at once his merry crooning was interrupted by a loud shout: "Stop singing and dancing around my station!"

Coyote looked around, and saw that the warning came from a mere buffalo skull. Unimpressed, he replied, "And who are you that I should be afraid?"

But there was good reason for fear. Marching robotlike after the coyote, the skull eventually devoured him and most of the inhabitants of an Indian village as well. The single Indian girl who contrived to escape fled at great speed from the village, but the skull continued to pursue her. At last the girl arrived, frantic, in front of a little hut. There the onrushing skull met its master, for living in the hut was a boy with special powers. He fired a little blue bead from his mouth in the direction of the skull; struck by the bead, the skull succumbed.

This tale was told to inspire awe and respect for the buffalo skull, which was deeply revered as a totem in Indian ritual and ceremony. Buffalo skulls, so the Pawnee storyteller warned his audience, have supernatural power and must not be called names or kicked around.

The skull legend has been found in many parts of North America and has even been traced as far as the center of South America, which would suggest that the story was dispersed like a ripple expanding concentrically; however, doubt is cast on such speculation by a puzzling absence of the same myth in various intervening regions.

The popular creation myth, which found its way into many areas of the plains, differed from tribe to tribe in the interpretation of the genesis of earth's creatures. In the Cheyenne version, which was recorded by anthropologist George Dorsey in Oklahoma in 1901, the ancestral herds dwelt deep within a magical spring. According to the tale, two youths plunged into this source one day, forging their way downward into a great cave. In the recesses of the cave, they found an old woman, who gestured excitedly to them and pointed toward the south. Turning their heads as she had bidden, they spotted in the distance a land covered with buffalo. Moved by the sight of the beasts, they sought her assistance to capture them; in reply, she promised to send the herd out of her cave sometime before sunset.

The pair passed back through the spring and returned to the Cheyenne camp, where they related their adventure and alerted their people to the old woman's promise. Toward sunset, the entire tribe went out to begin a vigil at the water's source.

A Cheyenne artist drew this rendition of his tribe's Creation myth, showing how two youths who waited at sunset by a magical spring were soon joined by hundreds of buffalo that had emerged from a cave deep in the ground.

"In a short time," the narrator continued,

they saw a buffalo jump from the spring. It jumped and played and rolled, and then returned to the spring. In a little while another buffalo jumped out, then another, and another, and finally they came out so fast that the Cheyenne were no longer able to count them. The buffalo continued to come out until dark, and all night and the following day the whole country out in the distance was covered with buffalo.

The emergence of a buffalo from the ground, a common plot in the oral traditions of Plains tribes, has some basis in fact. Anthropologists have speculated that the tale originated among the Indian inhabitants of the Staked Plain, an extensive grassy plateau of New Mexico and Texas. Each year these tribes abandoned their high, wind-ravaged plains to move for the winter into sheltered camps nearby; some days or weeks later, the scientists theorize, buffalo in the same region retreated to their own winter quarters in the adjacent canyons. Year after year, when the tribes returned in the spring to hunt the herds, they found nothing but barren plain. Soon, however, the swarms of animals would file out of the canyons and spread across the grassland. After witnessing such outpourings of buffalo from the earth, the Indians must have believed that they had seen a miracle.

While such myths chronicled the emergence of buffalo from the ground, others accounted for the appearance of the herds with tales of magic materializations. One Caddo myth held that the world was at first inhabited only by human beings. During a council meeting, these early people decided that some large beasts were needed to serve as prey for prospective hunters. Accordingly, they rolled a few of their comrades in the sod to affect a transformation. When the subjects arose, they were no longer Indians: the grass had stuck to them like hair, some of it even dangling down in long beards from their chins, and their bodies had taken on the shape of buffalo.

Among the Hidatsa, storytellers related how the dressed bones of slain buffalo reinvested themselves with flesh and came to life again. Their conception of reincarnation was reinforced by a tribal myth: when a local boy failed to return to camp after a hunt, Hidatsa warriors, believing that he had been slain by warring Sioux, assembled a martial party and struck out to avenge his murder. En route, they stopped to kill a buffalo for food. When they opened up the carcass, they were astonished to find the long-lost boy inside. As soon as the boy was released from his imprisonment, he recounted the tale of his strange incarceration. One rainy evening, while seeking shelter from a storm, he had come upon a dead buffalo. Thoroughly soaked, and desperate for protection from the rain, he eviscerated the carcass and crawled into the rib cage. Comfortably ensconced in his makeshift quarters, he soon fell asleep. During the night, however, the flesh reformed about the abdomen, and the dead animal came to life again. Thus imprisoned, the boy remained inside the buffalo for a year, until his avengers had a chance to slay the beast for food.

Whether regenerated from a carcass, evolved from a lump of sod, or issued forth from the earth, the buffalo of Indian myths were creatures of prodigious power and skill. The Pawnee knew of invulnerable animals that were enormous, sexless, and devoid of joints in their legs. These remarkable creatures could repulse all ordinary weapons, and succumbed only to missiles anointed with a magic potion that facilitated penetration of their armorlike skin.

Man-eating buffalo of an Arikara myth had horns and tails, but were otherwise human in form. Once a tribal youth, concealing himself under a buffalo robe, managed to sneak past some man-eaters guarding their chief's tipi and enter the lodge, only to hear one of the sentinels announce: "I smell human flesh." Soon the boy heard another beast reply: "It is because we have just had a killing." Terrified, the boy climbed to the top of a nearby funeral scaffold. There he discovered "fresh meat of humans and some bodies not yet cut up." After a frantic chase, the boy escaped and returned to his tribe. In the fullness of time, the Arikara managed to ambush the man-eaters, pursuing them until they turned into real—and innocuous—buffalo. As the tale drew to a close, Snowbird, the narrator, would add significantly, "When this story is told, everybody keeps quiet."

Several folktales stressed the closeness between buffalo and Indian with tales of marriages between the two. Tribesmen believed recital of these stories would cause the herds to approach and offer themselves for slaughter. Typical of such tales was the tradition of "The Man Who Married a Buffalo," which anthropologist George Dorsey obtained in 1899 from Wonderful-Sun, a Pawnee storyteller.

One day a youth, out walking by himself, discovered a buffalo cow firmly mired in a marsh. Glancing about to make sure no one was looking, he stripped off his clothes and mounted her. On leaving his temporary mate, he removed from his neck a small shell pendant and tied it to one of her horns.

Some time later, the cow gave birth to a male buffalo calf, the offspring of her impromptu dalliance in the marsh. The infant, though resembling his herd mates, was taunted or shunned by all the other calves because he didn't know his own father. He spent most of his days wandering the meadows alone.

One day, to buoy her son's spirits, the calf's mother arranged to take him on a journey to visit his Indian father. But when mother and calf arrived in "the people's country" and confronted the father, he failed to recognize them. The irate cow nudged her infant and turned to leave. Just then, the puzzled Indian spotted his shell pendant dangling from the calf's neck. As he paused to reflect on the significance of his discovery, the mother pulled her calf away and led him back toward the herd.

When the father at last recalled the scene in the marsh, he pursued the fleeing pair into the camp of the buffalo. There, the cow had already informed the ruling bulls that he had tried to disown his son, and the angry bulls were preparing their revenge. "We must kill him," they said. "We will have nothing to do with these straight-up people."

Despite their rage, the bulls gave the man a chance to redeem himself. Assembling ten identical calves, they commanded him to pick out his son from among them. It was an impossible task; but the clever calf, eager to save his long-lost father, found a way to reveal himself. As the Indian inspected the line-up, the calf began to signal, twitching his tail rapidly back and forth. In a moment the father placed a hand on the young buffalo's head and proclaimed, "This is my son." The bulls grunted in surprise. "He is a wonderful man," they marveled. "But still we will kill him."

Yet they could not bring themselves to kill him immediately. New trials were devised to test his courage and ingenuity. Again and again the beasts tried to stump the man, but with each new challenge he outwitted them.

At last the bulls realized they had met their match. Gathering in council, they agreed to transform the Indian into a buffalo. The wonderful deed was accomplished on the spot. Forming a circle, the great bulls invited the candidate inside. Then they tightened the ring and drew closer to him, some "breathing on him, rubbing him, others urinating and wallowing, grunting and bellowing . . ."

All at once they made a rush at him, and rolled and rolled him, until they had him in a buffalo wallow, rolling, getting some of the buffalo water on him so that he had a buffalo odor. Presently he was also trying to bellow like a buffalo. Now he felt he was becoming one. He could feel the horns coming out on him, and afterwards he knew he had a buffalo head. The buffalo saw it, and made haste in their work, tumbling him over and over in the buffalo wallow. Then he stood on his four legs and was a complete buffalo.

No sooner had the Indian become a beast than he was challenged by another bull, a former lover of his mate. But in his animal form, the father was strong and sturdy. Locking horns with his rival, he vanquished him instantly. At last he rejoined his family, to the delight of his buffalo son, who was now free to play happily with all the other calves, never again to be taunted about a "straight-up" father.

Closely related to accounts of buffalo marriages were tales of buffalo adoptions, in which orphaned boys, Mowgli-like, were raised by the herd. The Crow had a favorite story in this category: when the unwed daughter of a tribal chief gave birth to a baby boy, the girl's embarrassed father secretly crept out onto the prairie and dumped the infant into a buffalo wallow. Shortly afterward, the lad was discovered and adopted by seven buffalo bulls, who undertook the job of rearing him. After learning "animal ways" from his buffalo tutors, he returned to his Indian camp to perform wonderful deeds and teach his tribe the wisdom of the wild.

The beneficent acts of this youth raised him to the rank of a so-called culture hero, a mythological protagonist of rare accomplishment who tried his best to improve an imperfect world, delivering his people from hunger, overcoming enemies, and slaying monsters.

Another such hero was the "Poor-Boy" of a much-told Arikara myth. As the story unfolded, Poor-Boy, a humble lad, instructed his grandmother to make a bow and some arrows, so that he might join the men of the tribe on their buffalo hunt. The old woman sobbed as she carried out his request, certain that her charge would be humiliated during the outing: not only would he be unable to secure any of the highest rewards of the hunt—the buffalo hearts and tongues—but he would surely fail to strike a single buffalo. When Poor-Boy gathered his new bow and arrows and joined the group, the other men laughed at the neophyte, mocking his determination to set out with the experienced hunters. But Poor-Boy astonished them all. With the help of a supernatural buffalo, he brought down a number of animals; then, pulling off bunches of hair from the slain beasts, he transformed them by magic into additional piles of hearts and tongues. At the end of the outing he returned with the greatest treasures of the day. Awed by Poor-Boy's influence with the spirits, the tribe venerated him ever afterward. He led the men in their next hunt, married the chief's daughter, became a great warrior, and eventually rose to rule over the entire Arikara nation.

Another group of heroes had the role of "tricksters," peculiar characters with supernatural endowments that could be used for good or evil. In some tales they were noble benefactors, creating the world, eliminating great evils, and bettering the life of the tribes. In others they were unscrupulous rascals who took advantage of their companions and gained their ends by means of pranks and hoaxes. Their sly humor amused the audience, while their foibles of dishonesty, vanity, or greed often pointed up a moral.

Stars of the trickster tales varied among tribes. For several in the northwestern plains the protagonist was "Old Man," for others, largely in the southwest, it was "Coyote." The Assiniboin, Omaha, and Sioux featured a character called "Spider."

"Spider" was a likely trickster for the Sioux, who considered the eight-legged creature so devilish that he must have evolved from Sioux ancestors. Endowing "Spider" with remarkable supernatural traits, they made their trickster superior to all other animals, more cunning than man himself. One day, according to myth, the prodigious arachnid happened to step in the path of Buffalo. Affronted, Buffalo called Spider "a wee bit of a thing," and warned him that a single hoof would squash him into oblivion. Spider replied that it was not he but Buffalo who was in the way, and that Buffalo would have to step around. Buffalo was outraged, and retorted that he owned the whole earth and could stand where he pleased. Infuriated by this time, Spider spun a web over Buffalo's eyes. Soon Buffalo was staggering into trees, stumbling into holes, floundering wherever he moved. At last, totally handicapped, he was forced to give in. Begging forgiveness, he promised never to tease Spider again. Thus mollified, Spider removed the webs.

Trickster myths in the Blackfoot area featured the tribe's own "Old Man." In one of these, Old Man inveigled a fox into a conspiracy against four buffalo bulls. "My little brother," he said, "I can think of only one way to get these bulls. I will pluck all the fur off you except one tuft at the end of your tail. Then you go over the hill and walk up and down in sight of them, and you will seem so funny to them that they will laugh themselves to death."

This impossible scheme proved surprisingly successful: upon seeing the plucked fox, the impressionable buffalo began to giggle among themselves. Rolling over in hysterics, they soon laughed themselves to death. As Old Man butchered the victims, the fox sat nearby, his back humped up, his teeth chattering in the icy air. When the last bull had been cut up, Old Man looked at the hairless fox and remarked, "It's getting pretty cold, isn't it? Well, we don't care for the cold. We've got our winter's meat and we'll have nothing to do but feast and dance and sing until spring." The fox did not reply. Old Man prodded him, and the fox keeled over, frozen dead in the cold.

Despite the extravagant efforts of these tribal tricksters, their plots did not always succeed. Sometimes other characters, like Buffalo himself, got the better of them, as he did in the prevalent motif of the coyote who metamorphosed into a buffalo. In the Pawnee version, Coyote, famished, and envying the ease with which Buffalo grazed grass, asked the great beast to help him change his identity. Buffalo obliged, directing Coyote to stand in a wallow, then charging toward him. At the instant of contact, Coyote turned into a buffalo.

But "Coyote-Buffalo" grew overconfident. Before long he misused his special powers, attempting to change a fellow coyote into a buffalo by means of the same technique. When the dust had settled, his companion stood unchanged in the wallow, and he himself had suddenly shrunk in size. Instead of transforming his friend into a buffalo, he had turned himself back into Coyote. Now he pleaded with Buffalo to transform him again. Once more Buffalo obligingly consented. As Coyote placed himself in a wallow, Buffalo began to charge him as before. On impact this time, however, Buffalo tossed him up in the air and gored him to death.

"Ever since that time," the Pawnee raconteur would conclude, "Coyotes have been willing to be Coyotes, and Buffalo have always disliked Coyotes."

The Indians may have observed buffalo harassing coyotes in real life and attempted to justify their behavior with this story; or perhaps the tale was invented merely to amuse. But the stories as a whole had many functions—they entertained, instructed, cautioned, or advised, and they helped the Indians to explain puzzling phenomena in their world. Indians mentioned in myth all creatures and elements in the universe that were relevant to their lives, and depicted close unions between themselves and the animals with whom they were most intimately linked by fate. It was no accident that in the widely distributed creation myth, the buffalo was made next after man.

12

DAYS AMONG THE HERDS

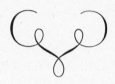

THE MYTHS AND FOLKTALES SAMPLED IN THE LAST
chapter have come to us from a native people who knew the
buffalo intimately. But, as legends, they shed little light on actual
buffalo behavior; and the tribes, lacking a written language, kept
no factual records about the animals they understood so well.
Thus we have had to learn much about the Indians and their relationship with the herds from the chronicles of early visitors to the
area. Their notes and journals contain a wealth of plains lore from
an era that has passed away for all time.

Valuable as historical records, these chronicles also contain
many passages that can help to illuminate the actions of today's
herds. In my writings on the behavior of the species, I have made
reference to such material from past centuries whenever feasible,
although I have drawn primarily from my own first-hand observations of various herds. The fabled throngs did indeed vanish in the
1870's, yet I had no trouble finding suitable subjects, for a number
of large herds still dwell in many North American refuges. After

visiting several of these areas, I decided to concentrate my studies on the animals in Yellowstone National Park. Unconfined by fences, agitated only rarely by human intruders, and uncorrupted by programs of differential herd reduction (at least at the time of my study), these animals lived under conditions that approximated those on the early plains.

Conducting studies on these herds was itself a pioneering experience. My numerous treks into buffalo country took me deep into Yellowstone Park, leading me to remote meadows seldom seen by the millions who visit the preserve each year.

Starting at the world-famed geyser Old Faithful and heading east on the "Grand Loop," the average visitor eventually arrives at West Thumb, where soft-colored paintpots bubble and emerald pools steam against a backdrop of Yellowstone Lake, the largest mountain lake on the continent (altitude 7,731 feet). Driving north along the shoreline for about twenty miles, the traveler comes to Fishing Bridge, where anglers stand elbow to elbow above the tempting waters at the lake's outlet. As the road continues north toward the chromatic Grand Canyon of the Yellowstone, it passes Black Dragons Caldron, a mud geyser with convulsive eruptions of pitchlike, steaming clay. A short distance beyond, the road enters an area of meadowland designated by the guidebook as "tranquil Hayden Valley." Indeed it is tranquil. Below the road to the right are sedge meadows bordering the Yellowstone River; to the left, a sagebrush-flecked grassland slopes toward the horizon. The rolling hills obscure the extensive size of the valley, which stretches seven miles from the highway to form a most significant meadowland in a park that is ninety per cent forest.

After a glance or two toward the apex of Hayden Valley, most tourists continue on to Canyon Village. The casual passerby may question the guidebook report of buffalo in this area, since the animals are seldom visible from the highway; yet several hundred buffalo, the largest herd in the park, dwell in the upper reaches of Hayden Valley. Along with other herds in the Pelican and Lamar Valleys to the east, these are the most important free-ranging herds in the nation.

More than half my field notes were gathered in Hayden Valley, where I spent three successive seasons at a period when it was inhabited by about 440 buffalo. (Because the range could not comfortably support so many animals, it later deteriorated to a condition of overuse, forcing park officials to initiate a program of annual herd reduction. The Hayden herd will probably never again be as large as it was when I conducted my study.)

On each visit to Hayden Valley, I entered through a service gate near the highway and drove several miles along an old fire road. Camping deep in the valley, I used my car as a base of operations, sleeping and preparing breakfast and dinner there. Each morning, after packing a knapsack with lunch, telescope, binoculars, notebook, and poncho, I set forth to stalk buffalo.

At times the animals would settle in a hollow adjacent to the car, bellowing throughout the night and disrupting my sleep with a boisterous reminder of their close presence. At other times, the hundreds simply disappeared. Often, after spending hours coursing over the valley, I would conclude that my subjects had retreated into the woods and abandon my search.

After two seasons of observing and note-taking, I began to document the behavior of buffalo on film. With the addition of the bulky photographic equipment, the scope of my Hayden Valley operation broadened. An assistant joined me to help with extra duties, and the once simple camp was expanded to include a large white canvas tent pitched on a timbered knoll bordering the main grassland. To transport ourselves, our cameras, and our tripods, we rented two saddle horses—"Dude" and "Stranger." Their value was established at seventy-five dollars apiece by the local wrangler, who hinted darkly at the accidents that could befall a horse in Hayden Valley.

We didn't have long to wait before the first unsettling encounter. After returning to camp on our second evening, we picketed Stranger on a hundred-foot tether and released Dude, who remained—as the wrangler had promised he would—within sight of his companion. We had just finished a light supper and were starting to wash our dishes when we noticed that both horses were staring intently toward the timbered end of the meadow. Two grizzly bears had emerged from the lodgepole pine and were slowly working their way through the sedge, hunting rodents. Observing that the direction of their quest would take them right past Dude and Stranger, I was reminded of the reputation of the grizzly for belligerence.

From moment to moment as the bears traipsed down the

meadow, one or the other would stop abruptly, perk its ears, and pounce into the sedge after a meadow vole or pocket gopher. Before long, one bear reared up on his hind legs, followed quickly by the other—they had spotted our horses. When both bears had reached a point about a hundred feet from the horses, Dude became nettled at the invasion of his territory. Head held high, he nickered, then charged toward the bears. They reared up and withdrew a short distance. Dude stood his ground fifty feet from the bears, forcing them to detour around him in order to pass on toward the lower valley. No grizzly was going to usurp *his* meadow.

Nor any buffalo bull, for that matter. While we were having breakfast one morning, an aged bull wandered down the road, spotted our camp, paused to stare for a moment, then ambled onward. Dude spied the bull and rushed toward him, stopping twenty feet away. Calmly, the buffalo lay down in a wallow and rolled several times. Dude waited until the animal rose, then marched still closer, raised his head and whinnied. The bull turned and glared at him, and Dude looked away as if wrongly accused; but when the buffalo walked on again, Dude followed for a few paces to assure himself that the interloper had left the meadow.

My assistant and I also had our problems with an occasional errant bull. Once an old veteran plodded blindly up the hill toward our camp, apparently failing to notice the tent sitting in the clump of pine at the crest. When he had tramped dangerously close, I heaved the only solid object at hand—a buffalo chip. It bounced futilely off his back and landed in the grass at his feet. He glared at us for a moment, then grudgingly altered his course and proceeded on his way. Some days later we repulsed another intruding bull by banging on pans and shouting.

Each evening we were lulled to sleep by a chorus of coyotes, which tuned up with sporadic yapping and then harmonized in howling contests that echoed back and forth across the hills; sometimes nearby buffalo bulls would contribute a few rumbling bellows to this refrain from bygone years. As we lay in our sleeping bags listening to the night sounds, we were reminded that our days in Hayden Valley were not much different from days on the plains over a century and a half ago.

Seventy-five miles south of Hayden Valley, within the borders of Grand Teton National Park, a 513-acre fenced enclosure confined the twenty-two or so buffalo of the Jackson Hole Wildlife Park. I studied this small band and the Hayden herds in alternation, gaining from each area a different perspective on the species. The small size of the herd in Jackson Hole made an intimate survey possible. I was able to identify each individual and follow its daily routine from dawn to dusk and even into the night. These close observations, combined with the more general records I made of the throngs of Hayden Valley, gave me a balanced view of the animals and provided the bulk of my field notes. Additional data came from Wind Cave National Park and five other refuges.

Most of these studies were conducted in spring, summer, and fall. As I felt that my field notes should include observations of herds under conditions of snow and cold, I also scheduled special winter expeditions into the same areas of Wyoming that I had visited in warmer seasons. Headquartered in the upper part of Jackson Hole a few miles outside the almost deserted village of Moran, I was close enough to the small herd in the Wildlife Park to make daily visits. From my base camp I also went on periodic outings to Yellowstone Park. Since the direct route to the park was buried under several feet of snow, I had to make a circuitous detour through Idaho and Montana in order to reach the only passable entrance. There, in the region of Mammoth Hot Springs, a single cleared road provided access to the buffalo herd in the Lamar Valley. The rest of the park, including Hayden Valley, was blocked each year by the heavy snowstorms of October or November, and remained inaccessible by automobile until May.

But an opportunity for an expedition into Hayden Valley soon developed. Walt Disney needed some footage on the midwinter activities of the herds for his film *The Vanishing Prairie*, and the photography was assigned to our crew. Shortly after the project was proposed, we rented two snowplanes for a trip into the snowbound heartland of Yellowstone Park.

A snowplane is a considerably more agile vehicle than its flimsy, homemade construction might indicate. It consists of a lightweight fuselage mounted on three oversized skis; attached to the rear is an airplane motor and prop, which can push the improbable contraption over snow at speeds up to ninety miles an hour.

After consultation with our snowplane drivers, we decided that an approach to Hayden Valley from the south might be too treacherous. Part of the route across frozen Yellowstone Lake passes over scattered hot springs that erode the ice from underneath, creating weakened patches liable to give way under the weight of a snowplane. We therefore planned to proceed through the West Entrance over firm, snow-covered ground.

Aerial reconnaissance in a single-engined private plane indicated clear snowplaning over this route from beginning to end, and we headed off expecting to reach our destination within two hours. We did not realize that we had made our survey flight immediately after a fresh snowfall, which had blanketed the entire road. By the time we drove our snowplanes in, widespread activity from hot springs had melted the snow down to bare pavement in countless patches. Fortunately, anticipating a few such spots, we had thought to bring along two sets of casters. To cross each patch, we had to lift the plane laboriously, fit the casters under the skis, guide the machine across the pavement and then remove the casters for the journey across the next expanse of snow.

Our first evening in the park found us barely more than halfway to the Hayden buffalo. As we sputtered around a long curve, we came within sight of the Norris Geyser Basin, where steam and thermal activity had melted snow from large stretches of the road. The only comforting feature of the Basin was an occasional shallow pool of hot water. Standing in one of these to warm our feet, we debated the uncertain status of our expedition. When we had departed from the West Entrance, we had been so sure of reaching Hayden Valley within two hours that we had jettisoned sleeping bags and extra provisions. Now, as night approached, we found ourselves low on gas and lacking food and shelter. It was time to decide whether to push on or turn back.

Suddenly one of the drivers piped up: "If John Colter made it through here in 1807 with only a rifle and snowshoes, we sure as hell can with our planes!"

Such a challenge left no alternative. We spent an icy night cramped in the seats of our snowplanes, and started off again at dawn. As we maneuvered the machines across the numerous bare spots, dense clouds of steam bellowed up from the geyser basin, condensing on nearby trees to transform them into giant, frosted ghosts. Farther on, we were slowed by sticky snow; but we managed to pull into Canyon Village before dark. Instead of two hours, the trek had taken us two arduous days.

Approaching the deserted tourist cabins of Canyon, we spotted a thin wisp of smoke wafting from the chimney of one of the buildings. As we·converged on the cabin, two winter caretakers, roused by the noise of our planes, came out to offer a royal welcome to our foursome—the first group of visitors from the "outside" in months. We broke our involuntary fast with a hearty meal of steak and potatoes, gassed the snowplanes from an emergency cache, and retired for a night of cozy sleep in a heated cabin.

Early the next morning, we revved the planes for the final lap of our journey. A heavy fog slowly lifted to reveal a clear sky as we skimmed over fast-running snow en route to the buffalo herds. When we crested a knoll at the edge of Hayden Valley, we spotted our quarry—a cluster of tiny black specks on a distant snowy rise. Within minutes we were schussing cornices, darting up and down hills, speeding to forty or fifty miles an hour in order to survey all the groups in the valley. After we had looked over the whole area, we began to record in notes and on film valuable information about the midwinter activities of the herd, documenting the elaborate system of paths and the struggles of a few trailblazing animals breaking a course through a morass of virgin snow.

The waning of the light in the late afternoon prompted our return to Canyon Village, where we spent a second night before heading back to the West Entrance. By evening our sunburned faces were a tingling reminder of the bright, free alpine country of the Yellowstone, with its cloudless sky, clear air, and dazzling winter sun. From our memorable day among the herds, we had come away with a gratifying number of field notes and exposed films. The day in Hayden Valley had also worked its wilderness magic on us. It had been remarkably still, a day of snowy quiet so profound that it rang in our ears, emphasizing the forsaken expanse of snow around us, a lonely meadowland harboring scattered wildlife—and not a single human being.

13

THE NATURE OF

THE BEAST

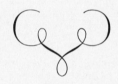

THE MANDAN INDIANS, CLOSE FAMILIARS OF THE BUF-
falo after countless hunting forays, were well aware that the vision
of their quarry was inferior. Attempting to explain this deficiency,
local storytellers devised a tale about Coyote, a patron animal of
the Mandan, and Buffalo, a major character in tribal mythology.

Coyote, according to the myth, observed that the Mandan were
at a disadvantage because of the keen vision of Buffalo, who could
spot hunters before they were able to approach for a kill. To assist
the favored Mandan, Coyote threw dust in Buffalo's eyes, then
kicked his head to make it hang down near the ground. "Now
Buffalo can see only about as far as from here to that hut over
there," the storyteller would remark in closing.

The Mandan myth was based on fact, for the buffalo's vision,
compared with the sense of smell, on which he relies so heavily for

detecting approaching enemies, is not sharply developed. But buffalo see well enough. From a range of one half and possibly three fourths of a mile, they can readily discern the difference between a mere horse and a horse with rider (they flee only on seeing a mounted steed). Even more acute is their perception of moving objects, which they can spot at a range of more than a mile.

Conversely, if an object is motionless and perhaps slightly camouflaged in bushes or trees, they may miss it altogether, even at close quarters. On certain occasions, I approached small groups of buffalo, keeping the wind in my favor to prevent them from catching my scent, crawling ahead when the animals were feeding intently or facing away from me. Whenever a buffalo looked up, I would freeze—and go unnoticed. On each occasion the ploy worked until an individual unexpectedly glanced up at the wrong moment and caught me creeping along.

Such an experiment could be conducted only against the wind. Had I approached with the wind at my back, the animals would soon have become aware of my presence and fled, for the buffalo's sense of smell is its main means of detecting danger. A wary buffalo will tear off at once if it picks up human scent, whereas it may keep only a vague eye on intruding humans detected by sight or sound.

During my stalking days in Hayden Valley, I often saw skittish individuals raise their heads from time to time to test the wind. When my scent drifted in they would quickly hasten off, even if they had not caught sight of me. In some cases they took flight after detecting my scent blowing in from as far away as a mile.

Plainsmen had observed the same behavior over a century before: "The inexperienced voyager will often be surprised to perceive the dense masses of these cattle urging their rapid flight across the prairie, at a distance of two or three miles, without any apparent cause of alarm; unaware as he is, of the fact that the tainted breeze has betrayed to them his presence, while still far away." Some even claimed buffalo were more alarmed by a white man's scent than by an Indian's.

Buffalo also have very sensitive ears, and can pick up extremely weak or distant sounds. On more than one occasion, their excellent hearing foiled my efforts to approach a herd. Once, while observing a group of buffalo from a distance of five hundred feet, I was astonished when the animals suddenly bolted—even at this range, they had detected the faint sound of a twig crackling under my foot.

Although we have ample reason to respect the keen senses of hearing and smell in buffalo, we may be tempted to question their sense of taste—especially in their selection of drinking water. As stagnant pools bake under the summer sun, they sour into hollows of algae-cluttered, foul-smelling liquid. Muddied by the tramping of buffalo, littered with excrement, such pools, as Meriwether Lewis remarked with just disdain, are "unfit for any purpose except the uce of buffaloe." But the buffalo seldom hesitate to drink the murky slime. Lowering their muzzles into the liquid, they suck it up with ease, for they can swallow without raising their heads.

Although buffalo will drink almost anything, they are more selective when it comes to grazing, cropping some patches of grassland quite closely and ignoring others. Most favored are a few broad-leaved nongrassy herbs and many species of grasses: grama, buffalo, wheat, blue, blue-joint, June, dropseed, and windmill, as well as several fescues. Only infrequently do the animals browse shrubs or trees.

Buffalo do use trees, however, in a favorite "touch" activity—body massage. They delight in rubbing their heads, necks, and sides on stumps, large trees, or even saplings and bushes. In addition to the pleasure they provide, these actions help to groom the body. The animals smooth and polish their horns through repeated stropping on trunks and rub off loose chunks of molted fur on branches or rough bark. Almost anything else that juts out from the ground serves as a convenient spot for rubbing—boulders, earthen banks, prairie dog craters, and mounds of snow.

Nothing, in fact, is exempt from the pleasure-seeking of buffalo, as a settler in western Pennsylvania once discovered to his chagrin. When a herd of several hundred came to sample a mineral lick near his plot, they were soon drawn to the inviting logs of his small cabin. Within a few hours "they rubbed the house completely down, taking delight in turning the logs off with their horns." The settler barely escaped being crushed to death in the ruins of his own house—or so said the dramatic report.

This insatiable instinct for rubbing also proved a hazard for the builders of the first cross-country telegraph lines. The slender telegraph poles, soon favored by rubbing buffalo, were eventually toppled in considerable numbers by the zealous scratchers. Then an ingenious employee of the company devised a system for repelling buffalo. He had the poles fitted with metal spikes, on the theory that they would prick and rout the rubbing animals. Instead of driving away the pesky behemoths, however, the barbed columns attracted them in ever greater numbers—the spikes apparently provided an exquisite fillip to the massage, and the buffalo came in swarms to struggle for the chance to rub themselves on the titillating points.

Although such rubbing helps to groom a buffalo by removing tufts of molted fur, the main grooming actions come in wallowing. The clouds of powdered earth stirred up by the rolling animal seem to cleanse the hair much as powdered spot remover draws dirt from clothing. The cleansing dust is raised by the buffalo's thrashing legs and thumping torso, as the animal struggles to gain enough momentum to roll up onto his hump. (Unlike a horse, a rolling buffalo does not turn all the way over.)

Wallowing and the associated actions of pawing and horning are connected, of course, with the buffalo's sense of touch, the last of the five major senses. Of these, the buffalo relies most heavily on vision, smell, and hearing for information about his environment—to detect possible predators, to select favored forage, or to rapidly identify nearby buffalo. Hearing, in particular, is a dominant sense that enables him to discriminate the pitch, tonality, rhythm, and other nuances of the so-called language of his herd mates, the varying kinds of grunts and bellows that serve as social signals.

During group travels, the sounds of communicating animals merge in a constant chatter. The buffalo seem to be saying to each other, "Here I am—where are you?" Mother and calf in particular keep track of each other by means of these calls. A cow who wishes to summon her calf uses a special, subdued grunt; the calf makes its own little "distress" grunts when it wants attention or assistance from its mother.

Sounds of this nature serve to draw the buffalo together; certain other calls are used to repel. Threat grunts warn off such intruders as buffalo stealing from a "private" food supply or venturing too close to a newborn calf. Prolonged, the threat grunt becomes a guttural, growling roar—the bellowing commonly heard between rival bulls during the rut.

And then there are the sounds of playing. During spirited gambols, buffalo break out in noises of apparent delight that range in style from a bawling grunt to a belching snort—including even a curt little sneeze. Youngsters buffeted by charges from elders will utter cries of pain, at times genuine and at times sham.

In addition to these so-called voiced sounds, which originate in the vocal cords, the buffalo makes three unvoiced noises that do not involve the larynx. A bull may occasionally snort, expelling sharp blasts of air through his nostrils. When about to mount his cow, a courting bull may give a brief, soft panting sound. And a cornered buffalo of either sex may produce a squeaky noise by grinding its teeth together.

These varied buffalo calls add up to a repertory of about ten. One is reminded of Leonardo da Vinci's remark: "Man has a great power of speech, which is to a large measure vain and false. The animals have little, but that little is useful and true, and a small and sure thing is better than a great lie." Naturally, the few "words" of buffalo vocabulary, like those in most animal languages, announce but a fragment of information at a time and can convey only simple emotions. Like laughing or screaming in humans, the sounds made by buffalo are spontaneous expressions of mood.

Since vocal conversation is so much the accepted means of communication between people, we tend to forget how expressive we can be in other ways. Our smiles, frowns, or clenched fists are often more telling than any number of words. Buffalo also express themselves in "body language," assuming certain positions or moving in a particular way. Thus the cow retreating in a bounding gait may seem to be simply ricocheting along in rapid hops, but the rhythmic thumps and the singular motions of her body act as signals to warn nearby companions of lurking danger.

In like manner, the posture of a buffalo may serve two functions, first as a channel for the animal's own emotions, and second —perhaps inadvertently—as a silent signal to others. Like the gaur or Indian bison, a buffalo perplexed by the intrusion of human beings stares motionless for several seconds, ears swung forward, head raised slightly and turned toward the disturbance.

Other animals may read the stance as a sign of danger and flee.

No aspect of the buffalo's body conveys so much as his busy tail. Twitching and jerking like a windshield wiper that has outrun its governor, its nervous activity betrays moods of excitement and pleasure. When buffalo chase each other in play or joust in sport, their tails switch rapidly back and forth; and during nursing, the calves of buffalo—and several other ungulates—whip their tails to and fro in similar fashion. Tail switching also occurs during the tension and conflict of rutting battles.

Motions of the tail reveal state of mind in other species, including a creature as unlike the buffalo as the house mouse, whose tail-lashing is likewise associated with conflict behavior. A mouse often wriggles its tail rapidly from side to side just before, during, or after a fight.

The tail of a buffalo may also express emotion by becoming rigidly erect in a vertical or near-vertical position. Although this tail-raising occurs during play, it is more typical of moments of stress or anxiety. Buffalo investigating strange or unfamiliar objects raise their tails, as do bulls either approaching rivals or preparing to mount their mates. (And of course the tail serves the purpose for which it must surely have been intended—that of a fly switch. It is indeed efficient for driving away swarms of biting insects that converge on the animal's thin-furred hindquarters.)

The whole gamut of buffalo positions and calls, in providing a means for the animals to relay simple messages between one another, assists in the organization of a complex herd structure. Buffalo are the most social big game animals on the continent, and, except for a few renegade bulls, mass together and remain in groups wherever they go—whether swimming rivers, traveling cross-country, or simply grazing a meadow.

To a great degree, the grouping habits of many grass-dwelling mammals are fostered by aspects of their environment, for only on the open plains can social animals find enough forage to maintain themselves in large numbers. In Africa, for example, studies of scores of bovine species have demonstrated a broad correlation between sociality and grasslands. Certain antelopes that pursue a solitary way of life dwell in scrub and thicket; species that congregate in large herds live mainly on the grassy veld. An extension of this principle of grouping operates in North America: in the largely forest environment of Wood Buffalo National Park, herds of buffalo generally number no more than thirty individuals, while on the open plains farther south, gatherings may range into the hundreds.

Although terrain and forage influence the groupings of buffalo, the animals often seem to gather simply to enjoy one another's company. When occasional animals stray off and lose track of the drifting herd, they quickly rush back to rejoin the rest as soon as they sense their predicament.

At times their desire for companionship is touchingly revealed in herds divided by destiny. Although a wire fence separates buffalo of Custer State Park from those of neighboring Wind Cave National Park, the two herds often cluster together in a large gathering as if no barrier separated them.

Buffalo bunch most closely together when they face conditions of adversity. Disagreeable weather like rain or snow draws the animals closer, and when they are disturbed by intruders, they swarm into a tight pack and hasten off together across the plain.

But there are limits to the pleasures of companionship. When an individual finds neighbors approaching too near, he may become hostile and drive them off. In this manner the herd spaces itself out, especially during grazing, when each animal will stake out a private feeding area and try to keep trespassers away. However, this antagonism toward herd mates is short-lived and mild. Although occasional buffalo may break away and depart, the majority remain together in a unified group.

The sociality of the animals carries over to other areas of herd life. Influenced by their companions, buffalo tend to carry on the same activity at the same time, whether grazing, traveling, sleeping, or ruminating.

The daily program of the animals usually starts soon after dawn. In small bands of three or four, the herd gradually rises, and before long all animals are grazing. Walking slowly along with muzzles close to the ground, they tear off mouthfuls of grass, barely chewing them before swallowing. After taking their fill of herbage, they loaf, some merely lazily standing, others totally collapsed on one side or the other, legs fully outstretched and heads resting on the ground. The loafing period is generally a time for cud-chewing, when the hastily swallowed grass is brought up, portion by portion, to be broken down more completely in a second chewing.

The day continues in much the same pattern, with alternations beween periods of feeding and periods of rest. A few animals will start each new activity and the rest of the herd will imitate them.

A similar tendency to imitate is a strong factor in leadership. The lead animal will move forward slowly, followed by others, until the whole group advances more or less as a unit. But leadership requires followers. A trailblazing buffalo cannot coerce others into following; he can only proceed a short distance at a time, glancing back now and then to check on the progress of his companions. If they lag, he advances for about a hundred feet and waits. When the other buffalo refuse to follow, the would-be leader gives up his attempt and returns to the herd.

But during times of possible danger, a buffalo that assumes leadership is seldom challenged. Any animal detecting the presence of an intruder is invariably followed from the area by its companions, as indicated in my field notes for late May in the Jackson Hole Wildlife Park: "I have remained hidden in timber watching the herd. A single cow at the tail end of the group grazes over to a spot forty feet from my hiding place and discovers me. Turning, she walks purposefully through the herd of twenty-two animals; the others, who have not spotted me, respond immediately, and retreat with her for some distance until they are out of sight."

Leadership is also absolute during the hasty flight of stampedes. The initiating animals, alarmed by some disturbance, dash off in headlong flight, thus giving the signal for retreat. Following by the others is virtually automatic. Some stampedes burst forth so suddenly that it is impossible to distinguish lead animals—if indeed there are any.

At the beginning of a stampede, the buffalo rush headlong into a tight bunch, massing together with a herding instinct so powerful that the group can seldom be divided. This same stubborn tendency to bunch often thwarts ranchers attempting to drive a buffalo herd onto a different range. No matter what the technique —pushing with a line of men, chasing with jeeps, or encircling with horsemen—the task is so difficult that many drives end in failure. Sooner or later one buffalo manages to outmaneuver its pursuers and squeeze through a minor break in the line, whereupon the rest of the animals quickly slip through the opening like so many links of a chain, and the drive falls apart. Men within touching distance of the stampeding herd may shout and whistle and frantically wave their hands, but to no avail.

Just as a single buffalo breaking through a line can disrupt a contemporary drive, a number of historic bison setting a determined course across the railroad tracks could derail a train. Once a few leaders had crossed, the rest of the herd would try to plunge after them, even when a train moved in to block the way. As Colonel Richard Irving Dodge observed in 1872, the result would be utter chaos:

> At full speed, and utterly regardless of the consequences, [the whole herd] would make for the track on its line of retreat. If the train happened not to be in its path, it crossed the track and stopped satisfied. If the train was in its way, each individual buffalo went at it with the desperation of despair, plunging against or in between locomotives and cars, just as its blind madness chanced to direct it. Numbers were killed, but numbers still pressed on, to stop and stare as soon as the obstacle had passed. After having trains thrown off the track twice in one week, conductors learned to have a very decided respect for the idiosyncracies of the buffalo . . .

It would be easy to equate the whim of a herd crossing the tracks with the motive of the legendary chicken that crossed the road. But it is quite possible that the buffalo had more in mind than merely reaching the other side. Disturbed by the train, they were perhaps attempting to retire to some haven of known security, and only became more desperate to reach it when the train blocked their way.

Many other wild animals behave in the same fashion when confronted by moving vehicles. In Africa, wildebeest, zebras, Cape buffalo, and other big game will gallop beside a car, then frantically speed up to dash across the road in front of it.

In their cross-country treks and in their milling about on the plain, the social buffalo are more ordered than their random assemblages might indicate. Close examination reveals that there is a definite pattern to the size and composition of their groups. Coronado, for one, remarked on the curious structuring of buffalo gatherings. For twenty leagues in May of 1541, he and his men saw "nothing but cows and the sky." Yet a month later they found that the number of bulls "without cows was something incredible." And still later they passed through plains where "there was such a multitude of cows that they were numberless."

Indeed, anyone who traveled for even a short distance over the virgin plains soon discovered that buffalo regularly formed distinctive groupings. They have the same tendency today, dividing into clusters composed mostly of males or of females. For the purposes of this discussion I have arbitrarily labeled these "bull groups" and "cow groups."

At first glance, the term "cow group" may seem a misnomer, for the assemblage often includes a few bulls. But cows make up a majority of the membership and are in almost complete control. The cow group is a definite matriarchy, and remains so even during the rutting season, when its ranks are swelled by numbers of bulls. No matter how boldly the visiting bulls may attempt to manage group affairs, they remain primarily followers, exerting little influence on the behavior of the gathering as a whole.

During the non-breeding season in plains refuges, membership in cow groups averages about twenty, and occasionally reaches as much as seventy. With the approach of the rut, however, it increases into the hundreds as several groups merge and are joined by numbers of mature bulls.

Bull groups are small in contrast, usually consisting of one to five members and seldom exceeding fifteen or twenty. Bulls four years or older predominate, and are joined only rarely by cows.

The two kinds of groups differ not only in membership but also in behavior. For instance, the females are more timid and watchful than the males. In Yellowstone Park they will flee when a man advances to within a thousand feet, whereas bulls will not move until the man comes to within three hundred feet. Some bulls are so obstinate that they can't be budged by an approach to within ten feet—even when pelted with stones.

Indians took account of this discrepancy in the wariness of cow and bull groups during the hunt, firing their first arrows at the cows in the expectation that they would be the first to flee. White hunters also adapted their techniques accordingly, often creeping past reclining bulls in order to get within range of the more desirable young cows.

Cow and bull groups also differ in the manner in which their members are spaced out on the prairie. Cows generally stick close together, and bulls scatter out over a larger area. When traveling, cow groups move as compact units while bull groups string apart for as much as two thousand feet, the lead animal disappearing from sight before the last straggler moves.

Whether bull groups or cow groups, most gatherings of buffalo, instead of traveling with a set roster of members, intermingle or split at random. At times, however, the merging of two unfamiliar groups is accompanied by elaborate ceremony. This is especially true if the meeting takes place in the vast reaches of Wood Buffalo National Park, where two herds may indeed be totally unfamiliar with each other. The approaching groups stop when they are about a hundred yards apart, at which point the ritual commences. One large bull advances from each herd, progressing step by step toward a rendezvous on neutral ground. There they lock horns and struggle briefly, almost gingerly, terminating their bout, as if by prearrangement, in a symbolic draw. Each bull then crosses over to the opposite herd, and the two groups merge.

Within the ranks of both cow and bull groups there are often little "clubs" of like individuals. For example, bulls tend to loiter at the edges of most herds, leading some writers to postulate that they are acting as sentinels. After spotting approaching peril, they are presumed to run back into the herd and warn their associates. This interpretation is probably unwarranted. Bulls located on the fringes act as lookouts only insofar as their peripheral location makes them privy to approaching danger. Also, since bulls are less vigilant than cows, they would be of limited use as sentinels.

To me, these small clubs of buffalo, whether composed of bulls, calves, or cows, seem nothing more than clusters of like individuals. Other observers, however, have asserted that many such clubs are family gatherings or "clans," whose members are all related to common ancestors. Used to refer to buffalo, the term "clan" describes a kin group, usually a cow and her progeny of three or four seasons. Naturalist Ernest Thompson Seton wrote feelingly of such a clan on the march, elaborating its membership to include "the old great-grandmother in advance; the young ones scattered through it, the father and grandfather behind; and the dethroned great-great-great grandfathers roaming along in the offing."

Such a conception, like so many extravagant claims about the buffalo, is largely guesswork. The idea of the clan seems to have been introduced on circumstantial evidence and promulgated by plains visitors who took a fancy to it. One of these, historian Henry Inman, wrote that "the resemblance of each individual of a family is very striking, while the difference between families is as apparent to the practiced eye as is the Caucasian from the Mongolian race of people."

I can but congratulate Mr. Inman on his extraordinary powers of recognition, remembering that it took me more than two weeks of careful scrutiny to differentiate between a mere sixteen individuals in one captive herd. I personally doubt that small clubs can be called clans, believing instead that they are formed voluntarily— even accidentally. The closest buffalo come to forming clans is in the pairing of each cow and her calf, a bond that normally dissolves by the end of the calf's first year and cannot properly be labeled a clan.

Even if we reject the concept of clan, we should not overlook the many other established intricacies of herd organization. Selective not only in their daily habits and activities but also in their choice of companions, buffalo live and travel in organized groups, each with a character as distinct and special as that of its separate members.

14

STATUS IN

BUFFALO SOCIETY

During each summer's rutting season, the bulls of a herd, by bluff or by battle, arrange themselves into an order of dominance that serves to divide the "spoils" of the rut. To the top-ranking male goes the first cow in heat; bulls with lower status get a chance at breeding only if more than one cow is available at a time. Bull number one is dominant over bull number two, who is dominant over bull number three, and so on down the scale, until the organization becomes a distinct class structure.

The first hierarchy of this nature to be carefully studied was that of domestic chickens. In 1922, a Norwegian named Thorlief Schjelderup-Ebbe published a report on class organization among fowl, a series of observations that would have profound impact on the study of animal behavior.

The Norwegian scientist undertook his research after becoming intrigued by the struggles of chickens vying for food. Watching a group in a small pen as they contested a limited supply of grain, he noticed that the competition sparked even the most phlegmatic hen into apparent life-or-death activity; in the struggle, some individuals pecked their comrades with such violence that they ripped out feathers and bloodied faces or combs.

Schjelderup-Ebbe analyzed all the pecks at each mealtime fray and soon made a significant discovery: hens were attacking each other not at random but in a distinct pattern. The flock was organized in a hierarchy of precedence in which one powerful hen pecked all subordinates. This pattern continued down the line until there was one hen at the bottom of the heap—a "cinderella," in Schjelderup-Ebbe's phraseology—with no underling to attack.

From this study emerged the term "pecking order" to describe precedence in groups of animals. Eventually the term entered everyday speech. We now talk about "pecking orders" among the editors of a newspaper, the characters of a Marquand novel, the officers of labor unions, or P.T.A. gatherings, and the staffs of universities or corporations.

Despite its common use, pecking order is a misleading term, since it overemphasizes the aspect of fighting. Although battles are known to erupt in animal societies, they are uncommon; precedence is not regularly contested, but mutually agreed upon and recognized. And the term pecking order is plainly inadequate to describe the attacks of species other than birds. Thus, "rank order" seems distinctly preferable.

After Schjelderup-Ebbe's discoveries among chickens, behaviorists began to investigate rank order in other species. Although it became apparent that invertebrates probably do not establish such hierarchies, researchers soon found that most higher groups of animals, including fish, turtles, and lizards, do develop definite systems of precedence in their societies. Even among certain snakes, individuals settle the question of rank by pushing each other with arched necks—a pose immortalized long ago in the caduceus symbol of the medical corps. Rank orders reach the highest complexity among birds and mammals, including species as diverse as canaries, pigeons, jungle fowl, rats, cottontails, cattle, sheep, horses, whitetail deer, and apes.

Fundamental to the establishment of rank order is the ability of each animal to recognize its associates as distinct individuals.

(Hens, for instance, have been known to identify every member of flocks numbering as many as ninety-seven.) As I started my own investigation, I realized that I would have to learn to distinguish between individual buffalo. I therefore selected as subjects for my study the herd of sixteen animals in the Jackson Hole Wildlife Park, where a fenced-in range limited the rambles of the herd, and the small number of buffalo simplified the task of identification.

But when I first observed the herd, several of the sixteen looked so much alike that I was forced to differentiate between them by the varying positions of their ear tags. After a few days, however, I managed to pinpoint some identifying features. Most helpful were minor irregularities in the curvature and texture of horns or slight differences in body shape and hide coloring. From these natural variations I was soon spotting some individuals by their horns ("Ring," "Straight," "Uneven"), their hides ("White Hump," "Dark Hump," "Scar"), or their facial features ("Thin").

Among the one- and two-year-olds, however, a virtual absence of distinguishing features soon forced me to create my own. At first I tried marking the animals by shooting arrows tipped with cloth-covered rubber balls into their coats; dipped in white paint and fired with a bow, these missiles left conspicuous marks on the buffalo. But the live targets did not appreciate being shot at and soon stampeded to a range that would have taxed the marksmanship of an expert bowman, a distinction I could not claim for myself.

I then enlisted a second tactic. Though simpler and quicker than arrow-marking, it could be used only during the winter, when the herd was artificially fed and could be attracted with fresh hay. Concealing myself in a shed, I used clumps of hay to entice the buffalo nearby, and then daubed patterns of paint on their heads as they ate. The resulting marks served to distinguish these juveniles somewhat impersonally as "2B" (two-year-old, paint on *back* of head), "2F" (paint on *front*), and so on.

When all the buffalo were clearly identified, I proceeded to record indications of rank between them. Almost three fourths of the interactions turned out to be peaceable. Dominant buffalo walked toward and displaced subordinates by their mere presence —without resorting to any apparent force or threat. In less easily observed interplay, low-ranking animals wended a careful course through the herd so as to avoid their superiors, revealing their rank by submission. Although these interactions were so subtle as to be almost imperceptible, the rank order they demonstrated was universally recognized and respected among the animals.

The remaining one fourth of the interactions, to the contrary, were purposeful and involved a threatened or actual use of force, which varied in style from mere warning motions to spirited battles, and, oddly, included mounting actions.

Mountings would seem to have no place in a discussion of rank, but on occasion they clearly signaled dominance. High-ranking buffalo (both males and females) would place their chins on the rumps of subordinates to force them to move away. Quite possibly the practice was picked up during the playful mountings of calfhood: the repeated withdrawal of young buffalo in the female position may have influenced a "male" to adopt mounting as a convenient means of forcing a companion to move. What had worked in play now proved equally useful in competition on the feedgrounds.

Mounting actions also indicate rank among other animals, sometimes even working in the opposite direction. Socially inferior monkeys may reveal their low rank by a sexually submissive pose, assuming a female position when confronted by a dominant animal; aggression on the part of the dominant is channeled into mounting behavior, and fighting is avoided. Mounting is thus the mark of the dominant, as the sexually submissive pose is of the subordinate. Since the displays, in monkey and buffalo alike, occur without regard to the sex of the individuals, the behavior cannot be considered strictly sexual.

In other forceful interactions between buffalo, dominants resorted to threatening motions. Sometimes they merely directed a steady stare toward subordinates, who recognized a quality of threat in the glance and moved away. At other times they applied stronger force by swinging their horns menacingly, even with occasional contact. On the few occasions when threats failed, battles resulted.

Once tabulated, all of these interactions established the linear rank order shown in Table 1 [page 164]. Bull 6 dominated Bull 5, who dominated White Hump, who dominated Scar, and so on down the scale to the lowest-ranking animal, yearling heifer 1B, who was subjected to blows from all other buffalo. So

TABLE #1

	Bull 6	Bull 5	White Hump	Scar	Ring	Thin	Dark Hump	Uneven	Straight	2F	2N	2B	♂ 1F	♂ 1L	♀ 1S	♀ 1B
				Cows						Heifers			Yearlings			
Bull 6																
Bull 5	2															
White Hump	2	5														
Scar	1	3	20													
Ring	2	4	24	22			1									
Thin		1	9	5	17											
Dark Hump	3	7	9	14	21	17										
Uneven	2	4	13	3	15	12	9									
Straight		2	5	6	6	8	6	17								
Heifers 2F	3	1	3	4	9	10	7	13	3							
Heifers 2N	2	1	3	4	2	10	3	4	5	13						
Heifers 2B			3	1	3	6	3	11	4	8	12					
Yearlings ♂ 1F	6	2	5	6	6	14	5	4	7	6	5	6				
Yearlings ♂ 1L	3	3	5	4	5	6	4	8	2	11	11	7	21			
Yearlings ♀ 1S	1	1	3	4	3	9	2	6	7		10	4	9	7		
Yearlings ♀ 1B	1	1	3	3	2	9	4	5	6	1	6	1	8	3	6	

Displays of dominance and subordination in the Jackson Hole Wildlife Park herd during a three-month period of observation indicated the rank order outlined in the above diagram. The figures from top to bottom show the number of times the animal at the head of a column exerted dominance over each other herd member. Figures from left to right, beginning with the name of each buffalo, show the attacks received by that animal.

readily did subordinates recognize and avoid their superiors that there was only one "temporary" reversal in a whole winter's observation: Thin momentarily jumped rank by repelling Ring with a thrust of her horns.

Underlying the system of rank order was the basic principle of the division of something limited in supply. In the Wildlife Park herd, as among Schjelderup-Ebbe's chickens, the commodity most frequently contested was food; thus rank was clearly revealed at the feedgrounds.

Not surprisingly, the period of greatest competition was winter, when heavy snows necessitated a daily dole of hay and biscuits. To permit each buffalo to eat by himself, attendants parceled food into a number of individual piles; each of these looked to my human eye as choice as any other, but the buffalo saw things differently. Often a dominant animal would shift capriciously to another pile, nudging away the animal feeding there and starting a chain reaction that soon shuffled at least half the herd.

Just as food was shared according to the rules of the rank order, so were other things in limited supply—a small waterhole, an object of curiosity, a mineral lick, a choice spot for lying or wallowing, and, of course, a cow in heat. By the same means buffalo even apportioned the limited shade under a clump of trees: dominants took shelter, leaving subordinates to bake in the hot sun.

The rank order was also evident during the herd's travels. A dominant might impel low-ranking buffalo to move on, or, by stopping, force others behind to stop as well. Once I watched as two dominant cows halted obstinately on a hard-packed trail through deep snow, stubbornly blocking all of the low-ranking buffalo in the rear. When the inferior buffalo decided to advance, they were obliged to detour around their superiors and flounder through the troublesome deep powder.

Among the privileges enjoyed by dominant buffalo one might expect to find the right of leadership, but this was by no means guaranteed. During herd travels, dominant buffalo could urge their subordinates on, but they could not necessarily *lead* them. In buffalo, it seems, as in men, a true leader directs the progress of his followers not by sheer force but by reasonable persuasion. Skillful in leadership as such were only three Wildlife Park buffalo: cow #3, cow #1, and cow #6, in that order. Plainly this ability to lead did not correspond with the winning of fights and thus the rise to high rank; nor did the ability to triumph over a herd mate in battle assure the chance to lead that same individual.

A similar lack of correlation between rank and leadership has been observed in other species, particularly in sheep and goats. Related behavior has even appeared among human children. Certain members of a group of young boys studied by a psychologist displayed a strong trait of leadership, obtaining voluntary cooperation from companions by means of their ability to explain a given situation. Conversely, a number of dominant boys proved unable to lead even after resorting to threats, commands, or attacks.

Human society resembles that of buffalo in other areas. Often in corporate class structures, a high-powered salesman will "jump rank," advancing over several of his associates to become vice president of the company. Such swift rises to influence and power also occurred among the buffalo of the Wildlife Park, particularly among the young bulls. Growing rapidly, these bulls became physically capable of dominating all cows in the herd by the time they were about two and a half years old. But the change in rank did not take place immediately; the bulls engaged in repeated battles with dominant cows before finally overwhelming them. Although the males clearly outweighed the females by the time they attained dominance, it would be an oversimplification to say that an advantage in size had tipped the scales in their favor. The past history of consistent conquest by the cows helped them to maintain an artificially high rank by a kind of "superiority complex." (The same pattern has been observed in chickens: a hen revolting against a recognized despot, aware of the past supremacy of her opponent, will fight less fiercely than she would against an underling.) Gradually, however, the buffalo bulls overcame the "mental set" of a low-ranking animal and began to use the advantage of their increased size and weight to dominate the cows.

Instead of toppling each successively stronger cow, however, the bulls advanced in irregular leaps; after overthrowing some high-ranking cows early in the game, they were unable to conquer certain low-ranking ones until a few weeks had passed. These fitful advances broke the normal straight-line succession into a pattern behaviorists call a triangle. To give an example, one bull dominated cow #2, which dominated cow #5, which in turn dominated the same bull.

Behavioral studies have shown that triangles are typical of an emergent or changing rank order. Thus, as might be expected, the triangles in the Wildlife Park herd ultimately disappeared when the rank-jumping bulls conquered all the cows.

In the hierarchy of the Wildlife Park herd, greater size and weight corresponded in general with higher positions of rank. But if two animals were very close in size, dominance was determined by other factors. Maturity in age fostered high status, as did strength, fighting skill, endurance, and, above all, aggressiveness.

I received my own lesson in aggression when I became engaged in a contest with a testy cow who seemed bent on routing me from the Wildlife Park. During my first two days inside the enclosure, she would often gallop directly at me, coming to a stop only a few feet away. Eventually I began to respond to her charges by throwing rocks and sticks at her. My repeated assaults were so successful that she—and only she among the herd— would back up whenever I so much as waved my hand. Thus it was evident that I had been a subordinate when I yielded, but had finally attained high rank by affirming my might, bluff though it may have been.

The normal means of attaining supremacy was bypassed in a few special instances when low-ranking buffalo temporarily ascended to dominance. The secret of the privileged underling was the careful choosing of companions—the animal climbed in rank by associating closely with a superior, thus "borrowing" its status. A calf quite naturally rose to the level of its mother, just as a cow rose to the rank of the bull who was courting her.

During the rut in the Wildlife Park and in other refuges, only top-ranking bulls succeeded in mating with cows in heat. In the language of evolutionary theory, this is survival of the fittest, or the process of natural selection. In any contest between two bulls, the superior animal triumphs, presumably because of stronger traits in his makeup. The hardiness of the species is thus assured as the blood of the strongest bulls flows in the veins of the next generation.

Natural selection among buffalo may favor the evolution of behavioral features as well as physical ones, also on the strength of their survival value to the species. For example, rank order works to control aggressive instincts that might otherwise lead to mortal combat and consequent depletion of the herds. Once estab- lished, the hierarchy minimizes such combat, enabling each indi- vidual to recognize his place in the herd. Subordinates thus retreat from superiors when threatened, submitting peacefully without fighting, reinforcing rather than disrupting group life.

Rank order, then, is important for the survival of a given spe- cies. It is also extremely useful to human beings in their dealings with animals. In chicken farming, a flock allowed to settle into a well-organized rank order performs significantly better than one continually disrupted by the addition of new members. Hens in the stable group peck each other less frequently, consume more food, gain more weight, and lay more eggs. The same principle is revealed with domestic cattle. Dairy herds upset by the introduction of unfamiliar cows respond with a decrease in output. As the new-comers joust to establish their positions in the hierarchy, the ensuing fighting and excitement reduce milk production by as much as five per cent.

Although buffalo keepers are hardly concerned with milk yields, they are likely to be aware of jockeying for rank in the herds. Their wards go through a complicated period of adjustment whenever new animals are introduced; and the birth of calves each spring sets in motion once again the gradual evolution of a new rank order.

I emerged from my study of the Wildlife Park herd much impressed by the complexity of the interactions I had witnessed. Research had showed that, far from being an arbitrary collection of similar animals, this society of buffalo was organized into a complex and discernible order of rank.

15

GROUP TRAVELS

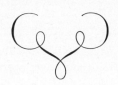

THERE IS NO MORE SPECTACULAR SHOW ON THE PLAINS than a buffalo stampede. Clouds of dust churned up by myriad grinding hoofs rise around the herd, at times enveloping the cataract of tumbling bodies; the pounding of hoofs swells until it becomes a continuous rumble, a sound that one both hears and feels, like the roar and vibration of a subway train passing beneath the street.

On and on the animals flee, often running for several miles in astonishing displays of endurance. I have seen groups in the Crow Reservation, shot at by hunters, dash across the plain for as much as seven miles, stopping only when blocked at the edge of their range by the steep-walled Bighorn Canyon.

Whether coursing over the prairie in a massive stampede or merely drifting from meadow to waterhole and back again, the buffalo in contemporary reserves summon visions of the once-teeming plains, and reward the spectator with a glimpse of the behavior of social mammals on the move. The wandering bison may even present the more knowledgeable observer with some clues to the puzzling migratory habits of the herds of yesteryear.

After the first rush of frenzied flight, stampeding buffalo often halt, stare back toward the source of their alarm, and proceed onward at a slower pace. During the course of their flight, they may use all of their principal gaits—walking, trotting, bounding, and galloping. A definitive analysis of these gaits and those of other mammals was made as long ago as 1872 by a man named Eadweard Muybridge, then a researcher in Sacramento, California. Muybridge was baffled by a question that had plagued artists from primitive cave daubers down through the Eygptians, Romans, and more recent animal painters: does a horse travel free from contact with the ground at any point during its stride?

Today the question is settled readily with a motor-driven camera and a study of the sequential shots it produces. Eadweard Muybridge had to experiment with materials available in 1872. Loading a twelve-lensed contrivance of his own design with wet collotype plates, he marched horses, camels, human sprinters, buffalo, and a host of other species before the battery of lenses, recording the footwork of each creature in sequence. Today the neatly arranged series of plates looks more like an exhibit of pop art than a scientific study, but when Muybridge's collection first appeared, it settled an age-old controversy, proving definitively that there are times in a horse's stride when the animal is entirely off the ground. The plates established their owner as the authority on the natural movements and gaits of numerous species.

In the buffalo, the four normal gaits are determined by the sequence in which the animal lifts and plants each of its hoofs. If a number is assigned to each hoof in logical order (with the buffalo viewed from directly overhead), the gaits can be easily broken down into their separate steps.

1. Left front   2. Right front
3. Left rear   4. Right rear

When walking, a buffalo moves his hoofs in a 3—1—4—2 sequence, a standard pattern for all of the four-legged animals investigated by Muybridge, including elephants, camels, and raccoons. (The same sequence applies when human beings attempt "four-legged" locomotion, a fact that you may easily prove for yourself—if you wish—by crawling across the living room floor. You will note that your left hand moves after your left knee, and so on.)

In the somewhat faster gait called the trot, each pair of diagonally opposite limbs is advanced and planted concurrently (1 and 4—2 and 3). Trotting exists in the same form in virtually all quadrupeds.

Bounding is an uncommon gait in which the buffalo springs forward by the more or less simultaneous extension of all four legs, much as the Thomson-gazelle or the whitetail deer bounces along when fleeing from danger. The gait is characteristic buffalo motion during intense play or in moments of sudden flight, as when an individual is spooked by the abrupt appearance of a human being.

The most rapid gait of a buffalo is the gallop, a progression from left to right, first of the front hooves and then of the rear. The 1—2—3—4 sequence distinguishes this running gait as a transverse gallop, a pattern that also occurs in horses, goats, bears, hogs, and camels. A smaller number of animals, including dogs, deer, and elk, travel by means of a rotatory gallop, in which the sequence runs smoothly clockwise: 1—2—4—3.

One would not expect the bulky buffalo to be a speedy runner, but actually the animal can course swiftly over the plains at thirty to thirty-five miles an hour. Bulls, cows, and month-old calves can maintain this pace for half a mile or more. Even infants a few hours old can keep up with the herd for short distances.

Surprisingly, speeds of buffalo are not far below those of top race horses, clocked at a little over forty miles an hour in quarter-mile stretches. The comparably swift horses of Indian and white hunters regularly outran groups of buffalo; but if the herd wasn't overtaken within a few hundred yards the hunters would abandon the chase, for although buffalo were a little slower at the outset, they had an edge over horses in their greater endurance (they sometimes continued a run for more than ten miles at a time) and their superior agility in rough country.

In view of their size and weight, buffalo are astonishingly nimble. They will venture into areas where no horse can be urged to go, and where a man can clamber only with difficulty. Seldom are they deterred by obstacles in the terrain, such as steeply cut banks along a river or rocky walls around a canyon. They have been known to climb high into the Rocky Mountains.

Even water will not daunt buffalo, for they are powerful swimmers, navigating skillfully with all but hump, muzzle, and top of the head submerged. Their swimming prowess once greatly inconvenienced Lieutenant William Clark and his party. In 1806, as the men descended the Yellowstone River on their homeward journey, they were forced to beach their canoes so that several "gangues of Buffalow" could continue across twin river channels totaling about half a mile in width. Even today, herds regularly swim the Peace and Slave Rivers, bucking a heavy current for as much as half a mile.

It appears that buffalo may also swim for the sheer fun of it. Sometimes animals wading out into a lake to drink will paddle into deeper water, apparently just for a dip. And during cross-country journeys, a few may plunge through ponds even when the detour around them would be far less strenuous.

Despite this fondness for aquatic exercise, swimming is a far from conventional mode of travel for contemporary buffalo. The herds follow normal overland routes through the most negotiable terrain. During their usual travels, animals in Yellowstone Park walk about two miles a day—provided sources for watering are plentiful and well dispersed. If not, the periodic round trip to a waterhole may extend the daily average to six miles or more.

Most herds in Yellowstone Park restrict their travels to specific ranges despite the absence of confining fences; but individuals have been known to straggle beyond these limits, and even to shift several miles outside the borders of the Park itself. At the time of my study, a group of three bulls drifted into Jackson Hole, forty-five miles south of their customary range.

These buffalo drifters are exhibiting the vagrant traits of bygone herds, whose members, unattached to any particular spot, wandered freely from range to range. "A home where the buf-fa-lo roam" might have indicated any area on the plains. The erratic traipsing of the herds taxed the ingenuity of Indians and professional hidemen alike. To the hidemen, coming across buffalo was as much a stroke of good fortune as winning a round at the local roulette table. Choice areas of prairie that trembled one week with the arrival of immense masses became silent and empty the next.

Throughout the plains the uneven ebb and flow in buffalo populations was an accepted phenomenon, although greenhorns fresh from the East often tried to lay the blame for the vanishing of a given herd to local hunting. Some of the fluctuation in buffalo numbers was caused by fickle wandering; at other times herds were forced to move on when they depleted local grass or ran out of water. Whatever their motivation, the travels were unpredictable, and forced the adoption of compensatory measures among the tribes that were dependent upon the herds for food and other staples.

To tide them over the periods when the herds were gone, Plains Indians stored quantities of buffalo meat by sun-drying or by conversion to pemmican. The neighboring Pawnee and Omaha tribes even made an intertribal treaty providing for reciprocal hunting privileges. When the herds withdrew into Pawnee territory, Omaha tribesmen were permitted to chase after them. The same provision worked in reverse if the buffalo went in the opposite direction.

But neither preservation of meat nor exchange of hunting domains could deal effectively with the problem created by the rambling of the herds. When the buffalo were near camp, the Indians feasted almost continually on the choicest cuts, but when the herds were scarce they made use of every scrap of the buffalo, including discarded bones, which the women pounded into small fragments and boiled for many hours to make soup. Faced with the prospect of starvation one winter, the desperate Hidatsa cut up and boiled their leather bull boats and the rawhide doors of their houses. Even more hard-pressed, the Assiniboin, in 1846, ate their dogs and horses, and, in some instances, their own children.

Most Plains tribes eventually adapted to the ways of their wandering prey by joining the herds. They became as nomadic as their roving quarry, not out of any natural leaning toward nomadism, but from sheer necessity. It was the only mode of life that could guarantee a fairly reliable food supply.

This erratic journeying by Indian nomads in search of buffalo prey furnishes evidence to dispute a long-standing notion about the behavior of the herds. For many centuries, observers of the animals have discussed the likelihood of an annual north–south buffalo migration in search of favorable conditions. By moving south for the winter, the animals presumably escaped driving blizzards and boreal cold while gaining plentiful, easily grazed forage. When they returned north the following spring, they avoided the sweltering southern summer and reaped juicy, tender grasses restored to lushness in their absence.

The benefits to the buffalo of such seasonal migrations are obvious. And surely the Plains Indians, skilled hunters that they were, would have been the first to discern such rhythmic alternations between summer and winter ranges. Stationing themselves along routes of migrating buffalo herds, they could have slaughtered enough during spring and fall treks to supply their yearly need, just as today's sportsmen conceal themselves in blinds along recognized flyways in order to gun down their limits of migrating ducks or geese.

But we know that the tribes did not hunt in such a seasonal manner, and, furthermore, that they were decidedly nomadic, wandering in irregular patterns across the plains; it was the very unpredictability of herd travels that had given rise to their nomadism in the first place. Thus the buffalo migration theory, which presupposes a reliable north–south shifting of the herds, is sadly discredited.

But the idea of buffalo migration appealed to many early observers. As far back as 1683, Father Louis Hennepin stated that buffalo "change their Country according to the Seasons of the Year; for upon the approach of the Winter, they leave the North to go to the Southern Parts." But the missionary qualified his observation: "These Bulls find in all Seasons Forrage to subsist by; for if they are surpriz'd in the Northern Countries by the Snow, before they can reach the Southern Parts, they have the dexterity to remove the Snow, and eat the Grass under it."

Almost a century and a half later, a zoologist reported on buffalo in the region of Monterrey, Mexico: "Each year in the spring, in April or May, they advance toward the north, to return again to the southern regions in September and October." He vaguely suggested that the Mexican buffalo traveled as far north as Michigan, but acknowledged that "these migrations are not general."

On the Great Plains, too, early hunters and pioneers believed that buffalo made extensive north–south migrations. For evidence they cited numerous well-worn trails, unaware that these north–south routes were natural watering paths for the animals. Plains rivers typically run from east to west, and thus the shortest and most logical routes between buffalo pastures and adjacent water ran perpendicular to the rivers, or from north to south.

Fur traders in this same region thought "the buffaloes that were found in summer on the plains of the Saskatchewan and Red River of the North spent the winter in Texas, and vice versa." But subsequent observers considered the wintering of Canadian buffalo in Texas "very improbable." Simple mathematics supports their objection. The distance between the two areas is about fourteen hundred miles. I estimate that buffalo could cover this stretch in about four and a half months, assuming ten miles of travel a day for this direct, purposeful journey. At such a rate, their round-trip time would be nine months, leaving only three months for luxuriating in the improved climate and savoring the lush forage at both ends. And even this brief period would be lost altogether if travel speeds dropped below an ambitious eight miles a day.

There is a modern example, however, which indicates that the Canada–Texas journey, though highly unlikely, is not inconceivable. If the animals had been able to move as rapidly and efficiently as the wildebeest on Africa's Serengeti Plain, which sometimes trek as much as thirty miles a day and twelve hundred miles a year, the migration would have been a reasonable venture. But we have little evidence to support the notion that buffalo made journeys of such length or traveled at such a rapid pace.

Zoologist William Hornaday proposed a more moderate buffalo migration for the early herds. Instead of insisting on the long Canada–Texas shift, he asserted that "at the approach of winter the whole great system of herds . . . moved south a few hundred miles, and wintered under more favorable circumstances than each band would have experienced at its farthest north."

But even this theory doesn't stand up to investigation. It would have each successive band trekking south into a region recently vacated by the adjacent group. Presumably the first animals would have deserted the area to escape parched pastures and a frigid climate—quite a surprise to the band moving south in search of rich pastures and a mild climate.

If we look at another species, however, it must be admitted that such short-distance southerly shifting is not impossible, and could have resulted in slightly more favorable conditions for each band. We know that certain birds migrate for only short hops.

Regional populations of the robin, for instance, shift southward from the area in which they nest. As a result, the robins spending each spring in Kentucky eventually migrate toward the Gulf of Mexico, only to be replaced during the fall by other robins moving in from their nesting grounds farther north.

But bird migrations, although they establish some basis for the idea of limited buffalo migration, only reveal the dearth of evidence to support it. Whereas travels of many species of birds are conclusively substantiated by visual sightings and recoveries of banded individuals, there is no matching proof for buffalo. There are, of course, some sight records, but early observers had an unscientific propensity to assume that buffalo moving northward or southward at the "proper" season were doing so as part of the Great Migration. And it is now more than a century late to mark buffalo for the purposes of tracking their precise movements across the open plain.

In their wake, the historic herds have left a confused trail of opinions on the question of long-range migration. The most competent final statement appears to have come from George Catlin, whose several years with the Plains tribes lend considerable authority to his opinion: "These animals are not migratory," he wrote. "They roam about and over vast tracts of country, from East to West and from West to East as often as from North to South." Catlin was aware that popular sentiment still favored the idea that the buffalo made a regular north–south migration, "which it has often been supposed they naturally and habitually did to accommodate themselves to the temperature of the climate in the different latitudes," but he disagreed, observing that buffalo within their range "seem to flourish, and get their living without the necessity of evading the rigour of the climate . . ."

Although the issue of a plains-wide seasonal migration may never be settled with finality, the preponderance of evidence is certainly against such migration. As we have seen, it is incompatible with the nomadism of Plains tribes. And reliable eyewitnesses indicated that the majority of the herds, rather than moving north and south in uniform alternation, roamed their range capriciously, unpredictably, wandering with little regard for season, direction, or climate.

We do know, however, that certain local groups of buffalo carried out seasonal shifts that, despite the relatively short distances involved, can still be classed as true migrations. The term "migration" may seem unsuitable because it has so often been applied to the more spectacular journeys of other species—the tiny calliope hummingbirds that nest in British Columbia and then fly three thousand miles south to Mexico, or the fur seals that bear their young in Alaskan waters and winter off the coast of California. Yet distance is not a primary condition of migration, for some species of plankton are migratory merely because they shift from a nighttime location near the surface of the sea to a daytime level at slightly greater depths. Their movements are classed as migrations because they are periodic round trips, with each leg of the journey undertaken in continued passage in one direction.

Buffalo herds in the northwestern portion of the Great Plains, especially Alberta and Saskatchewan, made short, seasonal migrations of this nature, abandoning the exposed plains to seek shelter in wooded areas during piercing winter storms. One of the most vivid descriptions of such a trek came from Alexander Henry, who encountered a group of migrating animals when bivouacking near the Saskatchewan River in 1776:

> . . . a storm of wind and snow . . . continued all the night, and part of the next day. Clouds of snow, raised by the wind, fell on the encampment, and almost buried it. I had no resource but in my buffalo-robe.
>
> In the morning, we were alarmed by the approach of a herd of oxen [buffalo], who came from the open ground to shelter themselves in the wood. Their numbers were so great, that we dreaded lest they should fairly trample down the camp; nor could it have happened otherwise, but for the dogs, almost as numerous as they, who were able to keep them in check. The Indians killed several, when close upon their tents; but neither the fire of the Indians, nor the noise of the dogs, could soon drive them away. Whatever were the terrors which filled the wood, they had no other escape from the terrors of the storm.

On these western Canadian plains, buffalo seeking shelter in wooded zones made a paradoxical fall migration some distance *north*, and west, in stark contrast to the alleged migrations of plains herds toward the temperate south. Scrub islands bordering open prairie on the north side provided the only significant tree shelter, and thus herds seeking protection from numbing snow squalls were forced to migrate northward.

Erratic and unpredictable as these migrations into sheltering scrub may have been, local Indians were able to plan hunts around them, apparently with some success. At the start of the winter, the Assiniboin stationed their camps along a likely stream and awaited the approach of buffalo into the adjacent timber. The Mandan slaughtered large numbers around their villages when icy blizzards drove the animals into refuge in nearby woods, from which haven it was "often almost impossible to drive them out . . ." Blackfoot and Cree tribesmen hunted in the same fashion.

Although we cannot study modern herds for evidence to settle the question of the Great Migration, we still know of herds that make seasonal treks into wooded areas as their forebears did, and the habits of these animals shed light on the short-range movements of bygone herds. Our most detailed observations on such behavior come from Wood Buffalo National Park, where herds journey some distance to escape the discomfort of wind and cold. When zero and below-zero temperatures are combined with active winds, the animals may travel several miles into wooded areas in search of shelter.

As these buffalo besieged by blizzard conditions move into the cover of trees, they are behaving just as oldtimers said they did—and the fortunate student of buffalo migration comes upon a rare harmony of current fact and historical record. He is watching the herds of bison journeying as they journeyed centuries ago.

16

THE CALVING SEASON

Winter in Hayden Valley, as in much of the high country of Yellowstone Park, is slow to fade. Although most of the snow on the main meadows has melted by mid-April, occasional ravines or wooded islands still harbor leftover drifts. Crystalline and mushy under the warm spring sun, the mounds of snow shrink visibly day by day, leaving in their place a soil sodden with moisture, which coaxes the first spring-green shoots to feel their way through last year's spent herbage.

As spring draws on, certain buffalo cows among the herds give indications that they are soon to calve. Heavy with the weight of their infants, which they have borne for some 270 to 285 days, they wander restlessly, at times ignoring their herd mates to strike out on lonely treks.

When the time comes for a cow to deliver her offspring, she may grunt, wallow, and paw in her discomfort, sometimes even tearing viciously into a young pine tree. Soon she stops, strains, and begins to hump her back in the first seizures of labor.

As the moment of delivery draws closer, the cow selects a site for the birth of her calf; very likely she will forsake all companionship and retire to the cover of a ravine or clump of trees, or she may continue with her herd, generally a small band of cows, the majority of them pregnant.

The birth itself takes from twenty minutes to almost two hours. The cow usually prepares to calve by flattening herself out, on one side, stretching her legs straight out and straining her neck backward. When the infant starts to emerge, she raises her upper hind leg to facilitate its passage, occasionally jerking the leg in violent spasms. The calf comes forth enveloped in a grayish-blue fetal membrane, portions of which tear and strip in the movements of labor. An occasional cow may give birth while standing; the emerging calf hangs suspended for a few minutes and then falls to the ground.

Once the birth is complete, the mother begins to devour the membrane surrounding her calf. Although these instinctive actions normally expose the infant within moments, I was alarmed once by the aspect of a calf that emerged with his face so tightly swathed he seemed in imminent danger of suffocation. His mother appeared unconcerned, and went about munching the membrane in systematic fashion, commencing not at his face, but at one hind leg, where the tissue had already ruptured. At long last she reached and consumed the wrapping about his head, and I was relieved when the infant gave a promising squirm.

For the first half hour following birth, the mother licks her calf avidly. An innate craving—not the desire to "clean" her calf —causes this behavior. The sudden carnivorous appetite, surprising in an animal whose normal diet is vegetarian, is an aspect of the same instinctive craving that induced her to consume the membrane enveloping him when he emerged and will find her devouring the afterbirth when it is expelled some time in the next few hours.

Shortly after the calf is born, nearby herd members meander over to inspect the new arrival, some to sniff him and lick his coat. His mother tolerates most of these visitors, although she may indicate irritation with a feeble horn swing, or chase an occasional caller away.

About twenty or thirty minutes after birth, a buffalo calf will try to rise for the first time. Anyone who has seen the first struggles of a domestic calf will be able to imagine his behavior. Early attempts at walking—or even just standing on all fours—are more spectacle than achievement, for the infant's desire outpaces his gangling ability. After propping his four weak, bowed legs into a precarious balance, he soon begins to totter, and eventually collapses in a disjointed heap. The spindly legs will not coordinate, and some of his attempts to stand terminate in headfirst tumbles or backward somersaults. Even when he manages a stable stance at last, his difficulties are not over, for he will have the same trouble coordinating when he tries to lie down. After a while, however, he learns to get up with fair skill, and weaves around in petite, spider-like steps.

Soon after he rises, the calf makes his first muddled efforts at nursing. Again like a domestic calf or any nursing animal, he pokes his muzzle here and there under his mother's belly, perhaps probing a little with his tongue. He is likely to test the region between her front legs, with naturally disappointing results. Eventually, as a rule unassisted by his mother, the calf directs his random searchings toward the rear, until at last he reaches a teat and is rewarded with milk. Thereafter he moves directly to the udder when hungry.

Suckling quite naturally establishes a close relationship between the infant buffalo and his mother. At the start, however, their association is mechanical, even accidental. The calf chooses to be with his mother simply because she is the first creature he meets. During a critical number of hours after birth, a "sensitive period," he is susceptible to falling into an attachment with any nearby animal—buffalo or other. Since his own mother is closest to him at this period, he is most likely to associate with her, but he might just as easily pair up with a nearby bull or even a human being. My field notes from Yellowstone National Park provide an example of such random selection:

A yearling bull approaches a mother and her five-hour-old calf, sniffs the calf and wanders on. The calf follows him. He breaks into a trot, evidently trying to get rid of the calf, which still tags along. Attempting to retrieve her calf, the mother runs after the fleeing pair. The bull continues his efforts to throw off the calf by prodding it lightly, but to no avail. After about a hundred feet of trotting, the trio comes to a stop, and the calf voluntarily returns to its mother.

When a newborn buffalo mistakes another creature for its own mother, it is exhibiting behavior found in the newborn of many other species. The phenomenon has received increasing notice in recent years, but it had already been documented as far back as 1873. In that year a British pioneer in the field of animal psychology published a study on the nature of instinct in young birds and mammals. Among his observations were some remarks about the selection of parent figures by the infants of various species: "Chickens, as soon as they are able to walk, will follow any moving object . . . When guided by sight alone, they seem to have no more disposition to follow a hen than to follow a duck, or a human being."

This tendency in newborn creatures to become attached, or *imprinted* to certain figures—usually their parents—is characteristic of species whose offspring arrive in a fairly advanced state of development. The fledglings of ground-nesting birds like chickens, geese, and ducks are able to move around shortly after hatching. At that time the young birds imprint to their parents automatically and without any special training. Likewise, the infants of many ungulates can walk and run minutes after birth, when they will instinctively trail behind their parents. This pattern is found in sheep, goats, cattle, elk, moose, and, of course, buffalo.

The rapidity of imprinting among the offspring of these animals contrasts with the relative helplessness of other infants, such as human babies or songbird fledglings. Born or hatched in an awkward state, the less-advanced infants require prolonged care or nursing. They develop slowly under the continued attention of their parents, who are largely responsible for cultivating family ties—a process involving several days at the very least. (Human infants form their primary ties between the ages of six weeks and six months. Thus, adoption is best undertaken before the third month; from then on, babies show increasingly severe emotional reactions to foster parents.)

In precocial species like buffalo, the union between infant and adult must take place shortly after birth. Otherwise the calf, advanced in development and without attachments, might run away. The necessary union is generally insured by imprinting, which offers the infant the best chance of survival by guaranteeing parental care.

Although imprinting operates normally to unite mother and offspring, it is more often remembered for its accidental quirks. With suddenness—and apparent blindness—some infants become imprinted to the most unlikely of parent figures. Goslings reared by human beings often ignore other geese and traipse after people. Freshly hatched ducklings will follow a ducklike decoy, as well as a box, a balloon, or even a model train. A substitute parent does not necessarily have to be in motion—chicks will go so far as to nestle around a prominently placed cardboard circle or triangle.

Young mammals are more discriminating in what they follow, usually selecting objects that are in motion. A newborn zebra or wildebeest will tag along behind a moving car. A lamb raised by a keeper may become so attached to people that it will shun other sheep. (Ranchers will do away with such an animal, aware that it won't stick with the herd once it has grown up.)

Imprinting, in addition to establishing the bond between parent and offspring, helps to establish other associations between members of the species. Just as the newborn calf cements his attachment to his mother, he forms lesser bonds with animals in the surrounding herd, taking his first steps toward communal living. As the maturing calf makes more and more acquaintances among his herd mates, he becomes imprinted—or socialized—to them in particular and to all buffalo in general.

Other species cling just as tenaciously to attachments formed by imprinting. Abnormal bonds, for example, may lead to some bizarre fixations, especially during the breeding season. Birds reared by hand often fail to reproduce: instead of responding to their own kind, they attempt to mate with their keepers. One bittern in the Amsterdam Zoo even performed the ritual of nest-relief in front of his attendant, thereby inviting him to step into the nest and incubate.

When young buffalo fail to imprint to their mothers, they straggle alone through the herd and eventually perish. An occasional orphan, however, may be adopted by a mother with a calf of her own, giving observers the impression that the cow has had twin offspring. Such adoptions probably explain the occasional reports of twins, as very few twin births have ever been substantiated.

In the immense historic herds, infant buffalo were occasionally orphaned during the turmoil of the chase. Often the young animals wound up in camp, as Father Louis Hennepin noted while hunting with the Illinois: "When they [the Indians] kill any Cows, their young Calves follow them, and lick their Hands. They bring them to their Children, who eat them, after having for some time play'd with them."

More than a century later Meriwether Lewis recounted an experience with an orphaned animal. "I met with a buffaloe calf," he wrote, "which attached itself to me and continued to follow close at my heels untill I embarked and left it."

Later visitors to the plains sometimes attempted to train such abandoned calves to follow them. Audubon placed a finger in the mouth of one of the creatures so that it could suckle for a time— presumably to see if it would accept human companionship. George Catlin held his hands over the eyes of another and breathed a few strong puffs into its nostrils, apparently trying to condition the calf to his own scent. By means of this ruse he was able to ride "several miles into the encampment, with the little prisoner busily following the heels of my horse the whole way, as closely and affectionately as its instinct would attach it to the company of its dam!" Some of Catlin's calves even followed "into the stable where our horses were led."

Perhaps such techniques for transferring motherhood were superfluous. There have been a number of accounts of young calves following horsemen for lack of any other beings to imprint to. A fur trader who came across some calves that had lagged behind the main herd during a stampede reported that they "remain quiet and allow themselves to be taken. Having been a little handled, they follow like dogs." Two of them, in fact, trailed the man's horse right into the trading post.

Recently, the head animal keeper of Yellowstone Park had a similar experience with a one-day-old calf. As he rode his horse past the baby animal, it ran over and began to follow him. It trotted along behind him with such persistence that he finally had to rope it, carry it back, and release it next to its mother.

For the first week or so of the calf's life, the buffalo cow distinguishes her own offspring from other infants not by sight but by

her finely developed sense of smell. So important is scent to ungulates in identification of their young that it can even be used to
deceive them. If, for instance, a ewe loses her lamb, she will accept
another if it is cloaked in the skin of her own dead infant; once she
gets used to the new lamb covered with the old scent, the skin may
be removed.

As the calf ages, his mother gradually learns to discern certain
of his physical characteristics, and thereafter can identify him by
sight alone. Also helpful in identification are the individual calls of
mother and calf. After a short time, the two animals can recognize
each other easily by sound alone.

During the first few days of his life, the calf remains close to
his mother. She regularly licks his coat, thus continuing to cement
ties between the two. She does not coddle him, but maintains a
gentle, firm control. When he fails to fall into line, she disciplines
with a well-aimed butt or a brief charge.

A mother buffalo will tolerate a certain amount of mischief
from her calf, especially when he is young and eager to nurse. He
may attempt to rouse her when she is lying down, placing his chin
across her back, rubbing against her, butting her or even climbing
on top of her. Eventually she will succumb to his demands and
rise to permit nursing. Later on, however, as her calf grows older,
the cow will be less receptive to such appeals, as a field note for
late June in the Wildlife Park illustrates:

Mother terminates seven minutes of nursing by moving away from
her calf and starting to graze. Calf tries to continue suckling, but
she blocks him repeatedly by lifting her leg. Soon she lies down,
but he remains standing and rubs his chin across her back. She re-
acts immediately, rising and kicking one leg so forcefully it hits
him in the head with an audible crack. Calf winces, twitches his
head a bit, then reclines, whereupon the mother lies down again.

As the calving season progresses, the accumulation of calves
leads in time to the formation of small "maternity clubs." These
bands of mothers with their new offspring drift within the main
herd, or, more likely, wander near its outer limits. The calves help
to initiate this grouping, for at an age of two or three weeks they
begin to keep company with one another as often as with their
mothers.

Maternity clubs govern the mood of the rest of the buffalo

herd. With the arrival of the season's first calves, the mothers become cautious, retreating from disturbances more precipitately
than at other times. Their influence on the entire herd is clearly
discernible in the number of stampedes they touch off.

One would expect an alarmed mother to lead her infant away
from danger, yet several historical chroniclers cited instances in
which fleeing cows actually abandoned their calves. Meriwether
Lewis once described "a large drove of buffaloe pursued by wolves
that . . . at length caught a calf which was unable to keep up
with the herd." He explained that "the cows only defend their
young so long as they are able to keep up with the herd, and seldom return any distance in surch of them."

In a scattering of historical accounts, however, buffalo mothers did return to look for lost infants. There is even one report of a
hunter who took advantage of their maternal instincts. While
chasing buffalo, the shrewd hideman roped and tethered several
calves, "thus causing the mothers of the respective calves to drop
out of the herd and stay with their offspring, whence they could be
killed at leisure."

In general, it seems that the buffalo mothers of bygone times
defended their offspring when they could, but sometimes abandoned their calves under severe pressure from enemies.

Present-day buffalo mothers, unlike the beleaguered creatures of the early days, live in a docile world, and present a picture
of faithful attention to their young. Sometimes when separated
from their calves, they will show remarkable persistence in attempting to rejoin them, as my field notes indicate:

Wichita Mountains Wildlife Refuge: After being released from
twenty hours of confinement inside a corral, a mother immediately
searched for and eventually found her month-old calf.

Wind Cave National Park: As a herd stampeded away, one cow
stopped abruptly and returned a hundred feet to retrieve her young
calf, who had become confused within a tangle of shrubs.

Yellowstone National Park: A cow kept vigil by her dead calf for
two days, departing only temporarily to graze, and returning to
drive off scavenging ravens and coyotes.

Such attention may also be accompanied by acts of apparent
courage, as a buffalo mother, when menaced by man or beast, is

likely to put up a vigorous defense. Without hesitation she will advance in slow, threatening steps or swiftly charge to protect her offspring against intruders. During my own observations, I recorded twelve attacks against people (mostly me), five against horses, two against ravens, and one each against an antelope and a porcupine.

Although early buffalo mothers are known to have abandoned their calves in the haste of flight, they would apparently stand and fight if cornered. "When a cow and her very young calf are attacked by wolves," wrote Audubon, "the cow bellows and sometimes runs at the enemy, and not infrequently frightens him away."

"Buffalo Jones" wrote of five instances in which his wranglers roped calves only to be charged by their irate mothers. His colorful copy portrayed one cow who "dashed at the enemy with all the ferocity of her outraged nature; her eyes looked like balls of fire; her hair bristled all over with battle . . . and her tail stuck straight out like the jib-boom of a yacht—the charging brute barely missed impaling him on her sharp horns . . ."

It was also said that buffalo bulls were staunch defenders of calves. Reports contributing to this view abound in historical and even scientific writings, but they appear to be little more than inflated hearsay. One impressive account told of a wolf attack in the spring of 1868. Although the writer did not set down his observations until years later, he managed to recall in meticulous detail how a pack of wolves had surrounded three sides of a herd and moved "quickly towards a lot of cows with young calves." It was at this point, according to his story, that the animals went into formation:

At once the cows started by pushing the calves, aided by the bulls, toward the center of the herd. The cows then formed a circle with the calves inside and the young bulls forming another circle outside of the cows, and the old and large bulls still making another circle outside their flanks, thus protecting the calves from the wolves.

Though musk oxen are known to form protective circles of this nature, there is scant evidence to support the idea of such a formation among buffalo. Buffalo do, however, fend off wolf attacks by massing into a tight group; such a bunching may have been the visual basis for the foregoing account of a defense system engineered by some highly canny early buffalo.

Other versions of a ringlike defense system have appeared from time to time. In one, plainsmen asserted that bulls traversed regular beats around the herd in order to guard their cows and calves, coursing around them repeatedly until they had trodden circular paths into the prairie. The men pointed for evidence to the "thousands of circles" left behind by these diligent bulls. But the circles had actually been produced by the action of several types of fungus. Expanding concentrically, these parasitic growths enriched the soil where they grew, inducing rings of luxuriant vegetation. More fanciful observers, instead of attributing the circles to buffalo, resorted to legend, giving them their common name—"fairy rings."

If accounts of the guarding efforts of bulls do not fall apart of their own failings, they are largely discredited by current observation. In several years of experience with the herds, I have never seen bulls defending cows or calves. Nor is such defense likely, since adult bulls do not normally join the cow groups until the rut begins in July, when most calves are at least six weeks old and no longer helpless.

Even when tiny, however, buffalo calves are not exactly defenseless. If cornered, they will counterattack readily—one three-day-old calf we captured charged and butted with spirit, though its frail assaults were more comic than fearsome. Older calves will also struggle to resist capture, and may be strong enough to knock a man off his feet.

At times, however, instead of confronting their enemies, infant buffalo will quietly secrete themselves in foliage. This hiding trait, common among young elk or pronghorn, is seldom reported in buffalo. I first observed it in the Wildlife Park after a group of us had just driven a herd from one enclosure to another. When a head count revealed one calf missing, we coursed back over the area, but found no trace of the lost infant. Twenty-eight hours later, a lone cow returned to the gate dividing the two enclosures. Her grunting and pacing prompted us to let her return to the original enclosure. When we opened the gate, she proceeded directly to a clump of sagebrush a hundred feet from the entrance. She grunted softly. At once a bedraggled calf rose from the brush near a fallen log, rushed over and started nursing greedily. By this time we realized that we had stepped over the log only ten feet from the calf without discovering the infant; the calf, of course, had not budged to betray its presence.

In the historic herds most of the calves that hid in the foliage had fallen behind when their herds were fleeing hunters. One early hunter described their pathetic attempts at concealment: "The calves," he wrote, "endeavor to secrete themselves when they are exceedingly put to it on a level prairie, where nought can be seen but the short grass of six or eight inches in height save an occasional bunch of wild sage in a few inches higher, to which the poor affrighted things will run, and, dropping on their knees, will push their noses under it, and into the grass, where they will stand for hours with their eyes shut, imagining themselves securely hid . . ."

The infrequent records of concealment by calves indicate that hiding animals are generally under two months of age. An older calf can keep up with most stampedes and thus has little reason to hide.

When the growing calf is about two months old, he takes on some marks of maturity. His back begins to arch into the characteristic hump and his grunt loses its nasal quality, deepening to the gruffer, more guttural voice of his elders. As he reaches an age of about two and a half months, his reddish-orange pelage—the salient characteristic of a young calf—begins to darken, and within another month the molt to a deep brown is largely completed.

As this color change progresses, the maturing calf comes to resemble his elders not only in general appearance but also in many patterns of behavior. No longer a pampered ward of his mother, he fits his daily activities into the rhythms of the group as a whole, grazing, resting, and drinking at the same time as his adult associates. In the next few months the bond with his mother gradually loosens as his periods of suckling become shorter and less frequent. When he is weaned at an age of about nine months, he is spending more time with other calves and yearlings than with his own mother.

At the end of his first year he weighs three or four hundred pounds—a tenfold increase over the thirty or forty he weighed at birth—and bears spike horns six or more inches long. By this time his mother is likely to give birth to another infant. Shortly after the arrival of the new offspring, she will chase off her old calf with frequent aggressive attacks. Although a few youngsters—usually females—may linger and follow their mothers for some additional months, the ties for most are firmly broken. They are now independent members of the buffalo society into which they were born.

With the arrival of another calving season, the sequence of birth and growth continues, paced by the reproductive cycle of the cow. After bearing her calf, the cow remains sexually inactive for several weeks. At the end of this period she again comes into heat, displaying a sexual fever that will initiate the new rutting season, the next important event in the round of buffalo life.

17

THE RUTTING SEASON

THOSE OF YOU WHO WOULD ENGAGE IN BUFFALO-watching could select no better time than July or August; two or three days of waiting and watching should surely reward you with a glimpse of a majestic and dramatic grassland pageant, the rut among the buffalo. The excitement begins slowly, as a restlessness spreads through the herds. First the cow groups clump together into larger gatherings, to be joined by bulls straggling in from their own bachelor herds, which are now beginning to dissolve. Cows and bulls alike stir with the mating fever that ushers in the rutting season, and a few individuals begin to move about in pairs. The courting has begun.

Most buffalo, at other times inclined to spend the greater part of each day idly grazing or ruminating, are intensely active during this period. Although you can scout them in any of several refuges, their activities will probably be most spectacular in the larger areas. You might want to choose Wind Cave National Park or the Wichita Mountains Wildlife Refuge if you appreciate the convenience—and protection—afforded by a car; but if you relish a little hiking in order to capture a sense of wilderness discovery, the best place will be Yellowstone Park.

The rut builds slowly from around the middle of June, varying a little in schedule from south to north. Activity is well under way in all regions by July, reaching its peak in the central plains in late July and early August and in the northern Canadian range in mid-August. (The later rut of northern herds seems to be an adaptation favoring the survival of newborn calves, who thus miss the worst of the raw weather of early spring.) In all areas, the rut wanes toward the end of September.

Throughout the season, the most frenzied rutting activity occurs in the cooler periods of the day—shortly after dawn and again near dusk, abating only in the event of strong winds or rain. Some bulls recognize no moratorium and remain standing long after most of the herd has settled down to a lazy rest, even carrying on their rutting behavior throughout the night.

Certain bulls court their cows so attentively that the couples ramble about the meadows like so many clockwork toys. Rival bulls hover, irritable and restless, at the fringes of the activity, wallowing at intervals, stirring up plumes of dust that spiral hazily into the hot, still air. Guttural bellowings rumble across the plains for miles. Chunks of sod vault skyward and saplings wither and bend as relentless fury is vented in attacks on earth and trees.

The cause of this remarkable behavior is the humble buffalo cow, who comes into heat at some time during the rutting season and remains in this condition for about two days. If she is not bred during this time, she comes back into heat after about three weeks. The bulls, by contrast, are sexually active during the entire rut.

When a cow first enters heat, her vulva becomes swollen and starts to ooze mucus and lymph. These changes are obvious to a trained observer, and must also be unmistakable to buffalo bulls. The aroused animals course back and forth through the herd, inspecting each cow by turn in search of one that is ready to mate.

Each time a bull completes his inspection of a cow, he wrinkles his face in a curious grimace that might be called "lip curling," although the name describes only the ending of a complex expression. With neck outstretched, head held level, and nostrils distended, the animal curls his upper lip to expose the gums, maintaining the pose for a few seconds.

A bull will curl his lip in this fashion after examining a cow's vulva, and sometimes after sniffing a cow's urine on the grass. (Even cows may lip-curl, usually after inspecting objects with strange or unfamiliar odors.) An animal wearing the expression looks as if he is both excited and repelled by the odor in his nostrils.

Lip-curling seems to be stimulated by scents. We do not know the precise reason for the expression or whether it serves a function; we do know, however, that it is flourished by many other ungulates, among them musk oxen, sheep, goats, cattle, camels, and llamas.

After a mature buffalo bull inspects several cows to determine their degree of heat, he selects one for courting. Standing parallel to her side or rump, he remains within five feet of her, warning off intruders with threatening postures, brief charges, or actual attacks. His serious rage is reserved for bulls, but he may even drive away the calf or yearling of his own mate. His close relative, the Indian bison or gaur, "tends" his chosen mate in much the same fashion.

A single bull with a single cow is the rule, a union zoologists refer to as "temporary monogamous mateship." Because the tending bull is usually challenged and may be displaced by a dominant bull, the pairing might last for only a few minutes; more often, it continues for one or two days. Whatever its duration, the bull will eventually move on to another mate, and thus may serve several cows during the season.

At any one time, however, a bull has quite enough to handle with a single cow, and will be content to trail closely beside her. On occasion a domineering bull may try to guide his mate by swinging his horns toward her or standing in front of her in a threatening manner until she moves in the desired direction; but even when he resorts to threats and persuasion, the cow remains essentially in control. She can dodge her mate's attentions and wander off on her own, or rush off with a stampede of neighboring buffalo, leaving her consort no choice but to join the group. At times she will elude his devotion and dash away for several hundred feet, only to be chased by him—and a bevy of eligible bachelors as well.

Many an amorous bull is rebuffed by a reluctant cow, his advances met with a swing of the head, a thrust of the horns, or a

swift kick. Thus harassed, he will either move out of her immediate range or ignore the attacks and continue to press his suit. Once
I watched an old veteran sustain a smashing blow in the nose from
the hind hoof of a prospective mate; he never blinked.

Initial reluctance from the mate-to-be is standard procedure in
several other mammalian species (including, of course, our own).
In wildebeest herds, the female in heat acts embarrassed by all the
attention she attracts, giving the impression that she desires nothing more than to be let alone. If too closely pressed by a bull, she
may even seek relief from his attention by lying down. But the
persistent efforts of a corps of attentive bulls ensures that most
wildebeest cows, no matter how reluctant, will eventually succumb to breeding.

Likewise, the determination of attending buffalo bulls guaran-
tees that most females in the herd will be bred. When a bull's first
advances are repelled, he will continue to make his intentions
known by standing and swinging his head toward his chosen cow.
Eventually he will try to put his chin on her rump, most likely to
be thwarted when she dodges away. He may even get so far as
to climb up on her and wrap his forelegs around her rump, only to
have her slip out from under him.

After some hours of this tending, the bull may lick his mate's
fur, and she may even return the favor. In the gaur of India, both
bull and cow commonly carry on licking for several minutes; in
the buffalo, however, prolonged licking is infrequent.

The courting buffalo bull often utters brief panting sounds
shortly before attempting to mount his cow. Thus warned of his
approach, the cow may shift away; but if she is receptive, he will
use his chin as a lever and swing himself up onto her rump, leaning his head against her side and pressing his forelegs together in
front of her flanks in the mounting position standard among
hoofed mammals. After he achieves insertion, he thrusts steadily
for a mere four to ten seconds until ejaculation; then he either
drops off voluntarily or releases his grip and allows his mate to
walk out from underneath.

Occasionally the mounting bull's preponderance in weight (he
may outweigh his mate by as much as a thousand pounds) and his
rough behavior during copulation will harm the cow. Damage is
most likely to occur on her flanks, where the striking and rubbing
of his front hoofs may leave bloody wounds. Among European

bison, heavy bulls have been known to mortally injure a young cow by breaking her spinal column.

Copulation in American buffalo is of such short duration that a person scanning one section of a large herd may well miss a mating going on in another; this may explain why few observers have ever witnessed the phenomenon. Brief copulation is the general rule among other grass-eating ungulates (Gerenuk antelope, to give an extreme example, accomplish the act at a trot while the male is balanced on the female's flanks). In contrast, wolves, lions, tigers, and bears may remain attached for hours. The prey species, then—the grass-eaters like buffalo and antelope, which are in constant danger of attack—copulate only momentarily, whereas their enemies, the large carnivores, can afford to take more time.

The moment of copulation among buffalo usually attracts the attention of nearby bachelor bulls. These soon converge on the mated couple and follow them wherever they go, to the annoyance of the courting male, who remains with his partner for some time after the coupling, repelling intruders with horn swings, short charges, or even vicious attacks.

When driving away such intruders, as well as when challenging rivals or guarding their mates, buffalo bulls emit loud bellows. The roars of the aroused animals blend together and roll away from the herd in a steady, guttural rumble, a striking animal call that has taxed the descriptive powers of many a plains journalist: ". . . like a foghorn—the earth seemed to fairly tremble with the vibration . . ." ". . . like the sound of distant thunder . . ." ". . . like the murmurs of the ocean waves beating against the shore . . ."

Indeed, in mid-roar, the buffalo bull seems to merit such effusions. Mouth wide open, tongue hanging way out, belly rising conspicuously with each utterance, he produces an impressive bellow that closely resembles the roar of a lion. Such is the force of the call that it carries three miles in still air, possibly even farther, although Canadian explorer Henry Youle Hind's assertion that the sound traveled "fully twenty miles" is extravagant. Hind also claimed that the sound was "best perceived by applying the ear to a badger hole." I cannot personally vouch for badger holes as megaphones, but I did frequently listen for the direction of the bellows in order to locate herds hidden among Hayden Valley's rolling hills. Surely lone stragglers or wandering groups homed in on rutting herds in the same way.

The bellows of a buffalo bull range from a soft purr to a fierce roar, varying in tone according to the emotional state of the animal. When alone or without competition, he bellows softly and briefly, but if his lone bellow elicits a response from another bull, he comes back with a long, echoing roar. The louder bellowing, like the growling of a dog, serves as a warning to rivals. If another bull answers the challenge, the first bull steps up the pace and increases the volume of his rumblings in an effort to bluff his rival into retreat.

A defending bull need not see his opponent to sense challenge —he will usually answer any bellow he hears, which may lead to some comical interchanges. I have heard bulls hurl a pugnacious response to each distant rumble of a thunderstorm; a few have even grumbled an answer to my own crudely voiced imitations of a bellow. (One is reminded of bull alligators that bellow in reply to low-flying airplanes or passing dump trucks.)

Certain bulls keep up this vocal show of force by bellowing constantly, even while stampeding, swimming, or ruminating. They may interrupt each roll of an energetic wallow to roar lustily through the dust. Even as they graze, the most vociferous bulls may forget the business at hand and stick out their tongues to bellow—often losing a mouthful of grass in the process.

In addition to bellowing frequently, rutting bulls increase certain grooming actions, customarily in a three-part sequence of pawing, wallowing, and horning. Although each act may be carried out by itself, all are likely to appear in combination. The pattern typically begins when the animal paws the earth with a front hoof, a logical first step, since it seems to have originated in the desire to scrape out a bare patch of ground for the grooming actions that follow.

One of these actions is wallowing, in which the bull lies down and rolls over on his back several times. Occasionally he thrashes so furiously that puffs of dirt shoot from his hoofs, and his hump slams into the ground with an audible thud.

The bull often completes his grooming treatment with some horning. Kneeling, he prods his horns into the earth or rubs his head back and forth on a bump on the ground. Trees, too, are jabbed; as ersatz opponents they receive deep gouges from the lethal horns. The bulls rub on them, butt them, thrash their branches, debark and sometimes even uproot them in their rage. The fury of such assaults is indicated in a few excerpts from my field notes: "Seven-foot-high lodgepole pine completely uprooted; two-inch diameter pine broken into three pieces; woody core of mature pine splintered to a depth of one inch."

Early observers of pawing, wallowing, and horning had a simple explanation for the activities. Clearly, the poor buffalo was undergoing seasonal molting. In his condition of near-nudity, his skin was irritated by the emergence of new pelage, scratched by prickly seeds and ravaged by the mosquitoes, black flies, and other winged tormenters that seemed to converge on him at this inopportune time. Surely he thrashed about in self-defense.

Pierre-Jean De Smet came to favor this theory after a curious adventure on the plains. Plagued by vast numbers of mosquitoes during a march through Montana, the missionary was astonished when the winged pests suddenly vanished—just as his party came across thousands of buffalo. De Smet queried his Indian companions about the disappearance of the mosquitoes, and was informed that they had all been drawn to the prodigious numbers of buffalo covering the plains for as far as the eye could see. When he saw rolling and thrashing animals in the distance, the priest's sympathies were naturally aroused. He jotted down his interpretation of the scene, expressing concern for "these noble animals throwing the earth on their bodies by means of their horns and feet, or rolling themselves in the dust . . . in the endeavor to rid themselves of their vexatious followers." Undoubtedly the insects had caused the wallowing.

There is a major flaw in this view. Only the bull buffalo engages in increased wallowing at this season. Since insects hover over the entire herd, one wonders why the molting cow should be exempt from attack.

In other ways the wallowing sequence fails to conform to the insect theory. Although rutting bulls use established wallowing craters if any are at hand, they will wallow almost anywhere, for the desire to wallow apparently outweighs the choice of location. Thus, when advancing toward a competitor, a bull will wallow right on his line of march instead of searching for a suitable patch of bare ground. Although he makes the gesture of tearing up a little sod beforehand, it seems curious, if we are to believe he is seeking relief from insect attack, that he will roll over on a grassy meadow where he cannot raise dust to soothe his distressed body.

In another strange quirk of wallowing activity, rutting bulls may sometimes stop to urinate feebly. Though at first this appears to be a completely irrelevant action, it acquires significance when compared with actions of Spanish bulls used for bullfighting. When these animals are transferred from the comparative calm of their home pastures to the hostile confines of an arena, they will urinate almost immediately. Behaviorists speculate that the desire to urinate at this time is triggered by conflict. Desperate to escape, the bulls are thwarted by the bullfighters and the walls of the arena. Buffalo bulls in the rut are faced with a different kind of conflict—when approached· by rival bulls, they must choose between advancing and taking flight.

An additional aspect of this urination may be an effort to mark out a territory, much as wolves warn trespassers by urinating along the boundaries of their hunting preserves or as dogs lift their legs on trees or hydrants to stake out their home ground. Bulls of the European bison are said to mark their own domain by urinating in wallows, rolling in the moistened earth, and then rubbing against trees with their urine-dampened fur, leaving this scent to notify other wisent of their claim to the area. American bison go through a similar wallowing ritual, yet their sequence of urinating, rolling, and rubbing (in the regions where trees are available) has not been interpreted as the actual marking of a territory. Additional observation and study may still confirm this trait in the species.

So far as we know, urinating in the buffalo bulls remains primarily related to conflict and tension, as does the whole pattern of pawing, wallowing, and horning. Thus a bull wallows when he may expect opposition from a rival—while courting his mate, confronting a strange herd, or approaching another bull. So automatic is the response that the moment two solitary bulls wander into each other's view, they may paw and wallow simultaneously.

Similar pawing among domestic bulls was given a novel interpretation by a French scholar writing in 1614. Each antagonist, he explained, pawed the ground until he had dug a large hole in which he could both conceal himself and remove his opponent from view. This would presumably eliminate further attacks.

The theory, however absurd, highlights an important aspect

THE

NATURAL HISTORY OF

THE BUFFALO

The three pictures at the left trace a buffalo calf from the moment of birth to his first attempts at walking a few minutes later. The infant begins to emerge enveloped in a grayish-blue fetal membrane, which usually ruptures slightly to release a portion of fluid and reveal the calf's tiny hoofs. As soon as the calf is born, the mother devours the membrane and then avidly licks the moist fur of her offspring. Prompted perhaps by this continued attention, the calf begins to lift his wobbly head and is soon making his first efforts to get up. Pushing upward with his hindlegs and attempting to straighten his forelegs, he manages to stand for a few moments, only to abruptly collapse into a sprawling heap. Before long his persistent efforts succeed, and he gets up and takes his first steps within ten minutes after birth, a shorter period than that reported for calves of domestic cattle. Shortly after standing, he probes between his mother's legs for the udder and starts to nurse when he finds it. Within an hour the precocious calf runs in circles around his mother.

Young buffalo commence their patterns of play (right) almost as soon as they can stand. The light-colored calf kicking his legs in the air is a few days old; similar bucking behavior has been observed in a newborn buffalo only thirty-five minutes after birth. The three calves in the center photograph have recently molted from the juvenile coat of reddish-orange to the usual dark-brown fur of their elders; in their playful battles they butt their heads together and shove each other back and forth. The bull "mounting" another bull (bottom) is about a year old; such play appears in calves only six days old.

During the rutting season, a cow in heat (above) is "tended" by a mature bull, who remains close to the side of his mate, following her every move. Another bull (below) examines the vulva and urine of the cow, then raises his head and wrinkles his face in a "lip-curling" expression after each inspection. Rutting bulls sometimes settle rank among themselves by vicious battles (opposite). The contests typically terminate after a few violent shoves, though some may end in a definite rout (lower right).

A cow firmly rubs her horns up and down the trunk of a lodgepole pine, which has already had much of the bark stripped off by the jabbing of other buffalo. Repeated horning like this can kill a tree.

Rolling up onto his hump in a dirt wallow, a bull stirs up clouds of dust with his vigorous actions. (In similar fashion, the bulls on Plate I have lined up to roll in the soft mud of a wet wallow.)

"Big Medicine," here standing beside a normally pigmented buffalo, was a partially albinistic bull. After his death in 1959, his skin was mounted for display in the Montana Historical Society at Helena.

The end point of bison evolution in the Old World is the European bison or wisent. The small group below is part of a herd of several hundred inhabiting the Bialowieza Forest of Poland.

Grizzly attacking a buffalo

Bull harassed by wolves

Pronghorn passing near a herd

Black-footed ferret at a burrow

Burrowing owls with rattlesnake

Prairie dog and buffalo herd

of bovine behavior. In the view of the Frenchman, the trench-digging bull is attempting to get rid of the conflict he feels on facing his rival. The pawing and wallowing of buffalo bulls is similarly related to conflict, for an advancing bull is struggling with two opposing urges—to attack and to flee. His inability to act resolves itself in a kind of compromise behavior, and he paws, wallows, or horns. These motions, of little use in the encounter with the rival, have no connection with their original function, the care of the body, and thus seem irrelevant. Behaviorists theorize

The community of animals that shares the grassland with the buffalo includes predators like the grizzly bear and wolf, other grazers like the pronghorn, and numerous smaller species like the varied inhabitants of a prairie dog town:

The crude pencil sketch of a grizzly attacking a buffalo was made by a Sioux Indian; predation by the grizzly has been reported by only a handful of observers.

Prey has momentarily turned on predator in George Catlin's portrayal of a band of wolves harassing an aged bull; the buffalo succumbed in time to the continued attacks of the wolves, but not before doing away with two of their number, which were, as Catlin said, "crushed to death by the feet or the horns of the bull."

The pronghorn passing calmly through an open corridor in a buffalo herd has no reason to be concerned about the larger, occasionally aggressive buffalo about him—he can nimbly outrun their charges within moments.

Poised at the entrance to a prairie dog burrow, the black-footed ferret is an important predator of the dogs; now so rare that it's listed as an "endangered" species, it has been decimated by poisoning campaigns mounted by ranchers and government trappers and has also suffered from a scarcity of dog towns on a grassland presently devoted to livestock.

Other residents of a prairie dog town are the two fledgling burrowing owls, here shown running from the strike of a prairie rattlesnake.

From the elevated rim of soil surrounding his burrow, a prairie dog surveys an approaching buffalo herd, barking in brief chirps that serve as an alarm signal.

that such "displacement activity" occurs when an animal is beset by urges he cannot satisfy. The nervous system of the frustrated animal helps him to find a compromise activity, and he grooms his body.

Displacement mannerisms resembling those of buffalo are found in many other mammals. In the stress of the rut, wildebeest bulls paw the ground, rub their faces in bare dirt, and horn trees. Pawing is also common in other ungulates—among them horses, musk oxen, ibexes, tapirs, and rhinoceroses. Swamp rabbits and cottontails vigorously rake the sod with their forepaws when confronting rival males. And goats, sheep, and Himalayan tahrs stamp their front hoofs under similar circumstances.

The displacement activities of many other species include actions normally used in caring for the body. Rival starlings may preen their feathers instead of actually battling each other. Fighting rats groom their fur between bouts of scuffling, as do cats hopelessly lost in an experimental maze. An elephant alone on the veld calmly pampers his hide, picking up water or earth with the end of his trunk and throwing it over his back; when he feels conflict at the approach of an intruder, however, the same action becomes a displacement activity, and he frenziedly throws stones, leaves, or chunks of earth over himself and into the air.

Human beings also engage in special "cosmetic" actions during moments of conflict. When ill at ease, we may groom ourselves simply for the sake of doing something—we scratch our heads, moisten our lips, or bite our nails. A nervous woman driver primps her hair while being questioned by a police officer; a shy job applicant constantly rubs his chin during a critical interview. These unconscious gestures that betray our inner feelings occur most frequently when we first meet others, a time when hidden fears and antagonisms are lurking just below the surface.

In buffalo, the pawing and horning of rutting bulls can also be considered in another light—they may be substitutes for actual fighting. Confronted by an adversary he doesn't dare attack, an angered bull smashes his horns into a sapling pine; even in the absence of a rival, he may release his pent-up rage in this manner. In domestic squabbles among human beings, husbands and wives will ordinarily take out their aggressive feelings on substitute targets—slamming a door, throwing a plate, or banging a fist on the table. An angered blackbird will redirect his aggressions to peck furiously at twigs or leaves instead of attacking his opponent (often a larger creature who might fight back).

As students of behavior, we can trace the origins of displacement activity in buffalo to conflict and frustration. To other buffalo, however, the actions serve as a direct indication of mood —a challenge and a threat. Thus they supplement other warning signals—bellowing, snorting, head-shaking, and charging. Warnings may also be issued in the form of an exaggerated, stiff-legged style of walking in which the riled bull advances ominously step by step.

These simple displays of threat are often themselves enough to settle disputes. A bull bellows; his intimidated opponent understands—and turns away, indicating his submission by lowering his head. Another bull carefully avoids moving too close to an irritable superior. Peace is maintained by a general reluctance to attack; the resulting counterpoise of bluffs leads to restrained, orderly encounters and minimizes violent fighting.

Yet like all bargaining, negotiation by threat occasionally fails. A warning goes unheeded; a challenger backs up bluff with force, and a vicious battle erupts.

When two bulls meet in combat, their encounter often begins with a spectacular charge. The enraged animals eye each other from a distance of a few yards; suddenly one rushes toward the other at top speed. The skulls connect with such a powerful impact that dirt flies from the pelts of both bulls.

As they collide, the two bulls lock their horns in head-to-head contact, the standard battling hold. From then on the contest is one of skill and strength. With humps arched in mighty curves of power and tails twitching rapidly, the great beasts shove each other back and forth, the stronger often pushing the weaker several yards in one direction. At times the sparring animals are completely screened by dust thrown up from their grinding hoofs. Horns clattering together like metal on metal, heads lowered until beards brush the earth, they remain locked in their primordial battle grip. Thus poised, they can exert—or resist—the greatest force, as they lunge upward in swift, violent jabs, each trying vainly to hook his opponent, each foiled again and again by the unyielding head-to-head hold.

This splendid headlock of the buffalo is a natural regulator of violence, in most cases establishing the victor without serious injury to either animal. Damage to skulls is slight because the shock of the constant battering is cushioned by a mat of long, dense hair on each combatant's crown. Even more important in reducing the risk of injury is the shape of the horns. Like the curved spikes of several battling African bovines, buffalo horns are structured in such a way as to lock readily into a "safe" hold and inhibit fatal stabbing. Their wide front surface has ample area for pushing, but the hooked tips prevent either opponent from sliding his horns around for a deadly flank attack. (By contrast, certain solitary African bovines are equipped with simple daggerlike horns, which they use not against each other but against their enemies.)

But these built-in safeguards are not foolproof. Although each buffalo strives to protect his flanks at all times, one animal may lose his footing, slip out of the headlock, and expose himself to the deadly stab of his opponent. Thrown off balance, he will step backwards in an effort to regain the head-to-head hold.

Eventually a clear victor emerges. If a female in heat has been the cause of dispute, the victor claims the desired cow at once. But he may not enjoy the fruits of victory for long; often a stronger bull will challenge his right of possession and duel him out of his prize. Not all fighting bulls are vying for a particular female, however. Other battles break out as bulls struggle simply to set up an order of dominance among themselves.

Bulls engaging in rutting combat are usually at least three years old; top-ranking males, winners of numerous contests, are older still. This natural evolution of rank ensures that only prime adult specimens have the opportunity to breed; though potent and fertile from an age of about two years, bulls are excluded from active participation in the rut until they are five or six years old.

In these dramatic rutting contests, serious gorings are infrequent, but an outmaneuvered bull may well sustain an injury before managing to escape. Battered eyes may remain swollen for days, or a bull may limp through the herd with fresh, open wounds. (I have even seen a bull with a horn broken off at the base.) And observers do not spot every injured animal; nor can they necessarily gauge the extent of injury in wounded bulls they see. Evidence of more extensive injuries comes to light during examination of the carcasses of animals slaughtered during annual herd reductions. In Yellowstone Park and the National Bison

Range I found that most mature bulls bore scars or abscessed sores on flanks or thighs. Signs of previous rib fractures in about one fourth of the animals gave further testimony to the effective aim of past antagonists.

Rare battles may even end in the death of one opponent. This is not surprising in captive herds, where fences prevent defeated bulls from escaping; but fatalities also occur in larger areas where confinement cannot influence the outcome. A few bulls, severely mutilated in battle, with pierced lungs, ripped hides, or bellies torn open to expose the viscera, either succumb to their wounds or have to be mercifully shot later. Other animals whose ravaged carcasses are occasionally found by park attendants are presumed to be casualties of rutting battles.

In a detail from George Catlin's drawing of a rutting herd, bulls are "plunging and butting at each other in the most furious manner." One victim, feet in air, has evidently been killed in combat.

Death is still the rare exception, not only in buffalo battles, but also in the battles of most species, for fighting mammals seldom destroy members of their own kind. Questions of rank among bulls or rights to the female are generally settled by means of thrashings rather than killings. Now and then, however, animals of the same species do kill each other. An occasional elephant is mortally wounded by an adversary's tusk, a rare hippopotamus stabbed in the heart by a rival's canine tooth.

When the battle is over, the contending buffalo bulls may merely separate and remain in each other's company—with a clearer sense of their relative strength. Or the loser may slowly back away from the thrust of his assailant's horns, guarding against a final flank attack until he has withdrawn to a safe distance. Then he may go off into voluntary seclusion for a time.

Such post-battle departures from the herd have given rise to the myth of the "lone bull," whose reputation in legend outruns that of any other patriarch in the animal kingdom: "The erstwhile czar was thenceforth excommunicated," wrote one myth-maker. Some described the loser variously as "an Ishmaelite," "a compulsory recluse," "one of the most pitiable objects . . ." According to other romantics, the solitary animal was "doubtless an outcast from the herd," "ostracized," "beaten and driven off by some rebellious young bull."

The appeal of such an image appears to have overwhelmed the evidence, for most bulls departing from their herds after battle leave voluntarily. On rare occasions a loser may be chased away by the repeated threats or aggressive charges of his adversary, but even he is free to return to his old group in time, or to join a new one, remaining an "outcast" only as long as he chooses to be by himself. In general, bulls wander freely from herd to herd during the rut. Some solitary bulls leave their groups capriciously, only to return a few hours later. Other loners wander near a strange herd, look and listen for a while, then continue on their way.

It was long thought that most lone bulls were in their old age, but careful research has shown otherwise. Only a third of the lone bulls in a Canadian survey turned out to be anywhere near old age, fixed at an early seven years for the purposes of the study. The remaining two thirds were from four to six years old—in other words, just reaching full maturity.

Why do such animals leave the herd? It may be that they are tired of family life, or that the commotion of rutting disturbs them; but most likely they are simply exhausted. Maintaining a standing among neighboring bulls and preserving the right to court cows in heat requires steady, fatiguing effort—most breeding males lose from one to two hundred pounds during the rut.

Recuperation may only be possible at a far remove from the hurly-burly of herd living.

Although the great majority of lone bulls rotate between bachelorhood and group life during the rut, an occasional aged veteran truly gives up all contact with the herd and enters monastic seclusion. Either alone or with a single companion, he drifts out of established buffalo range to seek solitude near a sedge-bordered pond deep in the timber or in the remote valleys of a nearby mountain range. Some near-wedded couples of oldsters remain faithful comrades for months, possibly even for years. Recognizing these grizzled veterans by certain peculiarities in their horns, coat, or face, I have spotted the same pairs drifting around the same meadows for weeks at a time.

Many wildebeest bulls pass their last years in similar isolation. While their youthful comrades range over hundreds of miles of African veld in search of the freshest grass, the aged recluses settle down on certain hilltops where a reliable waterhole is no more than a mile distant. One antiquated wildebeest bull, easily identified by his distinctive markings, was even known to have lived on the same hilltop for thirteen years.

Such recluses are behaving according to a pattern found in several other mammalian species. Prides of lions, which may contain as many as thirty individuals, are usually surrounded by a scattering of lone, aged males. Elsewhere on the African plains, single males are to be found among such species as the waterbuck, Cape buffalo, and elephant.

The lone American buffalo bull in his autumnal years leads a quiet life. He wanders wearily for short distances, grazing and resting when the mood suits him, and in general seems sullen and spent. For him the turbulent days of the rutting season are long past and forgotten.

18

PLAY AND AGGRESSION

As RUTTING BULLS LOCK HORNS IN VICIOUS COMBAT, other buffalo ignore the fierce bellows and flying sod to frolic with abandon just a few yards away. These buffalo, the yearlings and calves of the herd, are exhibiting the curious immunity of the young to the graver concerns of their elders.

I particularly remember a group of seven exuberant calves I watched at play one afternoon. They had been grazing quietly in one section of the herd when all of a sudden they perked up their tails, kicked their hind legs in the air, and bolted across the meadow to engage in what looked like a game of tag. As they milled chaotically, one calf bounded out of the little band, inviting another to follow. A companion came forth, and the leader broke into a rapid gallop, challenging him to a race around the herd. Before long all seven were tearing about in a frenzy of activity, butting, kicking, and bounding to and fro in carefree frolic. At last, thoroughly winded, they came to a stop and stood panting heavily with their tongues hanging out.

This frivolous romp was characteristic buffalo play, as aimless and free as the games and sport of children. The phenomenon of play in human beings, buffalo, and many other species has been observed and described in detail, its causes and consequences variously interpreted; but all the theories remain in the realm of speculation, for it is in the nature of play to elude the gravity of study.

Play cannot even be very clearly defined; we can only outline its characteristics, most of them plainly evident in the activities of the spirited little band. As might be expected, the seven animals were very young, for play is naturally most frequent among calves and tapers off as the animals approach maturity; older buffalo seldom sport with the intensity and abandon of the young. Whatever the age of the animal, play is utterly carefree, undertaken with no other aim than the pleasurable sensation of motion, the expression of unrestrained joy.

The phenomenon of play is so common in most birds and mammals that its absence in a few groups is all the more conspicuous. Platypuses, sloths, anteaters, armadillos, aardvarks, hyraxes, sea cows, and manatees have never been observed in play. And in all species of fish, amphibians, reptiles, or invertebrates, play simply does not exist.

Among the birds and mammals that do play, however, the repertory is almost endless. A lion cub pounces on the tail of its mother, and she in turn may join the game by switching the tuft of her tail back and forth. A young warbler tries to dislodge a companion from its perch in a tilting match. A coyote catches, frees, and then recatches a mouse before finally eating it, and a porpoise teases small fish. Pandas turn somersaults. Puppies and bears engage in wrestling contests. European badgers play leapfrog. Monkeys dive into ponds from the highest branches of trees. Over and over again, otters will climb to the top of a mud or snow bank and slide down. Even buffalo have been caught in a similar activity— once a traveler on the plains watched a number of them "amuse themselves by jumping off a steep bank into the water four feet below, running round to climb the bank at a low place, and repeating the performance many times."

The primary patterns of buffalo play, however, are sparring, mounting, and gamboling—or often a combination of all three. Other gestures may also express the gaiety and abandon of the moment—tails are frequently held half-cocked as the young animals buck and kick, prance and bound, or utter sounds as unique as they are difficult to describe. Glancing at my field notes, I find that one young buffalo at play "spouted a brief, loud, buzzing sneeze."

———◆◆———

Of the three patterns of buffalo play, sparring is the most common. The mock skirmishes of buffalo calves are much like the battle games of household pets and their masters. Although a dog may amuse himself by clamping his jaws around his owner's hand, he will not bite hard enough to pierce the skin, and the growls he produces are feigned. Buffalo use their spike-tipped horns in tussles, but refrain from the deliberate thrusting that inflicts wounds. Viciousness is rare; there is no decisive triumph or overthrow. The absurdly uneven matching of some contestants is testimony to the whimsical character of the battles: it is hard to take seriously a duel in which a bulky five-year-old bull fights a comparatively frail yearling cow to a draw.

Playful jousts convey a mood of unmistakable good humor. An animal lying down for respite is butted back into the game, or lazily returns the blows from a reclining position. A pair of young calves "shadow-butt," each prancing back and forth to attack the space just vacated by its opponent. And, finding no partner, a young buffalo persuades a springy sapling to fight back, as in my field notes for early October in the Jackson Hole Wildlife Park: "A calf plays with one branch on a windfall lodgepole pine. When he pushes his crown against the branch, it bounces him back. After three attacks, he strikes it with a hind hoof and departs in a bucking gait with all the bravado of a victor."

The second pattern of buffalo play is mounting. Though traditionally classified as a sexual act, mounting during play lacks a truly sexual function. Preconceived notions of male or female roles must be overlooked, for partners are chosen largely at random: females mount males, males mount other males, slight animals mount stout ones, and so on. Playful mounting does, however, begin in the manner of a true sexual advance. One individual places his chin on a partner's rump or actually jumps on, clasping his forelegs around the other's flanks and riding for a while. There is no suggestion of sexual drive—there is normally no unsheathing of the penis and no thrusting action. And even if the young Don Juans attempted more explicit sexual motion, they could accomplish little, for they are not sexually mature—calves make their initial mounting attempts at an age of six to twenty-one days. I particularly remember the first flings of one young buffalo, who walked up to the rear of a reclining cow and maneuvered himself onto her rump; to his dismay, she stood up immediately, dumping him on his rear end with a solid thump.

The third and last pattern of buffalo play is gamboling, which includes aimless racing, romping stampedes, and running games. The participants dash back and forth in short charges, gallop in circles, or play group games that look like chase and hide-and-seek.

Energetic races or social games of this nature are common in the gamboling of other species. Children love to tear through a house at top speed, just as kittens, lambs, kids, and colts dash about in their own domains. Instead of racing together, young foxes, weasels, and other carnivores playfully stalk a symbolic victim—a pebble, bone, or leaf. Gibbons swing through tree branches in a form of follow-the-leader, and chimpanzees refine this game into a rhythmic dance on the ground. King-of-the-mountain is favorite sport among lion cubs as well as young badgers and red deer.

Because people have always been fascinated by the play of animals, a great mass of material has accumulated on the subject; but in spite of efforts by numerous researchers, no completely satisfactory explanation for play has emerged.

One study stresses the resemblance between playful activities and their purposeful counterparts. Motions performed at other times with a specific objective are carried on in play simply for the pleasurable sensations involved. Buffalo sparring for fun have no desire to overthrow opponents; young animals mounting each other have no intention of copulating. Although some gambols resemble true flight, there is no enemy to escape from and no goal to reach; kicking used elsewhere in self-defense is harmless and whimsical in frolic.

Since playful activities achieve no visible objective, one is tempted to believe they have no function other than to amuse. But patterns of play may well prepare the individual for adult life. The repetition of certain energetic actions trains muscles and perfects coordination for later, more serious activities. The kitten stalking around the sofa to pounce on a catnip ball is perfecting the hunting technique of an efficient mouser. Puppies engaged in mock combat are sharpening their prowess for adult battles. And in the same way, the playful jousts of buffalo calves help to develop and polish skills for other battles, the crucial struggles of the rut. A young buffalo sparring in fun can practice his thrusts under conditions when mistakes are not critical; later, the penalty for sloppy dueling may be death.

Play in buffalo is often associated with another trait of the animals—the tendency to "explore," or approach and inspect unfamiliar areas or objects. Exploration is unhurried and studied, play vigorous and spirited, but the two activities are very likely controlled by the same basic mechanisms. Both emerge in the first few hours of a calf's life, reaching a peak of expression in the next year or two and tapering off as the animal approaches maturity. Both assist the maturing buffalo in his efforts to discover and thoroughly know his surroundings. And both are conducted when the animal is comfortable, which is to say when he has had his fill of food and water and is under no particular stress.

Although play has been observed only in birds and mammals, we know that exploration is more widespread in the animal kingdom. In lower animals, the activity is still rudimentary—an amoeba probes by extending a portion of its plastic form and a grasshopper scrutinizes with its antennae. Worker bees show great exploratory inclinations, bustling about for several hours a day investigating activities in the hive. And if novel or complex objects are introduced into the cages of laboratory rats, the animals rush over to inspect them immediately. Rhesus monkeys given a chance to open a door and look into a room filled with other monkeys have been observed to snoop for long periods each day.

The pronghorn, most inquisitive of all the buffalo's grassland associates, is fascinated by strange objects. Indians were even able to lure the animals within shooting range with the simple ruse of hiding behind a bush and waving a piece of cloth in the air. The same trick still works today.

Each species has its own manner of exploring novel objects. Primates typically grab the object in the forepaws, inspect it minutely, and then manipulate it by twisting, bending, rolling, or rubbing. Tigers or wolves chew, swat, or chase the object. The giant anteater uses its tongue and snout to explore; spider monkeys probe with their tails and llamas investigate with their lips.

The first steps of exploration in buffalo are tentative and cautious. Ears forward, the animals move slowly toward an object that has attracted their attention, focusing on it with a steady gaze. Advancing still closer, they sniff it carefully, perhaps even probing it with muzzle or tongue.

Buffalo making these exploratory probes are aroused by the "novelty" of an object—its quality of being unfamiliar, complex, or incongruous. Anything newly introduced into their territory will kindle curiosity. When I erected an observation platform in a tree in the Jackson Hole Wildlife Park, the herd stirred with impatience to come over and investigate. In another herd many buffalo had probably never examined a porcupine until I released one next to them. The prickly visitor soon attracted a dozen individuals, some of whom followed and sniffed at close range. Before long, one surprised bison reared up, his nose a pincushion of quills.

When something familiar to a buffalo is transplanted to a new setting, a semblance of novelty is created. Buffalo in Wind Cave National Park often passed through prairie dog towns, paying scant attention to the occupants. But my release of a single dog in another part of their range puzzled them—and several individuals came over to scrutinize the "new" stranger. Similarly, when I made daily visits to the Wildlife Park herd, the animals grew accustomed to the two-legged creature walking around in their domain, but when I decided to sit in a chair and take notes, they were absolutely stunned. Gathering about me to investigate, several buffalo approached to within two feet, and one young heifer came still closer, sniffing my boots and licking my pants.

Although buffalo will explore new situations or articles, their curiosity is limited by fear, and they are easily startled into retreat. The herds usually flee at the intrusion of human beings, although some tolerate a closer approach than others.

The response of past herds to human intrusion seems to have been quite arbitrary. Some early writers characterized the animals as extremely skittish: "Such is their timidity," wrote a plainsman, "that one man can put to flight the most numerous herd." Others found them strangely fearless. A traveler in Saskatchewan passing through a vast herd was astonished when the animals, instead of taking flight, "opened in front and closed behind the train of carts like water round a ship."

Meriwether Lewis, in his journey across the plains, met groups that exhibited both extremes of behavior. On May 4, 1805, he "saw immence quantities of buffaloe in every direction," and found them quite tame. "I passed them without firing on them; they are extreemly gentle—the bull buffaloe particularly will scarcely give way to you." But only about a month later, the temperament of the herds had changed remarkably, for Lewis wrote, "We cannot approach the buffaloe within shot before they discover us and take to flight."

The vacillation of buffalo between quiet, passive acceptance of human beings and jittery spookiness was best summmed up by historian Francis Parkman: "Sometimes they are so stupid and infatuated that a man may walk up to them in full sight on the open prairie, and even shoot several of their number before the rest will think it necessary to retreat. At another moment they will be so shy and wary, that in order to approach them, the utmost skill, experience and judgment are necessary."

Some present-day herds are virtually tame, particularly those in daily contact with cars and people. In a few parks, buffalo allow tourists to advance to within about five feet. Animals in other refuges permit the approach of cars to a distance of about twenty-five feet, but if the occupants get out they gallop away. In the more remote refuges the herds are as skittish as the most sensitive of their ancestors and retreat in a hasty stampede whenever people come within a few hundred feet.

Although a buffalo will usually flee as a man draws near, there is a point at which he may begin to feel cornered or annoyed. If the interloper trespasses beyond this point, the animal is likely to charge. Harrowing attacks by buffalo abound in the annals of history as well as in the records of present-day refuges. As far back as 1541, a letter from Coronado to King Charles told of efforts to slay animals for food "at the cost of several of our horses which [the buffalo] killed, because, as I wrote Your Majesty, they are very brave and fierce animals."

More than a century later, explorer Jacques Marquette added to the bison's reputation for belligerence: "Not a year passes without their killing some savages," he wrote. "When attacked, they catch a man on their Horns, if they can, toss Him in the air, and then throw him on the ground, after which they trample him under foot and kill him."

Ever since, scores of lurid tales and strong opinions have confirmed this portrayal of the buffalo as a crusty beast. Men who raised tame buffalo were later attacked and gored to death by their own pets. Naturalist Ernest Thompson Seton denounced the animals as "savage, treacherous . . . always a menace . . . never to be trusted." And an extravagant book entitled *Buffalo Land* described a formidable behemoth with "hair and mane enough to fit out half a dozen lions . . . fully as dangerous as the king of beasts."

In recent years the belligerent nature of bison has surfaced among the animals of the Jackson Hole Wildlife Park. During the time of my study, buffalo in the fenced confines of the park violently dispatched a pronghorn, a young moose, and an elk calf. Even on the open range of Yellowstone Park, a group of buffalo killed an elk calf they found hidden in the tall grass. Nearby, they slew one horse and gored three others and a mule. And an aged buffalo bull trapped inside a corral with some elk did away with a dozen before he could be removed.

On rare occasions, even wolves and grizzly bears—normally classed as predators of buffalo—have been killed by their own prey. George Catlin once painted a scene of a lone bull being attacked by a circle of wolves. In notes accompanying the painting, he explained how some of the wolves, "less lucky, had been crushed to death by the feet or the horns of the bull." Two other writers detailed similar episodes in which wolves attacked bulls only to be fatally gored themselves.

A buffalo bull has also been known to battle a grizzly bear to death, if we can accept two startling accounts by Indian witnesses. In both episodes, a bear lay in wait on a rise above a trail, pouncing on a cow as the herd passed underneath, and a bull eventually dispatched the assailant after prolonged battle. One of the Indians described the fracas he saw:

The bull would charge the bear, and when he struck him fairly would knock him off his feet, often inflicting severe wounds with his sharp horns. The bear struck at the bull, and tried to catch him by the head or shoulders, and to hold him, but this he could not do. After fifteen or twenty minutes of fierce and active fighting the bear had received all the punishment he cared for, and tried to escape, but the bull would not let him go, and kept up the attack until he had killed his adversary. Even after the bear was dead the bull would gore the carcass and sometimes lift it clear of the ground on his horns. He seemed insane with rage, and, notwithstanding the fact that most of the skin was torn from his head and shoulders, appeared to be looking about for something else to fight.

It is easier to confirm a more recent account of such a battle in the records of two Yellowstone Park rangers. While patrolling the Lamar Valley in June of 1951, the men discovered the mutilated carcass of a medium-sized female grizzly, dead for no more than three or four days. Both sides of the body were badly bruised and bloodied; all the ribs on one side were broken; and the belly was punctured by two holes whose size and spacing suggested the horns of a young buffalo. Near the carcass were several patches of buffalo fur and numerous hoofprints, but no dead or injured victim was ever found. The rangers concluded that a buffalo had struggled with and "in all probability killed" the grizzly.

Yellowstone Park has also been the scene of a number of hair-raising incidents involving buffalo and people. A thirty-year-old man was run down and trampled by a buffalo in 1971. "He wasn't gored," stated the assistant superintendent, "but the collision was about like being hit by a two-ton truck." He died.

In 1963, near Old Faithful Geyser, a solitary bull charged a man as he turned to stroll away. The bull's horns tore through the victim's buttocks, necessitating surgery and hospitalization. This assault was not only painful, but also especially embarrassing for the victim, an experienced African big game hunter who had often pooh-poohed the ferocity of American game.

About a year later, near Old Faithful, a fifteen-year-old boy and his two companions approached a grazing buffalo bull. When they were about ten feet away, the animal charged. "The boy was thrown into the air," went the report of the attending ranger, "and a severe abrasion was inflicted on the right side of the lower back. The buffalo made no further attempt to harm the boy and continued grazing." The victim received treatment from two park nurses, who were never paid for their services. After all, complained the boy's parents, "Buffalo should be fenced in."

Five days after this incident, a buffalo bull in the same general area charged a ten-year-old girl, fracturing two vertebrae and inflicting painful abrasions. Official park records contain the report of an eyewitness: "There were twenty to thirty people close to the buffalo. The girl was not as close as the rest, but it turned on her. It caught her from behind and threw her high in the air. When she landed she did not move. The buffalo started for her again, but a man distracted it with a hat."

The "twenty to thirty people" that had clustered within a few yards of this bull had given it ample cause for irritation; indeed, most attacks can be traced to some kind of provocation. In the National Bison Range, most encounters with charging buffalo occur as horsemen bear down on groups of animals to drive them from one pasture to another; individuals in the harassed herd may dash out and try to gore the horses. Cows, usually mothers with calves, charge more frequently than bulls. During recent drives in the B-Bar-B Buffalo Ranch, charging buffalo mutilated a couple of horses, prompting the manager to switch to pickup trucks for driving his herd. This measure did not eliminate the problem, however, for the buffalo took to attacking the trucks, marking the doors and fenders with occasional dents.

Even if unprovoked, buffalo are far from harmless. Any approach toward the beasts, no matter how judiciously undertaken, is risky. Influenced by the memory of a number of harrowing encounters, I recommend caution at all times.

Altogether, I have been charged outright on five occasions and had six other potentially dangerous confrontations. One May afternoon in Wind Cave National Park, for example, I was standing about sixty feet from a group of fifteen buffalo, scanning them through the narrowed field of my binoculars, when suddenly I was startled by a patter of hoofs and a soft snorting sound; I wheeled around to discover an aged cow galloping directly toward me. She stopped twenty feet away, then began to advance again. Fortunately I was able to retreat to the protection of my car.

Less than an hour later, as I observed another herd in the Park, a pregnant cow suddenly made a charge at me. She bore down on me at a rapid gallop, halting only fifteen feet away. I withdrew to the safety of a tree, keeping a vigilant eye on her all the way. She marched slowly after me for a few paces as if to assure herself of the sincerity of my retreat, then turned and went back to the herd.

A splenetic buffalo sometimes gives signals that warn of an intent to charge—a bull hoists his tail, paws the ground, bellows, or wallows. One cannot rely on such signals, however, for charges may occur with almost no warning. Old bulls in particular should be treated with utmost respect. Although they carry themselves with a certain aloof dignity in a posture of stiffening old age and appear as firmly rooted as stumps, they can suddenly spring to life and charge an unsuspecting visitor.

If you decide to go buffalo stalking, you must be ready for danger at all times and should plan a route of escape in case one of the animals charges. Of course, if a tree is handy, you can dodge behind it or climb into it; but many buffalo inhabit treeless plains where there is no hiding place and a charge may be a terrifying experience. The only thing you can do is confront your assailant and hope he will stop. Fortunately for you, the chances are very good that he will. In spite of the discrepancy in physical bulk, the contest is really between your will and his. A buffalo can be bluffed, as can other large animals like the elephant and the gorilla. Once you have won the initial face-off, you should walk backwards, still facing your antagonist, moving gradually at first and then quickening your pace.

Bluffing a buffalo may seem foolhardy, but is actually a sensible decision. Running would be sheer folly, for you could never sprint as fast as your adversary. And a hasty retreat might well invite pursuit. In standing your ground, you are being both brave and wise, as one bull-bluffing fur trader discovered in 1854:

When the buffalo turned, my horse, frightened out of his propriety, made a tremendous bound sidewise, and, alas, that I should tell it, threw me out of the saddle and within ten feet of the enraged monster! Here was a predicament! I was face to face with the brute, whose eyes glared through the long hair which garnished his frontlet like coals of fire—the blood streaming from his nostrils. In this desperate situation, I made up my mind that my only hope of escape was to look my adversary in the eye, as any attempt to fly would only invite attack. Holding my gun cocked to fire if he attempted a rush, I stood firmly although, I must confess, I thought my last hour had come! How long he stood there pawing and roaring, I have not now the least idea, but he was certainly slow in deciding what he should do. At length, he moved away, and I gave him a parting salute that let out the little blood remaining in his body. He walked a short distance and fell dead.

Steadfast confrontation is not the only stratagem that has been suggested for surviving buffalo charges. One self-proclaimed authority recommended hugging "Mother Earth as tight as may be," because "the probabilities are that the bull cannot pick the body up with his horns." His opinion is somewhat at odds with the remarks of a veteran hunter: "A buffalo can hook a pocket handkerchief to shreds from the ground, which is not at all pleasant to think of when drifting before an infuriated brute with nothing nearer than the North Pole to dodge behind."

Still another authority advised beating vigorously on a tin pan, producing a racket that would strike panic into the heart of the aggressor and put him to immediate flight.

If no tin pan is handy, the technique of tooth for tooth is indicated. Zoologist William Hornaday asserted that the only hope for a potential victim lay in the final second when the creature paused to aim its horns for a crushing toss. At that instant, he counseled, the terrified chap must deal his opponent a smashing blow close to the eye. To illustrate, Hornaday told the story of a keeper in the New York Zoological Park who once persuaded a charging cow to retreat. All it took was several smashing blows with a pitchfork on the side of her head, delivered "when she was just close enough."

19

THE GRASSLAND

COMMUNITY

To ALL CREATURES DWELLING ON THE OPEN PLAIN, THE
rigors of the winter blizzard or the searing heat of the summer sun
present a formidable challenge, harassing bison, hawk, and mouse
with no regard for size or strength. Grass-dwellers, unlike the inhabitants of surrounding forests, who can take cover beneath
shrub or tree, must depend for their survival on certain life patterns and physical traits developed over eons of evolution on the
plains.

Some residents seek shelter from the elements as well as from
their natural enemies by burrowing under the ground. Jackrabbits raise their young in dens beneath the surface, while ground
squirrels, prairie dogs, pocket mice, and kangaroo rats live in burrows all year round. Their efforts to hide are sometimes foiled by
predators—grizzly bears, coyotes, kit foxes, badgers, black-footed

ferrets, and a number of snakes—who capture them in their tunnels or dig them out. When wandering above ground these burrowing mammals become possible quarry for such airborne hunters as prairie falcons, short-eared owls, and ferruginous and Swainson's hawks.

Other grass-dwellers escape from their enemies by running. The pronghorn, with a top speed of fifty-five miles an hour, is the fastest mammal on the continent. With its keen, wide-ranging vision it can spot approaching predators and observe the warning signals of nearby pronghorn. In time of danger, the stiff hairs on the rump of a pronghorn bristle and rise, becoming a broad patch of white. Like flashing mirrors, these rump-puffs telegraph signals across the plains, enabling distant pronghorn to discern danger and relay the alarm.

Though no match for fleet pronghorn, buffalo are enduring runners and can reach speeds of thirty to thirty-five miles an hour. Equally swift are jackrabbits, whose oversized hind legs carry them over the plains in leaps of fifteen or twenty feet. (A similar hopping gait is common among several grassland animals, including kangaroo rats, pocket mice, jumping mice, and, of course, grasshoppers.)

Certain inhabitants of the grassland are screened from their enemies by their protective coloration, which blends closely with soil or local vegetation, permitting them to freeze and go undetected. Only if an enemy approaches too near do they burst forth and flee. In this group are nighthawks, sage grouse, and many small birds, as well as leaf hoppers and numerous other insects.

Group living provides protection for still another category of grass-dwellers, the social species, whose home in open country is well suited to large congregations; members can find their mates with ease, warn each other of approaching danger, and gain security in the strength of their numbers. Prairie chickens, sharp-tailed grouse, and sage grouse assemble each spring to strut and mate on their communal booming grounds, while their cousin, the ruffed grouse, courts in lonely seclusion in the forest.

Most elaborate of all social colonies on the plains, however, are those of the prairie dog. Each "dog town" is divided into a complex of wards and precincts, whose separate borders are strictly respected and whose members form their own closed societies, communicating with each other by means of an efficient system of gestures and calls. When an individual spots something suspicious, he gives a sharp bark that immediately sends all nearby dogs scurrying into the closest burrows; after the danger subsides, the first animals to emerge rise up and wheeze an all-clear signal, and the colony returns to its normal pursuits.

Widely known for their social communities, prairie dogs have also become stars of a popular Western legend. Dog towns are tenanted additionally by burrowing owls and prairie rattlesnakes, both of which find shelter in the burrows. This has given rise to the myth that the three creatures—dog, owl, and snake—live in fraternal harmony in cozy subterranean dens. The legend may have originated when an observer saw a dog and an owl dash together into the same hole—a cohabitation that occurs only in time of danger. Someone else may have added to this image of three-way fellowship after hearing the buzz of a rattlesnake coming from the entrance to an owl's tunnel, unaware that the warning notes of a burrowing owl are a close imitation of a snake's rattle.

In truth, the relation between the three species is anything but cozy. Of the trio, the prairie dogs fare worst in the arrangement, laboriously digging their complex burrows only to be confronted and shoved aside by numbers of invading rattlesnakes or owls. At first the dogs will attempt to drive out the invaders by bluff, but eventually they yield and retire to another section of their tunnels, sometimes even sealing off the usurped chambers. During the confrontation they may well lose some of their young to the marauding snakes and owls.

The most frustrating season for the dogs is the fall, when hundreds of migrating prairie rattlers may converge on their town to den up for the winter. Moving into the tunnels, the snakes coil up and prepare to hibernate in the comfortable inner passages. If a dog should snap at one of his unwelcome visitors, the snake will attempt to kill his antagonist with a few swift strikes. Most dogs eventually evacuate the area, and move off to construct a new village in nearby territory. Year after year, the rattlers return to the same denning burrows. In time, however, the favored tunnels, long untended by the fastidious dogs, fall into disrepair, and the snakes move on to take over still another town.

In the spring the dogs are again besieged, as mated pairs of burrowing owls set up housekeeping in their towns. When the owners of a stolen tunnel resist the takeover, the small, spindly-

legged owls puff up their feathers and spread their wings, presenting a fearsome aspect to the startled defenders; any dog left un-
convinced by the bluff is charged and pecked until he retreats.
After the dogs have relinquished the tunnel, the owls are free to
haul in shreds of buffalo dung and line the little hollow for nesting.

The burrowing owl is the only plains bird that rears its brood
below the ground; other species have adapted to their treeless environment by nesting on the grassland floor. And in a further
adaptation to the open plains, certain birds, for lack of a singing
post, soar into the air and pour forth their melodious song on the
wing. Among these are the bobolink, lark bunting, chestnut-
collared longspur, and Sprague's pipit. (The drab little pipit with
its delicate trill so impressed John James Audubon that he borrowed the name of a renowned European counterpart and dubbed
it the "Missouri skylark.")

The pipits, mice, grasshoppers, and other small creatures, as
well as the big game animals with whom they share the grassland,
are all links in a remarkably complex chain of species, an ordered
assemblage that has developed during eons of evolution on the
plains. By means of subtle adjustments, each evolving plant or
animal has adapted to its surroundings and to life among countless other species, linked to them by relationships of cooperation,
competition, and indifferent neutrality. All have acquired special
traits appropriate to the geologic and climatic forces of their environment—the earth they sink their roots into or press their hoofs
against, the winds that sweep the plains, the moisture from rain or
snow, the temperature of the air, and the changing patterns of
darkness and light. All of these forces and all of these species in-
teract under basic ecological laws to produce the self-sustaining
whole of the grassland "community," the habitat of the buffalo.

The foundation for this community is a layer of soil, a base for
grasses and other plants whose branching rootlets penetrate to a
depth of several feet. The dense tangle of rootlets—which bind the
sod so tightly that early settlers were able to slice out coherent
chunks for the construction of dwellings on the treeless plain—are
the supply lines for all food production, absorbing water from the
soil and transferring it to the plant layer. With the help of chloro-
phyll in blades and leaves, the sun's energy is harnessed to com-
bine water and carbon dioxide into glucose, which builds up a

store of nutrients in the foliage, thus endowing the grassland with life.

The nourishing leaves become primary links for most food chains, the channels through which energy flows from plant to animal and so on throughout the community. These relationships of consumed and consumer weave back and forth from one species to another, producing a complex web of dependencies, single strands of which might be traced as follows:

Foliage is eaten by buffalo, which then fall prey to wolves; or it is devoured by insects that are snared by spiders that are eaten by frogs that are swallowed by garter snakes that are caught by marsh hawks. In still other possibilities, foliage is nibbled by meadow voles, which are preyed upon by great horned owls, red-tailed hawks, weasels, ground squirrels, and coyotes.

In time, the terminal links of all chains die, releasing their final stores of energy to scavengers like carrion beetles and vultures and to the earth itself. There, fungi and bacteria extract additional sustenance by breaking down dead matter into minerals, which are returned to the soil for reuse by the plants of succeeding generations. In the eternal cycle of growth and decay, possibilities for different food chains are almost endless.

Grasses and other foliage supporting most food chains fall under the assault of numerous grazers, groups like insects, rodents, and ungulates, which keep the vegetation closely cropped. One would expect an animal so ponderous and plentiful as the buffalo to be the predominant force in reaping the greenery, but, surprisingly, in many preserves it is not.

In the tall-grass prairie of the northern plains, most of the grass is consumed not by the hulking buffalo, but by a ubiquitous rodent, the tiny meadow vole. And on the eastern prairie, a recent study has revealed that three dairy cows (the rough equivalent to three buffalo in grazing pressure), consume but a fraction of the aggregate forage yielded by a twenty-five-acre pasture. In this survey, although a fair amount of the abundant food went to the cows, an astonishingly large portion was eaten by about seventy-five million small invertebrates, who more than made up in numbers what they lacked in size. In the final tally, the army of small fry ate about twice as much as the three cows. During a similar study in Montana, grasshoppers feeding on three acres of range accounted for as much forage as a single domestic cow.

(These voracious grass-eaters reach their maximum numbers during periods of drought, assaulting the grassland in hordes to reduce the available forage still further; at times they will strip off every last bit of foliage, mowing down new growth as rapidly as it comes up.)

The collective feeding of invertebrates, rodents, and ungulates can thus cut down and greatly alter the grassland. Ecologists speculate that such feeding, especially by buffalo, may actually have changed the composition of certain arid tracts on the western plains. The characteristic short grasses of these areas, usually attributed to dry climate, may well have been caused by the grazing of vast herds of buffalo.

On a smaller scale, colonies of prairie dogs modify plots of grassland to suit their own needs. Each dog town is a warren of burrows, most of which terminate in a craterlike mound, a volcano of earth as much as three feet high and seven or eight feet wide. To mold such a structure, the industrious dogs scrape up and compact a pile of soil, tamping their feet or noses against it like so many air hammers. Their vigorous scraping and their ambitious clipping of vegetation soon denude the surrounding sod. Before long they have cleared out a series of sight paths for use in spotting approaching predators and observing the activities of nearby companions. In addition to grooming and uprooting the plant cover, the dogs also eat large quantities of grasses, eventually thinning these species and leading to an invasion of non-grass plants.

In time, the busy activities of the prairie dogs transform their towns into plots of barren earth or non-grass herbs, two types of terrain that are highly attractive to buffalo searching for spots to wallow or graze. It is not surprising, then, to find the herds bearing down like an ill-mannered army upon the poor prairie dog colony in search of these delights, ambling through the towns with total disregard for the handiwork of the inhabitants.

The worst damage occurs when a buffalo bull spots the provocative slope of a prairie dog crater, a ready-made wallowing place. Walking deliberately up to the mound, he paws it, pierces its crumbly rim with his horns and lies down to roll in the loose earth, flattening everything in a cloud of dust and a cascade of soil, sometimes even choking off the entrance to the burrow.

When the bull departs, the harried owner surfaces to take

stock of the damage. Bravely he commences repairs, reopening the entrance and diligently shaping the mound again. But once plundered, a prairie dog mound proves an irresistible target to the dust-loving buffalo, and the bulls inevitably return to demolish the renovated burrows. After repeated reconstructions, the prairie dogs finally relinquish the contested sites to their outsized opponents.

In the intricate web of relationships on the historic grassland, a system of checks and balances kept the varied animals in approximate equilibrium with each other and with their supply of food. Just as armies of meadow voles were held in check by snakes, shrews, weasels, skunks, badgers, foxes, and coyotes, the storied herds were controlled by their own predators—the wolf and the grizzly bear. Eventually, however, encroaching civilization swept both of these hunting species from most of their former range and all but eliminated them in their role as killers of buffalo. Today the grizzly is in a good position to prey upon buffalo only in Yellowstone National Park, and the wolf only in the remote reaches of Wood Buffalo National Park.

On the early plains, wolves were classed as the "most dangerous enemy of the buffalo" (outside of man, of course). The reputation rested on their long-range endurance and their efficiency when operating in a pack. Two accounts from the 1840's describe the group technique:

> . . . I have several times come across such gangs [50 to 100] of these animals, surrounding and torturing an old or a wounded bull, where it would seem from appearances that they had been for several days in attendance, and at intervals desperately engaged in the effort to take his life . . . the animal had made desperate resistance until his eyes were entirely eaten out of his head; the gristle of his nose was mostly gone; his tongue was half demolished, and the skin and flesh of his legs torn almost literally into strings . . .

> They . . . seem to act in concert and as if by understanding. First they post themselves at proper distances in a line in the direction the victim is supposed to take; then two or three charge into the middle of the herd, cut out the fattest and drive it toward the spot where their companions are waiting. The victim then runs between two ranks of wolves. As it goes on, fresh bands join in the chase, until at last, exhausted by fatigue, it stops and becomes their prey.

Similar teamwork is to be found today among packs of African hyenas, who often join forces to finish off an old or sick antelope. Elsewhere on the veld, hunting lions make use of the same technique. While some members of a pride lie in wait, others go out after game and drive the prey toward the concealed group. Once ambushed, the victim has almost no chance of escape.

Whatever their hunting tactics, wolves on the American plains were unquestionably the buffalo's most formidable foes. But, curiously, the buffalo themselves seemed oblivious to the danger, treating their potential assailants with a strange indifference. A possible explanation for this behavior was suggested by George Catlin, who wrote that the buffalo "are aware of their own superiority in combined force, and seem to have no dread of the wolf, allowing him to sneak amidst their ranks, apparently like one of their own family." We have seen how stalking Indians took advantage of this curious indifference, sometimes crawling boldly toward the herds under wolf skins.

The first modern studies of such indifference to wolves were made in Wood Buffalo National Park, where a zoologist carefully recorded the behavior of bison in the presence of wolves. On November 16, 1950, for example, one calf stood by unblinking as its companion thirty feet away was slaughtered and eviscerated by a pack of six wolves. On another occasion, the researcher carefully observed two bulls and two cows lying together in the grass as hunting wolves approached and prepared to make a kill. Three of the buffalo were strong, healthy specimens, and the fourth, a small cow, limped badly from an old bullet wound. In the course of an hour, eleven different wolves hunting in ones and twos crept toward the animals. As each wolf appeared, the maimed cow stared nervously at it. Whenever a breeze rustled a few nearby leaves, she raised her head and looked around in fear, and if a wolf appeared at the margin of her sight, she followed its motions with her eyes as if prepared to bolt at any time. During the entire period, her three companions reclined nonchalantly, ignoring the surrounding predators. At one point a solitary wolf peeked over a bank no more than twenty-five feet from one of the bulls; the buffalo did not even look up. The second bull rose and turned to glance at the wolf, but showed no fear, placidly continuing to ruminate. The lame cow, however, spotted the wolf immediately and turned to confront her antagonist on wobbly legs. A kill by the wolves was probably averted by the presence of the observer's truck.

This blasé attitude toward wolves is sometimes found in other prey species, like the barren-ground caribou. At times caribou pay no attention to nearby packs of wolves, but on other occasions they flee at the first appearance of a lone animal. Experience has evidently trained them to judge from the silhouette of a wolf whether or not the animal is hunting. When merely traveling cross-country, a wolf carries its head erect so that its perked ears are clearly silhouetted. When hunting, however, the animal lowers its head, flattening its ears back until they blend with the rest of the body, forming a smooth line against the horizon.

This relaxed behavior of caribou and buffalo in the presence of wolves is duplicated on the African plains by the herds of wildebeest, who often wander casually in the presence of their enemies. They may even trot up to within a hundred feet of a lion and stare at their hungry adversary, knowing they can dash away before he will be able to catch them. By careful stalking or ambushing, however, the tenacious lions manage to bring down their share of wildebeest; indeed, the lion is the wildebeest's most deadly foe.

In Canada's Wood Buffalo National Park, the one remaining reserve with a substantial wolf population, surveys have shown that wolves are clearly the principal enemies of the herds. In order to gain information on the methods of these highly effective predators, researchers studied the carcasses of eleven buffalo victims.

Of the eleven, five were very old animals, regarded by zoologists as "surplus"—not vital to the general welfare of the herd. But predation on this class of individuals was judged to be moderate. It was found that wolves felled some aged animals, but left a substantial number in the population.

Three kills were in the calf group, a category with a similar surplus. Zoologists consider such predation of little consequence to the population as a whole, since cows bear more calves each year than are necessary to maintain the herd at a status quo. (Infant losses from predation, disease, or other natural factors can still be considerable—a little more than half of each season's crop of calves is eliminated during the first year.) In past centuries, according to a Pawnee estimate, wolves brought down a third of the calves.

The last three victims in the Canadian survey were all physically handicapped. One was in the terminal stage of tuberculosis, one was crippled by a bullet wound, and the last appeared to have a broken leg. Although all these animals belonged to the herd's productive core of breeding buffalo, a segment normally immune to wolf predation, they perished because of their weakened condition.

The concentration of wolf predation upon the young, the aged, or the handicapped is the typical pattern not only for buffalo, but also for all North American ungulates, such as elk, moose, musk oxen, Dall sheep, and whitetail deer. The largest of these are formidable prey for the wolves, who dare attack only if the target animal is at a disadvantage.

Even if the buffalo under attack is young and frail, wolves may have difficulty bringing it down. In the Canadian survey, one pack of half a dozen had to pursue an orphaned, practically defenseless six-month-old calf for eight miles before they were able to stop it—and even then the calf put up a valiant fight, as indicated by the trampled ground at the site of the final encounter. On those occasions when wolves are able to move in rapidly, they may still fail in their first attack, only wounding their prey; in such cases they will hang around and wait for a chance to finish the job.

The ideal situation for a wolf is to surprise a buffalo alone on the open prairie, where the victim's chances are slim indeed. If the animal manages to reach heavy timber it may be able to dislodge its clinging enemy by rubbing against trees, but on the barren plain it is without hope.

When more than one buffalo is caught in the open, however, the animals' chances of withstanding attack are greatly improved. Under assault, they bunch together to prevent assailants from singling out individual animals. "Whilst the buffaloes are grouped together," observed Catlin in 1844, "the wolves seldom attack them, as the former instantly gather for combined resistance, which they effectively make."

Because Canadian wolves concentrate on the so-called surplus buffalo, their predation is not considered detrimental to the herds as a whole. The attacking animals do not eat themselves out of their supply, but merely prevent the prey species from increasing too rapidly. Thus they help to maintain an equilibrium on the range.

Although we can justify the presence of wolves by their beneficial effect on herd welfare, the wolves are of far greater importance in their own right. Before the white man ever appeared on the continent, they were a natural part of life on the plains, and it should be our duty to save some remnants of these complete animal communities. In this increasingly man-dominated world, it is heartening to note that Canadian officials believe in keeping wolves as essential members of the wilderness population of Wood Buffalo National Park.

Although predation by wolves on both modern and historical herds is well documented, our information about the hunting habits of grizzly bears is scant and will probably not increase. The great bears that once roamed from the Pacific Ocean eastward to the Mississippi have been severely reduced in numbers, and driven far back to mountain sanctuaries. Only in Yellowstone Park is their population large enough to pose any threat to the buffalo.

During my studies in this area, I ran across an occasional grizzly near the herds. One afternoon in Hayden Valley, for example, I trained my binoculars on a sow as she led her three cubs through the meadow on a hunting trek. From time to time she reared up on her hind legs, looked over the terrain, and loped on. Only seven hundred feet from her a herd of seventy-eight buffalo grazed calmly, paying no attention. They did not even seem to notice when she discovered and slaughtered a hidden elk calf.

In the months that followed, I watched many other grizzlies as they hunted over these meadows, but at no other time did I see a bear capture anything larger than a rodent. Since that time, zoologists Frank and John Craighead have conducted an intensive study on grizzlies in the same general area, trailing them throughout their range by means of electronic devices. After first drugging the bears with tranquillizing darts, they fitted each of them with a sturdy collar containing instruments to monitor bodily functions and a tiny radio transmitter. When the Craigheads focused their receiving antennas on the signals coming from the bears, they were able to plot their movements on a map of the area. By this means they located a few elk killed by grizzlies, but not one slain buffalo.

Total information on grizzly predation is thus inconclusive—in an area where bears could easily kill buffalo, they gave no indication of having done so. (They were still efficient scavengers of carcasses in the Yellowstone, however. A buffalo dead of natural causes often attracted as many as thirty or forty hungry grizzlies, who feasted until nothing remained but a few bones and tufts of fur.)

Among the scattered historical accounts on grizzly predation, the best evidence comes from the journals of Lewis and Clark. In one provocative entry, Lewis wrote: "These bears resort the river where they lie in wate at the crossing places of the game for Elk and weak cattle (buffalo); when they procure a subject of either they lie by the carcase and keep the wolves off untill they devour it."

The journals also reveal much by what they leave unsaid. Buffalo, wolves, and grizzlies ("white bears") are frequently listed as inhabitants of the same regions, but wolves alone are depicted as constant predators: "We have seen great numbers of buffaloe, and the usual attendants of these last, the wolves, who follow their movements and feed upon those who die by accident or who are too poor to keep pace with the herd; we also wounded a white bear . . ." Many of the predatory efforts undertaken by the bears were against the expeditionaries themselves, some of whom had narrow escapes from the beasts. "The White bear have become so troublesome to us," wrote Lewis, "that I do not think it prudent to send one man alone on an errand of any kind . . . I have made the men sleep with their arms by them . . ."

There are only two or three eyewitness accounts of grizzly predation against buffalo. Of these, the most detailed comes from a Canadian journal:

One bear [grizzly] killed at Hand Hills [Alberta] in 1877 required eight shots before he was disabled. His feet were eight inches across, and were armed with claws five inches long. He was caught in the act of killing a buffalo cow, and had just cracked her spine when he received the first shot. When stretched, his hide was as large as a buffalo bull . . .

Apparently grizzlies were capable of killing buffalo, but did so rarely.

Whether buffalo fall to grizzlies or to wolves, their end by such predation is usually expeditious and violent; the predators operate with tooth and claw and gorge themselves on the spot. But there is another group of organisms that prey subtly and steadily on buffalo, stealing their nourishment little by little over a period of days or even years. These are the tiny parasites that gather both within and upon the animals, transforming their hosts into veritable walking hostelries. Mites, lice, ticks, and several winged assailants—such as mosquitoes, gnats, black flies, and botflies—all find lodging in the ample fur. And within the body dwell an even greater variety of parasites, including several roundworms, tapeworms, and one-celled organisms. (See Appendix C.)

But parasites have little effect on the over-all well-being of a herd, since each species generally occurs in only a portion of the group, and in limited concentrations. On occasion, however, parasites can reproduce so fast that they become infestations, causing emaciation, anemia, and possibly even death. And victims weakened by parasites are more likely to succumb to secondary infections like pneumonia.

The most serious parasitic diseases are four infections caused by bacteria: hemorrhagic septicemia, brucellosis, malignant anthrax, and bovine tuberculosis. Originally transferred to buffalo from domestic stock, each one has inflicted striking—even epidemic—losses at one time or another.

The first, hemorrhagic septicemia, is a form of blood poisoning caused by bacteria closely related to agents of plague in both humans and rats. In the early part of the century, outbreaks of septicemia claimed the lives of 105 buffalo in Yellowstone Park. Once the herd was vaccinated, however, the disease disappeared.

The second bacterial disease is brucellosis, sometimes called contagious abortion. Human beings coming into contact with diseased animals or their discharges (such as milk) develop human brucellosis, or undulant fever. Female buffalo afflicted with brucellosis tend to abort partway through pregnancy; in the long run this lowers the birth rate of an infected herd.

Although the incidence of brucellosis has climbed to sixty per cent in some herds, most buffalo seem to develop an immunity that retards many of the disease's effects. Efforts by the U.S. Department of Agriculture to eliminate brucellosis in buffalo are carried out primarily to control undulant fever in humans. To this end, programs of vaccination have been started in most refuges.

The third bacterial disease, malignant anthrax, has a record of devastation dating back to the Middle Ages, when it took a heavy toll of livestock and people. How and when it arrived in America is unclear. It may have been transferred from the Nile valley to the Mississippi delta by ships docking at Gulf ports, or by early expeditions putting in along the Rio Grande.

In areas where anthrax has once killed livestock, the tenacious spores of the organism may account for outbreaks of the disease years later. On an abandoned island off the coast of Scotland, scientists have determined that anthrax spores are still alive and lethal more than twenty-five years after their introduction there in biological warfare tests conducted during World War II.

Although anthrax has been known on this continent since the eighteenth century, few cases were reported among buffalo until recent years. On July 28, 1962, however, a Canadian Wildlife Service biologist helicoptering over the northern edge of Wood Buffalo National Park spotted 32 dead buffalo; during the next three weeks he located another 249 victims. Laboratory examination of the carcasses confirmed that the epidemic had been caused by anthrax.

To halt the disease, the Canadian government initiated strict control measures. Carcasses were buried or cremated where they fell—an enormous task, since infection occurred over seven hundred square miles of remote country. Then the whole area was burned off to keep other buffalo away. Because there was no way to sterilize the soil itself, dormant spores have given rise to periodic outbreaks since the original epidemic.

In the fourth bacterial infection, bovine tuberculosis, germs are usually picked up by inhalation. Once within the body, the bacteria incite formation of a tubercle. If this enlarges and breaks into a blood vessel, the contamination is carried to other organs, bringing the disease to an acute, often fatal, stage. The disease may also take a slower course or be arrested by bodily defenses.

Tuberculosis has been intensively studied in Wood Buffalo National Park, where it kills between four and six per cent of the population annually. One out of every seven animals in the park has been found to be tubercular, leading authorities to suggest a program of eradication. But attempts to eliminate tuberculosis might necessitate the elimination of the buffalo themselves, and the disease is simply not serious enough to warrant such a course. Indeed, the small percentage of deaths is not unwelcome, as it acts to keep the population stable, preventing the animals from eating themselves out of their range.

The tuberculosis bacteria and a legion of other parasites sap nourishment from the buffalo in a one-sided arrangement in which the parasites gain abundant benefits, often harming the host in the process. In contrast, a more equitable relationship exists between buffalo and certain other species, most particularly the so-called buffalo birds. Although bird may gain more than buffalo, the partnership is profitable for both.

The most common buffalo bird is the cowbird; others involved in this unique collaboration are the Brewer's blackbird, redwing, magpie, and starling. A relative of the starling, the African tick bird, maintains a similar partnership with big game, especially rhinoceros and Cape buffalo. Another associate of African game is the cattle egret, a species that has recently moved into the southeastern United States, where it now haunts domestic cattle. Both the American and the African birds are noted for diligently picking parasites from their hosts. The performance of a cowbird described in my field notes from Wind Cave National Park is typical:

> A solitary, aged bull is lying in open meadow as a cowbird flies in and lights on his back. The bird hops around between back and forehead, busily seizing flies from the swarms that are hovering about the animal's body. When the buffalo rests his chin on the ground for a few minutes of solid slumber, the bird flits around his head to catch more flies, continuing to feed while the animal flattens out on one side. After 35 minutes of nearly uninterrupted feasting, the bird flies off—presumably gorged.

Although at such times it may appear that the birds are picking the parasites directly from the bodies of the animals, buffalo birds do not usually feed *on* their hosts' fur; instead, they hunt for insects on the ground *around* the buffalo, where an ever-present supply is concealed in the grass. As the buffalo move about, they stir up this hidden bonanza of leaf hoppers, grasshoppers, and other insects, which are immediately seized by the birds.

For the buffalo birds, however, the partnership is hardly limited to dining; the birds also use their giant companions for lodging and rest. During a downpour on the treeless prairie, the back of a buffalo makes a snug perch. Even in fair weather, I have seen as many as five cowbirds roosting on the "ridgepole" of an old bull's spine. And in winter the birds sink their feet deep into the fuzzy warmth of a buffalo's fur, fluffing out their feathers to seal in every calorie.

But the buffalo is not the exclusive donor in the partnership. To a lesser degree he profits from removal of flies or other parasites. And a few writers have even characterized the bird as a noble sentinel who remains "ever faithful to his friendship, at the sign of danger arousing his shaggy companion by fluttering and crying about him and picking at his head." In Africa, tick birds do indeed rouse their hosts by flying away abruptly with a chattering call, but I have never seen American bison alerted by their companions in a similar fashion. I doubt that they ever are.

Unlike the buffalo birds, who mix with their hosts in neighborly, even intimate, contact, countless other animals benefit from the herds indirectly. These are the species that inhabit a surprisingly rich source of nourishment and life—the ubiquitous piles of buffalo dung. Just as the famed buffalo chip served as fuel for Indian and frontiersman, the fresh dropping achieves distinction as a home for thousands of invertebrates, who exploit it for food, for shelter, and for the rearing of young.

The dank piles are in fact tiny settlements, each with its collection of inhabitants, including groups of parasites and hosts, predators and prey. Flies and beetles are common dung-dwellers, and wasps, earwigs, springtails, and mites often join the colony.

What looks like just another dungheap to the unpracticed eye turns out to be a bustling habitat with subtle gradations in form. As it slowly ages, the drying pile attracts different residents, who move in when the conditions suit them. Thus flies may congregate on nearby grass blades, slipping down on occasion to gingerly test the surface of the dung, waiting until it is dry enough for them to lay their eggs.

Finding the dropping in the first place takes a variety of talents. Some flies (*Haematobia*) stick so close to the herds that they can alight within seconds after each buffalo defecates. Other insects arrive within three minutes by flying or walking along a spoor of wind-blown odors (which have been described as changing rapidly "from a musky sweetness to an unpleasant stink"). Dung beetles come a bit later, often themselves carrying numbers of hitchhiking flies and mites.

Most species remain only long enough to deposit their eggs, departing before the maggots and grubs hatch and begin feeding.

The little colony is soon rife with all kinds of competition. Larvae of beetles and wasps devour or slowly kill fly maggots. Other species fight over space, often jostled by the clumsy maneuvering of a large dung-feeding beetle (*Aphodius*). Another beetle carts away so much of the cake's contents that fly maggots, if not killed in the transfer, are left to starve and dry up beneath an inedible crust; just one of these beetles can destroy the life of an entire dropping.

Most famous of all the dung-feeding beetles is the tumblebug. Gathering a large amount of manure, it works the mass into a ball, deposits an egg inside, and then rolls the contraption to a suitable nesting site, where the grub hatches and matures. Similar dung balls are rolled by a close relative, the sacred scarab of Egypt. (This beetle cousin is more renowned for its position in ancient Egyptian theology, where it was once worshipped as an emblem of planetary movements and the afterlife.)

In addition to subsidizing colonies of dung-feeding insects, the buffalo's droppings may enrich the soil—patches of greener herbage soon spring up in each fertilized area. On the other hand, buffalo also destroy vegetation, vigorously horning and rubbing against trees, sometimes stripping off so much bark that a tree will die, its crown deprived of nutrient channels. Persistent horning can halt proliferation of new trees and may even push back the border of a forest. (This phenomenon occurs only where herds congregate frequently—along major trails and near waterholes and mineral licks. The damage is localized, however, and has little over-all effect on the landscape; buffalo can hardly be given credit for clearing forested sections of the plains.)

Elsewhere in their environment, buffalo bring about marked changes in the prairie soil. Some of their wallows, deeply worn into the ground, fill up with rainwater and become havens for salamanders, toads, and aquatic insects, which may even breed in the stagnant pools. Especially when the soil is moist, the travels of the massed herds may impress distinct paths in the earth. These incipient routes are then broadened and packed with each successive trek, until they are virtual wilderness highways. It was such roads that proved indispensable to early wagon caravans.

Although some of the trailblazing feats attributed to the buffalo are open to question, there is no doubt that the animals choose efficient routes for their journeys. During my adventures with the herds, I hiked over most of the buffalo trails in Hayden

Valley and found that the extensive network offered the best available routes to any point in the area. In nearly straight lines, the trails cut·through confusing masses of timber from one meadow to another. They established surprisingly direct routes through a complex of rolling hills, forded streams at points with gradual approaches and shallow water, and crossed steep-walled canyons at the only negotiable passes.

In choosing the most feasible passages through the valley, these modern buffalo did not necessarily select the most comfortable climbs. Some of their trails are so precipitous that a horse and rider can negotiate them only by crossing back and forth in a series of sharp switchbacks. But the steep sections of the historic trails seldom discouraged travelers seeking passable routes through rough country. They simply bypassed the most difficult areas and rejoined the main trail when it became level again. And Plains Indians leading horses encumbered with travois also followed routes of the herds, along which they could easily find safe stream crossings.

The use of these trails by the tribes was but one more link between Indian and buffalo, further tying the tribes to the intricate web of life on the plains. The Indians were even more closely linked to the herds through their hunting activities. Their consumption of the buffalo classed them with the wolf and the grizzly as terminal links in some buffalo food chains. Harvesting a normal surplus from the herds, they fitted into the scheme on the grassland as unobtrusively as any other predator in the buffalo's community.

But the balance of grassland life was eventually upset by the arrival of professional hunters and fur traders, groups that would bring the buffalo to the brink of extinction, thereby disrupting the community of creatures whose lives were intimately linked with the ways of the herds. In an astonishingly short period of time, the network of species that had formed a smoothly functioning whole fell apart. Some of these animals were able to make the transition to the newly domesticated plains: buffalo birds shifted to cattle just as the tiny world of scavenging insects found a new home in cattle dung. But for many, the extirpation of the storied herds was the fall of the curtain. Grizzly bears and wolves shrank back to mountain fastnesses, and the Indians retired into a shadow of their former glory.

20

NATURAL CATASTROPHES

Before hidemen and other hunters arrived to lay waste to the great hordes of buffalo, the ravages of nature were taking a recurrent, at times disastrous, toll of the herds. In 1867, in one memorable incident, a herd of four thousand bison attempting to ford the Platte River in Nebraska walked into channels of loose quicksand at the water's edge. As animals in the rear, ignorant of the danger, pushed the lead animals onward, hundreds of bison slipped from the banks and sank into the sand. By the time the remnants of the herd reached the opposite shore, over two thousand bison lay mired and dying in the riverbed.

Such catastrophes were almost regular events in historic times and, to a lesser extent, they still occur today. Although the social life style of buffalo may often benefit herd members, this group living has certain disadvantages. Among less gregarious species, the Platte quicksands might have claimed only a handful of victims, but in the massed buffalo, they wiped out thousands at a stroke.

The inevitable bunching in the herds may also result in harmful competition, especially in periods of hardship, such as drought or heavy snow, when food supplies are severely limited. At times, the struggle may kill off weaker individuals, thereby reducing the over-all size of the herd.

Furthermore, crowding brings the animals into close contact with one another, furnishing an exceptionally easy route for the spread of parasites and disease. The two most dangerous buffalo diseases, anthrax and tuberculosis, pass rapidly through a bunched herd. After an outbreak of anthrax in Canada, for example, it was found that the most severely ravaged group had congregated in one limited area. The victims had sealed their own fate by their repeated use of contaminated wallows.

In the same fashion, epidemics of rinderpest yearly sweep through herds of wildebeest on the plains of East Africa, taking their heaviest toll when the animals are crowded into swarming throngs. As they roam the veld in herds that sometimes reach a strength of two hundred thousand, these antelope provide us with a contemporary picture of life as it might have been among the multitudes of historic buffalo. A study of the difficulties of modern wildebeest can throw light on the struggles of the American herds at the height of their population.

Wildebeest suffer their heaviest losses in the calf group, particularly among infants under two weeks of age. If a newborn lives in a small gathering of twenty-five or so cows, it has a good chance of survival; its chances decrease markedly as its herd increases in size—many calves in the larger groups become separated from their mothers during the milling of the multitude. Once lost, a calf is not apt to find its mother again; buffeted from one strange wildebeest to another, it soon weakens and succumbs to starvation or to the ubiquitous hyena. Almost half the calves in the larger groups die each year.

Observers of the historic herds of American buffalo recorded far fewer losses, which leads us to believe that buffalo calves fared better than wildebeest. Infant casualties may have been minimized by the mothers' preference for remaining in isolated groups during the calving season.

Older wildebeest are also killed in accidents within their own ranks; deaths among the animals are so routine that the herds attract a constant following of scavengers awaiting a supply of carcasses. Hyenas and jackals lurk hungrily around the edges of the huge gatherings, and vultures hover above in such dense concentrations that small planes dare not fly low.

The most frequent victims of accidents are wildebeest that have fallen as a result of the mass action of the herd itself. As thousands of animals crowd across rough terrain or through gullies, knocking down small trees in their haste, they jostle their own herd members, until some fall and are trampled in the surge of moving bodies. Every large herd trails a straggling band of cripples with broken legs, cracked horns, or crushed chests.

The welfare of individual animals in the historic herds of buffalo was also jeopardized in the vast concentrations of rapidly moving animals. More than four centuries ago, Coronado came across buffalo fleeing in such numbers that "they trampled one another in their haste until they came to a ravine. So many of the animals fell into this that they filled it all up, and the rest went across on top of them."

To survive such a stampede, each animal had to mesh his own speed and course into the ordered flow of the entire group. If he tried to change pace or direction too abruptly, he would be caught in the momentum of the fleeing throngs about him and became trampled underfoot, often to be injured or killed. Plains Indians put this blind surge of the stampeding herds to good advantage: when skilled hunters maneuvered the rushing animals off precipices, it was usual for an entire herd to perish.

Nor did it necessarily take human direction to steer a herd into disaster; many groups came upon it all by themselves. Quicksand regularly trapped large numbers of buffalo in mishaps like the South Platte River disaster. Some years earlier, George Catlin had run across a band of buffalo "standing with all legs fast, and one half of their bodies above the water, and their heads sunk under it, where they had evidently remained for several days; and flocks of ravens and crows were covering their backs, and picking the flesh from their dead bodies."

Individuals as well as groups fell prey to these bogs. Audubon observed one "unfortunate cow that had fallen into, or rather sunk into a quicksand only seven or eight feet wide; she was quite dead, and we walked on her still fresh carcass safely across the ravine which had buried her in its treacherous and shifting sands."

Even today, buffalo stumble into natural traps of this kind. In recent years, a bog in the northern part of Yellowstone Park snared a cow and a calf—apparently one animal followed the other onto the false sedge-covered bank protruding over the edge of the small pond. When the bank gave way, the victims were thrown into a layer of ooze at least six feet deep. Another marsh in the same region claimed the life of a bull, which had evidently been lured into the muck by some clumps of green sedge.

Yellowstone Park also has a treacherous scattering of boiling pools, whose waters yearly scald a few tourists and entrap a number of insects, snakes, birds, and ungulates. In 1869, reports of such hot springs were brought back by a band of early explorers, who discovered "the entire skeleton of a buffalo that had probably fallen in accidentally and been boiled down to soup." The depths of Ojo Caliente Springs, with a temperature of 202°, claimed buffalo in 1938 and 1945. A nearby spring known as the Queen's Laundry trapped a victim in 1949. And Buffalo Spring still holds the skeletal remains of some of its namesakes; the unsuspecting animals had probably broken through the pool's thin overhanging ledges, to be scalded before managing to regain solid ground.

Just as quagmires and hot springs claimed many victims, turbulent rivers caught scores of other buffalo. Meriwether Lewis, encamped near the Great Falls of the Missouri River, reported on the devastation he had seen:

. . . the fragments of many carcases of these poor animals daily pass down the river, thus mangled, I presume, in descending those immence cataracts above us. As the buffalo generally go in large herds to water and the passages to the river about the falls are narrow and steep, the hinder part of the herd press those in front out of their debth and the water instantly takes them over the cataracts where they are instantly crushed to death without the possibility of escaping. In this manner I have seen ten or a dozen disappear in a few minutes. Their mangled carcases ly along the shores below the falls in considerable quantities . . .

The strength of the current was often enough to clutch unsuspecting buffalo and carry them into the torrent heading for the falls. Only a few would sense the danger in time to fight the flow and paddle their way to shore. Even rivers without waterfalls took their toll in drowned buffalo when inattentive animals were swept into rapid currents.

To this day, buffalo continue to perish in drownings. In Wood Buffalo National Park, forty or fifty die in this manner almost every year; at times the loss may be disastrous. In the spring of 1958, for example, high water in the Athabasca-Peace River delta took the lives of nearly five hundred animals. And during the autumn and winter of 1960, severe flooding along the shores of Lake Claire was believed to have killed three thousand.

These numbers drowned in rivers or lakes are insignificant when compared to the multitudes trapped by breaking ice. Particularly treacherous were both the thin, newly formed ice of late autumn and the slushy, rotten ice of spring, especially the latter, since the herds were accustomed to crossing the winter surface without incident. Areas that could support a few individuals buckled under the weight of massed herds. Unable to regain a hold and clamber out, the victims became lodged under the ice and drowned, only to reappear in staggering numbers during the spring thaw. A fur trader's journal for May 18, 1795, gives a bewildering tally:

Observing a good many carcasses of buffaloes in the [Qu'Appelle] river and along its banks, I was taken up the whole day with counting them and, to my surprise, found I had numbered when we had put up at night, 7360, drowned and mired along the river and in it. It is true, in one or two places, I went on shore and walked from one carcass to the other, where they lay from three to five files deep.

Equally astounding are some notes written by Alexander Henry at his trading post on the Red River in 1801:

March 30th: Rain broke up the ice; it drifted in large masses, making a great noise by crushing, tumbling, and tossing in every direction, driven by a strong current. It continued to drift on the 31st, bearing great numbers of dead buffalo from above, which must have been drowned in attempting to cross while the ice was weak.

April 1st: The river clear of ice, but drowned buffalo continued to drift by in entire herds. It is really astonishing what vast numbers have perished; they formed one continuous line in the current for two days and nights.

April 18th: Rain; drowned buffalo still drifting down the river, but not in such vast numbers as before, many having lodged on the banks and along the beach.

April 25th: Drowned buffalo drift down river day and night.

April 30th: Drowned buffalo drift as usual.

May 1st: The stench from the vast numbers of drowned buffalo along the river was intolerable.

May 2nd: Two hunters . . . tell me the number of buffalo lying along the beach and on the banks above passes all imagination; they form one continuous line, and emit a horrid stench.

May 4th: Encamped at the Bois Perce with my people, I was actually prevented from taking supper by the stench of drowned buffalo that lay on the banks in a state of putrefaction.

The stench rising from ripe carcasses was considered one of the "disagreeable features" of a steamboat trip on the Missouri above Sioux City. Nonetheless, grizzlies, wolves, ravens, and a host of scavengers reveled in the waterborne feast, as did several tribes of Indians. Both men and women in the Mandan area were especially dexterous at diving naked into frigid waters to chase floating carcasses. Leaping or plunging among cakes of ice, they managed to land scores of drowned buffalo during the season. Apparently the putrefaction of the flesh did not diminish its appeal to the Indians, for we are told that such carrion was eaten with relish.

Even present-day herds fall prey to the perils of thin or rotten ice. Many accidents occur in Wood Buffalo National Park as groups of animals attempt to ford the Peace River during their seasonal migrations; the annual breakup in late spring yields from twenty to fifty carcasses. In Yellowstone National Park, a group of five fell through the ice while crossing Slough Creek in 1941, and thirty-eight crashed into the Yellowstone River in 1946; all of these animals, unable to work their way to shore, ultimately drowned.

In addition to the hazard of treacherous ice, the winter season brought severe temperatures and deep snows to trouble the herds at a time when their food supplies were severely reduced. Furthermore, much of the buffalo range lay in a plains area branded the homeland of blizzards. Settlers in the region had to withstand these sieges of wind and snow that blasted through every crack and crevice in their houses. Some even lost their way trying to pass from house to barn as driving blizzards blotted out all objects in sight. (Conditions haven't changed much since those days. Of the more than twenty people who perished in the monumental blizzard of 1966, one was a six-year-old girl who became lost between the chicken coop and barn of her family's farm in North Dakota and froze to death.)

Anyone traveling across the exposed prairie when a blizzard struck was certain to perish unless he was familiar with a plan of safety devised by the knowledgeable plainsman: scooping a deep pit in the snow, the foresighted voyager spread out buffalo robes or blankets brought against such an emergency, then lay down and covered himself with more robes. The snow drifting over his cocoon insulated him against freezing to death from exposure.

Tenderfoots who ridiculed holing up during blizzards soon foundered—dampened, chilled, and frostbitten. Those who didn't freeze to death often faced the eventual loss of a limb. A grim record of the severity of the worst storms was written out in the number of amputations—seventy were performed by the post surgeon at Fort Dodge after the blizzard of 1873.

Blizzards and other rigors of winter, so perilous to pioneers and their domestic stock, were often as great a trial for buffalo. Casualties among the herds have been recorded for as many winters as men have logged records on the animals. In the hundred-year period starting in 1779 a "killer" blizzard occurred about every eleven years. Two were particularly devastating. In 1821 or thereabouts, snow accumulated to a depth of fourteen feet in the Hay River country of northwestern Alberta. The flaky torrent "so enveloped the animals that they perished by the thousands . . ." The catastrophe was not discovered by white men until fifty years later, when two explorers portaging through the area hiked past "thousands of buffalo skulls." After querying local Indians about the dead animals, the voyagers eventually pieced together the details of the historic storm.

In 1865, winter weather was interrupted by a thaw and heavy rain in the area of what is now Wood Buffalo National Park. A subsequent freeze turned the water-sogged snow to a hard, unbreakable crust; unable to root down to their usual forage, large numbers of buffalo starved to death. A decline in population beginning at about the same period has been attributed to decimation by winter storms—justifiably, since the buffalo in this region, in contrast to those on the Great Plains, were never hunted to excess.

It is easy to accept these early records of winter deaths among the herds if one has observed the difficulties of animals attempting to graze under winter conditions. A buffalo feeding in deep snow presses his nose downward, swinging his head back and forth to clear a trench to the grass. The sides of his head and even his neck assist his excavating; on rare occasions he may use a front hoof to push aside stubborn chunks of snow.

This nasal snowplowing is rigorous work. Snow balls up on long hairs around the edge of the animal's mouth, eventually severing them to give him what might be described as an involuntary shave. Occasionally herds working in frozen crust leave evidence of their toils in tracings of blood. Yet the animals manage to tunnel down to forage in snow as deep as four feet, although they almost disappear in the process.

The survival of most buffalo through winter hardships that would devastate other breeds has given the animals an inflated reputation for stoicism. According to many admiring reports from plains witnesses, the brave beasts faced *into* storms like so many cadets standing at attention. Though such a description flatters the stalwart buffalo of legend, it fails to correspond with behavior I've seen in the herds. All the bison I've observed during storms have been facing in random directions. Records of Indian ritual also fail to support the romantic idea of blizzard-battling buffalo. The Blackfoot, Flathead, Mandan, and Hidatsa Indians held bison-calling ceremonies based on an accepted tendency of the beasts to move *away* from a storm. They appealed to their spirit helpers to bring blizzards blowing from the herds toward camp, thereby driving animals in with the wind. The stereotype is made still more questionable by the well-documented reports of winter migrations, which found the herds retreating into wooded areas to seek shelter from approaching storms.

Despite the inaccuracy of this cherished theory, the hardy buffalo have an extraordinary capacity for riding out foul weather. Their bodies help to fortify them against the rages of winter—the skin thickens, develops fatty deposits, and puts forth a marked increase of woolly hairs. Thus warmly insulated, the animals plow stubbornly through deep snow. Panting heavily from exhaustion, their tongues dangling even after short treks, they forge ahead, no matter how rough the going. If necessary they can negotiate astonishing depths. When our light plane frightened a group of twenty-five in Hayden Valley, the animals blundered into a cornice twenty feet deep. Although they floundered—one buffalo even clambered across the back of a neighbor—they all finally managed to wade through.

The annual assault of ice and snow was surely the greatest trial for the buffalo, but other elemental forces took their toll as well. The drought of 1276–1299, dated by evidence of hardship it inflicted on Indian populations in parts of the southwest, is suspected of having devastated herds in the same region; at about this time, especially in New Mexico, buffalo disappeared from some districts never to return. In 1875 drought was said to have resulted in the starvation of hundreds of buffalo in central Texas. (Although many victims of drought succumb to starvation immediately, the local population may be weakened for many more months by a shortage of Vitamin A. The only natural source of this vitamin, green forage, customarily dries up during a drought. The resulting vitamin deficiency—carefully documented in sheep—causes a lowering of the birth rate, and in time reduces numbers as surely as starvation.)

Other aspects of plains weather have been known to claim the lives of buffalo. On rare occasions, bolts of lightning knocked out an animal in the early herds. And buffalo caught in the path of a tornado were likely to be annihilated, as a hunter traversing the Kansas plains discovered in 1854:

> . . . we saw where the cyclone that had jumped us had stripped acres of sod and soil from the prairies. We also found two dead buffalo completely denuded of hair, and every bone in their bodies crushed. Those animals must have been picked up by the cyclone, carried to a great height, and then dashed to the earth.

A small war party of Sioux once watched another tornado carefully as the funnel descended toward a herd of buffalo; before the dark cone dipped into the herd, however, torrential rains forced the Indians to take shelter. Emerging after the storm, the men discovered "hundreds" of carcasses strewn over a quarter of a mile, the majority broken and twisted, some stripped of fur and mutilated, many stacked in heaps four and five deep.

Of all the forces on the grassland, however, the most terrifying were the great wind-driven fires. In the short-grass plains, where the tinder was sparse and thin, the fire crept along with a relatively feeble flame that men and animals could hop over; but in the lush foliage of the tall-grass prairie, including the rich meadowlands along major rivers, fire was a deadly, raging force. Whipped by the wind, the blaze raced over the grass with a terrifying roar, sometimes even overtaking fleeing Indians on their fastest mounts. (On September 11, 1971, a prairie fire running fast before the wind in northeastern Montana was clocked by a truck driver at twenty-five miles an hour. Flames leaping ten to twenty feet into the air then swept into the settlement of Oswego to destroy eighteen of the town's twenty-six buildings. It was the third time Oswego had been devastated by a prairie fire in the past half-century.)

Such fires were regular, natural forces in buffalo country, for the scorching summer sun turned the heated plain into an enormous tinderbox. Lightning started many blazes, which, nurtured by dry grasses, often flared out of control. And the Indians sometimes set the prairies afire, using such man-made conflagrations for a number of purposes—to send messages, to harass inimical neighbors, and to divert or drive buffalo.

Whether kindled by lightning or by man, prairie fires sometimes blossomed into holocausts that destroyed or maimed large numbers of buffalo. In 1850, a settler traversing the Oregon Trail just west of Council Bluffs viewed the aftermath of one such catastrophe:

> There had been a slope of the prairie burned and it had killed hundreds of buffaloes. We saw as many as three hundred lying together with the hair all burned off them while many were roaming around deprived of their eyesight by the fire. Many were shot to put them out of their misery . . .

An even more terrible scene was witnessed in southern Manitoba in 1804:

> Plains burned in every direction and blind buffalo seen every moment wandering about. The poor beasts have all the hairs singed off; even the skin in many places is shrivelled up and terribly burned, and their eyes are swollen and closed fast. It was really

pitiful to see them staggering about, sometimes running afoul of a large stone, at other times tumbling down hill and falling into creeks not yet frozen over. In one spot we found a whole herd lying dead . . . At sunset we arrived at the Indian camp, having . . . seen incredible numbers of dead and dying, blind, lame, singed and roasted buffalo. The fire raged all night toward the S.W.

The few buffalo that might have escaped unscathed from the giant holocausts were isolated on a scorched plain devoid of greenery for mile upon mile. Most eventually died of starvation.

Such conflagrations have become a lesser threat to prairie wildlife with the advent of modern fire-fighting practices. But, ironically, developing technology has also presented buffalo with a contemporary danger—the motor vehicle. In areas where highways cross through buffalo preserves, the animals risk encounters with cars, and vice versa. The hazard is greatest after dusk, when the dark fur of the beasts blends into the night. I once narrowly missed colliding with a large bull I met ambling across a road in Yellowstone Park at night. Only at the last moment was I able to detect a white glimmer of eyeball, a slight sheen on a shaggy coat. Although I swerved in time, others have been less fortunate. Collisions between vehicles and buffalo have occurred in most preserves—to the great detriment of both parties.

Although the buffalo's survival has been contingent on his very removal from the frenetic activities of men, it appears that even in his preserves, the great national beast is not immune to the pressure of modern times.

21

WESTWARD

THE HUNTERS

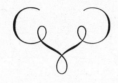

Natural disasters had been taking a heavy toll on the herds for centuries. Thousands of animals, their fate clearly documented in historical narrative, had perished in river, fire and storm. But in the 1800's there appeared a band of men who seemed intent on outdoing nature itself.

Among this band was St. George Gore, a rich nobleman who had left his native Ireland to sample "the wild delights of the chase" through America's buffalo country. Striking out from St. Louis in the spring of 1854, Sir George led an elaborately equipped expedition that was to set a standard of frontier luxury for some time to come.

Gore's trip lasted almost three years, cost some five hundred thousand dollars, and carried him over the plains for more than six thousand miles. His personal staff consisted of forty servants and several scientists; the expedition traveled with seventy saddle horses, three dairy cows, as well as "four six-mule wagons, two three-yoke ox wagons and twenty-one French carts, painted red, each drawn by two horses." One entire wagon was given over to the transport of firearms, among them seventy-five muzzle-loading rifles. Between forty and fifty dogs were brought along for chasing game.

The nobleman himself rode a Kentucky thoroughbred, switching to the comfort of a large carriage whenever he wearied of the saddle. He spent his nights under a linen tent decorated with a green and white striped lining and stocked with vintage wines and masterworks of English literature. An ornate rug served as his ground cloth, and he slept each night on a brass bedstead, which unscrewed to facilitate packing.

After hunting buffalo on the plains during the summer of 1854, Gore holed up for the winter at Fort Laramie. There he met the famed mountaineer Jim Bridger, who guided the party across the northwestern plains for the next year and a half. By the time Gore disbanded his outfit in the spring of 1857, his reckless slaughter had brought down two thousand buffalo.

Buffalo were considered enticing targets by other sportsmen, among them Washington Irving, who tried his luck on the central plains in 1832. Although the celebrated author felled a few animals with a gun, his aim with pen was surer:

> There is a mixture of the awful and the comic in the look of these huge animals, as they bear their great bulk forward . . . tail cocked up like the queue of Pantaloon in a pantomime, the end whisking about in a fierce yet whimsical style, and their eyes glaring venomously with an expression of fright and fury.

Eleven years later, William Drummond arrived from Scotland to organize a buffalo-shooting expedition. His white jacket and Panama hat were somewhat at odds with the rugged outfits of his guides, but Sir William managed to ride and shoot as well as any of them. Together, nobleman and guides left the prairie about the Platte River "strewn for miles" with the carcasses of slain buffalo.

For one English sportsman, Grantley F. Berkeley, the greatest titillation—greater even than the pleasures of the chase—was a face-to-face encounter with an American buffalo:

To see a bull of this sort halt on his native plain and dare the close approach of man, under the peculiarly ferocious aspect as well as power assigned him by nature, is absolutely a poem in itself, well worthy the contemplation of any lover of nature or scion of the chase, and I would not have missed its advent for a great deal. The solitude of the scene, the size and appearance of the game, the immense area of desert around you, and the fact that you are there dependent on your horsemanship and your aim with the *diminutive-looking* weapon in your hand for your life as well as for the successful issue of the chase, altogether makes the situation so beautiful that words fail to convey any idea of the pleasurable excitement of the hunter's position.

Buffalo hunting became the rage, its reputation swelled by the tales of returning eastern dudes, who had trooped to the plains in hordes to find out if reports of the celebrated herds were true. The railroads began to plug low-priced buffalo-hunting excursions across the Kansas prairies with exhibitions of live buffalo and advertisements headlining the numbers of animals shot on previous junkets.

Hunting from trains could hardly be considered sport. One observer called it "the most cruel of all bison-hunting pastimes," and gave a sorrowful description of the practice:

The rate per mile of passenger trains is slow upon the plains, and hence it often happens that the cars and buffalo will be side by side for a mile or two . . . During these races the car-windows are opened, and numerous breech-loaders fling hundreds of bullets among the densely crowded and flying masses. Many of the poor animals fall, and more go off to die in the ravines. The train speeds on, and the scene is repeated every few miles . . .

Most of the victims were left to rot by the tracks. Only infrequently did the train halt to permit the loading of a carcass onto a baggage car.

Full-blooded sportsmen frowned on such ungallant slaughter, preferring instead to chase and kill their quarry on horseback. Such was the method selected for a hunting trip organized by General Phil Sheridan for more than a dozen of his "millionaire" friends from the East. Though green in the ways of the chase, they found a ready guide in "Buffalo Bill" Cody, who led them to bison and other game for ten days of hunting in Kansas. The men tempered the adversities of life on the open plains with iced wine, and had for escort a hundred cavalrymen and a train of sixteen government wagons, including three horse-drawn ambulances to cater to saddle-sore hunters.

One of the members of the millionaire group was James Gordon Bennett II, publisher of the New York *Herald*. The newspaperman returned to write an enthusiastic description of flamboyant Buffalo Bill, the "beau ideal of the plains."

This notice was a mere prologue to the reams of publicity Cody was soon to receive for another hunt. On January 13, 1872, the famous guide greeted a special train as it steamed into the station at North Platte, Nebraska. Aboard were General Phil Sheridan, Lieutenant Colonel George Custer (who would gain lasting fame four years later at the Little Bighorn), and a highly touted royal guest—Grand Duke Alexis, third son of Czar Alexander II of Russia. Alexis and his entourage departed immediately for their base camp on Red Willow Creek, where Cody had made preparations to guide them on a great buffalo hunt.

The following day, Cody gave Alexis his celebrated buffalo-running horse, "Buckskin Joe," and told him he had only to "sit on the horse's back and fire away." But the instructions were somehow lacking, for the Duke's first shots passed on all sides of the buffalo. What followed is best described by Cody:

> I now rode up close beside him and advised him not to fire until he could ride directly upon the flank of a buffalo . . . We dashed off together and ran our horses on either flank of a large bull, against the side of which the Duke thrust his gun and fired a fatal shot. He was very much elated at his success . . .

Indeed he was. As the Kansas City *Times* reported the scene, the Duke

> . . . leaped from the saddle in a transport of astonishment, turned the horse loose, threw the gun down, cut off the tail as a souvenir, and then, sitting down on the carcass, waved the dripping trophy and as Custer later stated, "let go a series of howls and gurgles like the death-song of all the fog-horns and calliopes ever born." These cries penetrated the ears of the waiting party, and, among others, the Russians came galloping to see what was the matter. They first

solemnly embraced their prince by turns, then fell into each other's arms. The trophy was passed from hand to hand till all were plastered with blood and dirt. The timely arrival of an ambulance . . . put an end to the riot and enabled each to drown his joy in champagne.

Two days later, the party returned to North Platte, where the Russian bade his boisterous guide farewell, presenting him with a pin bristling with diamonds and a purse full of greenbacks.

Grand Duke Alexis continued his tour, stopping in eastern Colorado for a final buffalo hunt with Custer before heading back to rejoin his fleet, which lay at anchor off Pensacola. The Colorado stop was so hurriedly arranged that Alexis' army escorts were caught off guard without mounts for the distinguished sportsmen. Horses were borrowed from nearby Fort Wallace—but the only available animals were unaccustomed to running buffalo. Presented with the choice of using these horses or abandoning the venture, Alexis decided to take a chance on the raw steeds.

The decision almost proved disastrous. Custer and Alexis rode calmly out toward the herd, but when the inexperienced mounts caught their first sight of buffalo, they panicked and tore off out of control, taking their startled riders on a wild dash across the prairie. Eventually, however, the men managed to rein in the animals, and on a less hazardous second run into the herd, both brought down a respectable number of buffalo.

This unnerving experience was nothing new to Colonel Custer, who had had his share of difficulties when running buffalo on horseback. Once he had met disaster as he rode his wife's favorite saddle horse, "Custis Lee," into the chase. The Colonel later explained the "most unfortunate occurrence" in a letter to his wife:

I . . . was about to pull the trigger, when the buffalo again turned on me and so suddenly as to cause Lee to veer to the left. I drew up my pistol, intending to use both hands in controlling the horse, when, just as my hand was raised to the reins, my finger accidentally and in the excitement of the moment, pressed the trigger and discharged the weapon, the ball entering Lee's neck near the top of his head and penetrating his brain. Both horse and buffalo had been at full speed. The shot produced instant death . . . I was thrown heels over head, clean over Lee, but strange to say, I received not a scratch or bruise.

General Custer, confronted by bull, after shooting his wife's horse by accident.

Custer went on to assert that he had never lost his presence of mind. Nor had the buffalo, for that matter; after glaring at his prostrate assailant for a moment, he turned and trotted off across the plain.

Custer's accident was not unusual in buffalo-running, a sport as dangerous as it was exhilarating. Riding pell-mell after stampeding herds was a risky enterprise, as the Indians discovered soon after acquiring their first mounts. White hunters, many of them less skilled than the Indians, were even more likely to be undone by the hunt on horseback. Some lost life or limb from the unintentional discharge of firearms, or learned the hard way that an enraged buffalo would turn upon his pursuers; others suffered injurious or fatal tumbles when their mounts fell into ravines, stumbled over hillocks, or caught their legs in hidden animal burrows. Hospitals in buffalo territory contained a goodly number of "buffalo cripples"—men with gunshot wounds and broken bones sustained during the hunt.

But serious accidents occurred less frequently than one might expect. As historian Francis Parkman suggested, "in the recklessness of the chase, the hunter enjoys all the impunity of a drunken man, and may ride in safety over gullies and declivities, where, should he attempt to pass in his sober senses, he would infallibly break his neck."

Despite their reckless killing, these dude hunters had little effect on the vast buffalo population. It was a different breed of hunter, the professional hideman, who ushered in the threat of extinction with a wild massacre that was to last about a dozen years.

———◦———

Although the first big haul of the hidemen was shipped out in 1871, a local trade in buffalo skins had been thriving on the continent for thousands of years. Long before the arrival of the first Europeans, tribes were already bartering among themselves, exchanging the fruits of the chase for the products of the farm. Nomads offered buffalo hides, robes, fat, and dried meat in return for the vegetables and tobacco of the villagers.

The trade in furs expanded in the 1700's with the visits of early explorers, who swapped the white man's goods for the richly tanned buffalo robes of the Indians. This barter reached a peak in the first half of the 1800's, furnishing countless Americans with cozy, thick-furred buffalo robes for sled and sleigh, carriage and wagon, sofa and bed—even for overcoats and overshoes, as snug as they were cumbersome. Eventually, however, the traffic in shaggy robes gave way to a much more extensive trade in dry, raw hides.

Instrumental in the shift to hides was a breakthrough in tanning processes. By 1871, tanneries in Europe and America had devised new ways of treating dry buffalo hides, and the hide business boomed. Although the most thickly furred hides, taken in fall or early winter, were still tanned with the hair on for use as robes, coats, or overshoes, the rest of the hides were turned into fine, serviceable leather. One dealer's entire supply went to the British army, which considered buffalo leather more flexible and elastic than cowhide, and used it to replace many of the standard articles in a soldier's outfit. Buffalo leather was also in demand for the belting needed for the machinery of an expanding industrial complex. For interior decoration in affluent homes of the period, the latest mode was richly padded furniture and textured wall panelings, both made from buffalo leather. And for the cushions, linings, and tops of carriages, sleighs, and hearses, it was the best leather available. As the market for the product opened up, tanneries and hide dealers began to broadcast orders for large quantities of skins, and carload after carload started rolling eastward to supply the mounting trade.

Moving in the opposite direction was an army of hunters lured by the prospect of quick riches in the expanding hide business. They surged onto the Great Plains in droves, to play as vital a role in the opening of the West as the explorers, missionaries, trappers, fur traders, and goldseekers before them.

Buffalo hunters were a controversial lot, derided by some as uncouth barbarians, praised by others as pioneer heroes. A voice rising from the ranks of the hunters themselves labeled the group "the saltiest goddam men on the Western frontier." In truth, the men were a combination of all these things, leading lives so rich and full of adventure that they inspired many a colorful volume (among the best, Wayne Gard's *The Great Buffalo Hunt* and Mari Sandoz' *The Buffalo Hunters*).

To be sure, the hidemen's ruthless eradication of the herds starved out the Plains Indians, paving the way for stockmen and wheat farmers; but these tough professionals hardly pondered how they might affect the nation's destiny. They were out on the prairie for one purpose—to accumulate as many buffalo hides as they could, in as short a time as possible. Buffalo hunting was one of the few thriving businesses in the years of depression following the panic of 1873, and the men were there to milk it of every penny.

But for all their greed, buffalo hunters seldom made fortunes; many barely broke even. For each buffalo hide sold to a dealer, the hunter received anywhere from about one to three dollars, depending on the market. This was a good deal of money at the time, but because of the nature of their business, few hidemen realized high profits. Before even starting on a hunt, the men had to plunk down large sums of money for rifles, ammunition, horses, wagons, and other supplies. In the best of years they had to reckon with the unpredictable wandering of the herds, sometimes waiting for days before bringing in a good kill. And they were at the mercy of prolonged damp spells, which could spoil hides before they had a chance to dry.

The buffalo men fared poorly indeed when compared to other historical hunters. During the same period, hunters of passenger pigeons collected enormous sums for their labors—in just five weeks of intense effort, a skilled pigeon-netter could capture enough barrelfuls of the birds to earn a normal year's wages. And at the height of the ivory trade in Africa, a hunter got about five hundred dollars for the hundred pounds of ivory in an average bull's tusks; proficient hunters could travel over the veld in luxury and eventually retire in wealth.

American hide hunters, by contrast, worked for small remuneration under rough and dirty conditions, and their pursuits were fraught with danger. Caught on the open plain in blizzards, hunters could perish in drifting snow or iron cold; many were maimed by frostbite. Indians defended their hunting grounds against all intruders, especially buffalo men. Aware of the risk they ran, hunters kept as sharp a lookout for Indian ambushes as they did for herds; many carried capsules of cyanide to swallow if they should be confronted with inevitable capture. A quick end by poison was considered preferable to prolonged torture at the hands of the Indians.

Naturally the buffalo themselves contributed to the hidemen's troubles. Now and then wounded animals charged hunters, injuring some, killing others; occasional hunters were dispatched by "dead" buffalo that rose again to make a last, fatal lunge. In 1864 Charles Reynolds and a partner, walking up to butcher several buffalo they had just killed, spotted a cow stretched out on her side, still twitching nervously, though apparently close to death. As Reynolds' partner moved in to cut the animal's throat, she sprang up, charged, horned him with a sudden blow in the chest, and collapsed. Rushing to his companion, Reynolds found him ripped open from belly to throat so cleanly that he was able to view "the heart still expanding and contracting." The man died within minutes. After burying his friend on the spot, Reynolds rode into a nearby town and reported the accident, only to be accused of falsifying a murder. In order to establish his innocence he was forced to return to the grave and dig up his companion's body.

Despite the hardships, the dangers, and the middling pay, buffalo hunters loved their work and their wild, free lives. And there was always excitement in the nearby boom towns—Miles City, Dodge City, Fort Griffin, and others. Money that came in easily from a fortunate kill often went out just as easily, in the saloons, dance halls, gambling parlors, and "other evils" lurking in the frontier towns. "Hays City by lamplight," observed a writer of the day, "was remarkably lively and not very moral."

In addition to offering nightly diversion, the pioneer town served as depot and shipping point for raw hides and as headquarters for equipping hunting parties. Most outfits consisted of four to a dozen or more men, well organized to buck the competition, the Indians, and the elements. The leader of each outfit usually doubled as hunter, and was likely to be a skillful shot who could kill twenty-five to a hundred buffalo a day, enough to keep his team of more than five skinners busy from dawn to dusk, and often into the night. There was also a cook, two or three hide handlers, and a man to reload the cartridges.

Outfits were considerably more elaborate in the Red River country of Manitoba, where full-scale buffalo hunting had commenced decades before the hunting on the American plains. Chiefly responsible for these operations was Thomas Douglas, the fifth Earl of Selkirk. Early in the nineteenth century, during the Anglicizing of Scotland, numbers of his countrymen had been evicted from their small farms in the highlands so their grain fields could be pieced together into large sheep ranches. To accommodate these displaced farmers, Lord Selkirk had secured a land grant from the Hudson's Bay Company, a plot of 116,000 square miles lying south of Lake Winnipeg and embracing much of the valley of the Red River. Colonists began to arrive in 1812, intending to make their livelihood in farming. Their crops fared poorly, however, and the newcomers soon turned to buffalo hunting for a living.

In later years, the settlement of Red River hunters accepted a large influx of *métis*, or half-breeds, the progeny of Indian and French-Canadian unions. Though welcomed into the community, the new citizens were warned by the Scotsmen: ". . . remember, there is no field here for the pursuit of your savage life; you must settle down, cultivate the soil, and become Christians."

The *métis* made no conspicuous efforts to settle down, but they did duplicate on their own one Christian principle—they outlawed buffalo hunting on the Sabbath. This prohibition was one of a number of laws drawn up by *métis* leaders to ensure a military control over the hunt, a disciplinary system borrowed from the neighboring Plains Ojibwa. Like the tribes, the half-breeds deputized special police to enforce the rules of the hunt, which prohibited stalking apart from the main party and running buffalo before the signal for attack. Any half-breed who broke the laws had his saddle or clothing chopped to pieces; repeated offenders were flogged.

Red River hunting expeditions downed most of their buffalo on the plains of Manitoba and the Dakota Territory, headquartering between hunts in the area of present-day Winnipeg. These expeditions had a vital effect on the local community, involving large numbers of people and quantities of equipment. Following is a list of expenses for an outing of "1630 souls" who set forth on a two-month hunt on June 15, 1840:

620	hunters at $0.23 per day	$ 8,556
650	women at $0.18 per day	7,020
360	boys & girls at $0.08 per day	1,728
1210	carts at $6.75 each	8,167
403	buffalo-running horses at $67.50 each	27,202
655	cart horses at $36.00 each	23,580
586	draft oxen at $27.00 each	15,822
	Saddlery	3,810
740	guns, with ammunition	7,550
	Sundries "too tedious to be enumerated"	5,290
	TOTAL	$108,725

When this well-outfitted group returned from the hunting grounds in August, they had accumulated a little over a million pounds of buffalo meat—some nine hundred pounds per cart. A portion of this they saved to stock their own larders, but most of it had to be sold to traders at the Hudson's Bay Company in order to square the debts of the expedition and raise a little extra money for household necessities. Many hunters went out again for a second or third trip to round up enough meat to tide their families over the winter.

Before each assault on the buffalo, the Red River men gathered on the prairie in full force, "no less than four hundred huntsmen all mounted, and anxiously waiting for the word 'Start!' " A witness in 1840 described the ensuing chase:

In a moment more the herd took flight, and horse and rider are presently seen bursting in among them; shots are heard, and all is smoke, dust and hurry. The fattest are first singled out for slaughter, and in less time than we have occupied with the description, a thousand carcasses strew the plain. Those who have seen a squadron of horses dash into battle may imagine the scene, which we have no skill to depict. The earth seemed to tremble when the horses started; but when the animals fled it was like the shock of an earthquake.

Clearly the Red River hunters adored the sport of the chase as they rode at breakneck speed into the midst of stampeding herds, singling out one target after another. But the professional hidemen on the American plains were not interested in sport; they were seeking more practical ways to down large numbers of animals. Buffalo-running on horseback was poor practice, they argued; it frightened the herds out of the country, squandered ammunition and manpower, and generated too many casualties among the horsemen and their mounts. (The Red River chase just described, over a hunting plain riddled with rocks and badger burrows, had been a debacle. At one point, twenty-three horses and riders lay sprawled on the ground: "One horse, gored by a bull, was killed on the spot; two more were disabled by the fall. One rider broke his shoulder blade; another burst his gun and lost three of his fingers by the accident; and a third was struck on the knee by an exhausted ball.")

Furthermore, buffalo-running left carcasses scattered all over the prairie, and skinners had to waste valuable time traveling from one spot to another to handle them. The American hidemen preferred a hunting technique that would leave carcasses in convenient concentrations; they favored the "still hunt," in which participants stalked and shot at the herd from under cover. Some called this "sheer murder," but the hidemen were unconcerned. The method netted them as many buffalo as their skinners could handle.

Before a hunter advanced on the herd, he tested the direction of the wind, for as one veteran explained, "If Mr. Buffalo ever gets wind of you, his hide is lost for good." Picking a few blades of grass, he dropped them in mid-air and watched the direction they took as they fell to the ground. Then, keeping downwind from the herd, he began his stalk. To conceal his approach, he walked through ravines or took cover behind bushes, mounds, or other projections on the landscape. If he could find no natural cover, he might crawl slowly and steadily on his hands and knees in open view. Even when buffalo spotted him creeping along, they often ignored him (some, fascinated by the curious four-legged interloper, might even move closer to peer at him). Such an approach was easiest when the animals were lying down or busily grazing.

A successful stalk conveyed the hunter to within about 250 yards of the herd, more often much closer. Once within range, he positioned his rifle and began to fire. If his shooting spooked the herd, he jumped to his feet and "ran right after the buffalo as hard and fast as possible, to save every inch of that hard-earned ground. When the buffalo were running, they couldn't see that their pursuer was in motion."

If they stopped to look back, the animals obligingly positioned themselves broadside to the hunter, who would fire off a few quick shots to pick off stragglers before they had a chance to run. The herd might retreat again and again, moving a shorter distance each time. Chasing after each of these graduated withdrawals, the hunter could eventually down enough for his skinners.

The most coveted achievement for a hunter was a "stand." In this strange combination of luck and skill, the buffalo blindly stood their ground and allowed the rifleman to slay scores from one herd without ever changing his position.

A well-known hideman named John Cook, after three years of steady hunting, made the biggest kill of his career in a stand. Toward noon of a hot June day in 1875 on the southwestern plains, from a position of concealment, he studied a nearby group of about a thousand animals. Patiently waiting until they finished drinking and began to lie down, he noted that those still on their feet "seemed to be sound asleep." Cook stalked to within "eighty steps" and began shooting: "I shot a tremendously large bull first. All he did was 'cringe' a little. Not half of those lying down arose at the report of the gun. After [I had made] three good dead shots, those closest to me moved off a little toward the creek. Getting in a good shot at the leader, I stopped him and that stopped the rest." Cook went on to describe the kill in detail:

I now had what I had so often heard about but had never actually seen before, *a stand*. Charlie Hart, while I was with him, had given me some good pointers on how to manage "a stand," if I ever got one. He told me not to shoot fast enough to heat the gun barrel to an over-expansion; to always try to hit the outside ones; to shoot at any that started to walk off, unless I thought they were mortally wounded. He said that "with an over-expanded gun barrel the bullet would go wobbling, and would be liable to break a leg; and that would start a bolt."

After I had killed twenty-five that I knew of, the smoke from my gun commenced to hang low, and was slow in disappearing. So I shifted my position and in doing so, got still closer. And I know that many of the herd saw me move. I had shot perhaps half a dozen times, when, as I was reloading, I heard a keen whistle behind me. Looking around I saw Charlie Cook (John Cook's hunting partner). He was on his all-fours, creeping up to me. He said: "Go ahead; take it easy; I am coming with more cartridges." He crawled right up to my side with my gun (John had been using a borrowed gun) and an extra sack of ammunition for me, and a canteen of water. He asked if the gun was shooting all right. I told him "Yes; but the barrel is pretty warm." He told me to try my own gun a while and let his gun cool a little. We exchanged guns, and I commenced again.

Even while I was shooting buffaloes that had not been shot at all, some would lie down apparently unconcerned about the destruction going on around them. I fired slowly and deliberately. Charlie poured some water from the canteen down the muzzle of his gun; then pulled down the breech-block and let the water run out. He then ran a greased rag in the eyelet of the wiping-stick and swabbed the barrel out, leaving the breech-block open for a while, thus cooling the barrel, in order to have that gun ready for use when my own gun got too warm.

An hour and a quarter and two gun changes later, John Cook took aim and fired at a big bull, breaking its left leg, but failing to bring it down. Frantically hopping around, its disabled limb flopping back and forth, the bull crashed into several nearby buffalo, then headed directly through the center of the herd. Its panicky actions drew the herd into retreat, and the stand was broken. Cook went on firing for as long as the animals were in range:

I moved up to a dead buffalo and got in several good shots . . . I moved again, on through the dead ones, to the farthermost one, and fired three more shots and quit. As I walked back through where the carcasses lay the thickest, I could not help but think that I had done wrong to make such a slaughter for the hides alone.

In counting them just as they lay there, their eyes glassy in death, (I found) I had killed eighty-eight; and several left the ground with more bad than slight wounds.

Other hunters did even better than Cook, their records enduring as testimony to the awesome slaughter possible in a stand:

Wright Mooar	96
Kirk Jordan	100
Charles Rath	107
Vic Smith	107
Doc Zahl	120
Tom Nixon	204
Orlando A. "Brick" Bond	250 (some even said 300)

(Tom Nixon was perhaps better known for another stand in which he downed 120 in forty minutes. His rapid firing in this encounter overheated his rifle so badly that it was ruined by the end of the massacre.)

Most buffalo hunters killed only as many animals as their skinners could handle in a day. The men knew it would be wasteful to kill more, but as veteran Frank Mayer once admitted, it wasn't the waste of the animals that stayed their trigger fingers—they simply didn't want to squander ammunition.

In many stands, the buffalo themselves set the limit on the slaughter. John Cook's herd, for example, had stampeded when he wounded the big bull without killing him. Cook had violated the cardinal rule for a stand: Always Kill Cleanly. Most hunters aimed for the lungs instead of the heart. Hit in the lungs, the buffalo floundered briefly, then collapsed in death; but a buffalo struck in the heart often made a frantic dash for a hundred yards or more, sending the entire herd into panicky retreat.

In addition to aiming for vital organs and approaching the herd with caution, the hunter attempting a stand had to take two other important precautions. To avoid being detected by the buffalo, he positioned himself downwind from the herd and kept himself concealed at all times (some men even slipped into position just before dawn). A few hunters preferred remote stations because the distance muffled the crack of their rifles, but many stands were brought off at close range, where the herd could obviously hear the rifle's report. (John Cook was blasting away a mere eighty steps from the herd.) "The report of the gun and the noise made by the fall of the wounded buffalo," wrote a plains observer, "astound, but do not drive away, the rest."

Other hunters attributed much of their success in stands to early elimination of the herd's leaders, whom they spotted by their "distinctive behavior within the group." Among other things, so it was said, lead animals were the first to dash away. The men shot the "leaders" at once and continued to fire at fleeing individuals, until eventually the remainder of the herd thrashed about without direction.

A void in leadership could have caused the helpless milling of these besieged herds, but this claim is brought into question by the clear admission of most hunters that the gunned-down leaders were bulls. My studies of modern herds reveal that virtually all mixed herds are led by cows.

An important element in the creation of a stand was a strange curiosity in the buffalo themselves, a trait still exhibited in contemporary herds. During one recent hunt in the Crow Reservation, for instance, an Indian game warden carefully stalked close to the herd and remained concealed in shrubbery while shooting at individual animals; the herd did not run away, but remained to mill around and sniff at the slaughtered buffalo. And in a Wyoming herd raised commercially for meat, the owner killed some twenty animals each year by calmly driving up in a truck and shooting them one by one; unafraid of cars or people, and apparently untroubled by the rifle's report, the herd of 150 generally ignored the hunter and gathered inquisitively about slain companions.

This odd attraction to blood or carcasses is mentioned in so many historical reports that it emerges as a striking factor in stands.

Joel Allen:

> . . . sometimes he [the hunter] has to rise and drive away the stupid creatures to prevent the living from playfully goring the dead!

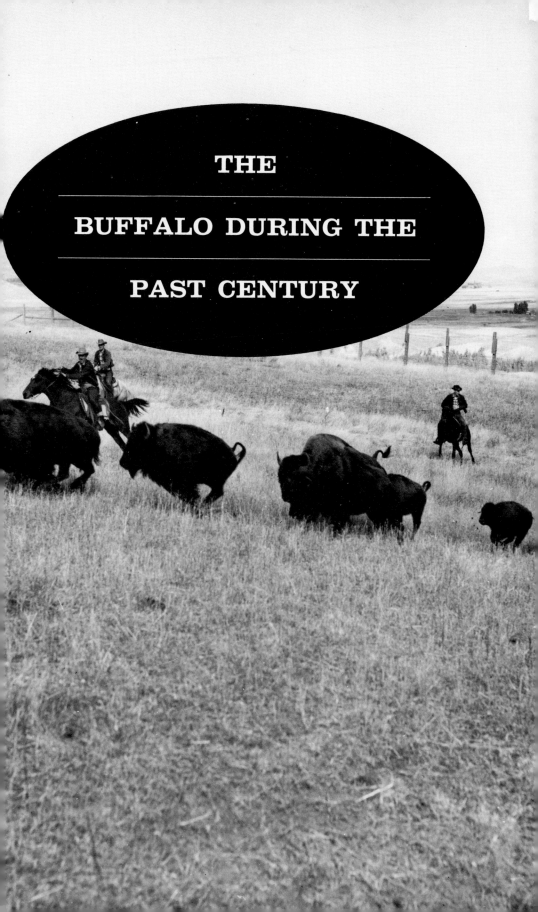

THE

BUFFALO DURING THE

PAST CENTURY

"Buffalo Bill" Cody is featured above in "The Great Royal Buffalo Hunt," painted in 1894 by Louis Maurer, a well-known Currier and Ives artist and a personal friend of Cody's. In the painting, Grand Duke Alexis is to the left of Cody and Lt. Col. George Custer is at the right, in buckskins. The Indian is probably Chief Spotted Tail of the Sioux, who acted as regional host to Alexis along with about one hundred of his tribesmen. Several years after Cody's exploits, when the buffalo were gone from the plains, he organized a Wild West Show, in which some half-wild buffalo (below) were featured.

"The Deadly Still Hunt," painted by James Henry Moser in 1888, depicts the hideman's most successful maneuver—a "stand." The hunter crawled toward buffalo under cover, keeping downwind. Once in position, he could often shoot scores before the herd finally fled.

Although this train was stopped to let passengers shoot, most engineers simply slowed their trains. Passengers could then shoot, as an observer in 1869 noted, "from every available window, with rifles, carbines, and revolvers. An American scene, certainly."

Hunting in northern Montana during the last big season for the hide-men, the winter of 1881–2, this hunter has very neatly felled all of his buffalo within a small radius. By the next fall, there were no more than a few stragglers in this entire region.

Although many Indians made their main slit down the hump, hidemen cut from the lower jaw down the belly to the tail. After loosening the skin around the edges, they often attached a noose to the neck and ears and quickly ripped off the entire hide with a horse.

Hidemen using a homemade press to compact robes for shipment.

Bison bones stacked along a rail siding for transfer to boxcars.

40,000 hides, a month's kill, piled at a landing on the Missouri.

A cattalo of 25 per cent bison parentage, sired by a Hereford bull.

A skittish cow that died in the transfer of the Pablo herd to Canada.

Ernest H. Baynes driving his team of six-month-old bison calves.

In Yellowstone Park, one cow laboriously breaks a new trail through Hayden Valley as the rest of her band patiently plod along behind in single file. During the winter, such trails soon build into a network that allows buffalo to move freely through the valley. Yellowstone bison consistently endure severe winters better than other big game in the area, not only because of an ability to maneuver in their snow-bound range, but also because of a rugged capacity to forage in deep snow. Like the bull below, they swing their heads from side to side until they work their way down to buried grass.

The author (above) approaches a herd under a buffalo hide to test the techniques of Indian decoys, who successfully lured buffalo into traps with similar masquerades.

In San Francisco (below), a worn buffalo head over the door advertises one restaurant's specialty.

Frank Mayer (in *The Buffalo Harvest*):

. . . the herd . . . would gather around her [a slain cow] and stupidly "mill"—which means poke her with their horns, strike her with their hooves, and just generally lose their heads when they smelled her blood.

William Hornaday:

They cluster around the fallen ones, sniff at the warm blood, bawl aloud in wonderment, and do everything but run away.

Colonel Richard Irving Dodge:

Attracted by the blood, they collect about the wounded buffalo. Another bullet is now sent in; another buffalo plunges, stops and bleeds. The others still stare, and, seeming to think the wounded animals responsible for the unusual noise, concentrate their attention on them. Again and again the rifle cracks. Buffalo after buffalo bleeds, totters and falls. The survivors stare in imbecile amazement.

Hugh Monroe:

Sometimes the smell of the blood from the wounded or dying would set the bulls crazy. They would run up and lick the blood, and sometimes toss the dead ones clear from the ground. Then they would bellow and fight each other, sometimes goring one another so badly they died. The great bulls, their tongues covered with blood, their eyes flashing, and tails sticking straight up, roaring and fighting, were terrible to see.

Although it is difficult to imagine a bull lifting the carcass of another from the ground, the rest of this last description tallies with an episode I witnessed—and influenced myself—in the Jackson Hole Wildlife Park herd. I must confess to having tampered with the herd, but my experiment elicited an interesting reaction and provided a modern example of the behavior of buffalo in the presence of blood or death.

To test the animals' reaction to gore, I poured some blood from a freshly killed porcupine on a pile of hay and positioned a rotting buffalo head nearby. When the two dominant bulls came over to sniff the blood and examine the head, I poked one of them in the flank with a pitchfork. The outcome of my meddling was a vicious battle, complete with wallowing and bellowing.

Similar curiosity over blood, and the attendant fighting, was evident on two other occasions when I had not provoked the incidents—the entire herd advanced to investigate a freshly killed buffalo, impeding the butchering of the slain animal by pressing so close to sniff and lick the body and viscera of the victim that attendants were afraid to move in. In addition, the birth of a new calf (on the occasions when I had the good fortune to observe this event in the Wildlife Park) was accompanied by the same exploratory and gladiatorial actions, perhaps because the delivery of the calf released a little blood.

In addition to these observations in the Wildlife Park, I have witnessed similar scenes in several other refuges, each incident involving blood or carcasses that provoked the curiosity of nearby buffalo. (African elephants also show a peculiar fascination for a corpse of their own kind, lingering around the dead animal, examining it carefully, and even burying it under a cover of soil and grass.) Thus in both contemporary and historical record, there is strong evidence for this strange attraction of buffalo to blood or death, and we are safe in considering it a key element in the creation of a stand.

Most important to this maneuver of the hideman was the efficiency of the weapon he used. By the Seventies, the single-shot breech-loading cartridge rifles had replaced the muzzle-loading Hawkins and other "plains rifles" made famous by the Mountain Men of the first half of the century. The decade of the hide-hunters, indeed, produced a bewildering proliferation of models, cartridges, and loads, owing largely to the new demands of the hunters themselves. Campfire talk of these ragtag and bobtailed men rang with arguments (sometimes resulting in violence) over the virtues of the Springfields, Sharps, Remingtons, Ballards, and Maynards that were in current use against the herds. "Store-bought" ammunition was expensive, so most hunters loaded their cartridges by hand, concocting pet reloads of varying sizes of bullets and powder charges from components made available by the suppliers; lead bullets ranged in weight from 300 to 550 grains and charges crammed into the long cartridge cases from 70 to 120 grains. Because the black powder of the period required long octagon-barreled guns to fully burn the big charges, such rifles weighed from nine to fifteen pounds.

In the late 1860's, it is likely that many of the earliest hunters out of Fort Hays, Kansas, used the U.S. Government .50–70, first available from Springfield but soon chambered by other rifle makers. By the early Seventies, a variety of models and loads was on the market, most of them in .44 caliber. Sharps, Remington, and other manufacturers brought out assorted "Creedmoor" models, named after the famous rifle range on Long Island. The "rolling block" .44–90 Remington and .44–90 "side-hammer" Sharps (also referred to as the .44–100 and .44–105) came along in 1873. That same year the government adopted the .45–70 Springfield as the army issue and soon the manufacturers dropped their .44's in favor of a variety of .45 cases and loads. The Sharps .45–100–550 (indicating caliber, powder weight, and bullet weight) shows up in the catalogue in 1876, when hidemen were still hunting on the plains. The same firm brought out an even more powerful .45 caliber cartridge (.45–120–500) in 1878, but it is unlikely that many of them got into the hands of the hidemen, for by then the supply of buffalo was running out.

The most famous of all buffalo guns, the so-called "Big Fifty," developed from the hide-hunters' demand for more and more powerful loads for the big animals. The suppliers responded, and in 1875 Sharps brought out the .50–90 (sometimes referred to as the .50–100 or .50–110, depending on the bullet weight and powder charge used in the reloads). When old buffalo hunters themselves spoke of the "Big Fifty," this was the load they were describing, although succeeding generations of Western writers have mistakenly used this famous name to refer to another model, the .50–140–170. This last load, most assuredly the "biggest" Fifty, was a special-order caliber that did not come along until about 1880, when the great herds had been exterminated from all but the northern plains. The only "buffalo" cartridge still being loaded today is the .45–70 Winchester (even now a first-rate, short-range powerhouse of a load). Its big boom may be thought of as a last faint echo from a tragic, if romantic, era of the Old West.*

With a good buffalo gun, the accomplished hunter could bring down the stoutest bull with a single shot aimed at a vital point—usually the heart or lungs, occasionally the spine or brain. If he missed all of these points, however, his shot was practically use-

---

* For those seeking more detail, see *Cartridges of the World* by Frank C. Barnes (the Gun Digest Company, Chicago, Illinois), the most authoritative source for firearms and cartridges of this bygone era.

less, so tenacious of life was the buffalo. (Audubon once described a victim "which during one of our hunts was shot no less than twenty-four times before it dropped.")

No part of a buffalo was more impermeable to bullets than the forehead. The skull bone of a large bull is overlaid with more than two inches of heavy skin and reinforced with a tangled cushion of long hairs. Altogether, the layers of bone, skin, and hair produce a tough head plate that came to be greatly respected by all buffalo hunters, including one inquisitive nineteenth-century sportsman:

> Against the frontal bone of the bison's skull, the lead falls harmless. To test this fully . . . I once approached a buffalo which stood wounded in a ravine. I took position upon the hillside, knowing that he could not readily charge up it, at a distance of only fifteen yards. I fired three shots from a Henry rifle full against the forehead, causing no other result than some angry head-shaking. I then took a Spencer carbine and fired twice with it. At each shot the bull sank partly to his knees, but immediately recovered again. I afterward examined the skull, and could detect no fracture.

Naturally the Sharps and similar rifles, though excellent in their day, are primitive in comparison with modern game rifles, which have a far greater killing power because their bullets travel at more than twice the speed and with much more accuracy. But even present-day rifles can be outmatched by a buffalo's forehead. There have been instances during annual herd reductions in Yellowstone National Park when .30/06 bullets fired into the forehead failed to penetrate the skull.

I myself saw a dramatic test of the buffalo's frontal armor while accompanying some Crow Indians on a hunting trip through their reservation. Late in the afternoon, as our jeep passed near a wounded bull, one of the Indians fired his .30/06 at the animal from the close range of thirty feet. The bullet smashed into the buffalo's head, bounced back and grazed the hand of a rider in the jeep, then landed on the ground nearby, a warped piece of lead and jacket bearing a trace of blood.

When the old-time hunters brought in their haul and the skins were ready for market, the railroads shipped them to the centers of trade. More than any other technical innovation of the age, the iron horse prepared the way for the elimination of the American bison from his native plain. Advancing lines of the major companies—the Union Pacific, the Kansas Pacific, the Northern Pacific, and the Sante Fe—hacked a passageway of commerce right into the heart of the buffalo country. To the hunters, who had arrived by train themselves, the twin steel bands were a lifeline of profit. Supplies for equipping the hunting outfits were freighted westward by rail, and the meat and hides were shipped back to markets in the East on the very same trains.

Ironically, the rail crews, builders of the lines destined to open the country to settlement and erase the virgin buffalo range, were almost as dependent on buffalo meat as the caravans of nomadic Indians whose regions they penetrated. Train gangs lived on fresh buffalo meat brought in by hunters hired expressly to supply them.

Of all the men involved in provisioning the railroad crews, the most colorful was William Frederick Cody, whose adventures in the meat trade were to prepare him for his eventual calling as plains guide for the rich and nobly born. The first phase of his career was launched in October 1867, when the twenty-one-year-old youth approached the firm of Goddard Brothers, a company under contract to board twelve hundred railroad workers for the Eastern Division of the Union Pacific. Cody, who had been reduced to driving his favorite buffalo-running horse in the menial task of grading a railway roadbed, bid for the job of providing the company's crews with meat. Goddard Brothers agreed to employ him, and he was contracted to furnish twelve buffalo per day. When the question of his salary arose, the hunter asked that certain things be taken into account:

As this was to be dangerous work, on account of the Indians, who were riding all over that section of the country, and as I would be obliged to go from five to ten miles from the road each day to hunt the buffaloes, accompanied by only one man with a light wagon for the transportation of the meat, I, of course, demanded a large salary. They could afford to remunerate me well, because the meat would not cost them anything.

Five hundred dollars a month was the figure agreed upon—large pay in those days, but a bargain for Goddard Brothers, for it balanced out to about a penny a pound for the meat.

Cody's work as a buffalo supplier came to a halt after only a few months, when suspension of construction work put an early end to the need for meat. But by that time he had set a record of sorts: "During my engagement as a hunter for the company—a period of less than eighteen months—I killed 4,280 buffaloes."

Since 1879, when Cody first announced this figure, these "4,280 buffaloes" have been mentioned in countless treatises on the beast and biographical notes about Cody. But it was not until 1960, and the publication of Don Russell's *The Lives and Legends of Buffalo Bill*, that anyone bothered to apply some elementary arithmetic to the total. Multiplying 547.5 (a year and a half, or Cody's "eighteen months") by 12 (the number Cody was contracted to kill each day), Russell arived at 6,570, a figure considerably above the announced total of 4,280. As Cody was scarcely apt to *under*estimate his kill, the persistent historian looked back into the record and traced the discrepancy to a typographical error in the original statement: the railroad hunting had lasted not for "eighteen" but only eight months. During this period, Cody should have delivered 2,916 buffalo. His alleged "4,280 buffaloes" exceeds this number by 1,364, or almost six per day.

Whatever the figure accepted for Cody's kill, it is based solely on his own word; no contemporary account has ever verified the number, despite the welter of testimony about the buffalo-hunting skill of William Cody.

Although the number of beasts he slew remains in doubt, Cody's stint with the railroads earned him a distinction that was to last for the rest of his life and link his name forever with that of his prey. Said Cody himself: "It was at this time that the very appropriate name of 'Buffalo Bill' was conferred upon me by the road-hands. It has stuck to me ever since, and I have never been ashamed of it." The name gained wider circulation in a popular jingle of the day:

> Buffalo Bill, Buffalo Bill,
> Never missed and never will;
> Always aims and shoots to kill
> And the company pays his buffalo bill.

Promoted in rhymes, yarns, and numerous dime novels and boosted by one of the best publicity agents of the day, Buffalo

Bill's reputation soon outran his frontier accomplishments to become legend. But at the peak of his conspicuous career, he performed actual feats almost as remarkable as the tales about him. In 1883 he climaxed these with his "Wild West Show," a rollicking extravaganza that played to millions during tours of the United States and Europe. It entertained royalty, including Queen Victoria and the Shah of Persia, and even prompted one staid New England newspaper to remark that the production "out-Barnumed Barnum." An authentic Western spectacle, the "Wild West Show" included cowboys and Indians, personalities like Annie Oakley and Sitting Bull, a Deadwood stagecoach that had been "baptized in blood and fire," and the most important feature of all—a herd of live buffalo.

Because of their ferocity, these rambunctious bison had already saddled Cody with several damage suits arising from "depredations" committed during transit between train and showgrounds. But as stars of the most spectacular daredevil act in the show, the animals were indispensable. Untamed and dangerous, they were mounted and ridden, bucking, wheeling, and snorting, to the great fascination and delight of the spectators. In show after show, Cody's most venturesome cowboys had braved the fury of every beast but one, the hulking, intractable Monarch.

One afternoon in Indianapolis, Cody, who as usual had been drinking heavily, decided to force his cowboys to ride Monarch in an effort to impress the local governor. For a while the men tried to talk their tipsy leader out of the scheme, but when their efforts failed and he scheduled the act in spite of them, they agreed among themselves to refuse the ride.

As the buffalo act entered the ring, Cody cantered in with his men, instructing Buck Taylor and Jim Lawson to rope Monarch. With two well-aimed throws, the cowboys pinned the bull in position for a man to mount. Cody called three different riders, each of whom declined. Exasperated, he jumped off his own horse, strode over to Monarch, climbed onto the hump of the beast, and shouted to Buck and Jim to release the ropes. Once freed in the ring, the bull leaped up, dashed forward, and began to buck violently, catapulting Cody high into the air. He fell to the ground with a heavy thud and lay there motionless.

Buffalo Bill's men carried him to the nearest carriage and

rushed him to a hospital. Miraculously, he recuperated from his bruises in two weeks—and it was said that he remained sober until the troupe hit Chicago.

Much renowned as a showman, Buffalo Bill was undoubtedly the most famous of all the buffalo hunters; during his days of supplying construction crews and conducting hunting parties, he downed thousands of the animals. But his sport and meat hunting had far less effect on the herds than the rampant slaughter of the hidemen. Encouraged by the enormous demand for furs and hides and assisted by the railroads, these men, in their quest for easy kills and ready money, went far beyond the carefully organized killing of the Indians and the colorful rampages of the dude hunters, until at last the day came when the numberless animals darkened the plains no more.

22

ON THE WAY TO

EXTINCTION

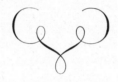

On a summer day in 1795, musicians playing vio-
lins, flutes, and oboes led a merry procession through the town of
Gallipolis, Ohio. After them came Charles Francis Duteil, marching with pride, a hunting rifle slung across his shoulder; and behind Duteil came his trophy, the inspiration for the celebration—a
large buffalo carcass. Borne through the town by several burly
men, its hoofs lashed to a long pole, the weighty hulk of the dead
beast swung from side to side. An excited crowd of townspeople,
mostly settlers of French ancestry who had emigrated to the area
only a few years earlier, paraded along behind.

After more singing and rejoicing, the merrymakers skinned
and dressed the buffalo, then prepared the meat "in such a variety
of ways and means as none but the French could devise." For some
years after, Duteil was idolized as the first person in Gallipolis

to kill a buffalo. He was also the last. And, for that matter, he was very close to the last to slay one anywhere in Ohio, for by the end of 1802 there was not a buffalo left in the state.

In previous years, settlers in Ohio had found the herds ample, if not as plentiful as on the plains. A few miles from Gallipolis, George Washington had shot some buffalo in 1770, and five years earlier a local chronicler had written that "buffaloes, bears, turkeys, and other game abounded" in the region.

In 1750 a French explorer describing the territory east of the Mississippi wrote of meadowlands "covered with an innumerable multitude of buffaloes—a species which will probably not run out for many centuries hence . . ." To be more precise, buffalo did range over most of the eastern United States, from the northern half of Florida up to central New York. Yet only sixty or seventy years after this report of multitudes, there were no more than a few stragglers in the entire area. Most had been wiped out by early pioneers, who had used the meat and hides to tide them over the first years of struggle in the wilderness. The establishment of a permanent settlement usually brought about the extermination of nearby herds within a few years. Two buffalo killed in western Wisconsin in 1832, according to the testimony of a local authority, appear to have been "the last specimens of the noble bison which trod, or will ever again tread, the soil of the region lying east of the Mississippi River."

About a year after this extinction in the East, explorer Josiah Gregg, traversing the Great Plains, reflected on the herds of bison around him. "Were they only killed for food . . . their natural increase would perhaps replenish the loss; yet the continual and wanton slaughter of them by travelers and hunters, and the still greater havoc made among them by Indians, not only for meat, but often for the skins alone . . . are fast reducing their numbers, and must ultimately effect their total annihilation from the continent."

But, save for a few words of assent, Gregg's voice rose alone in those early years of the nineteenth century. The evidence appeared overwhelmingly against him. How could a species that roamed in millions over the plains be rubbed out? No sir, the buffalo would be around forever, and there was nothing to keep hunters from swarming into the western territories to reap the harvest.

A decade later, John James Audubon noticed a "perceptible"

decline in the size of the herds and thought that "before many years the Buffalo, like the Great Auk, will have disappeared. Surely," he said, "this should not be permitted."

A few more protests of doom were heard early in the 1870's as the hidemen spread out over the Kansas plains like ants. Francis Parkman forecast that "a time would come when those plains would be a grazing country, the buffalo give place to tame cattle, farm-houses be scattered along the water-courses, and wolves, bears and Indians be numbered among the things that were." But Parkman's prophecies were lost in the great reaches of the buffalo territory. Most of the hunters firmly believed that they were eliminating not the original herds, but the annual increase.

Once the men warmed up to the task of liquidating the "overflow," they did a thorough job of it. Kansas marksman Thomas Linton downed more than three thousand buffalo in the 1872 season. George Reighard set a record of about a hundred a day for one month in 1872. During the last four months of the year, the three Clarkson brothers killed about seven thousand buffalo, occasionally shooting so many that their skinners had to work a hundred and fifty to two hundred carcasses a day.

Boosted by this rampant slaughter, shipments of hides reached a new peak. At Dodge City, in the heart of buffalo country, warehouses of the most prominent firm in the business often bulged with sixty to eighty thousand hides. The company shipped more than two hundred thousand in 1872–3, the first winter the Atchison, Topeka and Santa Fe operated out of Dodge. Other firms in the area probably handled an equal quantity of hides. And in addition to the vast shipments of hides, the railroads also carried substantial consignments of meat. An estimated two hundred carloads of hindquarters went out in the same season; two extra carloads contained nothing but cured tongues.

In the frontier towns along the rail lines, buffalo meat was a common staple, sold in local butcher shops or served in hotels and eating houses, usually labeled as buffalo, at times as beef. Fresh meat was also shipped to eastern cities in winter, and in all seasons the cured hams and tongues were popular items of traffic, commanding prices of twenty to thirty cents a pound in markets. In curing the meat, hunters first soaked it in a large vat, which was made by digging a hole in the ground and lining it with a green buffalo hide, the hair placed next to the earth and the edges held down with pegs; any bullet holes were "easily corked with a round stick." The men put about a thousand pounds of meat into the vat, poured in a brine solution, and laid another hide over the top to keep out dirt. After nine or ten days, the hunters transferred the meat to a smokehouse constructed of raw hides stretched over a framework of poles; smoke came from a steady fire of green wood or buffalo chips. For shipment by rail to eastern markets, the cured tongues were packed in barrels, and the hams were sewn into tight canvas wrappers.

As the shipments of meat and hides continued to mount, it was not surprising that Colonel Richard Irving Dodge began to notice a gradual decline in the buffalo herds around his army post in Kansas. In 1871–2, he had reported "apparently no limit to the numbers of buffalo," but by the fall of 1873 he found that "where there were myriads of buffalo the year before, there were now myriads of carcasses. The air was foul with a sickening stench, and the vast plain, which only a short twelvemonth before teemed with animal life, was a dead, solitary, putrid desert." In October of 1874, Dodge made another survey: "A few buffalo were encountered, but there seemed to be more hunters than buffalo."

By that time the Kansas herds had indeed been decimated, and Colonel Dodge began to calculate the extent of the slaughter, which had reached its height between 1871 and 1873. To obtain reliable statistics on the trade, he wrote to the officers of the Union Pacific, the Kansas Pacific, and the Sante Fe requesting figures on their traffic in meat and hides. From the Sante Fe he received a "prompt, full and clear statement," but from the other two lines he met only polite refusals. He soon realized that he "was treading on most delicate ground." The lines were clearly afraid that a disclosure of the size of their buffalo trade might stir up restrictive legislation. To Colonel Dodge such fears were ridiculous, since by 1874 their territory contained virtually no buffalo to be saved by legislation.

Ignoring the snubs from the other two lines, Dodge began computing a presumptive kill from the statistics of the Santa Fe. Between 1872 and 1874, according to the records, the railroad had shipped out 459,453 hides. Estimating an approximately equal trade for the secretive Union Pacific and Kansas Pacific, Dodge increased the Santa Fe tally by two hundred per cent, adjusting the total to compensate for waste and spoilage (in some cases, a single marketed hide represented three or more slain buffalo). The final, revised figure revealed that the hidemen had slaughtered at least three million buffalo during 1872, 1873, and 1874. Dodge then estimated that Indians hunting during the same interval probably killed over one million buffalo, and white settlers some hundred and fifty thousand. Altogether, the total of dead buffalo came to well over four million.

After this central part of the Great Plains had been cleared out—especially for the professionals, who could turn a profit only with an abundance of buffalo—hunters began to look elsewhere. A few career men had already moved to Texas by 1873, and word of large herds in the new region soon drifted back to the rest. But along with the encouraging reports came stories of angered Indian bands determined to prevent white hunters from wiping out any more of the herds that they considered their rightful heritage.

Not to be frightened out of a lucrative trade, the hidemen pressed south in the spring of 1874, many of them traveling in bands to improve their chances of repelling attack. Despite their precautions, militant tribesmen raided several camps, driving off stock and slaying the occupants. Since the hidemen had broken the Medicine Lodge Treaties of 1867 by moving into Indian Territory below the Arkansas River in Kansas, the tribes were out to protect what was left of their buffalo country.

Confrontation between Indians and hunters reached a climax with the Battle of Adobe Walls, from which Comanche Chief Quanah Parker eventually withdrew with severe losses. After this, army units stepped up their patrols, and by the spring of 1875 they had subdued the tribes. The southern range was now wide open to the hidemen. When the Texas and Pacific Railway completed a line into Fort Worth in 1876, hunters had a convenient outlet for shipping hides, and the curtain was ready to rise on another massacre. By the following winter the slaughter of the southern herds had reached its peak. Some fifteen hundred hunters and skinners ranged over the Texas plains, most of them operating out of Fort Griffin, a frontier town about a hundred miles west of Fort Worth.

Their success was clearly evident in the spoils accumulated at Fort Griffin by the next spring. One hide merchant had four acres of property blanketed with bales of hides waiting to be carted by wagon to Fort Worth. Later in the spring, some sixty thousand hides lay piled along the siding at the Texas and Pacific rail terminal in Fort Worth. For the entire 1876–7 season, Fort Griffin marketed two hundred thousand hides at $1.25 apiece.

In the fall of 1877, hunters headed out again to try their luck on the Texas range. Among them was Joe McCombs, who set forth from Fort Griffin with a crew of four. He returned to town in the spring with forty-nine hundred hides—the biggest catch of his career. But the following season he netted only eight hundred, and it became clear that the herds were dwindling fast. Indians in the same general region also found their trade in buffalo plummeting. In 1876, the agency for the Kiowa, Comanche, and Wichita handled a business of $70,000; sales dropped to $5,068 in 1879.

As the numbers of buffalo declined, the hidemen drifted away from Fort Griffin. Some, like Wright Mooar, who downed 20,500 buffalo during his nine years as a hunter, abandoned the business for cattle ranching. Others hearkened to reports of herds in Montana and headed north. By the summer of 1879, scarcely a hunter remained in Fort Griffin.

Plainly it was time for the professional hidemen to concentrate their activities in another region. The years 1870–3 had seen the best of the hunting on the Kansas plains; 1874–8 had marked the high point on the range farther south. The northern herd was now ripe for harvest.

A considerable commerce in buffalo robes had been going on in this region since early in the century, when fur companies had opened trading posts at key points in the Missouri basin. Largest of these was Fort Union, built in 1828 at the strategic junction of the Missouri and Yellowstone Rivers to accommodate tribal trade floated down by boat or carted overland by horse. In exchange for soft-tanned buffalo robes the Indians accepted coffee, sugar, flour, tobacco, cloth, gaudy blankets, trinkets, and, of course, whisky. The robes they brought to Fort Union were shipped on to St. Louis, at first in keelboats, later in steamboats. For several decades the traffic in this region exceeded eighty thousand robes a year.

By 1880 the activities of the hidemen had expanded so much that raw skins were beginning to outnumber the tanned robes of the Indians in the shipments coming down the Missouri. Downstream at Sioux City, the local *Journal* picked up word from passing boats that the same year had been the first big season for the Montana professionals:

> The past severe winter caused the buffalo to bunch themselves in a few valleys where there was pasturage, and there the slaughter went on all winter. There was no sport about it, simply shooting down the famine-tamed animals as cattle might be shot down in a barn-yard. To the credit of the Indians it can be said that they killed no more than they could save the meat from. The greater part of the slaughter was done by white hunters, or butchers rather, who . . . left the carcasses to rot.

The *Journal* went on to describe in detail a shipment that had passed Sioux City:

> Most of our citizens saw the big load of buffalo hides that the *C. K. Peck* brought down . . . a load that hid everything about the boat below the roof of the hurricane deck. There were ten thousand hides in that load, and they were all brought out of the Yellowstone on one trip . . .

Some of the boatloads of hides were transferred to boxcars at Bismarck after the Northern Pacific trackage was extended. The traffic manager of the line, who had observed the increase in these shipments by rail, later commented on the fate of the herds in the Upper Missouri:

> Up to the year 1880, so long as buffalo were killed only for robes, the bands did not decrease very materially; but beginning with that year, when they were killed for their hides as well, a most indiscriminate slaughter commenced and from that time on they disappeared very rapidly.

During the year 1881 the Northern Pacific laid additional trackage across the Montana plains, first to Glendive, then on toward Miles City. The extension of the line stimulated local buffalo hunting, just as earlier rail penetration into the plains to the south had spurred hunting in those regions. By 1882 there were at least five thousand hunters and skinners on the northern range. Taking note of their operations, one army lieutenant described "a cordon of camps, from the Upper Missouri, where it bends to the west, stretched toward the setting sun as far as the dividing line of

Idaho, completely blocking the great ranges of the Milk River, the Musselshell, Yellowstone, and the Marias, and rendering it impossible for scarcely a single bison to escape . . ."

The most memorable event of the next hunting season was the appearance of a teeming herd estimated at fifty to eighty thousand animals, which crossed the Yellowstone River not far from Miles City and headed north. By the end of the season the entire herd had disappeared. Most hidemen believed that the animals had merely passed north into Canada, an opinion shared by a locomotive engineer on the Northern Pacific: "They *couldn't* all have been killed so quickly," he said. "I saw them crossing the Yellowstone River. They darkened the plains with their numbers. Some of them must be living in the North."

But virtually all of them had been killed, succumbing to the barrage of gunfire from the army of hunters massed on the northern range. And there was no chance of replenishment from the north, for there were even fewer stragglers on the Canadian plains. Most herds in that area had been extinguished by 1880, before the start of the Montana slaughter.

Nevertheless, Miles City hunters outfitted routinely for the approaching season, spending hundreds of dollars on wagons, horses, mules, tents, utensils, provisions, guns, and ammunition. When at last they guided their outfits out from town in the fall of 1883, they found not a single herd. Refusing to believe that nothing remained of the millions, the thousands, even the hundreds, they persevered for mile upon mile, enountering only scattered stragglers. Within a few weeks they faced reality; by mid-season most had staggered into bankruptcy.

The following season, a fur buyer from Minneapolis scoured the northern plains for buffalo hides; after an exhaustive search he had found barely enough to make up one carload. It was hard to believe that only two years earlier, one Montana dealer had shipped 250,000 hides from the same region.

Almost every wild buffalo had been done away with; all that remained was the conspicuous leftover of carrion rotting on the prairie. In the northern range, as in the central and southern plains, this remnant attracted two groups of human scavengers— first the "wolfers" and later the bonepickers. Among these were a good many buffalo hunters who had suddenly found themselves out of work.

The wolfers operated by poisoning a few buffalo carcasses, then waiting a few days for their victims to devour the carrion and succumb. They were interested primarily in wolves, whose hides were worth a dollar or two apiece; but their mass poisoning also did away with other animals that fed on the carcasses, including coyotes, kit foxes, badgers, vultures, ravens, and several birds of prey.

When the wolfers, the hidemen, and innumerable animal scavengers abandoned the clutter of buffalo carcasses, nothing remained but bones, hoofs, horns, and scattered bits of dried skin. But even these unpromising leftovers were enough to launch the buffalo country into a final surge of activity, attracting hundreds of bone pickers, a few of whom made more profit than the hunters before them.

Buffalo bones brought an average of $8.00 a ton (the price fluctuated between $2.50 and $22.00 depending on the market). And the earnings could be inflated, for crafty traders knew that by soaking the sun-parched loads with water, they could increase the weight by as much as one fourth.

After shipment to St. Louis or cities farther east, the weathered bones were ground up for phosphorous fertilizer. Fresher bones were carbonized into bone char, which was used by sugar refineries for purging raw sugar liquor of its brownish coloration.

Bone pickers also gathered horns and hoofs, for which they received anywhere from six to thirty dollars a ton. (These were then converted into buttons, combs, knife handles, and glue.) Some scavengers even stripped off the long tufts of buffalo fur still clinging to the skulls and sold it for about seventy-five cents a pound; the coarse hair was used as stuffing for mattresses and cushions.

The booming bone business lifted several displaced buffalo hunters back into the money and pulled many a straggling sodbuster's family through the lean early years on the plains. One homesteader from Tennessee even made enough money off bone picking to settle a hefty down payment on a Texas sheep ranch.

Also trying a hand at bone picking were the Indians. Some tribesmen who had once burned the prairie to lure or drive herds of live animals now found themselves engaging in the same practice for a far less glorious purpose—to burn off the grass and expose the bones of the slain.

The trainloads of buffalo bones transported eastward at the height of the trade provide an appalling measure of the slaughter. To find out the approximate number of buffalo represented by these shipments, I made an estimate of the weight of an average skeleton (fifty-eight pounds) and divided this figure into the total weight of bones shipped over a given period. From 1872 to 1874, for example, the Santa Fe carried 10,793,350 pounds of buffalo bones; if the Union Pacific and Kansas Pacific handled approximately equal poundage, the total shipments for those three years represented at least 550,000 buffalo.

Shipping data from Texas revealed that the typical boxcar held 29,400 pounds of bones, the skeletons of some five hundred buffalo. Therefore, in a packed boxcar a single skeleton took up about 3.7 cubic feet of space. This figure is useful for analyzing the immense piles of bones that accumulated along railroad sidings awaiting shipment eastward. Beside a section of Santa Fe trackage in southeastern Colorado, for example, one rick of bones was "piled twelve feet high, nearly that wide at the base, and one-half mile long." That would make about 350,000 cubic feet, or some 94,000 buffalo skeletons. Ricks in other areas were reported "stacked up like cordwood" and ranging in length from one fourth to one half mile.

Early in the 1880's an enterprising Englishman named Jimmie Kilfoile began accumulating towering stacks of bones along his wagon route in northern Texas, tagging each new pile with a large buffalo skull and scrawling his initials across the frontal bones in charcoal. When the Fort Worth and Denver Railway completed its trackage through the area in 1887, Kilfoile had to hire a number of other freighters to help him haul his cargo to the nearest sidings. He sold the entire collection to a St. Louis entrepreneur for $25,000. At an average of $7.00 per ton, the lot accounted for over 100,000 buffalo.

These ghoulish bone harvests drew the curtain on the saga of wild buffalo. We can look back on the massacre and say that it was inevitable, that the buffalo and civilization were incompatible and one or the other had to go; if the hunters had not decimated the herds, the "nuisance value" of the beasts would eventually have necessitated their extermination. (We need only jog our memories with a report from the 1860's, when buffalo "were frequently so numerous right at Fort Ellice [Manitoba] as to require watchmen round the hay-yard to keep and drive them out . . .") The dilemma of a homesteader on a prairie swarming with buffalo would have been precarious indeed; one can easily visualize the havoc left in the wake of a stampede through treasured cornfields. Thus, we can say, if the virgin grassland was to be tamed by plow and fence, it was necessary for the buffalo to go.

And we know that the buffalo himself contributed to the swift pace of his downfall. Unquestionably he was an enticing target, a large mammal with a valuable hide enclosing hundreds of pounds of delicious meat. His chosen range was open grassland, where he found little in the way of bush or tree to hide behind, and where, consequently, he could be spotted from a good distance. Moreover, there were times when he displayed a surprising indifference to attack. And he was social, almost fatally social—the hunter who could shoot one individual from a herd was likely to bag scores more.

The buffalo was put at a further disadvantage by other circumstances—the intrusion of the railroads, the arrival of professional hidemen, increased hunting pressure from new settlers, and a virtual absence of protective laws. (Plains Indians were not overly destructive. Their numbers in the grassland were surprisingly few—about one per ten square miles—and their hunting ordinarily siphoned off no more than a normal surplus.)

But even if it was the buffalo's tragic destiny to be annihilated from his native grassland, we must never condone the nature of that annihilation—its ruthlessness, its greed, its extravagance. The animal's boundless abundance seemed to invite an equivalent waste. Although, as the Indians so cleverly proved, every part of a carcass could be used in one way or another, most hunters saved only about a third of each animal, often less. The following scene on the South Fork of the Republican River in 1874 was representative: ". . . six thousand five hundred carcasses of buffaloes, from which the hides only had been stripped. The meat was not touched, but left to rot on the plains. In fact, the whole plains were dotted with the putrefying remains of buffaloes." On the northern plains the waste of meat was even greater, for, as the traffic manager of the Northern Pacific once stated, "The number of pounds of buffalo meat shipped over our line has never cut any figure, the bulk of the meat having been left on the prairie as not being of sufficient value to pay the cost of transportation."

Although hidemen turned their backs on wasted meat, certain farmers in eastern Texas looked at the abandoned carcasses with a sharper eye. Driving their hogs out onto the plains, they fattened them on the rotten carnage, and returned with herds of plump porkers that brought good prices on the block.

To keep a tally on the number of buffalo shot by two teams of officers on a one-day hunting contest near Fort Hays, Kansas, the men simply removed the tongues as evidence. The remainder of the meat on the final twenty-three kills was left to rot.

Even the hunters who killed chiefly for meat saved only the choicest cuts, leaving the rest to rot on the prairie. When Buffalo Bill was provisioning the railroad crews, he "took only the hindquarters and hump of each buffalo." Many took even less. Thousands of buffalo were slain for their humps alone, and thousands more for their tongues.

Once, when Chief Satanta of the Kiowa was escorting an army group to a treaty conference, some "indiscriminate slaughter" occurred along the line of march. In violation of orders, several soldiers and camp followers began a wanton shooting of buffalo, salvaging only a few tongues from the animals. Such capricious massacre on tribal lands sorely grieved Satanta. With eyes flashing and lips curled in scorn, he complained to the commanding general: "Has the white man become a child, that he should recklessly kill and not eat? When the red men slay game, they do so that they may live and not starve."

This proud and eloquent accusation was justified. Since the early days, most Indians had used the animals thriftily, setting aside usable parts of a slain buffalo, from teeth to tail, and permitting waste only when superstition dictated—for example, in impounding and drives over cliffs, when all trapped animals were slain for fear escapees would steer other herds away from the sites. For as long as the tribes ruled their own destinies, they used the great beast that sustained life with economy and care.

But tribal life, too, was fated to alter when new ways reached the plains. Indian wastefulness increased as the white man began to offer tempting goods in exchange for buffalo products. In 1832, for instance, when George Catlin first arrived at Fort Pierre, South Dakota, he was informed that a few days earlier "a party of five or six hundred Sioux Indians . . . came into the Fort with *fourteen hundred fresh buffalo tongues* . . . for which they required but a few gallons of whiskey, which was soon demolished, indulging them in a little, and harmless, carouse." When the traders became more numerous and offered more attractive barter, some Indians started to kill buffalo for their hides alone, thus degrading themselves to the level of white hunters.

As the decimation of the herds continued, the immensity and wastefulness of the slaughter began to stir up protest. Some objected to the sheer butchery, others feared for the very survival of the species. One newspaper called the bloodshed "wantonly wicked," and went on to warn that "killing these noble animals for their hides or to gratify the pleasure of some Russian duke or English lord is a species of vandalism which cannot too quickly be checked." Plains Indians sent delegations to Washington to complain that buffalo hunters were appropriating game that had been a tribal birthright for centuries. Even army officers protested. "The theory that the buffalo should be killed to deprive the Indians of food is a fallacy," said one, "as these people are becoming harmless under a rule of justice." Another remarked that the buffalo slaughter had given the Indians "their strongest incentive to declare war." (One is tempted to add that it had also given them just cause.)

In Congress there were at least a few men who agreed that the country's westward expansion should be pursued with some decency. In 1871 they started action to limit the butchery of what one representative called "the finest wild animal in our hemisphere." But little came of their efforts until 1874, by which time the Kansas herds had already been decimated. On January fourth of that year, Illinois Representative Greenburg Fort introduced a bill aimed at saving the buffalo. The first section of his measure prohibited the killing of a female buffalo by anyone except an Indian; the second made it illegal to kill more animals at one time than could be used for food. Two months later, the Committee on Territories released the bill with the urgent recommendation that it be passed.

Much of the ensuing debate concerned the matter of sexing. One representative opposing the bill charged that hunters would never be able to distinguish the sex of a running buffalo. Representative Fort insisted that this was untrue. (Some years afterward, zoologist William Hornaday commented, "I know of no greater affront . . . to the intelligence of a genuine buffalo-hunter than to accuse him of not knowing enough to tell the sex of a buffalo 'on the run' by its form alone.")

Fort's bill finally passed House and Senate, and was sent on to President Ulysses S. Grant. And there it languished in a pigeon-hole on his desk. Grant's inaction may have been influenced by his Secretary of the Interior, Columbus Delano, whose feelings on the matter had been expressed in the previous year's Annual Report: "I would not seriously regret the total disappearance of the buffalo from our western prairies, in its effect upon the Indians, regarding it rather as a means of hastening their sense of dependence upon the products of the soil and their own labors."

One year after the pocket veto, Delano's Bureau of Indian Affairs was rocked by scandal, and the Secretary of the Interior, succumbing to his own mismanagement, was forced to resign. (Historians later examined Delano's record and found him to have been woefully ill-suited to high public office.)

Once Delano was out of the picture, Representative Fort reintroduced his bill, which was still framed to give maximum protection to cows and outlaw the killing of bulls except for meat. Within a month the bill passed the House by a vote of 104 to

36. But when it was sent on to the Committee on Territories in the Senate it was shunted aside and never even released to the floor.

This ended the efforts of Congress to rescue the dwindling herds. But several state legislatures, undaunted, continued to discuss the question of protection for the buffalo. In Texas, while the buffalo hunters were busily eliminating the last herds in the state, local lawmakers drew up a measure to save the survivors.

When word of the bill reached General Phil Sheridan, he left his regional military headquarters at San Antonio and hurried over to address a joint assembly of the House and Senate at Austin. During his oration, Sheridan allegedly told the lawmakers that "instead of stopping the hunters they ought to give them a hearty, unanimous vote of thanks, and appropriate a sufficient sum of money to strike and present to each one a medal of bronze, with a dead buffalo on one side and a discouraged Indian on the other."

Sheridan could not contain his praise for the buffalo hunters: "These men have done in the last two years, and will do in the next year, more to settle the vexed Indian question than the entire regular army has done in the last thirty years. They are destroying the Indians' commissary; and it is a well-known fact that an army losing its base of supplies is placed at a great disadvantage. Send them powder and lead, if you will; but for the sake of a lasting peace, let them kill, skin and sell until the buffaloes are exterminated. Then your prairies can be covered with speckled cattle and the festive cowboy, who follows the hunter as a second forerunner of an advanced civilization."

Sheridan's counsel was heeded, the Texas bill was shelved, "and for the next three years the American bison traveled through a hail of lead." By the time the last of the great herds was wiped out, the "Indians' commissary" was indeed destroyed. And the effect on the tribes was far more calamitous than even cocksure Phil Sheridan could have fancied.

The Plains Indians, who had thrived for centuries on a bountiful supply of buffalo, suddenly found their larders bare. Some struggled along on muskrats, gophers, and grass; a few survived by butchering their once-prized horses and mules. Conditioned since childhood to buffalo meat and the life of the hunt, the Indians resisted changing their ways even if the alternative was starving. A party of twenty-nine Cree was reduced in one winter to three survivors, "on account of starvation and consequent cannibalism." The abrupt extermination of Montana buffalo in 1883–4 resulted in six hundred deaths by famine among the Blackfoot. Beef could have prevented some of the casualties, but many Indians found it unpalatably "sweet." They also believed that the meat of cattle carried the epidemic diseases that had actually been introduced by white men. (The tribes had begun to sample beef just before their first outbreak of mumps in the 1700's, and they refused to abandon the notion that cattle had caused the malady.)

The passing of the teeming herds brought the traditional Indian way of life to an end. Plains Cree who had been aloof and arrogant in their former dealings with whites eventually besieged every trading post and settlement with piteous requests for food. Once adequately, if not richly, clothed, they soon came to depend on the castoff uniforms of army soldiers. And their erstwhile weathertight and commodious shelters gave way to leaky sod and timber hovels.

Ultimately the whole Plains culture shifted. The change might have taken decades, even centuries, in the normal course of tribal evolution, but with the disappearance of the buffalo it took less than two years; within that time most tribesmen were forced to abandon their nomadic way of life as food collectors and become sedentary food producers. They found the life of a farmer irksome and devoid of adventure, but they had no other choice—their buffalo-centered economy had been totally wrecked.

Although depletion of the herds caused serious physical discomfort, its effect on the minds and spirits of the Indians was even more debilitating. Many of the most important social and religious customs—outgrowths of centuries of cultural development—ceased to have meaning, and the Indians came to experience a tribal loss of identity. The death of the Plains culture was danced to the staccato rhythms of the hidemen's constant gunfire.

So swift and terrible was the extermination that many Indians could not believe it had actually happened. They viewed it rather as a sorrowful dream, a supernatural misfortune called forth as a punishment for their wrongdoings, and attempted to pacify the spirits and bring back the herds with resolute prayer and sacrifice.

Their patriarchs had told of years when buffalo had been scarce or remote, but never—except in the beginning of the world—of years when there were none at all. Tribal leaders were convinced that buffalo must still be living deep in caves or beyond the horizon, whence they would return bringing renewed prosperity and freedom for the tribes.

The impoverished Omaha sought to call the herds forth from these remote places with ritual ceremony. Technically, the ceremony of "Anointing the Sacred Pole" required buffalo meat, but when none could be had, the Indians sought to fulfill the provisions of the rite by substituting beef. From monies acquired through federal land transfers in 1882, they lavished a thousand dollars on the purchase of thirty head of cattle, which they immediately killed for an offering to the Sacred Pole. When this offering did not produce the herds, they squandered more tribal funds on a second band of cattle, then still more on a third. After the repeated failure of such efforts, they resigned themselves to a life of cultivating maize and raising chickens, pigs, and cattle. For years they shunned the Sacred Pole, disillusioned by its failure to control the white man's evil and recall the departed herds.

The vanishing of the buffalo plunged the Kiowa into a succession of equally desperate predicaments, all clearly charted in the last years of a pictographic calendar that ran from 1833 to 1892. Each year for six decades, *Sett'an*, or "Little Bear," had drawn a sketch representing the most significant happening of the season. Painted in crude detail on a series of tanned hides, the collection of scenes was intended to instill in the young men of the tribe a respect for their heritage. (Later, in 1892, as civilization made inroads into the private world of the Indians, the aged chronicler would request that a copy of his journal be taken to Washington along with other tribal relics, in order that "the white people might always remember what the Kiowa had done.")

In Little Bear's calendar, each year was represented by a drawing of the medicine lodge, the central structure in the annual Sun Dance; superimposed on the lodge was a pictograph of the most important event of the year. Thus 1879 was the year of the "Horse-eating Sun Dance," represented by a sketch of a horse's head suspended over a medicine lodge. This signified that the Kiowa had gone on their regular hunt during the preceding winter, but had

Sketches in pictographic calendar drawn by Little Bear documented the most significant annual events of the Kiowa tribe.

1879

1880

found so few buffalo that they were obliged to fend off starvation by killing and eating their own mounts. In effect, that year marked the disappearance of the great herds from Kiowa country.

The following year, the tribe could not find the single buffalo needed for the main offering of the Sun Dance, and the ritual could not be held. On his calendar Little Bear drew only a leafy tree growing out of an empty square, to indicate that he had stayed home because of the cancellation of the ceremony.

In 1881 the Sun Dance had to be postponed for two months while the tribe scoured the plains for a buffalo. Only after an exhaustive search was a solitary bull finally found and shot.

The necessary buffalo could not be located in 1882, and no Sun Dance was held that year; Little Bear's calendar took note instead of the attempts of one shaman to bring back the herds by means of witchery. The spiritual leader, "Keeps-His-Name-Always," was featured in the pictograph in position for the buffalo-calling rituals. Draped in a red blanket trimmed with eagle feathers, he squatted in his medicine tipi beside a ceremonial buffalo skin.

Keeps-His-Name-Always attracted a willing audience with extravagant promises to bring back the herds. According to Kiowa legend, the buffalo had originated in a cave long years ago; now, maintained the shaman, the herds had been driven back underground by the white man in an evil plot to subdue the tribe. Unable to conceive of the extermination of the herds, the Kiowa placed great faith in the mystic conjurations of their shaman. When Keeps-His-Name-Always claimed to have received divine guidance in a vision, the tribe joined him in prayer and ceremony, beseeching the spirits to send forth the herds from the underground caves.

After assuming his position of spiritual leadership, Keeps-His-Name-Always rather inappropriately changed his name to "Buffalo-Bull-Coming-Out" in recognition of his new powers. Most of the shaman's followers continued to believe in his prophecies, for they thought success in this venture depended more on the sanction of the spirits than on their own special efforts. They manifested their faith by giving blankets, money, and other property to Buffalo-Bull-Coming-Out, whose vision had clearly conferred upon him the divine mission of bringing back the herds. Although younger men in the tribe opposed his pretensions and used all their influence against him, he continued to hold a strong following. At last, however, after nearly a year of ritualizing failed to produce a single buffalo, he was forced to declare that his medicine had been inactivated for five years because someone had violated one of the ritual's innumerable regulations.

In the continuing chronicle of Little Bear's calendar, 1887 indicated a Sun Dance, the first in some time. Unable to find the required buffalo in the wild, the hunters had bought a single bull from a captive Texas herd.

The same year also marked the end of the five-year waiting period specified by Buffalo-Bull-Coming-Out; but the shaman's medicine was never renewed, since he had died in the meantime. His promises were taken over and considerably amplified by another shaman, "In-The-Middle," whose wild prophecies soon attracted considerable notice.

In-The-Middle made a divination that a whirlwind would blow away all white people as well as all Indians living among them or following their customs. After that would come a great prairie fire, which would consume all the buildings and schools erected by the whites on Kiowa territory. Then In-The-Middle would personally restore all buffalo and other game, along with the traditional Kiowa way of life. By the summer of 1888, the

1881

1882

1888

shaman had stirred up a considerable following with these au-
guries.

When the day fixed for the reckoning arrived and passed without incident, In-The-Middle's followers began to sense that they
had been duped. The only apparent material transformation involved the belongings of In-The-Middle himself; once poor and obscure, the shaman had grown quite rich through all the horses and
blankets donated by the faithful.

Although In-The-Middle failed to bring off his day of deliver-
ance, he was soon able to claim that his prophecies were being
fulfilled in the emergence of a new cult. A popular native messiah
had begun to gather an enthusiastic following with his predictions
of the forthcoming extermination of whites and the resurrection of
all deceased friends and departed buffalo. Reunion of the cultists
with their dead, or ghosts, was to be accomplished through the
performance of a ritualistic Ghost Dance. Frustrated and unhappy
because of their dreary, confined lives in reservations, followers
held mass revivalist meetings and danced themselves into trances.
After regaining consciousness they described visions of deceased
kinfolk and teeming herds of buffalo.

Nurtured by the feeling of hardship caused by the disappearance of the buffalo, the Ghost Dance religion thrived on many
reservations for more than two years. But the trances and visions
were the closest the Indians ever came to bringing back their be-
loved herds or their departed relatives. The new cult eventually
precipitated unrest that led Washington to order the seizure of
Sioux medicine man Sitting Bull. On the morning of December
15, 1890, Sitting Bull was put under arrest by Indian police and
dragged bodily from his tent. A scuffle followed, and the Sioux
leader was fatally shot.

Two weeks later, a skirmish broke out as federal troops attempted to disarm a band of Sioux camping along South Dakota's
Wounded Knee Creek. In the senseless shooting that ensued,
around two hundred men, women, and children were slain. This
massacre destroyed forever the Indians' dreams of restoring their
buffalo. The plains had seen the last of the great herds, and tribal
culture, the heritage of centuries, would soon pass into memory.

23

RETURN TO

THE PLAINS

EARLY IN 1886, WILLIAM HORNADAY, THEN CHIEF TAX-idermist at the U.S. National Museum, took inventory of the buffalo skins in his collection. To his surprise he found that "the Museum was actually without presentable specimens of this most important and interesting mammal." He relayed word of the deficiency to his superiors, who quickly formulated plans to send him into the field to collect some buffalo before the species became extinct.

In making arrangements for the trip, Hornaday wrote to contacts throughout the west asking them to help him pinpoint relict groups of buffalo. Replies were discouraging—in fact, so few sightings were reported that he was prompted to speed preparations for the expedition, although he would have preferred to wait until autumn, when pelts would be prime. It had become clear that even a few weeks' delay might be fatal to the enterprise. He left Washington on the sixth of May, arriving three days later in Miles City, Montana, ready to track down some buffalo.

His first days in town confirmed the pessimistic reports: no buffalo had been seen in the vicinity for some time. Hornaday organized a wagon train and set forth to explore the uninhabited country to the north. Days later, with a base camp established on the divide between the Yellowstone and Missouri Rivers, he began a systematic combing of the area. "It was our custom to ride over the country daily, each day making a circuit through a new locality," he wrote in his subsequent report of the expedition. After almost four weeks of persistent searching, he had collected only three buffalo. But conversations with cowboys in the territory convinced him that there was a herd of thirty-five ranging over the badlands farther north. Hornaday "resolved to leave the buffaloes entirely unmolested until autumn, and then, when the robes would be in the finest condition, return for a hunt on a liberal scale." After making concrete plans for the second outing, he departed for Washington.

On September twenty-fourth, Hornaday returned to Miles City "fully equipped for a protracted hunt for buffalo." Within thirty-six hours he had his outfit rolling north toward the Missouri–Yellowstone divide. He set up camp and began another systematic search of the area, this time with the assistance of three local cowboys, who had hired on as guides and hunters. Day after day the men ranged back and forth across butte country "scored by intricate systems of great yawning ravines and hollows, steep-sided and very deep, and badlands of the worst description." This barren and tortuous region, though ideally suited to harboring remnant buffalo, was extremely wearing on the horses.

For seventeen days the men coursed over this rough country without sighting a single buffalo. Then, on the eighteenth day, a lone cowboy freighting supplies into camp happened upon a group of seven. He fired into the band, but his shots went wild, and after a short pursuit, he gave up and returned to camp. Early the next morning, Hornaday and his men took up the chase and managed to bring down four animals.

Two days later the hunters killed another four buffalo, the last an immense bull that had led his pursuers twelve miles before he succumbed. By now it was late in the afternoon, and the men were unable to finish skinning this fine kill before darkness forced them to return to camp. Shortly after dawn the next morning, Hornaday and his assistants left with a wagon to finish work on the carcass: "When we reached it we found that during the night a gang of Indians had robbed us of our hard-earned spoil. They had stolen the skin and all eatable meat, broken up the leg-bones to get at the marrow, and even cut out the tongue. And to injury the skulking thieves had added insult. Through laziness they had left the head unskinned, but on one side of it they had smeared the hair with red war-paint, and the other side they had daubed with yellow, and around the base of one horn they had tied a strip of red flannel as a signal of defiance. Of course they had left for parts unknown . . ."

Hornaday's bruised ego soon recovered and the hunt was resumed. After eight weeks in the field the expedition had collected twenty-five buffalo, "as complete and fine a series as could be wished for." The largest specimen was an old stub-horned bull that weighed about sixteen hundred pounds. "I was delighted with our remarkably good fortune in securing such a prize," Hornaday said, "for, owing to the rapidity with which the large buffaloes are being found and killed off these days, I had not hoped to capture a really old individual. Nearly every adult bull we took carried old bullets in his body, and from this one we took four of various sizes . . . One was found sticking fast in one of the lumbar vertebrae."

Hornaday returned to the National Museum in Washington and started work on a new exhibit, a habitat group featuring the big bull. When the exhibit opened, it brought raves from the local *Star*, which headlined

A SCENE FROM MONTANA—SIX OF MR. HORNADAY'S BUFFALOES FORM A PICTURESQUE GROUP—A BIT OF THE WILD WEST REPRODUCED AT THE NATIONAL MUSEUM—SOMETHING NOVEL IN THE WAY OF TAXIDERMY—REAL BUFFALO-GRASS, REAL MONTANA DIRT, AND REAL BUFFALOES.

One year after Hornaday's Montana hunt, the authorities at the American Museum of Natural History realized that they, too, lacked a representative series of buffalo skins. To remedy this situation, Dr. D. G. Elliot assembled a hunting outfit in the fall of 1887 and struck out for the Yellowstone–Missouri divide, the very country in which Hornaday had taken his specimens one year earlier. He searched back and forth through the region for three months and found not one buffalo. At last he gave up and returned to New York.

The failure of this expedition came as a shock to naturalists and hunters alike. How could a species that had numbered in the millions a decade earlier have been eliminated so quickly? But the impossible had indeed happened. When William Hornaday censused the free-ranging—and unprotected—buffalo surviving in the United States in January 1889, he could account for no more than eighty-five. Elsewhere on the continent, he listed 200 under lax federal protection in Yellowstone National Park, some 550 in the vicinity of Great Slave Lake, and 256 scattered in various zoos or private herds.

The future looked grim indeed, particularly since taxidermists were offering up to fifty dollars for the heads alone. In 1889 Hornaday declared, "There is no reason to hope that a single wild and unprotected individual will remain alive ten years hence." As it turned out, his prediction was conservative. Eight years later, poachers ranging through the mountain valleys of Colorado's Lost Park slew a calf, a cow, and two bulls, probably the last wild, unprotected buffalo in the United States.

Even the supposedly sheltered herd in Yellowstone National Park was dwindling under pressure from poachers. Although regulations forbade the killing of these animals, punishment for an offender was hardly severe: after confiscating his hunting outfit, officials simply expelled him from the park. Most poachers returned with a new outfit a short time later. As taxidermists in nearby Montana demanded increasing numbers of skins, poaching soon became a lucrative business. The most profitable season was the winter of 1893–4, when poachers succeeded in slaying 116 buffalo that had shifted westward out of the park.

When a subsequent count turned up only twenty or so survivors, agitation for the preservation of the Yellowstone herd increased. Congress swiftly passed a law forbidding the killing of buffalo under penalty of a thousand-dollar fine or imprisonment. The measure, signed by Grover Cleveland in May 1894, was the first effective protection the federal government had ever granted buffalo.

Nevertheless, the scattered survivors in Yellowstone Park continued to hover perilously close to extinction. By 1901 they still numbered no more than twenty-five. Alarmed by their failure to increase, the park superintendent urged the establishment of a new herd. Fifteen thousand dollars was quickly appropriated by Congress, permitting the park to purchase twenty-one buffalo from private refuges in Montana and Texas. Care of these animals was entrusted to the newly appointed game warden, Charles Jesse "Buffalo" Jones, who had acquired his nickname some twenty-five years earlier, in recognition of his escapades roping and training wild calves for promotional stunts.

Jones' calf-roping skills had even played a role in the saving of the species. This important phase of his career had begun in the spring of 1886, when there were only scattered remnants of the herds on the Texas plains. Braving occasional counterattacks from irate mothers, Jones rode among the buffalo and captured calves alive in what must have looked like a comic imitation of present-day rodeo roping.

Never a man to miss a chance for publicity, Jones invited reporters along on a chase. "I heard him call for his charger like a knight of old going out to battle," wrote an impressionable newsman, "and his voice roared over the plain until it was enough, alone, to have terrified the buffalo and brought them to a standstill."

"I roped eight calves and saved them," Jones himself explained, "although the wolves and coyotes were there by hundreds." He went on to describe his formula for snatching calves from the jaws of doom:

As soon as I caught one, I tied my hat to it, as I knew the brutes never touched anything tainted with the fresh scent of man. The next, my coat, then my vest, then my boots, and last, my socks, thus protecting 7. The 8th I picked up in my arms and rode back to the 7th as it was surrounded by wolves and coyotes. When I arrived where it was bound down, I saw the vicious brutes snapping at the 6th one, so reached down and drew up the 7th one and galloped back to the 6th to protect it. I let the two calves down, one with the legs tied and the lasso around the 8th calf's neck, the other end of the rope around my horse's neck. The strain was so great, I fainted, but revived when my boys came up and gave me some whiskey we had for snake bites.

Buffalo Jones, lariat dragging behind his horse, holds two of the "perishing" buffalo calves that he has just gallantly rescued from marauding wolves and coyotes.

In addition to burnishing Buffalo Jones' reputation, the calf roping was to prove surprisingly lucrative. When first caught, the calves were nursed by foster mothers—dairy cows dragged along by Jones on each of four roping expeditions; once weaned, the young buffalo were turned out onto Kansas pastures. And at last, five years after the first captures, Jones sold ten grown bison for a thousand dollars each—a conspicuous improvement on the $2.50 paid for a buffalo hide only a decade earlier.

The buyer of Jones' buffalo was Austin Corbin, a railroad magnate eager to add some new blood to a private herd he kept in his private game preserve in southwestern New Hampshire. After Corbin died four years later, his family became concerned about the mounting expense of maintaining the herd, which numbered 160 head by June of 1904. In the same month, a man named Ernest Harold Baynes moved into a house on the borders of Corbin's reserve. Baynes was a conservation-minded journalist, and "the sight of these splendid creatures made a deep impression on him, and excited his interest in the fate of their race . . ."

During the ensuing months, the journalist launched a vigorous campaign to stir up interest in the plight of the buffalo. He realized that the concern of the Corbin family over the increasing expense of their herd pointed up a general problem: by now most buffalo in the United States were in private herds, where their future was decidedly insecure. Baynes began writing letters to prominent individuals, recommending that the federal government establish several permanent herds.

Response quickly swelled. From the White House, Theodore Roosevelt wrote: "I am much impressed with your letter, and I agree with every word you say." Thus encouraged, Baynes continued his efforts, publishing some forty articles in magazines and newspapers. His labors culminated in a meeting of fourteen interested conservationists, zoologists, and editors, on December 8, 1905, in the Lion House of the New York Zoological Park. Together the men organized the American Bison Society, electing William Hornaday president and Baynes secretary; Theodore Roosevelt was named honorary president.

With the official blessings of the newly formed society, Ernest Harold Baynes redoubled his efforts, recruiting fifty new members, giving exhibitions of buffalo robes and artifacts, and delivering free lectures about the dwindling herds. In additional newspaper and magazine articles, he admonished his readers that they had waited "until the eleventh hour" to attempt the rescue of their "finest native animal." His pleas were urgent: "This is literally 'the last call'—[the buffalo] must be saved at once or he will pass forever . . ."

In his zeal Baynes turned the deposed monarch of the plains into a symbol of the world's persecution, a hero of the American frontier. He also began to trumpet the untapped potential of the creature as a work animal.

This idea of the buffalo as a beast of burden was not new, however. More than two centuries earlier, Father Louis Hennepin had observed that "these young Calves might be easily tam'd, and made use of to plow the Land, which would be very advantageous to the Savages." Although the "Savages" probably never trained the animals to turn the sod, a few tame buffalo were actually broken to plow or wagon in plains settlements.

Buffalo Jones had even gone so far as to draw up plans and start training prototypes for a buffalo-drawn streetcar system for his native Garden City, Kansas. The project was never carried to completion, however, because the beasts proved too difficult to handle. As a zoologist later remarked, draft buffalo, "though strong and serviceable . . . were at times rather unmanageable."

But the prospect of recalcitrant buffalo didn't stop Ernest Harold Baynes. In his search for new projects for the American Bison Society, the indefatigable secretary soon wangled a loan of two young calves from the Corbin herd with the idea of testing them as beasts of burden. He raised his spirited wards on cow's milk and made a careful record of their progress. At first they were "inclined to be very aggressive . . . jumping into me and butting vigorously at the slightest provocation," but this did not discourage him. ". . . I liked to see this spirit of self-protection, and I admired the splendid courage of these handsome little beasts; it would surely prove an important factor in the effort being made to preserve the race from extinction."

The calves eventually quieted down enough for Baynes to attempt to break them. "When they were ten weeks old I put a calf-yoke on them, but in ten seconds they turned it inside out and broke it. I got a stronger one, and in less than an hour the calves were jogging along the road so steadily that I scarcely thought of the fine black eyes they had given me as I was adjusting the bows."

When the animals were four months old, Baynes hitched them to a stone-laden sledge and tested their abilities on a country road. He found that they exhibited "such splendid strength and courage as I could not have believed possible for youngsters still in their first summer." Even their stubbornness did not trouble him. "To be sure, they were a trifle headstrong, and once they ran clean away with the drag; but then, even domestic steers will do this if they get the chance."

As his draft buffalo grew in size, Baynes began exhibiting them at local fairs. "All the farmers present admitted that no team of steers of the same age could begin to match it for either speed or strength," he once boasted. Soon he had a chance to prove his team's superiority at the Central Maine Fair, where he was challenged by a man who had broken a steer to a sulky. When the steer was pitted against the improbable team in a half-mile race, the buffalo won a "decisive victory." (Baynes' report of this triumph was the last public mention he ever made of his cherished draft animals. Some years later, another writer let out the secret. Apparently the two buffalo, increasing in size and strength as they aged, had become impossible to handle, and Baynes had been forced to return them to the Corbin herd.)

To drum up greater interest in the cause of the American Bison Society, Baynes began publicizing the virtues of buffalo wool. Indian successes with the product had long before influenced Louis XIV to urge the development of a new wool industry in the French colony on the Mississippi. And a later effort had been launched in 1821 in the Red River settlement, where the "Buffalo Wool Company" was founded after the sale of $8,880 worth of stock and a loan of $20,000 from the Hudson's Bay Company. With this lavish backing, funds were plentiful, wages high, and prospects golden. Eventually the factory produced a few samples of buffalo-wool cloth and sent them to England for appraisal. In a short time word came back that the yard of cloth would bring $1.00 on the London market. Since the same yard cost $11.12 to fabricate, the great Buffalo Wool Company soon collapsed in bankruptcy.

Ernest Harold Baynes' efforts with buffalo wool were somewhat more successful than those of the Canadian venture. Gathering tufts of the fuzz as it was shed from the beasts, he spun it into yarn. Gloves knitted from the thick yarn proved warm and durable. Samples offered to wool companies elicited the report that "buffalo wool was very closely akin to sheep's wool; that it was stronger, grade for grade, than the average wool; and that for a long time it would demand a high price as a novelty." In later years the American Bison Society even arranged to have the wool knitted into a blanket, which was submitted to the U.S. Bureau of Standards for comparison testing with the standard army blanket. Although the buffalo wool blanket proved to be as warm as the army one, it was more porous and thus had the disadvantage of being a bit breezy.

The widespread enthusiasm over buffalo wool overlooked a small problem. As a later report expressed it, "The question of how to obtain the wool from the living buffalo has not been clearly solved." We may assume that shearing buffalo would be more adventurous than shearing sheep.

Baynes' gimmicks with wool and draft buffalo, while not successful commercial ventures, helped to stimulate a lively interest in the species. Membership in the American Bison Society had swelled to 236 by the time of the first annual meeting in January 1907. But the rest of that year was clouded by two setbacks in the Society's efforts at buffalo preservation.

The first came when Montana's Flathead Indian Reservation was 'opened to public settlement. The change in the title of the land forced resident Michel Pablo to sell his private herd of some six hundred buffalo. Pablo offered the herd to the U.S. government, but his terms were rejected. Shortly afterward he approached Canadian officials with a similar proposal. When the Canadians bid $250 for each animal, Pablo accepted, and by the end of 1907 he had managed to round up and ship 410 animals. The remainder of the herd was sent north in following years. This sale of buffalo to Canada, though inevitable under the circumstances, was a blow to the pride of the American Bison Society.

Also in 1907, the Society attempted to establish a state herd in New York's Adirondack Mountains. A bill was submitted to Albany calling for the appropriation of twenty thousand dollars for the new herd. The measure was received by the Finance Committee "in the most friendly spirit" and soon passed both houses of the legislature unanimously. After this gratifying success, the Society received a "profound and painful surprise" when Governor Hughes vetoed the bill. "It is doubtful, to say the least, whether there ever have been any Bison in the Adirondacks," the Governor stated, "and the policy of attempting to maintain Bison there is questionable." (His objection was valid, for it is unlikely that buffalo ever ranged as far as the Adirondacks.)

These two reverses were offset later in the year when a newly benevolent Congress appropriated fifteen thousand dollars to stock the first federal buffalo range. Eight thousand acres of prairie in what was once Oklahoma's Apache, Comanche, and Kiowa Reservation were fenced off for the animals. William Hornaday selected fifteen specimens from the New York Zoological Society's herd and sent them off to Oklahoma in royal style in two Arms Palace Horse Cars. After an enthusiastic reception by local cowboys, ranchers, and Indians, the buffalo were released into an enclosure that would one day be enlarged into the most important plains preserve in the nation, the fifty-nine thousand acre Wichita Mountains Wildlife Refuge.

Spurred by the success of this Oklahoma refuge, the American Bison Society made plans to establish a similar haven in Montana, engaging a local biologist to select the most suitable site in the state. Early in 1908, the scientist submitted a report indicating his choice of a twenty-nine-square mile plot a short distance north of Missoula. The paper contained detailed information on all aspects of the site, including possible buffalo enemies ("There are occasional rattlesnakes reported, but during the several days that I walked and rode over the range I did not see any") and local feelings ("There will not be a dissenting man, unless perhaps it may be someone who wants a portion of the range to himself").

With the help of Montana Senator Joseph M. Dixon, the American Bison Society sent Congress a bill proposing the establishment of the new reserve. After a brief discussion in committee, the bill was submitted to the floor with an enthusiastic endorsement. "The Committee believes that no more meritorious measure has been presented during the present session of Congress, and are unanimous in the recommendation that the bill pass." Boosted by a little lobbying from the Society, the measure sped through both houses and was signed by President Roosevelt on May 23, 1908.

Now the Bison Society went to work on a national campaign to raise ten thousand dollars for the purchase of a nucleus herd. In January 1909, the drive topped its goal by $560.50, and William Hornaday expressed the Society's surprise and pleasure at "the *splendid* support that the undertaking received from the women of America." Their widespread interest in birds was well known, but they had never been expected to respond with "unflagging industry" to gather contributions for a brutish mammal.

Although the response from women's groups had been gratifying, Hornaday was disappointed by the weak support from the West. Aside from a good showing in Montana, the project received only paltry sums from the Great Plains states. And from Texas, Kansas, and the Dakotas, where butchery of the historic herds had been wanton, it got not one cent.

But in spite of this shocking indifference, enough money had been brought in to bankroll the purchase of thirty-four buffalo from a private Montana herd. The animals were shipped by rail and wagon and released into the new National Bison Range on October 17, 1909, to the delight of William Hornaday: "As the crates were opened, the bison backed out of them, looked about for a moment, saw their Paradise Regained looming up . . . and climbed up into their new home . . . the richest and the most beautiful grazing grounds ever trodden by bison hoofs."

During his early appeals for the rescue of the buffalo, Ernest Harold Baynes had customarily clinched his argument with a tug on sentiment: "The buffalo . . . saved the lives of thousands of American pioneers and early settlers, and there are many living now whose relatives or friends would have suffered great hardship, if not death itself, but for the presence of buffaloes on the plains. Let us act at once . . . and save . . . this noble animal, which up to date has been repaid chiefly with brutality and with persecution to the very brink of extermination." Those who had helped to rescue the buffalo refused to forget the specter of past cruelty and slaughter and went to extremes in coddling their new wards. The animals released in the new preserves were not just herds of buffalo—they were distinct individuals: in Montana there was the dominant bull, "Kalispell Chief," and his "understudy," later named "Ravalli Chief," and in the Wichita Refuge, "Geronimo," "Lone Wolf," "Quanah," and "Black Dog."

The animals in Yellowstone Park's "tame herd" were equally pampered. Each buffalo was guarded and cared for tenderly, and any natural instincts that ran counter to the safety of members of the herd were suppressed. When the bulls seemed to be endangering some of the calves with their fighting, the unruly males were removed to separate pastures. Wardens even separated a few delicate calves from their mothers and bottle-nursed them to shield them from possible harm. Twice a day the main herd was carefully shepherded out of its enclosure to give the animals a chance to sample fresh forage. Shelters were erected to protect the buffalo from inclement weather.

Much loving care was also lavished on another group of buffalo, a Texas herd owned by Major Gordon "Pawnee Bill" Lillie. His concern for the animals revealed itself during negotiations in 1906 over the sale of seven choice bulls. The prospective buyer, a Señor José Banjio, ostensibly planned to breed the bulls with domestic cattle in Mexico. Pawnee Bill received a large down payment and was about to ship the animals when his clipping service sent him an item from El Paso. A local paper there had picked up news that the town of Juarez, just across the border, was soon to be the scene of a corrida pitting "seven of the largest and most ferocious buffalo bulls" against a group of Mexico's "most savage Spanish bulls and skillful matadors." Shocked by the "murderous purpose" planned for his darlings, Bill quickly returned Banjio's down payment and censured him for "deceitful tactics."

As the herds in the Wichita Refuge and the National Bison Range thrived and multiplied, William Hornaday began to receive chummy letters from his correspondents in the field. From Oklahoma, the local warden wrote that his buffalo had "plenty of good green grass and pure running water. They did not have a tick on them last summer." And the range manager in Montana sent a generally glowing report: "I suppose you would like to know how your pets are by this time. I am proud to say that they wintered well and are . . . all in fine condition except one yearling bull that got bitten by a rattlesnake when a calf. He has a stiff leg, and has never done very well." (Evidently the bull had run into one of the "occasional rattlesnakes" mentioned in the initial survey of the range.)

The American Bison Society continued its fight to create new government reserves. In 1906 the army had abandoned its Fort Niobrara Military Reservation in Nebraska, since the fort was no longer needed to control Sioux Indians, cattle rustlers, horse thieves, and "other lawless persons." The land soon found another use when presidential decree set the whole area aside for the protection of native birds. Shortly afterward, the American Bison Society checked the property and found it ideally suited to buffalo as well. When a local Nebraskan volunteered his private herd of six buffalo, the establishment of a new reserve seemed assured; but the animals could not be accepted until the range was fenced. Funds to meet this emergency were quickly contributed by the citizens of nearby Valentine, the Chicago and Northwestern Railway, and the National Association of Audubon Societies, and the Nebraska herd was moved into its new range on January 21, 1913.

In the same year, the Society stocked the recently fenced Wind Cave National Park with fourteen buffalo, all gifts of the New York Zoological Society. And just north of Wind Cave, thirty-six buffalo were released into the newly established Custer State Park.

By 1915, the members of the American Bison Society could reflect happily on the accomplishments of their first ten years. During this decade they had overseen a general population increase of about 270 per cent. Buffalo were now established and thriving in the new Wichita, Niobrara, Wind Cave, and Custer preserves, and even Yellowstone Park's "wild herd," once almost abandoned because the twenty-two survivors seemed beyond rescue, had doubled its ranks. Reviewing these gratifying gains in all herds, the officers of the Society proclaimed that "the future of the species now seems assured."

In the years that followed, the officers expanded their sphere of interest to champion pronghorn preservation. But in 1918 their favorite cause was threatened once again, when a wartime shortage of beef and mutton prompted livestock interests to campaign for grazing rights in some of the preserves occupied by buffalo. Even in the critical days of the war, the Society considered the possibility of such usurpation "nothing short of a national calamity," and successfully rallied support to protect both preserves and occupants.

Weathering such difficulties, the herds continued to increase in numbers, and by 1922 the Society was able to issue the following proud report: "It is a matter of gratification that the buffalo are becoming so numerous in some of the government herds that it presently will become necessary to treat the surplus bulls as so many domestic cattle." In 1930 the American Bison Society published its last annual report. The rescue of the species had been accomplished.

In the meantime, Michel Pablo's buffalo, whose sale to Canada in 1906 had been so sorely lamented by the Society, were prospering in their new home. Pablo had finally delivered 672 animals, after the longest, wildest, costliest, and most frustrating buffalo roundup ever held. The venture had taken six years and involved as many as seventy-five cowboys; but in the end it proved worthwhile for Pablo, who raked in a total of $177,000 by the time the last buffalo was delivered.

Ultimately, all of Pablo's animals wound up in the Buffalo National Park at Wainwright, Alberta. By 1921 they had increased to 4,609, and they continued to multiply by about twenty-five per cent each year. The authorities soon realized that if they were to be kept from overgrazing their range, measures would have to be taken to dispose of over a thousand individuals annually. Consequently, 2,409 buffalo were killed between 1922 and 1924.

The following year, the Canadian Department of the Interior, speaking through Maxwell Graham, came up with a new plan for disposing of the overflow. Graham proposed the annual shipment of one or two thousand buffalo north into Wood Buffalo National Park. Since the transfer would mean mixing the plains with the wood race, Graham wisely anticipated opposition and attempted, however lamely, to justify his proposal.

Although only two years earlier he had stated that wood buffalo were "the finest specimens of their species, superior in pelage, size and vigour to those of the plains," he suddenly began to express doubts about the desirability of maintaining the animals as a separate subspecies. And, besides, he added, a portion of the supposed wood race would still remain intact on the northern part of the range, separated from the body of introduced plains animals by natural barriers of swamp and muskeg. Furthermore, the new arrivals could multiply to provide a future source of food for the natives.

Maxwell Graham must have been dumbfounded by the storm of protest that quickly descended upon his proposals. One of the first replies came from Dr. Francis Harper, a charter member of the American Bison Society and a zoologist who had undertaken more than one expedition into wood buffalo territory. Harper noted that since adequate protection had allowed wood buffalo to increase from a onetime low of three hundred to a current population of fifteen hundred, they would eventually multiply to saturate their range. There was thus no valid reason for introducing any more buffalo. He also argued that there was no impenetrable natural barrier to prevent wood and plains races from interbreeding, and he warned that the introduced buffalo would contaminate the wood population with new diseases.

Two months later the American Society of Mammalogists, an international organization with over seven hundred members, reaffirmed Harper's objections and cautioned that "serious results would occur" if the proposed transfer were carried out. In renewed pleas, both Canadian and American naturalists advised that it would be better to shift the surplus buffalo to virgin range or even kill the entire Wainwright herd than to risk tampering with the last remnant of wood buffalo.

Officials in the Canadian Department of the Interior were unmoved. They admitted to having received "protests from zoologists and mammalogical societies of the United States and Canada," but reaffirmed their intention to proceed with the transfer, insisting that "their own experts are better qualified to judge the policy, because of experience and practice, than are zoologists at a distance . . ." These "experts," however, were never identified.

On June 25, 1925, the first group of buffalo left the rail siding at Wainwright. For two days and more than four hundred miles they traveled in custom cars carrying plentiful rations of water and feed. On reaching the end of the line at Waterways, Alberta, they were turned into corrals to rest for a day and a half. Finally they were loaded onto two special barges and pushed by steamboat for four days, from the Athabasca River to the Slave River, a distance of 257 miles. There, at last, they were released into Wood Buffalo National Park.

The curious flotilla made the journey seven times in 1925; still more buffalo were shuttled to the new region during the following three summers. The group-style accommodations permitted the transport of those animals up to a maximum age of three years—fully grown bison could not be carried because provision had not been made for individual crating. By the end of the transfer in 1928, 6,673 plains buffalo had been relocated.

During the initial discussions about the project, Minister of the Interior Charles Stewart had claimed that "it is not the intention to mix breeds in any way." But within a few months his own department published a brochure stating the transplanted animals were "mingling with the Wood Buffalo." The newcomers soon infected the residents of Wood Buffalo National Park with both tuberculosis and brucellosis. And in the very first year of the project, interbreeding between the two races did indeed occur, giving Harvard zoologist Thomas Barbour good reason to label the transplant "one of the most tragic examples of bureaucratic stupidity in all history." The four-to-one preponderance of plains animals almost completely wiped out the wood buffalo as a pure race, transforming the park population into hybrids with a bulk of plains characteristics.

Despite continued crossbreeding over the next thirty years, biologists from the Canadian Wildlife Service held out hope that a remnant of pure wood buffalo lay hidden in an isolated corner of the Park. At last, during an aerial survey of the herds in 1957, they found just such a group, a number of animals separated from the mass of hybrids by a strip of inhospitable timber and bog. But the area was as inaccessible as it was isolated.

In the winter of 1958–9, however, the men managed to make their way into the remote region with the aid of snow tractors. After setting up a base camp, they tracked down a total of some two hundred buffalo. In order to check the subspecific identity of the group, they collected five specimens, including one twenty-three hundred-pound bull. Subsequent examination at the National Museum of Canada verified the original supposition—the animals were indeed wood buffalo.

Having rediscovered their "lost" race, the Canadian Wildlife Service set about transferring most of the animals into new ranges where they could never cross with plains buffalo. When the selected wood animals had been safely moved to Elk Island National Park and a range bordering the Great Slave Lake, the scientists issued a final communique: "We gain some satisfaction in knowing that although we have not discovered a new subspecies, perhaps we have saved an old one."

Some four decades earlier, during the uproar over the suggested transplant, certain critics had even recommended total annihilation of the plains animals at Wainwright. Although their drastic proposals were soon forgotten, overgrazing in the pastures and a high incidence of tuberculosis and liver flukes eventually forced officials to kill off the herd and "give the range a rest." And so, ironically, some twelve years after the damaging transplant that had been undertaken with great difficulty to save them, the entire Wainwright herd was liquidated after all.

After the elimination of the controversial herd, the Canadian Department of Agriculture continued to operate an enclosure at Wainwright for the breeding of "cattalo"—hybrid animals produced by mating buffalo with domestic cattle.

These attempts to develop a superior breed of cattalo, begun in 1915, were hardly new. In what was perhaps the first proposal for such breeding, Captain Vicente de Zaldívar, in 1598, speculated that the "wild cattle" of the American plains might be tamed by "crossing them with those from Spain." Actual crossbreeding did not occur until about 1750, when colonists in "Carolina and other provinces to the south of Pennsylvania" began to raise buffalo calves with their tame cattle; the two species mated "and by this means generated, as it were, a new breed." About thirty-six years later, in the northwestern counties of Virginia, "the mixed breed was quite common . . . and the cows, the issue of that mixture, propagated like all others."

Various breeders in the years to come tried crossing buffalo and domestic cattle, producing a known tally of 345 hybrids by 1908. Most famous of the experimenters was the colorful Buffalo Jones, who gave the breed its name.

Jones had high hopes for his hybrids. "They are surely destined to be of great value," he proclaimed, "for there are yet over six hundred million acres of unclaimed government land, so sterile that domesticated animals cannot utilize it, but sufficiently fertile to provide a living for the catalo." (This spelling was changed to "cattalo" some years later.)

With dreams of dazzling success, Jones formed a company, sold stock, and drove a herd of about 120 buffalo into the House Rock Valley near the north rim of the Grand Canyon. There he began a program of crossing buffalo with Galloway cattle.

Three years later the operation folded quietly, with little more than red ink and overblown publicity to its credit. The glorious destiny of Jones' cattalo was not to be realized.

In spite of these early failures, it appears that a worthwhile breed of cattalo can be developed. Considerable progress was made not long ago in a research program involving a hundred cows at the Range Experimental Farm in Alberta. Crossbreeding was aimed at generating a range beef animal combining the superior meat qualities of domestic cattle and the rugged traits of buffalo. Such a combination was expected to produce a new, hardier breed of animal that could better endure the severe blizzards that regularly rake the northern plains, for as William Hornaday wrote in 1889, "A buffalo will survive where the best range steer would literally freeze on foot, bolt upright, as hundreds did in the winter of 1886–87."

Theoretically, buffalo-cattle hybrids can be obtained by crossing a buffalo bull with a domestic cow or vice versa. The first combination was abandoned early in the testing, however, because it led to births often fatal to both mother and calf. (The deaths were associated with an excessive accumulation of fluid in the birth sac, and were not, as some early breeders believed, due to overexertion of the domestic cow in delivering a calf with a hump.) Such losses were avoided by the reverse mating. The main difficulty in this combination was psychological, not physical, for some of the farm-pampered domestic bulls shied from mating with their wild cousins.

Of the hybrids produced in these matings, only the females were fertile. The sterility of the males seriously hindered development of a breed of cattalo capable of reproducing itself.

When the female offspring were backcrossed to either parent species, however, the descendants usually demonstrated an improved fertility. Successive backcrossing of these individuals produced cattalo of about sixteen per cent buffalo parentage. By repeated selection of superior breeders from this group, researchers made steady progress toward achieving a reliable male fertility.

Some of the winter hardiness of buffalo was indeed transmitted to the Canadian cattalo, for they displayed outstanding tolerance to cold and excellent foraging ability on the exposed winter range. They were willing to feed during bad weather, rooting through snow with their muzzles, grazing on open prairie more doggedly and more effectively than domestic breeds. Some of their winter vigor could be attributed to the warmth of their coats, whose thickness and quality were inherited from the buffalo's side of the family.

Once the cattalo had attained this winter hardiness, further breeding experiments were aimed at improving the quality of the meat. But after several years of additional breeding, cattalo meat was still not up to the high standard of beef. The hybrid animals yielded slightly inferior carcasses—generally grade "B" instead of grade "A" under the rating system used for cattle. This inferiority was attributed in part to the hunchbacked shape of the buffalo, a feature that carried over to the cattalo, making them somewhat heavy in the shoulders and light in the hindquarters, traits undesirable in high-grade beef animals.

Despite the accomplishments of the Canadian cattalo project, research was discontinued in 1964, and the entire herd was slaughtered. By this time most ranchers on southern Canadian prairies were feeding their range cattle in winter instead of turning them out to pasture, and the government no longer considered it necessary to develop a breed with a tolerance for extreme cold.

Cattalo may yet prove useful on more northerly ranges, however. Should the need arise again, ranchers will be able to consult the Alberta research for the fastest means of achieving a superior breed.

During the course of the Alberta experiment, the quality of cattalo meat was sampled by a panel of tasters. Evaluating different cuts for aroma, flavor, texture, tenderness, and juiciness, these experts determined that meat from a cattalo of fourteen per cent buffalo parentage was indistinguishable from that of a Hereford. They concluded that marketing meat from cattalo would involve no difficulties.

A newspaper advertisement from Safeway Stores in California features a sale of buffalo meat, which was obtained from a ranch in Oregon.

Even the meat from pure plains buffalo finds a ready outlet in today's markets. This is not surprising when one considers that fur traders, sportsmen, railroad crews, and explorers alike survived on it for years.

A number of modern ranches and refuges supply buffalo meat, most of it tender and juicy (the best quality coming from bulls under about three years and cows under five or six years). It is possible to buy a quarter of a carcass from one of the preserves that disposes of surplus animals each fall—the Wichita Mountains Wildlife Refuge, the Fort Niobrara National Wildlife Refuge, the National Bison Range, or Custer State Park. Depending on the form of processing and packaging selected, a quarter will run around sixty-five dollars (information may be obtained from the Bureau of Sport Fisheries and Wildlife, Washington, D.C. 20025). The refuges recommend writing early in the year, as they usually sell out long before the meat is ready for delivery. For smaller portions, one can try the meat counters of certain supermarket chains, especially in the late fall (Safeway stores on the West Coast have been known to carry special sales of the meat). Prices run about ten to thirty per cent higher than comparable cuts of beef.

Despite the greater cost, buffalo meat is not overpriced, for its marked leanness entails less fatty marbling and less trimming. In roasting, a standing rib of buffalo reaches the rare stage at a lower temperature than a beef roast because it is insulated with less fat. Otherwise, buffalo meat can be cooked in much the same manner as beef.

A recent feature in *Sunset* magazine described the taste of the meat as "often indistinguishable from beef, although buffalo tends to have a fuller, richer flavor." (From my own experience, I would agree; buffalo can be quite tasty. But because the meat is not graded as carefully as beef, it can also be a bit tough or stringy at times.) The magazine offered special buffalo recipes, among them baked buffalo ribs and savory noodles, buffalo in tomato-wine sauce, buffalo stroganoff, and "buffaloaf."

In preparing the article, *Sunset*'s home economist worked closely with Wyoming's B-Bar-B Buffalo Ranch (now Durham Meat Company), the nation's largest commercial supplier of buffalo meat. At the end of the testing, she expressed the staff's gratitude to the ranch, and volunteered an opinion on the meat: "Our tasters want me to pass along their enthusiasm for the roast buffalo. That mammoth standing rib roast was just about the most magnificent meat any of us have ever tasted."

Many restaurants now feature buffalo meat, either as a standard dish or as a seasonal specialty. Near Denver, for instance, The Fort advertises buffalo steaks "charbroiled Blackfoot style over

3 1 1

aspen." But no eating establishment vaunts its buffalo meat more proudly than Tommy's Joynt, a colorful cosmopolitan eatery in San Francisco. At Tommy's, gourmets may sup contentedly on buffalo stew, assured that they are not contributing to the decimation of this fine American breed, but instead fostering harmonious matrimonial life among the beasts. A large plaque inside the establishment reads: "The meat is secured from slaughtering the excess bulls annually. As many male as female calves are born, but if the ratio of bulls is not cut to one for every ten adult cows, the males fight and gore one another so unmercifully that they neglect their job of fathering a progeny, and the herd does not increase as it should." With this curious piece of rationale, they soothe the consciences of their customers and sell a lot of buffalo stew.

Even buffalo jerky has made a comeback in recent years—two meat packing plants in Wyoming sell it locally and by mail order for seven to eight dollars per pound. The manufacturer of "Injun Ben" jerky insists that his product has tremendous food value, is sweeter and more pliable than beef jerky, and is, of course, nonfattening. The producer of the other brand, Jackson Cold Storage and Distributors, draws its sales pitch from pioneer history: "Once the staple of Indians, mountain men and settlers. Still prepared and cured by the old fashioned mountain process."

In addition to the preserves that kill surplus buffalo for meat, a few areas allow shooting of the animals for sport. In the Big Delta area of Alaska, the state is swamped each year with three thousand applications for its annual quota of fifty permits. Arizona, Colorado, Utah, South Dakota, and the Northwest Territories also allow a small number to be shot each season. Elsewhere, hunting is permitted on some private ranches, where a man who wants to brag about having potted a buffalo can become eligible to do so for about five hundred dollars. In most of these places, the chase is about as exciting as gunning down a neighbor's cow: the sharpshooter simply plugs away until he dispatches the chosen animal. In the Copper River Region of Alaska, however, the hunt is considerably more sporting. Penetrating this wilderness with a buffalo safari is said to be quite an adventure, though still a far cry from the horseback buffalo-running of the past century.

The not inconsiderable numbers of buffalo slaughtered annually for meat and sport give some indication of the size of the populations now ranging over portions of North America. The current total is about thirty thousand, the majority grouped in seventeen prominent herds. In the summer of 1970, their numbers were as follows:

Wood Buffalo National Park, N.W.T.	12,000
Range east of the Slave River, N.W.T.	3,000
Ponderosa Ranch, Burns, Oregon	2,700
Durham Meat Company, Gillette, Wyoming (formerly B-Bar-B Buffalo Ranch)	2,000
Triple "U" Enterprises, Pierre, South Dakota	2,000
Custer State Park, South Dakota	1,935
Lazy YX Ranch, Murdo, South Dakota	1,400
Wichita Mountains Wildlife Refuge, Oklahoma	910
Elk Island National Park, Alberta	735
Yellowstone National Park, Wyoming	625
National Bison Range, Montana	410
Fort Niobrara National Wildlife Refuge, Nebraska	325
Big Delta, Alaska	250
Wind Cave National Park, South Dakota	240
House Rock, Arizona (1969)	228
Raymond Ranch, Arizona	217
Maxwell Game Refuge, Kansas	210

The present population marks a twenty-five-fold increase over the sparse numbers of 1901. In that year, as the pounding of endless hoofs vanished in a disconcerting silence, the U.S. Treasury issued a ten-dollar note that bore the image of a lordly buffalo bull. Today the buffalo note is out of circulation, a rarity worth many times its face value. The artist's models, on the other hand, are outliving the art, for the herds of buffalo are undeniably here to stay—living legends that summon a nostalgia for the early west.

Their rescue from the brink of extinction must give inspiration and courage to conservationists struggling to save the more than five hundred birds and mammals now listed, as the buffalo once was, on the roster of rare and vanishing species. Six close relatives of the buffalo, in particular, are threatened. Designated as "rare" are the wisent of Europe, the dwarf water buffalo of Celebes, and the wild Indian buffalo of Assam, Nepal, and India. In even greater danger are the seladang of Malaya, the kouprey of Cambodia, and the tamarau of the Philippines, whose numbers have been reduced to no more than two or three hundred each.

Neither time nor history is on the side of those working to rescue these endangered animals, for our civilization is wiping out species at a rate of at least one a year, and the figure is accelerating rapidly. For mammals alone, the rate of extinction has increased fifty-five-fold in the last century and a half. If the killing should continue to speed up at this quickening pace, all of the remaining 4,062 species of mammals would disappear within thirty years. Even now, over two hundred are officially listed as "endangered," or fighting a losing battle with extinction.

Such losses cannot be redeemed later; once an animal is gone from the earth, it is gone forever. In an effort to save the threatened species, a few men are working to undo the errors of the many. They are engaged in a fierce struggle against our culture's reckless disregard for rare wildlife, primitive peoples, and irreplaceable timberlands, marshes, seashores, and other natural domains. Fortunately, these conservationists are as dedicated as their predecessors—men like Ernest Harold Baynes, William Hornaday, and the members of the American Bison Society. But present-day naturalists cannot shoulder alone the trusteeship of our wildlife. All of us are answerable to future generations for the preservation of the dazzling variety of our natural environment.

With each passing year man draws his world of concrete and steel more closely around him. In the fight to reverse this trend, the rescue of the buffalo has been a dramatic and encouraging success, but it marks no more than a beginning. If man cannot make a passionate commitment to the preservation of his fellow creatures, many more will vanish in time, and our world, ironically enough, will become a cold, inhuman place to live.

APPENDIXES

Appendix A

Principal Wildlife Conservation Agencies

The World Wildlife Fund
910 Seventeenth Street, N.W.
Washington, D.C. 20006

The National Audubon Society
1130 Fifth Avenue
New York, N.Y. 10028

The International Union for the Conservation of Nature
Morges
Switzerland

The Royal Society for the Protection of Birds
The Lodge
Sandy, Bedfordshire
England

National Wildlife Federation
1412 Sixteenth Street, N.W.
Washington, D.C. 20036

The Sierra Club
1050 Mills Tower
San Francisco, California 94104

A P P E N D I X B

Hoofed Kin

Within the classification of mammals, the bison is related to a group of our most prominent big game and domestic species. Its position can best be understood from the following key, which includes the distinguishing features of some important relatives and their North American representatives, listed in parentheses.

Order *Artiodactyla:* Main axis of foot running between third and fourth digits; toes generally numbering two or four; hoofed.

Suborder *Suiformes:* Horns or antlers absent; upper incisors present.
Superfamily *Suoidea:* Snout piglike.
Family *Tayassuidae:* (Peccaries.)

Suborder *Ruminantia*—the ruminants: Horns or antlers generally present, at least in males; upper incisors absent and supplanted by a callous pad against which the lower teeth bite; stomach four-chambered.
Superfamily *Cervoidea:* Mainly browsers; antlers, usually only on males, shed each year.
Family *Cervidae:* (Elk, deer, moose, caribou, and brockets.)
Superfamily *Bovoidea:* Mainly grazers; horns, usually on both sexes, protruding from skull as permanent bony outgrowths covered by horny sheaths.
Family *Antilocapridae:* Horny sheaths shed each year. (Pronghorn.)
Family *Bovidae:* Horny sheaths never shed. (Wild species: Bison, musk ox, bighorn and white sheep, and mountain goat. Domestic species: Domestic cattle and humped cattle—or zebu, sheep, and goats.)

Appendixes

PARASITES

Within and without its body, a buffalo plays host to an army of lilliputian spongers.

Swarming about any thin-furred portions are mosquitoes, black flies, gnats, and several other winged menaces, all of which can cause irritating abrasions through their repeated biting.

Buffalo wounds are likely to attract egg-laying by screw-worm flies (*Cochliomyia macellaria*), named after their screw-like larvae, maggots three fourths of an inch long with rings of bristles between each pair of body segments. The developing larvae find shelter and nourishment in wounds, eventually agitating the lesions into festering sores. Buffalo lick these sores—presumably in an effort to remove the worms, sometimes assisted in reaching out-of-the-way parts of the body by their herd mates. Even more insidious than the screw-worm fly is the botfly (*Hypoderma*), whose larvae burrow beneath the skin to feed internally on the animal's flesh; once grown, they bore out, drop to the ground, and pupate, emerging later as fully developed flies.

The hide may be further overrun by lice (*Damalinia sedecimde-cembrii*). Severe infestations result in a loss of hair that can predispose the host, in its weakened condition, to death from predation or other causes.

Ticks (*Dermacentor andersoni*) also infest the hide, crawling onto buffalo from foliage and then working down through the dense hair about the horns and neck to bite into the skin. Heavy infestations of a hundred or so may bring on "tick paralysis" in yearlings (older animals seem more resistant to attacks). When first afflicted, the youngsters develop an unsteady gait and twitch their legs and heads. Eventually they stagger and collapse, struggling once or twice to get up, only to settle into a quiet stupor. This progressive paralysis of the muscles is probably brought on by a nerve poison injected by the feeding ticks. Prompt removal or destruction of the ticks results in dramatically rapid recovery with no impairment to health. Evidently any poison left in the buffalo soon breaks down and ceases to produce any further paralysis. Conversely, if the ticks are not eliminated within a few hours after collapse, the victim dies.

Elsewhere on buffalo, small mites (*Speleognathus australis*) may inhabit nasal passages. Farther down, lungs may be infested with lungworms (*Dictyocaulus viviparus* and *filaria*) or the bacteria that cause pneumonia (*Asterococcus mycoides*). (In 1887, pneumonia claimed Buffalo Bill Cody's entire herd of twenty while they were performing in his Wild West Show at Madison Square Garden.)

The muscles of buffalo may house *Sporozoa*, a class of protozoa that reproduces by formation of spores, bringing on anemia or general ill health. The body is also vulnerable to actinobacillosis, a disease caused by bacteria (*Actinobacillus lignieresii*) that form radiating structures in the tissues. The peritoneal cavity may harbor round-worms (*Setaria labiato-papillosa*); if numbering in the dozens, these cause lesions that can be harmful.

Portions of a buffalo's digestive tract play host to a rich fauna of parasites. The stomach and small intestine house three species of roundworms (*Ostertagia bisonis, Cooperia bisonis,* and *Haemonchus contortus*). The intestine can shelter two more species (*Oesopha-gostomum radiatum* and *Trichuris ovis*) as well as one kind of tape-worm (*Moniezia benedeni*) and several protozoa—two flagellates (*Cercomonas* and *Copromonas*), two amoebae (*Sappinia diploidea* and *Vahlkampfia*), and a *Monas*. Stomach and intestines may also contain a bacillus that causes inflammation (it produced ten deaths in the National Zoological Park in 1898). And two kinds of liver fluke (*Fasciola magna* and *hepatica*) dwell in buffalo in one phase of their life cycle, relying on certain species of snails as hosts for another phase.

Even the blood of buffalo may harbor its own types of specialized parasites: One type of bacteria secretes poisons that produce the multiple abscesses of pyemia. Other bacteria (*Anaplasma*) infect red blood corpuscles to bring about a disease known as anaplasmosis. Also infectious in the corpuscles are protozoa (*Babesia bigemina*) that give rise to Texas fever; they are introduced by bites from a tick (*Boophilus annulatus*).

Besides playing innkeeper to this legion of parasites and their accompanying diseases, buffalo develop a number of other disorders with such familiar names as arthritis, pleurisy, cirrhosis of the liver, hardening of the arteries, peritonitis, cysts, abscesses, fatty tumors, and even kidney stones.

Appendixes

A P P E N D I X   D

Picture Credits

Sources listed with a date from which drawings or photographs were taken will be found in the bibliography.

Photographs taken by the author appear through the courtesy of Photo Researchers, Inc., of New York City.

All photographs credited to "Disney" are from the Walt Disney True-Life Adventure motion picture The Vanishing Prairie, *copyright Walt Disney Productions.*

Album I, The Ancient Bison, the Early Hunters, and the Plains Indian Culture

    I   author, at Museum of the American Indian.
   II   *top:* author. *bottom:* author, at Field Museum of Natural History.
 III *left:* author. *right:* University of Colorado Museum, Joe Ben Wheat.
 IV *top:* Courtesy of the National Collection of Fine Arts, Smithsonian Institution. *bottom:* William Andrews Clark Memorial Library, University of California, Los Angeles.
   V Thwaites, 1904–7, Vol. 25.
 VI Courtesy of the American Museum of Natural History.
VII *top:* Franklin, 1823. *bottom:* Hornaday, 1887.
VIII *top:* author, at Field Museum of Natural History. *bottom:* Gilcrease Institute of American History and Art.
 IX *top:* author, at Museum of the American Indian.
  X *top:* Catlin, 1844. *center:* Catlin, 1844. *bottom:* Courtesy of the National Collection of Fine Arts, Smithsonian Institution.
 XI *top:* Field Museum of Natural History. *bottom:* author, at Natural History Museum of the Smithsonian Institution.
XII *top and bottom pairs:* author, at Museum of the American Indian. *center pair:* author, at Natural History Museum of the Smithsonian Institution.
XIII author, at Museum of the American Indian.
XIV author, with Reginald Laubin.
XV *top:* William Andrews Clark Memorial Library, University of California, Los Angeles. *bottom:* Field Museum of Natural History.
XVI *top:* Field Museum of Natural History. *lower left:* Courtesy of the National Collection of Fine Arts, Smithsonian Institution. *right center:* Museum of the American Indian.

Album II, The Natural History of the Buffalo

    I Courtesy of the National Collection of Fine Arts, Smithsonian Institution.
   II Disney.
 III *top:* Harry Engels from National Audubon Society. *center and bottom:* Yellowstone National Park.

Appendixes

BIBLIOGRAPHY

Allee, W. C. *The Social Life of Animals.* Boston: Beacon Press; 1958.

Allen, Durward L. *The Life of Prairies and Plains.* New York: McGraw-Hill; 1967.

Allen, Joel A. "The American Bison, Living and Extinct." Museum of Comparative Zoology, Harvard University, *Memoirs,* 4(10): 1–246, 1876.

————. "Northern Range of the Bison." *American Naturalist,* 11:624, 1877.

Altmann, Margaret. "Seniors of the Wilderness." *Animal Kingdom,* 66(6):181–3, 1963.

American Bison Society. *Annual Reports,* 1905–30.

Anonymous. "If You Hunger for Buffalo." *Sunset,* 135(4):213–216, 1965.

Armstrong, Edward A. "The Nature and Function of Displacement Activities." *Symposia of the Society for Experimental Biology,* 4:361–84, 1950.

Aubrey, Charles. "Memories of an Old Buffalo Hunter." *Forest and Stream,* 71(4):133–4, 71(5):173–4, 71(6):216–17, 1908.

Audubon, John James, and the Rev. John Bachman. *The Quadrupeds of North America,* Vol. 2. New York: V. G. Audubon; 1849.

Baggley, George F. "The Survival of the Fittest." *Yellowstone Nature Notes,* 10(9–10):39, 1933.

Bailey, Vernon. "A Biological Survey of North Dakota." *North American Fauna,* 49:1–226, 1925.

Bancroft, Hubert Howe. *Native Races of the Pacific States,* Vol. 2. San Francisco: A. L. Bancroft and Co.; 1883.

Bibliography

Banfield, A. W. F., and N. S. Novakowski. "The Survival of the Wood Bison (*Bison bison athabascae* Rhoads) in the Northwest Territories." *National Museum of Canada, Natural History Papers*, 8:1–6.

Barnes, Frank C. *Cartridges of the World*. Chicago: The Gun Digest Company; 1969 (2nd edn.).

Baynes, E. H. "In the Name of the American Bison." *Harper's Weekly*, 50:404–6, 1906.

Beach, F. A. "Current Concepts of Play in Animals." *American Naturalist*, 79:523–41, 1945.

————, ed. *Sex and Behavior*. New York: John Wiley & Sons; 1965.

Beal, Merrill D. "Losses of Animal Life Due to Gaseous Emanations and Boiling Pools in Yellowstone National Park." *Yellowstone Nature Notes*, 29(2):1–3, 1955.

Beckwith, Martha W. "Mythology of the Oglala Dakota." *Journal of American Folk-Lore*, 43:339–42, 1930.

————. "Mandan-Hidatsa Myths and Ceremonies." *Memoirs of the American Folk-Lore Society*, 32:1–327, 1938.

Beidleman, Richard G. "An Altitudinal Record for Bison in Northern Colorado." *Journal of Mammalogy*, 36:470–1, 1955.

Berkeley, Grantley F. *The English Sportsman in the Western Prairies*. London: Hurst and Blackett; 1861.

Berlyne, D. E. "Curiosity and Exploration." *Science*, 153(3731): 25–33, 1966.

Bhambhani, R., and J. Kuspira. "The Somatic Karyotypes of American Bison and Domestic Cattle." *Canadian Journal of Genetic Cytology*, 11(2):243–9, 1969.

Blish, Helen H. *A Pictographic History of the Oglala Sioux*. Lincoln: Univ. of Nebraska Press; 1967.

Boller, Henry A. *Among the Indians. Eight Years in the Far West: 1858–1866*. Philadelphia: T. E. Zell; 1868.

Bowers, A. W. *Mandan Social and Ceremonial Organization*. Chicago: Univ. of Chicago Press; 1950.

Bradley, James H. "Sir George Gore's Expedition." *Contributions to the Historical Society of Montana*, 9:246–51, 1923.

————. "Characteristics, Habits and Customs of the Blackfeet

Bibliography

Indians." *Contributions to the Historical Society of Montana*, 9:255–299, 1923.

Branch, E. Douglas. *The Hunting of the Buffalo*. Lincoln: Univ. of Nebraska Press, 1962.

Brown, Barnum. "The Buffalo Drive." *Natural History*, 32(1): 75–82, 1932.

Brownlee, A. "Play in Domestic Cattle in Britain: An Analysis of Its Nature." *British Veterinary Journal* 110(2):48–68, 1954.

Burlingame, Merrill D. "The Buffalo in Trade and Commerce." *North Dakota Historical Quarterly*, 3(4):262–91, 1929.

Burroughs, Raymond Darwin, ed. *The Natural History of the Lewis and Clark Expedition*. East Lansing: Michigan State Univ. Press; 1961.

Bushnell, David I. Jr. "The Various Uses of Buffalo Hair by the North American Indians." *American Anthropologist*, N.S.11:401–25, 1909.

Busnel, R. G. *Acoustic Behaviour of Animals*. New York: Elsevier Publishing Co.; 1963.

Cahalane, Victor H. "Restoration of Wild Bison." *Transactions of the North American Wildlife Conference*, 9:135–43, 1944.

Carthy, J. D., and F. J. Ebling. *The Natural History of Aggression*. London: Academic Press; 1964.

Catlin, George. *Illustrations of the Manners, Customs and Condition of the North American Indians*. London; Chatto & Windus; 1841.

―――――. *North American Indian Portfolio*. London: George Catlin, C. and J. Adlard, printers; 1844.

―――――. *O-Kee-pa: A Religious Ceremony*. Philadelphia: J. B. Lippincott & Co.; 1867.

Christman, Gene M. "The Mountain Bison." *The American West*, 8(3):44–7, 1971.

Cloudsley-Thompson, J. L. *Animal Behaviour*. Edinburgh: Oliver and Boyd; 1960.

―――――. *Animal Conflict and Adaptation*. London: G. T. Foulis & Co., Ltd.; 1965.

Cody, William F. *Life and Adventures of Buffalo Bill*. Chicago: John R. Stanton Co.; 1917.

Bibliography

Cole, James E. "Buffalo (*Bison bison*) Killed by Fire." *Journal of Mammalogy*, 35:453–4, 1954.

Collias, N. E. "Statistical Analysis of Factors Which Make for Success in Initial Encounters Between Hens." *American Naturalist*, 77:519–38, 1943.

Collins, Henry H. Jr., *1951 Census of Living American Bison (Bison bison)*. Bronxville: Blue Heron Press; 1952.

Cook, John R. *The Border and the Buffalo*. Topeka, Kansas: Crane and Co.; 1907.

Corner, A. H., and Robert Connell. "Brucellosis in Bison, Elk and Moose in Elk Island National Park, Alberta, Canada." *Canadian Journal of Comparative Medicine and Veterinary Science*, 22(1):9–21, 1958.

Cornwall, Ian W. *Prehistoric Animals and Their Hunters*. London: Faber; 1968.

Costello, David F. *The Prairie World*. New York: Thomas Y. Crowell Company; 1969.

Cottam, Clarence, and C. S. Williams. "Speed of Some Wild Animals." *Journal of Mammalogy*, 24(2):262–3, 1943.

Coues, Elliott. *The Manuscript Journals of Alexander Henry and of David Thompson*. 3 vols. New York: Francis P. Harper; 1897.

Craighead, Frank Jr., and John Craighead. "Trailing Yellowstone's Grizzlies by Radio." *National Geographic*, 130(2):252–67, 1966.

Custer, Elizabeth B. *Tenting on the Plains or General Custer in Kansas and Texas*. New York: C. L. Webster; 1889.

Davis, Theodore H. "The Buffalo Range." *Harper's Monthly*, 38:147–63, 1869.

Day, James M. "A Preliminary Guide to the Study of Buffalo Trails in Texas." *Western Texas Historical Association Yearbook*, 36:137–55, 1960.

Deakin, Alan, G. W. Muir, and A. G. Smith. "Hybridization of Domestic Cattle, Bison and Yak." *Canada Department of Agriculture, Publication 479, Technical Bulletin 2*, 1935.

Deakin, A., G. W. Muir, A. G. Smith, and A. S. MacLellan. "Progress Report of the Wainwright Experiment, 1935–41." *Animal Breeding Abstracts*, 10:88, 1942.

Denig, Edwin T. "Indian Tribes of the Upper Missouri." *Annual*

Bibliography

Report of the Bureau of American Ethnology, 46:375–654, 1928–1929.

de Vos, A. "Ecological Conditions Affecting the Production of Wild Herbivorous Mammals on Grasslands." *Advances in Ecological Research*, 6:137–83, 1969.

Dobie, J. Frank. "Bison in Mexico." *Journal of Mammalogy*, 34: 150–1, 1953.

Dodge, Colonel Richard Irving. *The Hunting Grounds of the Great West*. London: Chatto & Windus; 1877.

Dorsey, George A. *The Mythology of the Wichita*. Washington: The Carnegie Institute; 1904.

———. *Traditions of the Arikara*. Washington: The Carnegie Institute; 1904.

———. "Traditions of the Skidi Pawnee." *Memoirs of the American Folk-Lore Society*, 8:1–366, 1904.

———. "The Cheyenne." *Field Columbian Museum Anthropological Series*, 9(1–2):1–186, 1905.

———. *Traditions of the Caddo*. Washington: The Carnegie Institute; 1905.

———. *The Pawnee Mythology*. Washington: The Carnegie Institute; 1906.

Dorsey, George A., and Alfred L. Kroeber. "Traditions of the Arapaho." *Field Columbian Museum, Publication 81, Anthropological Series, Vol. 5*, 1903.

Driver, Harold E. *Indians of North America*. Chicago: Univ. of Chicago Press; 1969.

Ebert, Hugh B. "Buffaloes Frozen in the Yellowstone River." *Yellowstone Nature Notes*, 20(2):8, 1946.

Egan, Gail N., and George A. Agognino. "Man's Use of Bison and Cattle on the High Plains." *Great Plains Journal*, 5(1):35–43, 1965.

Egerton, P. J. Marjoribanks. *The Cow-Calf Relationship and Rutting Behavior in the American Bison*. University of Alberta: Master's thesis for the Department of Zoology, 1962.

———. "The Bison in Canada." *Oryx*, 7(6):305–14, 1964.

Ellison, Lincoln. "Influence of Grazing on Plant Succession of Rangelands." *Botanical Review*, 26(1):1–78, 1960.

Bibliography

Elrod, Morton J. "The Montana National Bison Range." *Journal of Mammalogy*, 7:45–8, 1926.

Errington, Paul L. *Of Predation and Life*. Ames: Iowa State Univ. Press; 1967.

Etkin, W., ed. *Social Behavior and Organization among Vertebrates*. Chicago: Univ. of Chicago Press; 1964.

Ewer, R. F. *Ethology of Mammals*. New York: Plenum Press; 1968.

Ewers, John C. *Blackfeet Crafts*. Washington: Bureau of Indian Affairs; 1945.

————. "The Last Bison Drives of the Blackfoot Indians." *Journal of the Washington Academy of Sciences*, 39:355–60, 1949.

————. *The Blackfeet: Raiders on The Northwestern Plains*. Norman: Univ. of Oklahoma Press; 1958.

Farb, Peter. *The Land and Wildlife of North America*. New York: Time Inc.; 1964.

————. *Man's Rise to Civilization*. New York: E. P. Dutton & Co.; 1968.

Fischer, Wayne A. "Observations on Behavior of Lone Bull Bison." *Proceedings of the Iowa Academy of Science*, 74:87–91, 1968.

Fish and Wildlife Service. *Management of Buffalo Herds*. Washington: Wildlife Leaflet 212; 1951.

Flerov, K. K., and M. A. Zablotskii. On the Causative Factors Responsible for the Change in the Bison Area. *Moskovskoe Obshchestvo Ispytatelei, Biulleten*, 66(6):99–109, 1961. (In Russian)

Fletcher, Alice C. "The White Buffalo Festival of the Uncpapas." Harvard University, *Sixteenth Report of the Peabody Museum of American Archaeology and Ethnology*, 260–75, 1882.

————, and Francis La Flesche. "The Omaha Tribe." *Annual Report of the Bureau of American Ethnology*, 27:15–672, 1905–6.

Fox, H. Munro, and Gwynne Vevers. *The Nature of Animal Colours*. London: Sidgwick and Jackson Ltd.; 1960.

Franklin, John. *Narrative of a Journey to the Shores of the Polar Sea in the Years 1819, 20, 21, and 22*. London: J. Murray; 1823.

Fraser, A. "The State of Fight or Flight in the Bull." *British Journal of Animal Behaviour*, 5(2):48–9, 1957.

Frison, George C. "The Buffalo Pound in Northwestern Plains Prehistory: Site 48 ca 302 Wyoming." *American Antiquity*, 36(1): 77–91, 1971.

Bibliography

Fryxell, Fritiof M. "A New High Altitude Limit for the American Bison." *Journal of Mammalogy*, 7(2):102–9, 1926.

—————. "The Former Range of the Bison in the Rocky Mountains." *Journal of Mammalogy*, 9:129–39, 1928.

Fuller, W. A. "The Horns and Teeth as Indicators of Age in Bison." *Journal of Wildlife Management*, 23:342–4, 1959.

—————. "Behaviour and Social Organization of the Wild Bison of Wood Buffalo National Park, Canada." *Arctic*, 13(1):1–19, 1960.

—————. "The Ecology and Management of the American Bison." *La Terre et la Vie*, 108(2–3):286–304, 1961.

—————. "The Biology and Management of the Bison of Wood Buffalo National Park." *Wildlife Management Bulletin*, 1(16):1–52, 1962.

—————, and L. A. Bayrock. "Late Pleistocene Mammals from Central Alberta, Canada." *Vertebrate Paleontology in Alberta*, pp. 53–63. Edmonton: Univ. of Alberta, 1965.

Galdikas, Birute. "The Shift from Mammoth to Bison in Paleo-Indian Subsistence: a Reappraisal." *Anthropology, UCLA*, 2(1):1–18, 1970.

Gard, Wayne. *The Great Buffalo Hunt*. New York: Alfred A. Knopf; 1959.

Garretson, Martin S. *The American Bison*. New York: New York Zoological Society; 1938.

Gilmore, Melvin R. "Old Assiniboin Buffalo-Drive in North Dakota." *Indian Notes*, 1:204–11, 1924.

—————. "Buffalo-Skull from the Arikara." *Indian Notes*, 3:75–9, 1926.

—————. "Methods of Indian Buffalo Hunts." *Papers of the Michigan Academy of Science, Arts and Letters*, 16:17–32, 1931.

Glickman, Stephen E., and Richard W. Scoges. "Curiosity in Zoo Animals." *Behaviour, International Journal of Comparative Ethology*, 26(1–2):151–88, 1966.

Glover, Richard. "The Wisent or European Bison." *Journal of Mammalogy*, 28(4):333–42, 1947.

Goodnight, Charles. "My Experiences with Bison Hybrids." *Journal of Heredity*, 5:197–9, 1914.

Goodwin, George G. "Buffalo Hunt—1935." *Natural History*, 36: 156–64, 1935.

Graham, Maxwell. "Finding Range for Canada's Buffalo." *Canadian Field Naturalist*, 38:189, 1924.

Gray, A. P. *Mammalian Hybrids—A Checklist with Bibliography*. Edinburgh: Technical Communication No. 10, Commonwealth Bureau of Animal Breeding Genetics; 1954.

Gray, Prentiss, ed. *Records of North American Big Game*. New York: The Derrydale Press; 1932.

Grinnell, George Bird. "The Last of the Buffalo." *Scribner's Magazine*, 12:267–86, 1892.

———. "Some Early Cheyenne Tales." *Journal of American Folk-Lore*, 20:169–94, 1907.

———. *Blackfoot Lodge Tales*. New York: C. Scribner's Sons; 1913.

———. *The Cheyenne Indians*. 2 vols. New York: Cooper Square Publishers; 1962.

Guthrie, Russell D. "Pelage of Fossil Bison—A New Osteological Index." *Journal of Mammalogy*, 47(4):725–7, 1966.

———. "Bison Evolution and Zoogeography in North America during the Pleistocene." *Quarterly Review of Biology*, 45(1):1–15, 1970.

Hadley, James Albert. "A Royal Buffalo Hunt." *Transactions of the Kansas State Historical Society*, 10:564–80, 1907–8.

Hafez, E. S. E. *The Behaviour of Domestic Animals*. Baltimore: Williams and Wilkins Co.; 1962.

Haines, Francis. *The Buffalo*. New York: Thomas Y. Crowell Co.; 1970.

Hall, E. Raymond, and Keith R. Kelson. *Mammals of North America*. Vol. 2. New York: Ronald Press; 1959.

Halloran, Arthur F. "American Bison Weights and Measurements from the Wichita Mountains Wildlife Refuge." *Proceedings of the Oklahoma Academy of Science*, 41:212–18, 1961.

Harper, Francis. "Letter to the Canadian Field Naturalist." *Canadian Field Naturalist*, 39:45, 1925.

Hassrick, Royal B. *The Sioux*. Norman: Univ. of Oklahoma Press; 1964.

Bibliography

Hediger, H. "Säugetier-Territorien und ihre Markierung." *Bijdragen tot de Dierkunde*, 28:172–84, 1949.

Heldt, F. George. "Narrative of Sir George Gore's Expedition, 1854–1856." *Contributions to the Historical Society of Montana*, 1:128–31, 1876.

Hennepin, Father Louis. *A New Discovery of a Vast Country in America.* Chicago: A. C. McClurg & Co.; 1903.

Herrig, Daniel M. "Behavior of the Lone American Bison Bull." *Iowa Cooperative Wildlife Research Unit, Quarterly Report*, 34(1): 36–44, 1968.

————, and Arnold O. Haugen. "Bull Bison Behavior Traits." *Proceedings of the Iowa Academy of Science*, 76:245–62, 1970.

Hibbard, C. W. "The Jinglebob Interglacial (Sangamon?) Fauna from Kansas and its Climatic Significance." *Univ. of Michigan Museum of Paleontology, Contributions*, 12(10):179–228, 1955.

Hind, Henry Youle. *Narrative of the Canadian Red River Exploring Expedition of 1857 and of the Assiniboine and Saskatchewan Exploring Expedition of 1858.* 2 vols. London: Longman, Green, Longman and Roberts; 1860.

Hodge, F. W., ed. *Handbook of American Indians, North of Mexico.* Washington: Govt. Printing Office; 1905.

Hornaday, William T. "The Extermination of the American Bison, with a Sketch of its Discovery and Life History." *Report of the U. S. National Museum, 1887 (Washington, 1889)*, Part 2, pp. 367–548.

————. *The Minds and Manners of Wild Animals.* New York: C. Scribner's Sons; 1922.

Hough, Walter. "The Bison as a Factor in Ancient American Culture History." *Scientific Monthly*, 30(4): 315–19, 1930.

Howell, A. Brazier. "Letter to the Canadian Field Naturalist." *Canadian Field Naturalist*, 39:118, 1925.

————. *Speed in Animals.* Chicago: Univ. of Chicago Press; 1944.

Hulbert, Archer Butler. *Paths of the Mound-Building Indians and Great Game Animals.* Cleveland: A. H. Clark Co.; 1902.

Inman, Colonel Henry. *Buffalo Jones' Forty Years of Adventure.* Topeka, Kansas: Crane and Co.; 1899.

Irving, Washington. *A Tour on the Prairies.* London: John Murray; 1835.

Bibliography

Jablow, Joseph. "The Cheyenne in Plains Indian Trade Relations 1795–1840." *Monographs of the American Ethnological Society*, 19: 1–100, 1951.

Jacobs, John Cloud. "The Last of the Buffalo." *The World's Work*, 17:11098–100, 1909.

Jakle, John A. "The American Bison and the Human Occupance of the Ohio Valley." *Proceedings of the American Philosophical Society*, 112(4):299–305, 1968.

Jenness, Diamond. *The Sarcee Indians of Alberta*. Ottawa: National Museum of Canada, Bulletin No. 90, Anthropological Series No. 23.

Jennings, J. D., and E. Norbeck. *Prehistoric Man in the New World*. Chicago: Univ. of Chicago Press; 1964.

Johnson, Charles W. "Protein as a Factor in the Distribution of the American Bison." *Geographical Review*, 41:330–1, 1951.

Jones, C. J. "Breeding Cattelo." *American Breeders' Association Annual Report*, 3:161–5, 1907.

Keast, Allen. "Evolution of Social Structure in African Bovids." *Proceedings of the XVI International Congress of Zoology*, 2:26, 1963.

Kendeigh, S. Charles. *Animal Ecology*. Englewood Cliffs: Prentice-Hall; 1961.

King, John A. "Social Behavior, Social Organization and Population Dynamics in a Black-tailed Prairiedog Town in the Black Hills of South Dakota." *Contributions from the Laboratory of Vertebrate Biology, Univ. of Michigan*, 67:1–123, 1955.

Klauber, Laurence M. *Rattlesnakes*. 2 vols. Berkeley: Univ. of California Press; 1956.

Kroeber, Alfred L. "Cheyenne Tales." *Journal of American Folk-Lore*, 13(25):161–90, 1900.

————. "Ethnology of the Gros Ventre." *Anthropological Papers of the American Museum of Natural History*, 1(4):141–281, 1908.

Krysiak, Kazimierz. "News of the European Bison in Poland." *Oryx*, 7:94–6, 1963.

Kurtén, Björn. *Pleistocene Mammals of Europe*. Chicago: Aldine Publishing Co.; 1968.

La Flesche, Francis. "The Omaha Buffalo Medicine-Men." *Journal of American Folk-Lore*, 3:215–21, 1890.

————. "The Osage Tribe: Two Versions of the Child-Naming Rite." *Annual Report of the Bureau of American Ethnology*, 43:23–164, 1925–6.

Langford, N. P. "Letter Written to Mr. W. J. Doolittle." *Yellowstone Nature Notes*, 29:13–16, 1955.

Lanyon, W. E., and W. N. Tavolga. *Animal Sounds and Communication*. Washington: American Institute of Biological Science; 1960.

Larson, Floyd. "The Role of the Bison in Maintaining the Short Grass Plains." *Ecology*, 21(2):113–21, 1940.

Lemon, Paul C. "Fire and Wildlife Grazing on an African Plateau." *Proceedings of the Annual Tall Timbers Fire Ecological Conference*, 8:71–88, 1968.

Leroi-Gourhan, André. *Treasury of Prehistoric Art*. New York: Harry N. Abrams, Inc.; 1968.

Lewis, Meriwether. *Journals of the Lewis and Clark Expedition, 1804–1806*. 8 vols. New York: Dodd, Mead & Co.; 1904–5.

Lott, Dale F. "Postural Aspects of Threat and Submission Signalling in Mature Male American Bison." *American Zoologist*, 9(4): 1071, 1969.

Lowie, Robert H. "The Assiniboine." *Anthropological Papers of the American Museum of Natural History*, 4(1): 1–270, 1909.

————. "Societies of the Crow, Hidatsa and Mandan Indians." *Anthropological Papers of the American Museum of Natural History*, 11(3):141–358, 1913.

————. "Myths and Traditions of the Crow Indians." *Anthropological Papers of the American Museum of Natural History*, 25 (1):1–308, 1918.

————. "Material Culture of the Crow Indians." *Anthropological Papers of the American Museum of Natural History*, 21(3):203–70, 1922.

————. *Indians of the Plains*. New York: McGraw-Hill; 1954.

MacTavish, Newton. "The Last Great Round-Up." *Canadian Magazine*, 33:482–91, 34:25–35, 1909.

Martin, Paul S. "Pleistocene Overkill." *Natural History*, 76(10): 32–8, 1967.

Matthews, Washington. "Ethnography and Philology of the Hidatsa Indians." *U. S. Geological and Geographic Survey, Miscellaneous Publications, No. 7*, 1877.

Bibliography

Mayer, Frank H., and Charles B. Roth. *The Buffalo Harvest.* Denver: Sage Books; 1958.

McCracken, Harold. "The Sacred White Buffalo." *Natural History,* 55(7):304–9, 341, 1946.

————. *George Catlin and the Old Frontier.* New York: Bonanza Books; 1959.

McCreight, Major Israel. *Buffalo Bone Days.* Dubois, Pennsylvania. (Published by the author)

McGee, W. J. "The Siouan Indians, A Preliminary Sketch." *Annual Report of the Bureau of American Ethnology,* 15:153–204, 1893–4.

McGill, Thomas E., ed. *Readings in Animal Behavior.* New York: Holt, Rinehart and Winston; 1965.

McHugh, Tom. "Social Behavior of the American Buffalo (*Bison bison bison*)." *Zoologica,* 43(1):1–40, 1958.

Meagher, Mary. "Snow as a Factor Influencing Bison Distribution and Numbers in Pelican Valley, Yellowstone National Park." *Office of Natural Science Studies, Yellowstone National Park, Wyoming, Report No. 9,* 1971.

Michelson, Truman. "The Mythical Origin of the White Buffalo Dance of the Fox Indians." *Annual Report of the Bureau of American Ethnology,* 40:23–289, 1925.

Mohr, C. O. "Cattle Droppings as Ecological Units." *Ecological Monographs,* 13(3):275–98, 1943.

Mohr, E. "The Studbook of the European Bison." *International Zoo Yearbook,* 7:187–8, 1967.

Mooney, James. "Calendar History of the Kiowa Indians." *Annual Report of the Bureau of American Ethnology,* 17(1):129–468, 1895–6.

————. "The Cheyenne Indians." *Memoirs of the American Anthropological Association,* 1(6):357–442, 1907.

Moore, Ely. "A Buffalo Hunt with the Miamis in 1854." *Transactions of the Kansas State Historical Society,* 10:402–9, 1908.

Müller-Beck, Hansjürgen, "Paleohunters in America: Origins and Diffusion." *Science,* 152:1191–1210, 1966.

Murdock, George P. *Ethnographic Bibliography of North America.* New Haven: Human Relations Area Files; 1960.

Bibliography

Muybridge, Eadweard. *Animals in Motion.* London: Chapman and Hall; 1907.

Novakowski, N. S., J. G. Cousineau, and G. B. Kolenosky. "Parasites and Diseases of Bison in Canada. II. Anthrax Epizooty in the Northwest Territories." *Transactions of the North American Wildlife and Natural Resources Conference,* 28:233–9, 1963.

Novakowski, N. S., and W. E. Stevens. "Survival of the Wood Bison, *Bison bison athabascae* Rhoads, in Canada." *Presented to the 45th Meeting of the American Society of Mammalogists,* June 21, 1965.

Olsen, Stanley J. "Post-Cranial Skeletal Characters of *Bison* and *Bos.*" *Papers of the Peabody Museum of Archeology and Ethnology, Harvard University,* 35(4): 1–15, 1960.

Orr, R. T. *Animals in Migration.* New York: Macmillan; 1970.

Oviedo y Valdés, Gonzalo Fernández de. *Historia General y Natural de las Indias, Islas y Tierrafirme del Mar Océano.* Madrid: Real Academia de la Historia; 1851–5.

Parkman, Francis. *The Oregon Trail.* Boston: Little, Brown, & Co.; 1903.

Peters, H. F. "Experimental Hybridization of Domestic Cattle and American Bison." *Atti del Quinto Congresso Internazionale per la Riproduzione Animale e la Fecondazione Artificiale,* 7:326–32, 1964.

Pruitt, William O. "A Flight Releaser in Wolf-Caribou Relations." *Journal of Mammalogy,* 46(2):350–1, 1965.

Pucek, Zdzislaw, ed. "The European Bison, Current State of Knowledge and Need for Further Studies." *Acta Theriologica,* 12 (19–35):323–501, 1967.

Purchas, Rev. Samuel. *Purchas his Pilgrimes.* 4 vols. London: W. Stansby; 1625.

Pyper, J. F., and L. Willoughby. "Anthrax Outbreak Affecting Man and Buffalo in the Northwest Territories." *Medical Services Journal of Canada,* 20(6):531–40, 1964.

Radin, Paul. "The Winnebago Tribe." *Annual Report of the Bureau of American Ethnology,* 37:35–550, 1915–16.

Raup, H. M. "Range Conditions in the Wood Buffalo Park of Western Canada with Notes on the History of the Wood Bison." *Special Publication of the American Committee for International Wild Life Protection,* 1(2):1–52, 1933.

Reed, Erik K. "The Myth of Montezuma's Bison and the Type Locality of the Species." *Journal of Mammalogy*, 33:390–2, 1952.

———. "Bison beyond the Pecos." *Texas Journal of Science*, 7(2):130–5, 1955.

Rhoads, S. N. "Notes on Living and Extinct Species of North American Bovidae." *Proceedings of the Academy of Natural Sciences of Philadelphia*, 49:483–502, 1897.

Riggs, Thomas L. "The Last Buffalo Hunt." *Independent*, 63:32–38, 1907.

Roe, Frank Gilbert. *The Indian and the Horse*. Norman: Univ. of Oklahoma Press; 1955.

———. *The North American Buffalo*. Toronto: Univ. of Toronto Press; 1970.

Ross, Alexander. *The Red River Settlement: Its Rise, Progress, and Present State*. London: Smith, Elder and Co.; 1856.

Ross, S., and J. P. Scott. "Relationship between Dominance and Control of Movements in Goats." *Journal of Comparative Physiology and Psychology*, 42:75–80, 1949.

Rowell, C. H. Fraser. "Displacement Grooming in the Chaffinch." *Animal Behaviour*, 9(1–2):38–63, 1961.

Rush, W. M. *Wild Animals of the Rockies*. New York: Harper and Brothers; 1942.

Russell, Don. *The Lives and Legends of Buffalo Bill*. Norman: Univ. of Oklahoma Press; 1960.

Ruth, Clara. "Preserves and Ranges Maintained for Buffalo and Other Big Game." *Biological Survey, Wildlife Leaflet No. 95*, 1937.

Sampson, Arthur W. *Range and Pasture Management*. New York: John Wiley & Sons, Inc.; 1923.

Sandoz, Mari. *The Buffalo Hunters*. New York: Hastings House; 1954.

Schaller, George B. *The Deer and the Tiger*. Chicago: Univ. of Chicago Press; 1967.

Schein, Martin W., and Milton H. Fohrman. "Social Dominance Relationships in a Herd of Dairy Cattle." *British Journal of Animal Behaviour*, 3(2):45–55, 1955.

Schjelderup-Ebbe, Thorleif. "Beiträge zur Sozialpsychologie des Haushuhns." *Zeitschrift für Psychologie*, 88:225–52, 1922.

Bibliography

Schloeth, Robert. "Quelques Moyens d'Intercommunication des Taureaux de Camargue." *La Terre et la Vie*, 2:83–93, 1956.

———. "Cycle Annuel et Comportement Social du Taureau de Camargue." *Mammalia*, 22(1):121–39, 1958.

———. "Das Scharren bei Rind und Pferd." *Zeitschrift für Säugetierkunde*, 23:139–48, 1958.

———. "Das Sozialleben des Camargue-Rindes." *Zeitschrift für Tierpsychologie*, 18(5):574–627, 1961.

Schoolcraft, Henry R. *Narrative Journal of the Travels from Detroit Northwest through the Great Chain of American Lakes to the Sources of the Mississippi River in the Year 1820*. Albany: E. & E. Hosford; 1821.

Schorger, A. W. "The Validity of *Bison bison pennsylvanicus*." *Journal of Mammalogy*, 25:131–5, 1944.

Schultz, C. B., and W. N. Frankforter. "The Geologic History of the Bison in the Great Plains (A Preliminary Report)." *Bulletin of the Univ. of Nebraska State Museum*, 3(1):1–10, 1946.

Schultz, James Willard. *Apauk, Caller of Buffalo*. Boston: Houghton Mifflin Co.; 1916.

———. *Blackfeet and Buffalo*. Norman: Univ. of Oklahoma Press; 1962.

Scott, John Paul. *Aggression*. Chicago: Univ. of Chicago Press; 1958.

Seton, E. T. *Lives of Game Animals*. 4 vols. Garden City: Doubleday, Doran & Co.; 1929.

Shaw, Don H., and J. R. Patel. "Demonstration of Antigenic Difference between the American Bison (*Bison bison*) and Domestic Cattle (*Bos taurus*)." *Nature*, 196(4853):498–9, 1962.

Shelford, Victor R. *The Ecology of North America*. Urbana: Univ. of Illinois Press; 1963.

Sherman, H. B. "The Occurrence of Bison in Florida." *Quarterly Journal of the Florida Academy of Science*, 17(4):228–32, 1954.

Shirley, Glenn. *Pawnee Bill*. Albuquerque: Univ. of New Mexico Press; 1958.

Shoemaker, Henry W. *A Pennsylvania Bison Hunt*. Middleburg, Pennsylvania: The "Middleburg post" Press; 1915.

Shult, Milo J. "Breeding Biology and Behavior of the American

Bibliography

Bison." *Iowa Cooperative Wildlife Research Unit, Quarterly Report,* 34(1):25–35, 1968.

Sibley, Henry H. "The Sport of Buffalo-Hunting on the Open Plains of Pembina." Pages 94–110 in vol. 4 of Henry R. Schoolcraft's *Information Respecting the History Conditions and Prospects of the Indian Tribes of the United States.* Philadelphia: Lippincott, Grambo & Co.; 1854.

Simms, S. C. "Traditions of the Crows." *Field Columbian Museum, Publication No. 85, Anthropological Series,* 2(6):277–324, 1903.

Skinner, Alanson. "Political Organization, Cults, and Ceremonies of the Plains-Ojibway and Plains-Cree Indians." *Anthropological Papers of the American Museum of Natural History,* 11(6):475–542, 1914.

Skinner, M. R., and O. C. Kaisen. "The Fossil *Bison* of Alaska and Preliminary Revision of the Genus." *Bulletin of the American Museum of Natural History,* 89(3):125–256, 1947.

Sluckin, Wladyslaw. *Imprinting and Early Learning.* London: Methuen & Co., Ltd.; 1964.

Smet, Father Pierre Jean de. *Life, Letters and Travels, 1801–1873.* 4 vols. New York: Francis P. Harper; 1905.

Smith, F. V. "The 'Critical Period' in the Attachment of Lambs and Ewes." *Animal Behaviour,* 14(1):120–5, 1966.

Soper, J. Dewey. "History, Range and Home Life of the Northern Bison." *Ecological Monographs,* 11(4):347–412, 1941.

Spencer, Robert F., Jesse D. Jennings, *et al. The Native Americans.* New York: Harper & Row; 1965.

Spier, Leslie. "The Sun Dance of the Plains Indians." *Anthropological Papers of the American Museum of Natural History,* 16(7):447–527, 1921.

Steele, Samuel Benfield. *Forty Years in Canada.* Toronto: McClelland; 1915.

Stefansson, Vilhjalmur. "Pemmican." *Military Surgeon,* 95(2):89–98, 1944.

————. *Not by Bread Alone.* New York: Macmillan; 1946.

Stewart, J. C., and J. P. Scott. "Lack of Correlation between Leadership and Dominance Relationships in a Herd of Goats." *Journal of Comparative and Physiological Psychology,* 40:255–64, 1947.

Bibliography

Stoddart, Laurence A., and Arthur D. Smith. *Range Management*. New York: McGraw-Hill; 1955.

Strickland, Rex W. "The Recollections of W. S. Glenn, Buffalo Hunter." *Panhandle-Plains Historical Review*, 22:15–64, 1949.

Strong, W. D. "Plains Culture in the Light of Archaeology." *American Anthropologist*, 35:271–87, 1933.

Tadeusz, Szczdsny, ed. *Progress in European Bison Restitution*. (In Polish and Russian, with English summaries.) Warsaw: Panstwowe Wydawnictwo Naukowe; 1969.

Talbot, Lee M., and Martha H. "The Wildebeest in Western Masailand." *Wildlife Monographs, No. 12*, 1963.

Thevet, André. *Les Singularitez de la France Antarctique, Autrement Nommée Amerique, et Isles Decouvertes de Nostre Temps*. Paris: Maisonneuve et Cie; 1878.

Thorpe, W. H. *Learning and Instinct in Animals*. London: Methuen; 1963.

————, and O. L. Zangwill, eds. *Current Problems in Animal Behaviour*. Cambridge: Univ. Press; 1961.

Thwaites, Reuben Gold. *Early Western Travels*. 32 vols. (especially volumes 5–7, 14–17, 19, 21–5.) Cleveland: A. H. Clark Co.; 1904–7.

Tilghman, Z. A. "Source of the Buffalo Origin Legend." *American Anthropologist*, N.S.43:487–8, 1941.

Tinbergen, N. *Social Behavior in Animals*. New York: John Wiley & Sons; 1953.

Türcke, F. "Zu Territorium und Markierung bei den Wisenten in Springe." *Zeitschrift für Säugetierkunde*, 33(2):124–5, 1968.

Turney-High, Harry H. "The Flathead Indians of Montana." *Memoirs of the American Anthropological Association*, 48:1–161, 1937.

————. "Ethnography of the Kutenai." *Memoirs of the American Anthropological Association*, 56:1–202, 1941.

Utley, Robert M. *The Last Days of the Sioux Nation*. New Haven: Yale Univ. Press; 1963.

Walker, J. R. "Sun Dance and Other Ceremonies of the Oglala Division of the Teton Dakota." *Anthropological Papers of the American Museum of Natural History*, 16(2):49–221, 1917.

Bibliography

Wallis, W. D. "Beliefs and Tales of the Canadian Dakota." *Journal of American Folk-Lore*, 36:36–101, 1923.

Walsh, Richard J. *The Making of Buffalo Bill*. Indianapolis: The Bobbs-Merrill Co.; 1928.

Wardrop, J. C. "Studies in the Behaviour of Dairy Cows at Pasture." *British Journal of Animal Behaviour*, 1(1):23–31, 1953.

Warren, Edward Royal. "Altitude Limit of Bison." *Journal of Mammalogy*, 8:60–1, 1927.

Way, Joe J. "Survival of the Fittest." *Yellowstone Nature Notes*, 25(4):46, 1951.

Weaver, J. E. *North American Prairie*. Lincoln: Johnsen Publishing Co.; 1954.

————, and F. E. Clements. *Plant Ecology*. New York: McGraw-Hill; 1929.

————, and F. W. Albertson. *Grasslands of the Great Plains*. Lincoln: Johnsen Publishing Co.; 1956.

Webb, Walter Prescott. *The Great Plains*. Boston: Ginn and Co.; 1931.

Webb, William E. *Buffalo Land*. Philadelphia: Hubbard Brothers; 1872.

Wedel, Waldo R. *Prehistoric Man on the Great Plains*. Norman: Univ. of Oklahoma Press; 1961.

Welker, W. I. "An Analysis of Exploratory and Play Behavior in Animals." Chapter 7 in *Functions of Varied Experience*, edited by Donald W. Fiske and Salvatore R. Maddi. Homewood, Illinois: Dorsey Press; 1961.

Wheat, Joe Ben. "A Paleo Indian Bison Kill." *Scientific American*, 216(1):44–52, 1967.

Wilson, Gilbert L. "The Horse and the Dog in Hidatsa Culture." *Anthropological Papers of the American Museum of Natural History*, 15(2):125–311, 1924.

Winship, George Parker. "The Coronado Expedition, 1540–1542." *Annual Report of the Bureau of American Ethnology*, 14(1): 329–613, 1892–3.

————. *The Journey of Coronado, 1540–1542*. New York: Allerton Book Co.; 1904.

Wissler, Clark. "Material Culture of the Blackfoot Indians." *Anthropological Papers of the American Museum of Natural History*, 5:1–175, 1910.

Bibliography

————. "Ceremonial Bundles of the Blackfoot Indians." *Anthropological Papers of the American Museum of Natural History*, 7(2): 65–289, 1912.

————. *North American Indians of the Plains.* New York: American Museum of Natural History; 1920.

————. *The American Indian.* New York: Macmillan; 1938.

————, and D. C. Duvall. "Mythology of the Blackfoot Indians." *Anthropological Papers of the American Museum of Natural History*, 2(1):1–163, 1908.

Wolcott, G. N. "An Animal Census of Two Pastures and a Meadow in Northern New York." *Ecological Monographs*, 7:1–90, 1937.

Wormington, Hannah Marie. *Ancient Man in North America.* Denver: Denver Museum of Natural History; 1949.

Zablocki, M. "Territorium und Markierung biem Wisent." *Zeitshrift für Säugetierkunder*, 33(2):121–3, 1968.

(Current references will be found in *Biological Abstracts*, in "Recent Literature of Mammalogy" in the *Journal of Mammalogy*, and in the *Wildlife Review*. Articles on the European bison are regularly published in *Acta Theriologica*, Bialowieza, Poland.)

INDEX

Index

Index

Index

Index

A Note on the Author

At an early age in his hometown of Cleveland, Ohio, Tom McHugh started a career in biology by working at the Cleveland Museum of Natural History. His continued interest in the natural sciences led him to study zoology and wildlife management while he attended Oberlin College, Miami University, and the University of Wisconsin, from which he was graduated with a B.A., M.A., and Ph.D. Mr. McHugh was the principal photographer for Walt Disney's *Vanishing Prairie* and *White Wilderness* and also worked on five other Academy Award winning films in this True-Life Adventure series. As camerman-director for the Jack Douglas Organizations, he has traveled to every continent except Anarctica while preparing over one hundred television documentaries. Mr. McHugh is a life member of the American Society of Mammalogists, and his photographs and articles on wildlife have appeared in *Natural History*, *Audubon*, *Sports Afield*, *National Geographic*, *Time*, *Life*, and the Encyclopedia Britannica. He makes his home in Los Angeles.

A NOTE ON THE TYPE

This book was set in Monticello, a Linotype revival of the original Roman No. 1 cut by Archibald Binny and cast in 1796 by the Philadelphia type foundry Binny & Ronaldson. The face was named Monticello in honor of its use in the monumental fifty-volume *Papers of Thomas Jefferson*, published by Princeton University Press. Monticello is a transitional type design, embodying certain features of Bulmer and Baskerville, but it is a distinguished face in its own right.

Composed and bound by H. Wolff, Inc., New York, New York. Printed by Halliday Lithograph Corp., West Hanover, Massachusetts. Typography and binding design by Guy Fleming.